Mercedes-Benz E-Class
Owners Workshop Manual

Martynn Randall

(5710 - 288)

Models covered

Mercedes-Benz E-Class (W211 Series) Saloon & Estate with diesel engines
E220 CDI, E270 CDI, E280 CDI & E320 CDI

2.2 litre (2148cc) 4-cyl, 2.7 litre (2685cc) 5-cyl, 3.0 litre (2987cc) V6 & 3.2 litre (3222cc) in-line 6-cyl

Does NOT cover petrol models, or four-wheel-drive ('4Matic') models
Does NOT cover new E-Class range (W212 Series) introduced during 2009

© J H Haynes & Co. Ltd. 2015

ABCDE
FGHIJ
KLMNO
PQ

A book in the **Haynes Owners Workshop Manual Series**

Printed in Malaysia

ISBN 978 0 85733 710 8

J H Haynes & Co. Ltd.
Sparkford, Yeovil, Somerset BA22 7JJ, England

British Library Cataloguing in Publication Data
A catalogue record for this book is available from the British Library.

Haynes North America, Inc
859 Lawrence Drive, Newbury Park, California 91320, USA

Printed using NORBRITE BOOK 48.8gsm (CODE: 40N6533) from NORPAC; procurement system certified under Sustainable Forestry Initiative standard. Paper produced is certified to the SFI Certified Fiber Sourcing Standard (CERT - 0094271)

Contents

LIVING WITH YOUR MERCEDES-BENZ E-CLASS

Roadside repairs

Weekly checks

Lubricants and fluids

Tyre pressures

MAINTENANCE

Routine maintenance and servicing

Contents

REPAIRS AND OVERHAUL

Engine and Associated Systems

Transmission

Brakes and suspension

Body equipment

Wiring diagrams

REFERENCE

Index

The W211 Series Mercedes-Benz E-Class replaced the popular W210 Series in June 2002. Available as a 4-door Saloon, or Estate, it was launched with a range of in-line diesel engines, with 4-, 5-, or 6-cylinders. Theses engines are developments of well-proven engines used in many Mercedes-Benz vehicles. In June 2005, a V6-diesel engine was introduced, with greatly improved output and emissions levels. Both of these engines are fitted, longitudinally with the transmission mounted behind the engine. Both manual and automatic transmissions are available.

Fully independent suspension is fitted front and rear, with MacPherson type front suspension, and multi-link rear suspension with separate coil springs and dampers. On various models, air suspension was offered as an option, with either air springs just at the rear, or front and rear.

All models feature anti-lock brakes, traction control, ESP, along with a multitude of equipment to enhance the safety, convenience and efficiency of the vehicle.

Provided that regular servicing is carried out in accordance with the manufacturers recommendations, the E-Class should prove very reliable and durable. The engine compartment is well designed, and most of the items requiring frequent attention are easily accessible.

This manual covers the following models:
- *4-, 5-, 6-cylinder in-line, and V6 diesel engines*
- *Two wheel drive Saloon and Estate models*
- *Manual and automatic transmissions*
- *Does not cover petrol engines, or 4 wheel drive models*

Your Mercedes E-Class manual

The aim of this Manual is to help you get the best value from your vehicle. It can do so in several ways. It can help you decide what work must be done (even should you choose to get it done by a garage). It will also provide information on routine maintenance and servicing, and give a logical course of action and diagnosis when random faults occur. However, it is hoped that you will use the manual by tackling the work yourself. On simpler jobs it may even be quicker than booking the car into a garage and going there twice, to leave and collect it. Perhaps most important, a lot of money can be saved by avoiding the costs a garage must charge to cover its labour and overheads.

The manual has drawings and descriptions to show the function of the various components so that their layout can be understood. Tasks are described and photographed in a clear step-by-step sequence. The illustrations are numbered by the Section number and paragraph number to which they relate – if there is more than one illustration per paragraph, the sequence is denoted alphabetically.

References to the "left" or "right" of the vehicle are in the sense of a person in the driver's seat, facing forwards.

Acknowledgements

Thanks are due to Draper Tools, who provided some of the workshop tools, and to all those people at Sparkford who helped in the production of this manual.

This manual is not a direct reproduction of the vehicle manufacturer's data, and its publication should not be taken as implying any technical approval by the vehicle manufacturers or importers.

We take great pride in the accuracy of information given in this manual, but vehicle manufacturers make alterations and design changes during the production run of a particular vehicle of which they do not inform us. No liability can be accepted by the authors or publishers for loss, damage or injury caused by any errors in, or omissions from, the information given.

Project vehicles

The main vehicle used in the preparation of this manual, and which appears in many of the photographic sequences, was a 2006 E320 with a V6 diesel engine.

Mercedes-Benz E-Class

Working on your car can be dangerous. This page shows just some of the potential risks and hazards, with the aim of creating a safety-conscious attitude.

General hazards

Scalding

• Don't remove the radiator or expansion tank cap while the engine is hot.
• Engine oil, transmission fluid or power steering fluid may also be dangerously hot if the engine has recently been running.

Burning

• Beware of burns from the exhaust system and from any part of the engine. Brake discs and drums can also be extremely hot immediately after use.

Crushing

• When working under or near a raised vehicle, always supplement the jack with axle stands, or use drive-on ramps.
Never venture under a car which is only supported by a jack.
• Take care if loosening or tightening high-torque nuts when the vehicle is on stands. Initial loosening and final tightening should be done with the wheels on the ground.

Fire

• Fuel is highly flammable; fuel vapour is explosive.
• Don't let fuel spill onto a hot engine.
• Do not smoke or allow naked lights (including pilot lights) anywhere near a vehicle being worked on. Also beware of creating sparks (electrically or by use of tools).
• Fuel vapour is heavier than air, so don't work on the fuel system with the vehicle over an inspection pit.
• Another cause of fire is an electrical overload or short-circuit. Take care when repairing or modifying the vehicle wiring.
• Keep a fire extinguisher handy, of a type suitable for use on fuel and electrical fires.

Electric shock

• Ignition HT and Xenon headlight voltages can be dangerous, especially to people with heart problems or a pacemaker. Don't work on or near these systems with the engine running or the ignition switched on.

• Mains voltage is also dangerous. Make sure that any mains-operated equipment is correctly earthed. Mains power points should be protected by a residual current device (RCD) circuit breaker.

Fume or gas intoxication

• Exhaust fumes are poisonous; they can contain carbon monoxide, which is rapidly fatal if inhaled. Never run the engine in a confined space such as a garage with the doors shut.
• Fuel vapour is also poisonous, as are the vapours from some cleaning solvents and paint thinners.

Poisonous or irritant substances

• Avoid skin contact with battery acid and with any fuel, fluid or lubricant, especially antifreeze, brake hydraulic fluid and Diesel fuel. Don't syphon them by mouth. If such a substance is swallowed or gets into the eyes, seek medical advice.
• Prolonged contact with used engine oil can cause skin cancer. Wear gloves or use a barrier cream if necessary. Change out of oil-soaked clothes and do not keep oily rags in your pocket.
• Air conditioning refrigerant forms a poisonous gas if exposed to a naked flame (including a cigarette). It can also cause skin burns on contact.

Asbestos

• Asbestos dust can cause cancer if inhaled or swallowed. Asbestos may be found in gaskets and in brake and clutch linings. When dealing with such components it is safest to assume that they contain asbestos.

Special hazards

Hydrofluoric acid

• This extremely corrosive acid is formed when certain types of synthetic rubber, found in some O-rings, oil seals, fuel hoses etc, are exposed to temperatures above 400OC. The rubber changes into a charred or sticky substance containing the acid. *Once formed, the acid remains dangerous for years. If it gets onto the skin, it may be necessary to amputate the limb concerned.*
• When dealing with a vehicle which has suffered a fire, or with components salvaged from such a vehicle, wear protective gloves and discard them after use.

The battery

• Batteries contain sulphuric acid, which attacks clothing, eyes and skin. Take care when topping-up or carrying the battery.
• The hydrogen gas given off by the battery is highly explosive. Never cause a spark or allow a naked light nearby. Be careful when connecting and disconnecting battery chargers or jump leads.

Air bags

• Air bags can cause injury if they go off accidentally. Take care when removing the steering wheel and trim panels. Special storage instructions may apply.

Diesel injection equipment

• Diesel injection pumps supply fuel at very high pressure. Take care when working on the fuel injectors and fuel pipes.

⚠️ *Warning: Never expose the hands, face or any other part of the body to injector spray; the fuel can penetrate the skin with potentially fatal results.*

Remember...

DO

• Do use eye protection when using power tools, and when working under the vehicle.
• Do wear gloves or use barrier cream to protect your hands when necessary.
• Do get someone to check periodically that all is well when working alone on the vehicle.
• Do keep loose clothing and long hair well out of the way of moving mechanical parts.
• Do remove rings, wristwatch etc, before working on the vehicle – especially the electrical system.
• Do ensure that any lifting or jacking equipment has a safe working load rating adequate for the job.

DON'T

• Don't attempt to lift a heavy component which may be beyond your capability – get assistance.
• Don't rush to finish a job, or take unverified short cuts.
• Don't use ill-fitting tools which may slip and cause injury.
• Don't leave tools or parts lying around where someone can trip over them. Mop up oil and fuel spills at once.
• Don't allow children or pets to play in or near a vehicle being worked on.

The following pages are intended to help in dealing with common roadside emergencies and breakdowns. You will find more detailed fault finding information at the back of the manual, and repair information in the main chapters.

If your car won't start and the starter motor doesn't turn

☐ If it's a model with automatic transmission, make sure the selector is in 'P' or 'N'.
☐ Open the boot lid or tailgate, lift up the floor panel, and unclip the battery cover. On Estate models, unclip the cover from the battery on the right-hand side of the spare wheel well.
☐ Check the condition and security of the battery connections.
☐ Switch on the headlights and try to start the engine. If the headlights go very dim when you're trying to start, the battery is probable flat. Get out of trouble by jump starting using a friends car.

If your car won't start even though the starter motor turns as normal

☐ Is there fuel in the tank?
☐ Is there moisture on electrical connections under the bonnet? Switch off the ignition, then wipe off any obvious dampness with a dry cloth. Spray a water-dispersant aerosol product (WD-40 or equivalent) on ignition and fuel system electrical connectors like those shown in the photos.

A Check the security of the fuel injection system/pre-heater system components wiring plugs

B Check the mass air flow sensor(s) wiring plug

C Check the engine compartment fuses

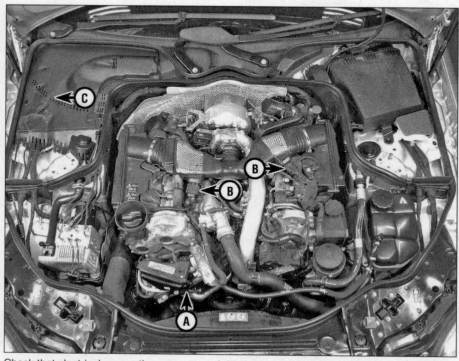

Check that electrical connections are secure (with the ignition switched off) and spray them with a water-dispersant spray like WD-40 if you suspect a problem due to damp

D Check the security and condition of the battery terminal clamps (battery is located under the floor in the luggage compartment)

Identifying leaks

Puddles on the garage floor or drive, or obvious wetness under the bonnet or underneath the car, suggest a leak that needs investigating. I can sometimes be difficult to decide where the leak is coming from, especially if the engine bay is very dirty already. Leaking oil of fluid can also be blown rearwards by the passage of air under the car, giving a false impression of where the problem lies.

⚠️ **Warning: Most automotive oils and fluids are poisonous, Wash them off skin, and change out of contaminated clothing without delay.**

HAYNES HiNT *The smell of a fluid leaking from the car may provide a clue to what's leaking. Some fluids are distinctly coloured. I may help to clean the car carefully and to park it over some clean paper overnight as an aid to locating the source of the leak. Remember that some leaks may only occur while the engine is running.*

Sump oil

Engine oil may leak from the drain plug...

Oil from filter

...or from the base of the oil filter.

Gearbox oil

Gearbox oil can leak from the seals at the inboard ends of the driveshafts.

Antifreeze

Leaking antifreeze often leaves a crystalline deposit like this.

Brake fluid

A leak occurring at a wheel is almost certainly brake fluid.

Power steering fluid

Power steering fluid may leak from the pipe connectors on the steering rack.

Towing

When all else fails, you may find yourself having to get a tow home – or of course you may be helping somebody else. Long-distance recovery should only be done by a garage or breakdown service. For shorter distances, DIY towing using another car is easy enough, but observe the following points:

☐ Use a proper tow-rope – they are not expensive. The vehicle being towed must display an ON TOW sign in its rear window.

☐ Always turn the ignition to the 'on' position when the vehicle is being towed, so that the steering lock is released, and that the direction indicator and brake lights will work.

☐ The front towing eye socket is located in the front bumper. Press-in the lower section of the cover (see illustration).

☐ The rear towing eye socket cover is located in the rear bumper. Press-in the mark on the cover.

☐ Before being towed, release the handbrake and make sure the transmission is in neutral. On automatic transmission models, if necessary the selector lever can be released from position by depressing the catch at the rear of the selector lever housing, after having pulled up the insert from the storage compartment behind the selector panel (see illustration).

☐ Note that greater-than-usual pedal pressure will be required to operate the brakes, since the vacuum servo unit is only operational with the engine running, and no power assistance will be available for the steering.

☐ The driver of the car being towed must keep the tow-rope taut at all times to avoid snatching.

☐ Only drive at moderate speeds, and keep the distance towed to a minimum. Drive smoothly, and allow plenty of time for slowing down at junctions.

☐ Mercedes state that the vehicle should be towed at a speed of no more than 50 mph (80 kmh) for a distance of no more than 50 miles (80 km). If being towed a longer distance, the propeller shaft must be removed as described in Chapter 8 Section 7.

Press-in the mark on the front towing eye cover

Use a long, thin screwdriver to depress the catch at the rear of the selector lever housing

Jump starting

When jump-starting a car using a booster battery, observe the following precautions:

✓ Before connecting the booster battery, make sure that the ignition is switched off.
✓ Ensure that all electrical equipment (lights, heater, wipers, etc) is switched off.
✓ Take note of any special precautions printed on the battery case.
✓ Make sure that the booster battery is the same voltage as the discharged one in the vehicle.

✓ If the battery is being jump-started from the battery in another vehicle, the two vehicles MUST NOT TOUCH each other.
✓ Make sure that the transmission is in neutral (or PARK, in the case of automatic transmission)

HAYNES HINT *Budget jump leads can be a false economy, as they often do not pass enough current to start large capacity or diesel engines. They can also get hot.*

HAYNES HINT *Jump starting will get you out of trouble, but you must correct whatever made the battery go flat in the first place. There are three possibilities:*

1 The battery has been drained by repeated attempts to start, or by leaving the lights on.

2 The charging system is not working properly (alternator drivebelt slack or broken, alternator wiring fault or alternator itself faulty).

3 The battery itself is at fault (electrolyte low, or battery worn out).

Saloon models

1 Lift the luggage compartment floor

2 Connect one end of the red jump lead to the positive (+) terminal of the flat battery

3 Connect the other end of the red lead to the positive (+) terminal of the booster battery.

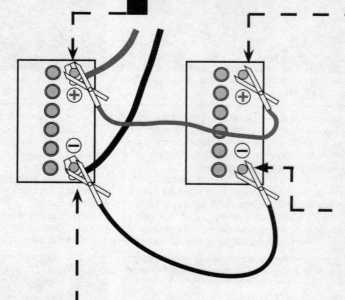

4 Connect one end of the black jump lead to the negative (-) terminal of the booster battery

5 Connect the other end of the black jump lead to the negative (-) terminal of the flat battery.

Estate models

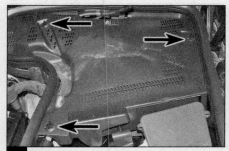

1 Open the bonnet, rotate the catches 90° and remove the plastic cover in the left-hand corner of the engine compartment.

2 Open the cover and connect one end of the red jump lead to the positive (+) terminal at the engine compartment bulkhead.

3 Connect the other end of the red jump lead to the positive (+) terminal of the booster battery.

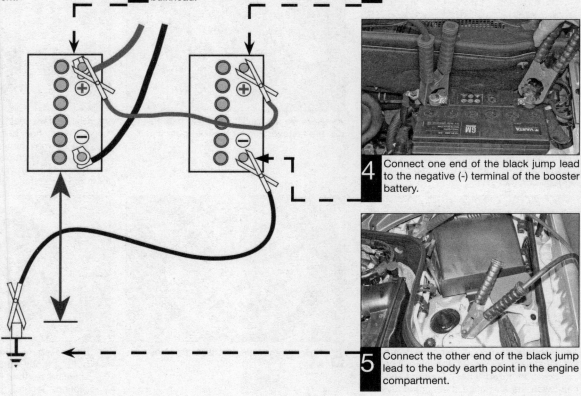

4 Connect one end of the black jump lead to the negative (-) terminal of the booster battery.

5 Connect the other end of the black jump lead to the body earth point in the engine compartment.

All models

6 Make sure that the jump leads will not come into contact with the fan, drive-belts or other moving parts of the engine. Start the engine using the booster battery and run it at idle speed. Switch on the lights, rear window demister and heater blower motor, then disconnect the jump leads in the reverse order of connection. Turn off the lights etc.

Wheel changing

 Warning: Do not change a wheel in a situation where you risk being hit by another vehicle. On busy roads, try to stop in a lay-by or a gateway. Be wary of passing traffic while changing the wheel – it is easy to become distracted by the job in hand.

Preparation

☐ When a puncture occurs, stop as soon as it is safe to do so.

☐ Park on firm level ground, if possible, and well out of the way of other traffic. If jacking on a slope is unavoidable, chock the wheel diagonally opposite the one to be removed on the downhill side, using the chock provided in the toolkit.

☐ Use hazard warning lights if necessary.

☐ If the ground is soft, use a flat piece of wood to spread the load under the jack.

Changing the wheel

1 The vehicle jack, toolkit and spare wheel are located under the luggage compartment floor panel. Lift the panel then rotate the catch clockwise and remove the toolkit cover from the left-hand side of the luggage compartment.

2 Remove the toolkit and jack, then release the fastener and lift out the spare wheel.

3 Using the wheel brace supplied, slacken the roadwheel bolts half a turn each. The wheels may have special locking bolts – these are removed with a special tool, which should be provided with the wheelbrace (or it may be in the glovebox).

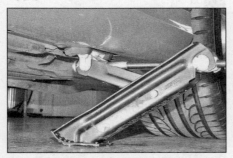

4 Position the jack head beneath the jacking point under the sill closest to the punctured wheel. Engage the jack head with the sill flange, then smoothly raise the vehicle undo the tyre is clear of the road surface.

5 Unscrew the wheel bolts, and remove the wheel.

6 Fit the spare wheel, and screw-in the bolts. Lightly tighten the bolts with the wheelbrace, then lower the vehicle to the ground. Securely tighten the wheel bolts. Note that the wheel bolts should be slackened and retightened to the specified torque at the earliest possible opportunity.

Caution: If a temporary 'space-saver' spare wheel is fitted, do not exceed 50 mph (80 kmh), and take particular care when cornering.

Finally . . .

☐ Remove the wheel chocks.

☐ Stow the punctured wheel and tools back in the luggage compartment, and secure them in position.

☐ Check the tyre pressure on the tyre just fitted. If it is low, or if you don't have a pressure gauge with you, drive slowly to the next garage and inflate the tyre to the correct pressure. In the case of the narrow 'space-saver' spare wheel this pressure is much higher than for a normal tyre.

☐ Have the punctured wheel repaired as soon as possible, or another puncture will leave you stranded.

Introduction

There are some very simple checks which need only take a few minutes to carry out, but which could save you a lot of inconvenience and expense.

☐ These Weekly checks require no great skill or special tools, and the small amount of time they take to perform could prove to be very well spent, for example:

☐ Keeping an eye on tyre condition and pressures, will not only help to stop them wearing out prematurely, but could also save your life.

☐ Many breakdowns are caused by electrical problems. Battery-related faults are particularly common, and a quick check on a regular basis will often prevent the majority of these.

☐ If your car develops a brake fluid leak, the first time you might know about it is when your brakes don't work properly. Checking the level regularly will give advance warning of this kind of problem.

☐ If the oil or coolant levels run low, the cost of repairing any engine damage will be far greater than fixing the leak, for example.

Underbonnet check points

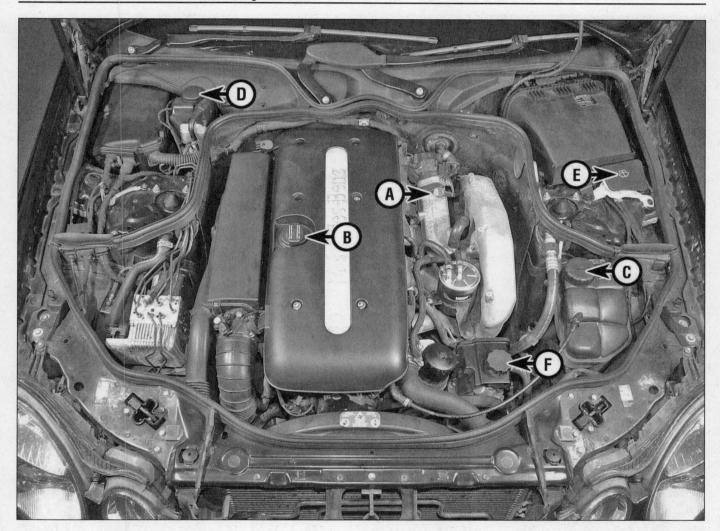

▲ **In-line engine shown – V6 is similar**

A *Engine oil level dipstick*

B *Engine oil filler cap*

C *Coolant expansion tank*

D *Brake fluid reservoir (unclip the cover for access)*

E *Screen/headlight washer fluid reservoir*

F *Power steering fluid reservoir*

Engine oil level

Before you start
✔ Make sure that your car is on level ground
✔ Check the oil level before the car is driven, or at least 5 minutes after the engine has been switched off.

 HAYNES HINT *If the oil is checked immediately after driving the vehicle, some of the oil will remain in the upper engine components, resulting in an inaccurate reading on the dipstick!*

The correct oil
Modern engines place great demands on their oil. It is very important that the correct oil for your car is used (See "*Lubricants and fluids*").

Car care
● If you have to add oil frequently, you should check whether you have any oil leaks. Place some clean paper under the car overnight, and check for stains in the morning. If there are no leaks, the engine may be burning oil (see "*Fault finding*").

Vehicles with an engine oil level dipstick
● Always maintain the level between the upper and lower dipstick marks. If the level is too low severe engine damage may occur. Oil seal failure may result if the engine is overfilled by adding too much oil.
● On all diesel models it is located on the left-hand rear side of the engine. See "*Underbonnet Check Points*" for the exact location of the dipstick.

Vehicles without an engine oil level dipstick
● Some models have a red cap fitted to the dipstick tube, and not a dipstick. The engine oil level is checked on the multi-function display unit on the instrument panel. By pressing the up and down buttons repeatedly, the ENGINE OIL LEVEL, MEASURING NOW! will appear on the display. Follow the instructions shown to achieve the correct level.

1 Withdraw the dipstick. Using a clean rag or paper towel, wipe all the oil from the dipstick. Insert the clean dipstick into the tube as far as it will go, then withdraw it again.

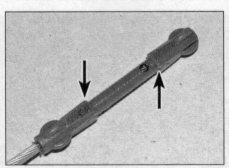

2 Note the oil level on the end of the dipstick, which should be between the upper MAX mark and the lower MIN mark.

3 Oil is added through the filler cap on top of the engine. Rotate the cap through a quarter-turn anti-clockwise and withdraw it. Top-up the level. A funnel may help to reduce spillage. Add the oil slowly, checking the level on the dipstick often. Do not overfill.

Coolant level

 Warning: DO NOT attempt to remove the expansion tank pressure cap when the engine is hot, as there is a very great risk of scalding. Do not leave open containers of coolant about, as it is poisonous.

Car care
● With a sealed-type cooling system, adding coolant should not be necessary on a regular basis. If frequent topping-up is required, it is likely there is a leak. Check the radiator, all hoses and joint faces for signs of staining or wetness, and rectify as necessary.
● It is important that antifreeze is used in the cooling system all year round, not just during the winter months. Don't top-up with water alone, as the antifreeze will become too diluted.
● The coolant level varies with the temperature of the engine. When the engine is cold, the coolant level should be level with the marker bar withing the filler neck. When the engine is hot, the level will rise approximately 15 mm.

1 If topping-up is necessary, wait until the engine is cold, then slowly unscrew the expansion tank filler cap anti-clockwise, to release any pressure in the system, and remove it.

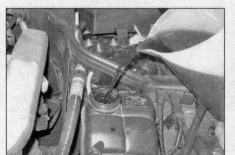

2 Add a mixture of water and antifreeze through the expansion tank filler neck . ...

3 ... until the coolant is level with the marker bar in the filler neck. Refit the cap, turning it clockwise as far as it will go until it is secure.

Brake/clutch fluid level

Warning: Brake fluid can harm your eyes and damage painted surfaces, so use extreme caution when handling and pouring it.
Caution: Do not use fluid that has been standing open for some time, as it absorbs moisture from the air, which can cause a dangerous loss of braking effectiveness.
Note: *The fluid level in the reservoir will drop slightly as the brake pads wear down, but the fluid level must never be allowed to drop below the "MIN" mark.*

Before you start

✔ Make sure that your car is on level ground.

Safety first!

● If the reservoir requires repeated topping-up this is an indication of a fluid leak somewhere in the system, which should be investigated immediately.

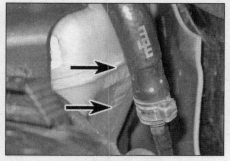

3 The MAX and MIN levels are shown on the side of the reservoir

1 The brake master cylinder and fluid reservoir are mounted in the engine compartment on the right-hand side of the bulkhead. On some models, rotate the fasteners anti-clockwise and remove the cover from above the master cylinder

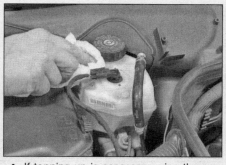

4 If topping-up is necessary, wipe the area around the filler cap with a clean rag before removing the cap. It's a good idea to inspect the reservoir. The fluid should be changed if dirt is visible.

2 On other models, remove the cover over the fluid reservoir

5 Carefully add fluid, avoiding spilling it on surrounding paintwork. Use only the specified hydraulic fluid; mixing different types of fluid can cause damage to the system and/or a loss of braking effectiveness. After filling to the correct level, refit the cap securely. Wipe off any spilt fluid.

Screen/headlight washer fluid level

● Screenwash additives not only keep the windscreen clean during foul weather, they also prevent the washer system freezing in cold weather – which is when you are likely to need it most. Don't top up using plain water as the screenwash will become too diluted, and will freeze during cold weather.

Warning: On no account use coolant antifreeze in the washer system – this could discolour or damage paintwork.

1 The reservoir for the windscreen and rear window, and healight (where applicable) washer systems is located in the front right-hand corner of the engine compartment. If topping up is necessary, open the cap.

2 When topping-up the reservoir a screenwash additive should be added in the quantities recommended on the container.

Power steering fluid level

Before you start
✔ Park the vehicle on level ground
✔ Set the steering wheel straight-ahead
✔ The engine should be cold and turned off

Safety first!
● The need for frequent topping-up indicates a leak, which should be investigated immediately.

Note: *For the check to be accurate, the steering must not be turned once the engine has been stopped.*

1 In-line engines – undo the fasteners and remove the cover from the top of the engine. The reservoir is mounted at the left-hand side of the engine compartment.

2 V6 engines – pull the cover up from the rubber mountings and remove the cover from the top of the engine. The reservoir is mounted at the left-hand side of the engine compartment.

3 Wipe clean the area around the filler cap, then unscrew it from the reservoir.

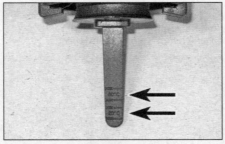

2 The level should be at the MAX mark on the dipstick, depending on the temperature of the fluid. MAX and MIN marks on the dipstick are given for 80°C and 20°C

3 If topping-up is necessary, use the specified type of fluid – do not overfill the reservoir. Take care not to introduce dirt into the system when topping-up. When the level is correct, securely refit the cap.

Wiper blades

● Screenwash additives not only keep the windscreen clean during foul weather, they also prevent the washer system freezing in cold weather – which is when you are likely to need it most. Don't top up using plain water as the screenwash will become too diluted, and will freeze during cold weather.
Warning: On no account use coolant antifreeze in the washer system – this could discolour or damage paintwork.

Front wiper blades
● Set the wipers in the 'Service position' by switching on the ignition, setting the wiper switch to continuous slow wipe, then when the arms are in the vertical position, turn off the ignition.
● Fold the wiper arms away from the windscreen.
Caution: Do not attempt to fold the arms away from the windscreen when they at not at the vertical position, otherwise damage to the bonnet may result.

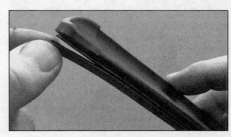

1 Check the condition of the wiper blades. If they are cracked or show any signs of deterioration, or if the glass swept area is smeared, renew them. For maximum clarity of vision, wiper blades should be renewed annually, as a matter of course.

2 Position the blade at 90° to the arm...

3 ... and slide it from the arm.

4 On rear wiper blades, Pull the blade away from the screen, rotate it 90°, depress the clip and slide it from the arm.

Battery

Caution: Before carrying out any work on the vehicle battery, read the precautions given in "Safety first" at the start of this manual.

✔ Make sure that the battery tray is in good condition, and that the clamp is tight.

Corrosion on the tray, retaining clamp and the battery itself can be removed with a solution of water and baking soda. Thoroughly rinse all cleaned areas with water. Any metal parts damaged by corrosion should be covered with a zinc-based primer, then painted.

✔ Periodically (approximately every three months), check the charge condition of the battery as described in Chapter 5A, Section 3.
✔ If the battery is flat, and you need to jump start your vehicle, see "Jump Starting".

1 The battery is located under the luggage compartment floor panel. Lift the floor panel, and on Estate models, pull up the cover over the batter. The exterior of the battery should be inspected periodically for damage such as a cracked case or cover.

2 Remove the electrostatic protection from the top of the battery.

3 Check the tightness of the battery cable clamps to ensure good electrical connections. You should not be able to move them. Also check each cable for cracks and frayed conductors.

HAYNES HiNT

Battery corrosion can be kept to a minimum by applying a layer of petroleum jelly to the clamps and terminals after they are reconnected.

4 If corrosion (white, fluffy deposits) is evident, remove the cables from the battery terminals, clean them with a small wire brush, then refit them. Automotive stores sell a tool for cleaning the battery post...

5 ... as well as the battery cable clamps

Electrical systems

✔ Check all external lights and the horn. Refer to the appropriate Sections of Chapter 12 for details if any of the circuits are found to be inoperative.

✔ Visually check all accessible wiring connectors, harnesses and retaining clips for security, and for signs of chafing or damage.

 HAYNES HiNT *If you need to check your brake lights and indicators unaided, back up to a wall or garage door and operate the lights. The reflected light should show if they are working properly.*

1 If a single indicator light, brake light or headlight has failed, it is likely that a bulb has blown and will need to be replaced. Refer to Chapter 12 Section 6 for details. If both brake lights have failed, it is possible that the stop-light switch operated by the brake pedal has failed. Refer to Chapter 9 Section 18 for details.

2 If more than one indicator light or headlight has failed, it is likely that either a fuse has blown or that there is a fault in the circuit (see Chapter 12). The main fusebox is located behind the end of the drivers side of the facia. A further fusebox is located in the left-hand side of the engine compartment, with a further fusebox beneath the luggage compartment floor. To access the main fusebox, prise the cover from the drivers end of the facia.

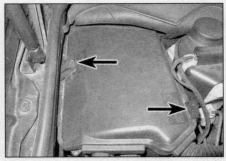

3 Slide the engine compartment fusebox lid clips to the unlocked position

4 Prise open the cover to access the fusebox on the left-hand side of the luggage compartment – Saloon models

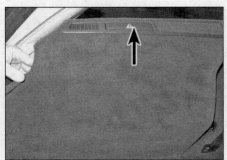

5 Depress the button and remove the side panel – Estate models

6 To replace a blown fuse, pull it out directly from the fusebox. Fit a new fuse of the same rating, available from car accessory shops. It is important that you find the reason that the fuse blew (see "Electrical fault finding" in Chapter 12 Section 2).

Tyre condition and pressure

It is very important that tyres are in good condition, and at the correct pressure – having a tyre failure at any speed is highly dangerous. Tyre wear is influenced by driving style – harsh braking and acceleration, or fast cornering, will all produce more rapid tyre wear. As a general rule, the front tyres wear out faster the the rears. Interchanging the tyres from front to rear ("rotating" the tyres) may result in more even wear. However, if this is completely effective, you may have the expense of replacing all four tyres at once!

Remove any nails or stones embedded in the tread before they penetrate the tyre to cause deflation. If removal of a nail does reveal that the tyre has been punctured, refit the nail so that its point of penetration is marked. Then immediately change the wheel, and have the tyre repaired by a tyre dealer.

Regularly check the tyres for damage in the form of cuts or bulges, especially in the side walls. Periodically remove the wheels, and clean any dirt or mud from the inside and outside surfaces. Examine the wheel rims for signs of rusting, corrosion or other damage. Light alloy wheels are easily damaged by "kerbing" whilst parking; steel wheels may also become dented or buckled. A new wheel is very often the only way to overcome severe damage.

New tyres should be balanced when they are fitted, but it may become necessary to re-balance them as they ear, or if the balance weights fitted to the wheel rim should fall off. Unbalanced tyres will wear more quickly, as will the steering and suspension components. Wheel imbalance is normally signified by vibration, particularly at t certain speed (typically around 50 mph). If this vibration is felt only through the steering wheel, then it is likely that just the front wheels need balancing. If, however, the vibration is felt through the whole car, the rear wheels could be out of balance. Wheel balancing should be carried out by a tyre dealer or garage.

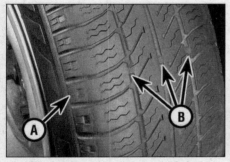

1 Tread Depth - visual check
The original tyres have tread wear safety bands (B), which will appear when the trad depth reaches approximately 1.6 mm. The band positions are indicated by a triangular mark on the tyre sidewall (A)

2 Tread Depth - manual check
Alternatively, tread wear can be monitored with a simple, inexpensive device known as a tread depth indicator gauge

3 Tyre Pressure Check
Check the tyre pressures regularly with the tyres cold. Do not adjust the tyre pressures immediately after the vehicle has been used, or an inaccurate setting will result

Tyre tread wear patterns

Shoulder Wear

Underinflation (wear on both sides)
Under-inflation will cause overheating of the tyre, because the tyre will flex too much, and the tread will not sit correctly on the road surface. This will cause a loss of grip and excessive wear, not to mention the danger of sudden tyre failure due to heat build-up.
Check and adjust pressures
Incorrect wheel camber (wear on one side)
Repair or renew suspension parts
Hard cornering
Reduce speed!

Centre Wear

Overinflation
Over-inflation will cause rapid wear of the centre part of the tyre tread, coupled with reduced grip, harsher ride, and the danger of shock damage occurring in the tyre casing.
Check and adjust pressures

If you sometimes have to inflate your car's tyres to the higher pressures specified for maximum load or sustained high speed, don't forget to reduce the pressures to normal afterwards.

Uneven Wear

Front tyres may wear unevenly as a result of wheel misalignment. Most tyre dealers and garages can check and adjust the wheel alignment (or "tracking") for a modest charge.
Incorrect camber or castor
Repair or renew suspension parts
Malfunctioning suspension
Repair or renew suspension parts
Unbalanced wheel
Balance tyres
Incorrect toe setting
Adjust front wheel alignment
Note: *The feathered edge of the tread which typifies toe wear is best checked by feel.*

Lubricants and fluids

Engine oil
Models without diesel particulate filter. . . . . 5W/30 meeting Mercedes specification 228.3/228.5/228.51/229.3/
229.31/229.5/229.51. Eg. Castrol Edge 5W30
Models with diesel particulate filter . . . . 5W/30 meeting Mercedes specification 228.51/229.31/229.51.
Eg. Castrol Edge 5W30

Coolant. . . . . Mercedes Benz Long life coolant to specification M325.6*

Transmission
Manual gearbox . . . . Mercedes Benz specification MB345.0 part No. A 001 989 24 03*.
Eg. Pentosin CHF 11 S
Automatic gearbox: . . . . Mercedes Benz ATF specification MB 236.14 part No. A 001 898 68 03.
Eg. Sheel ATF 134
Final drive. . . . . Mercedes Benz 75W-85 specification MB 235.7/237.74 Hypoid gear
oil part No. A 001 898 33 03*. Mobilube FE 75W-85

Brake/clutch fluid . . . . Hydraulic fluid DOT 4 Plus

Power steering fluid. . . . . Pentosin hydraulic fluid. MB part No. A 001 989 24 03 10
Check with dealer for latest specifications.

Tyre pressures

The pressures for the standard fitment tyres are given on a sticker attached to the inside of the fuel filler flap.

Chapter 1
Routine maintenance and servicing

Contents

Degrees of difficulty

| Easy, suitable for novice with little experience | | Fairly easy, suitable for beginner with some experience | | Fairly difficult, suitable for competent DIY mechanic | | Difficult, suitable for experienced DIY mechanic | | Very difficult, suitable for expert DIY or professional | |

Lubricants and fluids. . . . .   Refer to *'Weekly checks'*

Capacities

Engine oil (with filter):
  4-cylinder engines . . . .   6.5 litres
  5-cylinder engines . . . .   6.5 litres
  6-cylinder in-line engines . . . .   7.3 litres
  V6 engines . . . .   8.5 litres
Cooling system:
  4-cylinder engines . . . .   10.2 litres
  5-cylinder engines . . . .   11.25 litres
  6-cylinder in-line engines . . . .   12.0 litres
  V6 engines . . . .   13.0 litres
Fuel tank . . . .   65, 70 or 80 litres model/specification dependent
Manual transmission:
  716.60, 71661, 716.62 and 716.63 gearbox . . . .   1.2 litres
  716.64, 716.65, 716.66 gearbox. . . . .   1.5 litres
Automatic transmission (initial dry fill):
  7-speed transmission. . . . .   9.0 litres
  5-speed transmission. . . . .   7.5 litres
Final drive. . . . .   1.0 to 1.6 litres model/specification dependent

Cooling system

Protection at mixture of 50% anti-freeze and 50% water . . . .   -40°C

Braking system

Brake pad friction material minimum thickness (front and rear). . . . . .   2.0 mm

Torque wrench settings

	Nm	lbf ft
Automatic transmission:		
Drain plug.	47	35
Filler plug	39	29
Level plug	7	4
Cylinder block drain plug	23	17
Engine oil drain plug:		
M12	30	22
M24	45	33
Engine oil filter cap.	25	18
Manual transmission		
Drain plug.	30	22
Filler plug	35	26
Roadwheel bolts.	130	96

1 Maintenance schedule

1 The maintenance intervals in this manual are provided with the assumption that you, not the dealer, will be carrying out the work. These are the minimum maintenance intervals recommended by us for cars driven daily. If you wish to keep your car in peak condition at all times, you may wish to perform some of these procedures more often. We encourage frequent maintenance, because it enhances the efficiency, performance and resale value of your car.
2 The E-Class is equipped with a time/condition dependent service interval display system (ASSYST PLUS – Active Service System). Owners may wish to follow the service schedule indicated by this system, or follow the schedule detailed below.
3 If the car is driven in dusty areas, used to tow a trailer, or driven frequently at slow speeds (idling in traffic) or on short journeys, more frequent maintenance intervals are recommended.

Every 250 miles or weekly
☐ Refer to 'Weekly checks'

Every 6000 miles or 6 months, whichever occurs first
☐ Renew the engine oil and filter (Section 4).

Note: Frequent oil and filter changes are good for the engine. We recommend changing the oil at the mileage specified here, or at least twice a year if the mileage covered is less.

Every 12 000 miles or 12 months, whichever occurs first
In addition to the item listed in the previous service, carry out the following:

☐ Check the battery and clean the terminals (Section 5).
☐ Check the auxiliary drivebelt (Section 6).
☐ Check the electrical system (Section 7).
☐ Check under the bonnet for fluid leaks and hose condition (Section 8).
☐ Check the condition of all engine compartment wiring (Section 9).
☐ Check the condition of the air conditioning components (Section 10).

Every 12 000 miles or 12 months, whichever occurs first (continued)
☐ Check the seat belts (Section 11).
☐ Check the antifreeze concentration (Section 12).
☐ Check the steering, suspension and roadwheels (Section 13).
☐ Check the driveshaft rubber gaiters (Section 14).
☐ Check the exhaust system (Section 15).
☐ Check the underbody, and all fuel/brake lines (Section 16).
☐ Check the braking system (Section 17).
☐ Check the doors and bonnet, and lubricated their hinges and locks (Section 18).
☐ Road test (Section 21).
☐ Drain the fuel sedimentor (Section 20).
☐ Reset the service indicator (Section 22).

Every 24 months or 24 000 miles, whichever occurs first
☐ Remove the roadwheels, and apply anti-seize grease to the hubs (Section 23).
☐ Renew the air cleaner element (Section 24).
☐ Renew the fuel filter element (Section 25).
☐ Renew the pollen filter (Section 19).

Every 2 years, regardless of mileage
☐ Renew the brake fluid (Section 26).

Once at 37 000 miles
☐ Renew the manual transmission oil (Section 27).
☐ Renew the automatic transmission oil (Section 28).
☐ Renew the rear final drive oil (Section 29).

Every 10 years, regardless of mileage
☐ Renew the coolant (Section 30).

Front underbonnet view – In-line engines

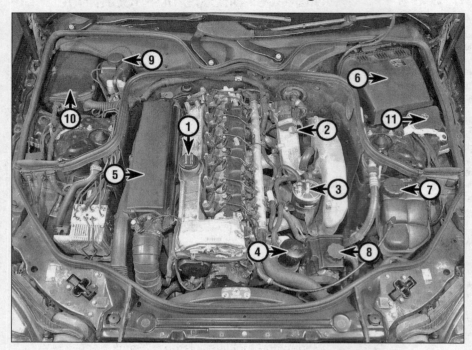

1 Engine oil filler cap
2 Engine oil level dipstick
3 Fuel filter
4 Engine oil filter cap
5 Air filter housing
6 Pollen filter housing
7 Coolant filler cap
8 Power steering reservoir cap
9 Brake/clutch fluid reservoir cap
10 Engine compartment fusebox
11 Screenwash reservoir cap

Front underbonnet view – V6 engines

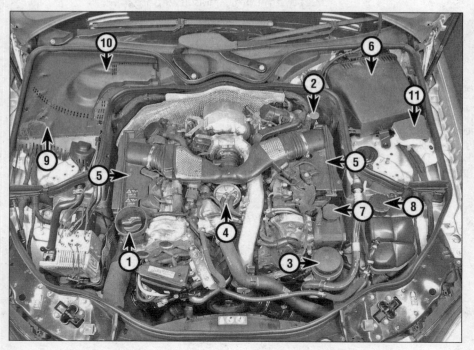

1 Engine oil filler cap
2 Engine oil level dipstick
3 Engine oil filter cap
4 Fuel filter
5 Air filter housings
6 Pollen filter housing
7 Power steering fluid reservoir
8 Coolant filler cap
9 Engine compartment fuse box (under cover)
10 Brake/clutch fluid reservoir (under cover)
11 Screenwash reservoir cap

Front underbody view – V6 shown (others similar)

1 Engine oil drain plug
2 Transmission fluid drain/filler plug
3 Anti-roll bar
4 Torque strut
5 Spring control arm
6 Track rod end
7 Brake caliper
8 Particulate filter
9 Engine oil temperature sensor

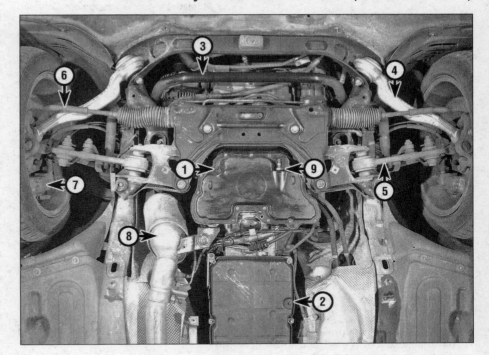

Rear underbody view

1 Propeller shaft
2 Final drive drain plug
3 Final drive filler plug
4 Tie-rod
5 Driveshaft
6 Air spring
7 Parking brake cable
8 Fuel filler pipe
9 Anti-roll bar

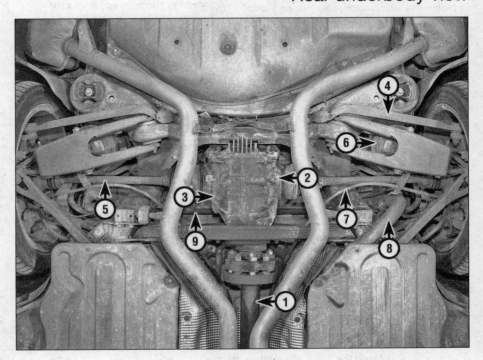

2 Introduction

1 This Chapter is designed to help the home mechanic maintain his/her vehicle for safety, economy, long life and peak performance.

2 The Chapter contains a maintenance schedule, followed by Sections dealing specifically with each task in the schedule. Visual checks, adjustments, component renewal and other helpful items are included. Refer to the accompanying illustrations of the engine compartment and the underside of the vehicle for the locations of the various components.

3 Servicing your vehicle in accordance with the above recommendations and the following Sections will provide a planned maintenance programme, which should result in a long and reliable service life. This is a comprehensive plan, so maintaining some items, but not others at the specified service intervals, will not produce the same results.

4 As you service your vehicle, you will discover that many of the procedures can – and should – be grouped together, because of the particular procedure being performed, or because of the proximity of two otherwise-unrelated components to one another. For example, if the vehicle is raised for any reason, the exhaust can be inspected at the same time as the suspension and steering components.

5 The first step in this maintenance programme is to prepare yourself before the actual work begins. Read through all the Sections relevant to the work to be carried out, then make a list and gather all the parts and tools required. If a problem is encountered, seek advice from a parts specialist, or a dealer service department.

3 Regular maintenance

1 If, from the time the vehicle is new, the routine maintenance schedule is followed closely, and frequent checks are made of fluid levels and high-wear items, as suggested throughout this manual, the engine will be kept in relatively good running condition, and the need for additional work will be minimised.

2 It is possible that there will be times when the engine is running poorly due to the lack of regular maintenance. This is even more likely if a used vehicle, which has not received regular and frequent maintenance checks, is purchased. In such cases, additional work may need to be carried out, outside of the regular maintenance intervals.

3 If engine wear is suspected, a compression test (refer to Chapter 2A Section 2, or Chapter 2B Section 2 as applicable) will provide valuable information regarding the overall performance of the main internal components. Such a test can be used as a basis to decide on the extent of the work to be carried out. If, for example, a compression test indicates serious internal engine wear, conventional maintenance as described in this Chapter will not greatly improve the performance of the engine, and may prove a waste of time and money, unless extensive overhaul work is carried out first.

4 The following series of operations are those most often required to improve the performance of a generally poor-running engine:

Primary operations

a) Clean, inspect and test the battery (see 'Weekly checks' and Section 5).
b) Check all the engine-related fluids (refer to 'Weekly checks').
c) Check the condition and tension of the auxiliary drivebelt (Section 6).
d) Check the condition of all hoses, and check for fluid leaks (Section 8).
e) Renew the fuel filter (Section 25).
f) Check the glow plugs (Chapter 5B Section 3).
g) Check the condition of the air filter, and renew if necessary (Section 24).

5 If the above operations do not prove fully effective, carry out the following secondary operations:

Secondary operations

6 All items listed under Primary operations, plus the following:
a) Check the charging system (Chapter 5A Section 5).
b) Check the fuel system (Chapter 4A Section 9).

4 Engine oil and filter renewal

Note: A new engine oil drain plug sealing washer will be required.

1 Frequent oil and filter changes are the most important preventative maintenance procedures, which can be undertaken by the DIY owner. As engine oil ages, it becomes diluted and contaminated, which leads to premature engine wear.

2 Before starting this procedure, gather together all the necessary tools and materials. Also make sure that you have plenty of clean rags and newspapers handy, to mop-up any spills. Ideally, the engine oil should be warm, as it will drain better, and more built-up sludge will be removed with it. Take care, however, not to touch the exhaust or any other hot parts of the engine when working under the vehicle. To avoid any possibility of scalding, and to protect yourself from possible skin irritants and other harmful contaminants in used engine oils, it is advisable to wear gloves when carrying out this work. Access to the underside of the vehicle will be greatly improved if it can be raised on a lift, driven onto ramps, or jacked up and supported on axle stands as described in 'Vehicle jacking and support' in Reference. Whichever method is chosen, make sure that the vehicle remains level, or if it is at an angle, so that the drain plug is at the lowest point. Where necessary, remove the undershields from under the engine (see illustrations).

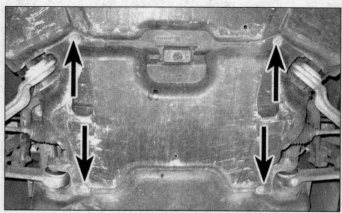

4.2a Undo the bolts and remove the front...

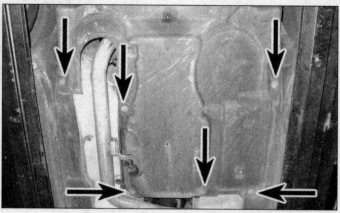

4.2b ...and rear sections of the engine undershield

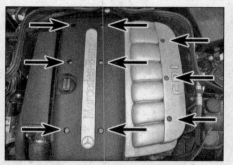

4.3a Undo the screws and remove the covers – in-line engines

4.3b On V6 engines, pull the cover up from the rubber mountings

4.4 Unscrew the oil filter cap

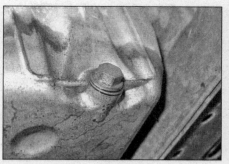

4.6a Engine oil sump drain plug – in-line engines...

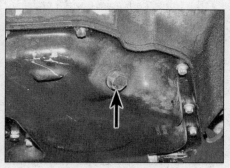

4.6b...and V6 engines

3 Remove the plastic covers from the top of the engine **(see illustrations)**.

4 Locate the oil filter/housing on the front left-hand side of the engine **(see illustration)**. Place a wad of rag around the housing to absorb any spilt oil, and then unscrew the oil filter cap.

Note: *By removing the cap, the oil will drain from the housing into the sump.*

5 Lift the old oil filter element out from the housing, and discard it.

6 Working under the vehicle, unscrew the sump drain plug about half a turn. Position the draining container under the drain plug, and then remove the plug completely **(see illustrations)**.

If possible, try to keep the plug pressed into the sump while unscrewing it by hand the last couple of turns. As the plugs releases from the threads, move it away sharply, so that the stream of oil issuing from the sump runs into the container, nut up your sleeve.

7 Recover the sealing washer from the drain plug.

8 Allow some time for the old oil to drain, noting that it may be necessary to reposition the container as the oil flow slows to a trickle. Remove the oil filler cap from the camshaft cover.

9 After all the oil has drained from the engine, wipe off the drain plug with a clean rag and renew the sealing washer. Clean the area around the drain plug opening, then refit and tighten the plug to the specified torque.

10 Remove the old oil and all tools from under the car, then refit the undershield and lower the car to the ground.

11 Wipe out the oil filter housing and cap using a clean rag, then fit new O-rings to the cap **(see illustration)**.

12 Fit the new filter element into the cap, then refit and tighten the cap to the specified torque **(see illustration)**.

13 Refit the plastic cover(s) to the top of the engine.

Models with a dipstick

14 Remove the oil level dipstick then fill the engine, using the correct grade and type of oil (see *Lubricants and fluids*). An oil can spout or funnel may help to reduce spillage. Pour in half the specified quantity of oil first, and

then wait a few minutes for the oil to run to the sump. Continue adding oil a small quantity at a time until the level is up to the lower mark on the dipstick. Finally, bring the level up to the upper mark on the dipstick. Insert the dipstick, and refit the filler cap.

15 Start the engine and run it for a few minutes; check for leaks around the oil filter cap and the sump drain plug. Note that there may be a delay of a few seconds before the oil pressure warning light goes out when the engine is first started, as the oil circulates through the engine oil galleries and the new oil filter before the pressure builds-up.

16 Switch off the engine, and wait a few minutes for the oil to settle in the sump once more. With the new oil circulated and the filter completely full, recheck the level on the dipstick, and add more oil as necessary.

17 Dispose of the used engine oil safely, with

reference to *General repair procedures* in the Reference section of this manual.

Models without a dipstick

18 Add the correct quantity and grade type of oil (see *Lubricants and fluids*). An oil can spout or funnel may help to reduce spillage. It would be prudent to add the specified quantity, less 0.5 litres to eliminate the possibility of over-filling.

19 Start the engine, and allow it to idle for a few minutes, then switch off the engine, and wait for at least 5 minutes.

20 Make sure the key is in position 2 in the ignition lock.

21 Operate the control lever up or down to select the message: 'Engine oil level Measuring now: '.

22 The measurement will take a few seconds, then a message will be displayed confirming

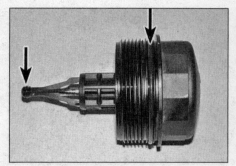

4.11 Renew the O-ring seals

4.12 Fit the new element into the cap

the level is correct, or suggesting an amount to add.

23 If necessary, add the suggested amount of oil, and re-check.

24 Dispose of the used engine oil safely, with reference to *General repair procedures* in the Reference section of this manual.

5 Battery maintenance and charging

⚠ *Warning: Certain precautions must be followed when checking and servicing the battery. Hydrogen gas, which is highly flammable, is always present in the battery cells, so keep lighted tobacco and all other open flames and sparks away from the battery. The electrolyte inside the battery is actually dilute sulphuric acid, which will cause injury if splashed on your skin or in your eyes. It will also ruin clothes and painted surfaces. When disconnecting the battery, always detach the negative (earth) lead first and connect it last.*

Note: *Before disconnecting the battery, refer to Battery disconnection in Chapter 5A Section 4.*

General

1 A routine preventive maintenance programme for the battery in your car is the only way to ensure quick and reliable starts. For general maintenance, refer to 'Weekly checks' at the start of this manual. Also at the front of the manual is information on jump starting. For details of removing and installing the battery, refer to Chapter 5A Section 4.

Battery electrolyte level

2 On models not equipped with a sealed or 'maintenance-free' battery, check the electrolyte level of all six battery cells.

3 The level must be approximately 10 mm above the plates; this may be shown by maximum and minimum level lines marked on the battery's casing.

4 If the level is low, use a coin or screwdriver to release the filler/vent cap, and add distilled water. Do not overfill – this can actually render the battery useless. To improve access to the centre caps, it may be helpful to remove the battery hold-down clamp.

5 Install and securely retighten the cap, then wipe up any spillage.

Caution: Overfilling the cells may cause electrolyte to spill over during periods of heavy charging, causing corrosion or damage.

Charging

⚠ *Warning: When batteries are being charged, hydrogen gas, which is very explosive and flammable, is produced. Do not smoke, or allow open flames, near a charging or a recently-charged battery. If the battery is being charged indoors, ensure this is done in a well-ventilated area. Wear eye protection when near the battery during charging. Also, make sure the charger is unplugged before connecting or disconnecting the battery from the charger.*

6 Slow-rate charging is the best way to restore a battery that's discharged to the point where it will not start the engine. It's also a good way to maintain the battery charge in a car that's only driven a few miles between starts. Maintaining the battery charge is particularly important in winter, when the battery must work harder to start the engine, and electrical accessories that drain the battery are in greater use.

7 Check the battery case for any instructions regarding charging the battery. Some maintenance-free batteries may require a particularly low charge rate or other special conditions, if they are not to be damaged.

8 It's best to use a one- or two-amp battery charger (sometimes called a 'trickle' charger), or a 'Smart/intelligent' charger. They are the safest, and put the least strain on the battery. For a faster charge, you can use a higher-amperage charger, but don't use one rated more than 1/10th the amp/hour rating of the battery (ie, no more than 5 amps, typically). Rapid boost charges that claim to restore the power of the battery in one to two hours are hardest on the battery, and can damage batteries not in good condition. This type of charging should only be used in emergency situations.

9 The average time necessary to charge a battery should be listed in the instructions that come with the charger. As a general rule, a trickle charger will charge a battery in 12 to 16 hours.

6 Auxiliary drivebelt check and renewal

Check

1 Due to its function and construction, the belt is prone to failure after a period of time, and should be inspected periodically to prevent problems.

2 The drivebelt is used to drive the coolant pump, alternator, power steering pump and air conditioning compressor.

3 To improve access for belt inspection, remove the cooling fan shroud as described in Chapter 3 Section 6.

4 With the engine stopped, using your fingers (and an electric torch if necessary), move along the belt, checking for cracks and separation of the belt plies. Also check for fraying and glazing, which gives the belt a shiny appearance. Both sides of the belt should be inspected, which means the belt will have to be twisted to check the underside. If necessary turn the engine using a spanner or socket on the crankshaft pulley bolt so that the whole of the belt can be inspected.

5 If the belt shows signs of damage, or significant deterioration, renew it as described in this Section.

Tension

6 The auxiliary drivebelt is tensioned by an automatic tensioner; regular checks are not required, and manual 'adjustment' is not possible.

7 If you suspect that a drivebelt is slipping and/or running slack, or that the tensioner is otherwise faulty, it and/or an idler pulley must be renewed.

Renewal

In-line engines

8 Remove the cooling fan shroud as described in Chapter 3 Section 6.

9 Engage a socket or Torx T60 bit with the tensioner body below the pulley, and then lever the tensioner anti-clockwise to relieve the tension in the belt **(see illustrations)**.

10 Hold the tensioner in position with the spanner/socket, and slide the belt from the pulleys. If necessary, the tensioner can be retained in its released position by inserting a suitable bolt or metal dowel (4 mm

6.9a Into the socket in the tensioner body...

6.9b...engage a T60 Torx bit

6.10 Use a 4 mm diameter rod to lock the tensioner in place

6.11 Auxiliary drivebelt routing – in-line engines

6.16 Air duct clip, air channel retaining bolts and upper bolt/retaining plate

diameter) through the holes provided **(see illustration)**.

11 Fit the new belt around the pulleys, starting with the crankshaft pulley. Check that the belt is correctly seated on all the pulleys **(see illustration)**. Where applicable, remove the metal dowel/bolt from the tensioner.

12 Release the spanner/socket, and allow the tensioner to move into position against the belt.

13 Refit the cooling fan shroud as described in Chapter 3 Section 6.

V6 engines

14 Pull the plastic cover on the top of the engine upwards to release it from the rubber mountings.

15 Although not strictly necessary, to improve access remove the cooling fan shroud as described in Chapter 3 Section 6.

16 Disconnect the charge air duct from the intercooler to the air channel at the front of the engine **(see illustration)**.

17 Undo the bolt, and remove the retaining plate securing the air channel to the duct that runs across the top of the engine.

18 Undo the 2 retaining bolts, unclip the coolant hose, and manoeuvre the air channel from place.

19 Rotate the tensioner anti-clockwise to relieve the tension in the belt **(see illustration)**.

20 Hold the tensioner in position with the spanner/socket, and slide the belt from the pulleys. If necessary, the tensioner can be

retained in its released position by inserting a suitable bolt or metal dowel (4 mm diameter) through the holes provided **(see illustration)**.

21 Fit the new belt around the pulleys, starting with the crankshaft pulley. Check that the belt is correctly seated on all the pulleys **(see illustration)**. Where applicable, remove the metal dowel/bolt from the tensioner.

22 Allow the tensioner to move into position against the belt.

23 The remainder of refitting is a reversal of removal.

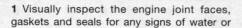

7 Electrical system check

1 Check for satisfactory operation of the instrument panel, its illumination and warning lights, the switches and their function lights.

2 Check the horns for satisfactory operation.

3 Check all other electrical equipment for satisfactory operation.

4 If a fault is suspected, proceed as described in Chapter 12 Section 2.

8 Underbonnet check for fluid leaks and hose condition

1 Visually inspect the engine joint faces, gaskets and seals for any signs of water or

oil leaks. Pay particular attention to the areas around the camshaft cover, cylinder head, oil filter and sump joint faces. Bear in mind that, over a period of time, some very slight seepage from these areas is to be expected – what you are really looking for is any indication of a serious leak. Should a leak be found, renew the offending gasket or oil seal by referring to the appropriate Chapters in this manual.

2 Also check the security and condition of all the engine-related pipes and hoses. Ensure that all cable-ties or securing clips are in place and in good condition. Clips that are broken or missing can lead to chafing of the hoses, pipes or wiring, which could cause more serious problems in the future.

3 Carefully check the radiator hoses and heater hoses along their entire length. Renew any hose which is cracked, swollen or deteriorated. Cracks will show up better if the hose is squeezed. Pay close attention to the hose clips that secure the hoses to the cooling system components. Hose clips can pinch and puncture hoses, resulting in cooling system leaks.

4 Inspect all the cooling system components (hoses, joint faces, etc) for leaks. A leak in the cooling system will usually show up as white- or antifreeze-coloured deposits on the area adjoining the leak **(see Haynes Hint overleaf)**. Where any problems of this nature are found on system components, renew the component or gasket with reference to Chapter 3.

6.19 Use a bi-hex socket to rotate the tensioner

6.20 Lock the tensioner in place using a 4 mm diameter bolt/rod

6.21 Auxiliary drivebelt routing – V6 engines

HAYNES HiNT

A leak in the cooling system will usually show up as white-or antifreeze coloured deposits on the area adjoining the leak.

5 Where applicable, inspect the automatic transmission fluid cooler hoses for leaks or deterioration.

6 With the vehicle raised, inspect the fuel tank and filler neck for punctures, cracks and other damage. The connection between the filler neck and tank is especially critical. Sometimes a rubber filler neck or connecting hose will leak due to loose retaining clamps or deteriorated rubber.

7 Carefully check all rubber hoses and metal fuel lines leading away from the petrol tank. Check for loose connections, deteriorated hoses, crimped lines, and other damage. Pay particular attention to the vent pipes and hoses, which often loop up around the filler neck and can become blocked or crimped. Follow the lines to the front of the vehicle, carefully inspecting them all the way. Renew damaged sections as necessary.

8 Closely inspect the metal brake pipes, which run along the vehicle underbody. If they show signs of excessive corrosion or damage they must be renewed.

9 From within the engine compartment, check the security of all fuel hose attachments and pipe unions, and inspect the fuel hoses and vacuum hoses for kinks, chafing and deterioration.

10 Check the condition of the power steering fluid hoses and pipes.

9 Engine compartment wiring check

1 With the car parked on level ground, apply the handbrake firmly and open the bonnet. Using an inspection light or a small electric torch, check all visible wiring within and beneath the engine compartment.

2 What you are looking for is wiring that is obviously damaged by chafing against sharp edges, or against moving suspension/transmission components and/or the auxiliary drivebelt, by being trapped or crushed between carelessly-refitted components, or melted by being forced into contact with the hot engine castings, coolant pipes, etc. In almost all cases, damage of this sort is caused in the first instance by incorrect routing on reassembly after previous work has been carried out.

3 Depending on the extent of the problem, damaged wiring may be repaired by rejoining the break or splicing-in a new length of wire, using solder to ensure a good connection, and remaking the insulation with adhesive insulating tape or heat-shrink tubing, as appropriate. If the damage is extensive, given the implications for the car's future reliability, the best long-term answer may well be to renew that entire section of the loom, however expensive this may appear.

4 When the actual damage has been repaired, ensure that the wiring loom is rerouted correctly, so that it is clear of other components, and not stretched or kinked, and is secured out of harm's way using the plastic clips, guides and ties provided.

5 Check all electrical connectors, ensuring that they are clean, securely fastened, and that each is locked by its plastic tabs or wire clip, as appropriate. If any connector shows external signs of corrosion (accumulations of white or green deposits, or streaks of 'rust'), or if any is thought to be dirty, it must be unplugged and cleaned using electrical contact cleaner. If the connector pins are severely corroded, the connector must be renewed; note that this may mean the renewal of that entire section of the loom – see your local Mercedes dealer for details.

6 If the cleaner completely removes the corrosion to leave the connector in a satisfactory condition, it would be wise to pack the connector with a suitable material which will exclude dirt and moisture, preventing the corrosion from occurring again; a Mercedes dealer may be able to recommend a suitable product.

7 Check the condition of the battery connections – remake the connections or renew the leads if a fault is found (see Chapter 5A Section 4). Use the same techniques to ensure that all earth points in the engine compartment provide good electrical contact through clean, metal-to-metal joints, and that all are securely fastened.

10 Air conditioning system check

1 The following maintenance checks will ensure that the air conditioner operates at peak efficiency:
a) *Check the auxiliary*
a) *drivebelt (see Section 6).*
b) *Check the system hoses for damage or leaks.*
c) *Inspect the condenser fins for leaves, insects and other debris. Use a clean paint brush to clean the condenser. The condenser is mounted in front of the radiator.*
d) *Check that the drain tube from the evaporator housing is clear – the hose is located under the drivers side of the facia, and connects the housing to the engine compartment bulkhead. Note that it is normal to have clear fluid (water) dripping from this while the system is in operation, to the extent that quite a large puddle can be left under the car when it is parked.*

2 It's a good idea to operate the system for about 30 minutes at least once a month, particularly during the winter. Long term non-use can cause hardening, and subsequent failure, of the seals.

3 Because of the complexity of the air conditioning system and the special equipment necessary to service it, in-depth fault diagnosis and repairs are not included in this manual.

4 The most common cause of poor cooling is simply a low system refrigerant charge. If a noticeable drop in cool air output occurs, the following quick check will help you determine if the refrigerant level is low.

5 Warm the engine up to normal operating temperature.

6 Place the air conditioning temperature selector at the coldest setting, and put the blower at the highest setting. Open the doors – to make sure the air conditioning system doesn't cycle off as soon as it cools the passenger compartment

7 With the compressor engaged – the clutch will make an audible click, and the centre of the clutch will rotate – feel the inlet and outlet pipes at the compressor. One side should be cold, and one hot. If there's no perceptible difference between the two pipes, there's something wrong with the compressor or the system. It might be a low charge – it might be something else. Take the car to a dealer service department or an automotive air conditioning specialist.

11 Seat belt check

1 Check the seat belts for satisfactory operation and condition. Inspect the webbing for fraying and cuts. Check that they retract smoothly and without binding into their reels.

2 Check that the seat belt mounting bolts are tight, and if necessary tighten them to the specified torque wrench setting (Chapter 11).

12 Antifreeze concentration check

1 The cooling system should be filled with the recommended antifreeze and corrosion protection fluid. Over a period of time, the concentration of fluid may be reduced due to topping-up (this can be avoided by topping-up

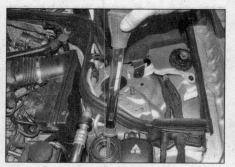

12.3 Check the anti-freeze concentration with a hydrometer

13.4 Check for wear in the hub bearings by grasping the wheel and trying to rock it

with the correct antifreeze mixture) or fluid loss. If loss of coolant has been evident, it is important to make the necessary repair before adding fresh fluid. The exact mixture of antifreeze-to-water which you should use depends on the relative weather conditions. The mixture should contain at least 40% anti-freeze, but not more than 70%. Consult the mixture ratio chart on the antifreeze container before adding coolant. Use antifreeze which meets the car manufacturer's specifications.

2 With the engine cold, carefully remove the cap from the expansion tank. If the engine is not completely cold, place a cloth rag over the cap before removing it, and remove it slowly to allow any pressure to escape.

3 Antifreeze checkers are available from car accessory shops **(see illustration)**. Draw some coolant from the expansion tank and observe how many plastic balls are floating in the checker. Usually, 2 or 3 balls must be floating for the correct concentration of antifreeze, but follow the manufacturer's instructions.

4 If the concentration is incorrect, it will be necessary to either withdraw some coolant and add antifreeze, or alternatively drain the old coolant and add fresh coolant of the correct concentration.

13 Steering, suspension and roadwheel check

Front suspension

1 Raise the front of the vehicle and support it securely on axle stands (see *Vehicle jacking and support*).

2 Visually inspect the balljoint dust covers and the steering linkage gaiters for splits, chafing or deterioration. Any wear of these components will cause loss of lubricant, together with dirt and water entry, resulting in rapid deterioration of the balljoints. Also check that the steering rack mountings are tightened to the specified torque settings (see Chapter 10).

3 Check the power steering fluid hoses for

chafing or deterioration, and the pipe and hose unions for fluid leaks. Also check for signs of fluid leakage under pressure from the steering rack, which would indicate failed fluid seals within the steering rack.

4 Grasp the roadwheel at the 12 o'clock and 6 o'clock positions, and try to rock it **(see illustration)**. Very slight free play may be felt, but if the movement is appreciable, further investigation is necessary to determine the source. Continue rocking the wheel while an assistant depresses the footbrake. If the movement is now eliminated or significantly reduced, it is likely that the hub bearings are at fault. If the free play is still evident with the footbrake depressed, then there is wear in the suspension joints or mountings. Note that the front hub bearings are adjustable (See Chapter 10 Section 2).

5 Now grasp the wheel at the 9 o'clock and 3 o'clock positions, and try to rock it as before. Any movement felt now may again be caused by wear in the hub bearings or the steering track rod balljoints. If the inner or outer balljoint is worn, the visual movement will be obvious.

6 Using a large screwdriver or flat bar, check for wear in the suspension mounting bushes by levering between the relevant suspension component and its attachment point. Some movement is to be expected as the mountings are made of rubber, but excessive wear should be obvious. Also check the condition of any visible rubber bushes, looking for splits, cracks or contamination of the rubber.

7 With the car standing on its wheels, have an assistant turn the steering wheel back-and-forth about an eighth of a turn each way. There should be very little lost movement between the steering wheel and roadwheels. If this is not the case, closely observe the linkage joints and mountings previously described, but in addition, check the steering column universal joint/coupling for wear, and the steering rack itself.

Rear suspension

8 Chock the front wheels, then jack up the rear of the vehicle and support securely on axle stands (see *Vehicle jacking and support*).

9 Working as described previously for the front suspension, check the rear hub bearings,

the suspension bushes and the strut or shock absorber mountings (as applicable) for wear.

Shock absorber

10 Check for any signs of fluid leakage around the shock absorber body, or from the rubber gaiter around the piston rod. Should any fluid be noticed, the shock absorber is defective internally, and should be renewed. **Note:** *Shock absorbers should always be renewed in pairs on the same axle.*

11 The efficiency of the shock absorber may be checked by bouncing the vehicle at each corner. Generally speaking, the body will return to its normal position and stop after being depressed. If it rises and returns on a rebound, the shock absorber is probably suspect. Examine also the shock absorber upper and lower mountings for any signs of wear.

Roadwheels

12 Periodically remove the roadwheels, and clean any dirt or mud from the inside and outside surfaces. Examine the wheel rims for signs of rusting, corrosion or other damage. Light alloy wheels are easily damaged by 'kerbing' whilst parking, and similarly, steel wheels may become dented or buckled. Specialist firms do exist who will repair alloy wheels, but sometimes renewal of the wheel is the only course of remedial action possible.

13 The balance of each wheel and tyre assembly should be maintained, not only to avoid excessive tyre wear, but also to avoid wear in the steering and suspension components. Wheel imbalance is normally signified by vibration through the car's bodyshell, although in many cases it is particularly noticeable through the steering wheel. Conversely, it should be noted that wear or damage in suspension or steering components may cause excessive tyre wear. Out-of-round or out-of-true tyres, damaged wheels and wheel bearing wear/maladjustment also fall into this category. Balancing will not usually cure vibration caused by such wear.

14 Wheel balancing may be carried out with the wheel either on or off the car. If balanced on the car, ensure that the wheel-to-hub relationship is marked in some way prior to subsequent wheel removal, so that it may be refitted in its original position.

15 At this time, also check the spare wheel for damage.

14 Driveshaft rubber gaiter check

1 With the vehicle raised and securely supported on stands, slowly rotate the rear roadwheel. Inspect the condition of the outer constant velocity (CV) joint rubber gaiters, squeezing the gaiters to open out the folds. Check for signs of cracking, splits or

14.1 Check the condition of the rubber gaiters on each end of the driveshafts

15.2a Check the security of the various exhaust brackets...

15.2b...and mountings

deterioration of the rubber, which may allow the grease to escape, and lead to water and grit entry into the joint. Also check the security and condition of the retaining clips. Repeat these checks on the inner CV joints **(see illustration)**. If any damage or deterioration is found, the gaiters should be renewed (see Chapter 8 Section 6).

2 At the same time, check the general condition of the CV joints themselves by first holding the driveshaft and attempting to rotate the wheel. Repeat this check by holding the inner joint and attempting to rotate the driveshaft. Any appreciable movement indicates wear in the joints, wear in the driveshaft splines, or a loose driveshaft retaining nut.

15 Exhaust system check

1 With the engine cold, check the complete exhaust system from the engine to the end of the tailpipe. The exhaust system is most easily checked with the vehicle raised on a hoist, or suitably supported on axle stands, so that the exhaust components are readily visible and accessible.

2 Check the exhaust pipes and connections for evidence of leaks, severe corrosion and damage. Make sure that all brackets and mountings are in good condition, and that all relevant nuts and bolts are tight **(see illustrations)**. Leakage at any of the joints or in other parts of the system will usually show

up as a black sooty stain in the vicinity of the leak.

3 Rattles and other noises can often be traced to the exhaust system, especially the brackets and mountings. Try to move the pipes and silencers. If the components are able to come into contact with the body or suspension parts, secure the system with new mountings. Otherwise separate the joints (if possible) and twist the pipes as necessary to provide additional clearance.

16 Underbody and fuel/brake line check

1 With the car raised and supported on axle stands (see *Vehicle jacking and support*), thoroughly inspect the underbody and wheel arches for signs of damage and corrosion. In particular, examine the bottom of the side sills, and any concealed areas where mud can collect. Also check the inside edges at the base of all doors.

2 Where corrosion and rust is evident, press and tap firmly on the panel with a screwdriver, and check for any serious corrosion which would necessitate repairs.

3 If the panel is not seriously corroded, clean away the rust, and apply a new coating of underseal. Refer to Chapter 11 for more details of body repairs.

4 At the same time, inspect the PVC-coated lower body panels for stone damage and general condition.

5 Inspect all of the fuel and brake lines on the underbody for damage, rust, corrosion and leakage. Particularly check the rear brake pipes where they pass over the fuel tank. Also make sure that the pipes are correctly supported in their clips. Where applicable, check the PVC coating on the lines for damage.

17 Braking system check

Front brakes

1 Apply the handbrake, then jack up the front of the car and support it on axle stands (see *Vehicle jacking and support*). For better access to the brake calipers, remove the wheels.

2 Look through the inspection window in the caliper, and check that the thickness of the friction lining material on each of the pads is not less than the recommended minimum thickness given in the Specifications **(see illustration)**.

3 If it is difficult to determine the exact thickness of the pad linings, or if you are at all concerned about the condition of the pads, then remove them from the calipers for further inspection (refer to Chapter 9 Section 5).

4 Check the caliper on the other side in the same way.

5 If any one of the brake pads has worn down to, or below, the specified limit, all four pads at that end of the car must be renewed as a set.

6 Check both front brake discs with reference to Chapter 9 Section 7.

7 Before refitting the wheels, check all brake lines and flexible hoses with reference to Chapter 9 Section 3. In particular, check the flexible hoses in the vicinity of the calipers, where they are subjected to most movement. Bend them between the fingers and check that this does not reveal previously-hidden cracks, cuts or splits **(see illustration)**.

8 On completion, refit the wheels and lower the car to the ground. Tighten the wheel nuts to the specified torque.

Rear brakes

9 Chock the front wheels, then jack up the rear of the car and support on axle stands

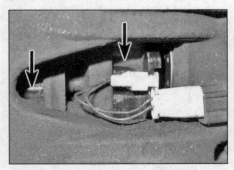

17.2 Check the friction material thickness through the window in the caliper

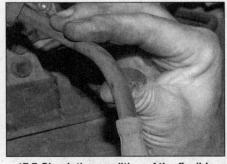

17.7 Check the condition of the flexible hoses

(see *Vehicle jacking and support*). Remove the rear wheels.

10 The procedure for checking the rear brakes is much the same as described in paragraphs 1 to 8 above.

Parking brake

11 With the car on a slight slope, firmly apply the parking brake lever, and check that it holds the car stationary, then release the lever and check that there is no resistance to movement of the car. If necessary, the parking brake should be adjusted as described in Chapter 9 Section 14.

18 Door and bonnet check and lubrication

1 Check that the doors, bonnet and tailgate/boot lid close securely. Check that the bonnet safety catch operates correctly. Check the operation of the door check straps.
2 Lubricate the hinges, door check straps, the striker plates and the bonnet catch sparingly with a little oil or grease.

19 Pollen filter renewal

1 Rotate the clips anti-clockwise, and remove the cover (where fitted) above the pollen filter housing in the left-hand corner of the engine compartment **(see illustration)**.
2 Undo the nut, release the clips and manoeuvre the pollen filter housing from place **(see illustration)**.
3 Remove the filter from the housing, noting its fitted position **(see illustration)**.
4 Clean any debris from the filter housing, then fit the new filter.
5 The remainder of refitting is a reversal of removal.

20 Fuel sedimetor draining

Note: *A filter drain port is only fitted to some*

models. *None of the vehicles we examined were equipped with a drain port.*
1 Remove the plastic cover from the top of the engine.
2 A drain port is provided on the fuel filter housing to enable draining water from the filter. On some models the port is controlled by a screw valve, whilst on others, a plug is fitted to the port.
3 On models with a screw, attach a hose to the port, and position the other end of the hose in a suitable container. Slacken the screw.
4 On models with a plug, remove the plug and attach a hose to the port. Position the other end of the hose in a suitable container.
5 On all models, have an assistant switch on the ignition, and observe the flow of fluid from the hose. When clean fuel emerges, have the ignition switched off.
6 Tighten the port screw, and disconnect the hose, or disconnect the hose and refit the plug as applicable.
7 Refit the cover to the top of the engine.
8 Start the engine, and allow it to idle for at least 3 minutes. Check for leaks.

21 Road test

Instruments and electrical equipment

1 Check the operation of all instruments and electrical equipment.
2 Make sure that all instruments read correctly, and switch on all electrical equipment in turn, to check that it functions properly.

Suspension and steering

3 Check for any abnormalities in the steering, suspension, handling or road 'feel'.
4 Drive the vehicle, and check that there are no unusual vibrations or noises.
5 Check that the steering feels positive, with no excessive 'sloppiness', or roughness, and check for any suspension noises when cornering and driving over bumps.

Drivetrain

6 Check the performance of the engine, clutch (where applicable), gearbox/transmission, propeller shaft and driveshafts.
7 Listen for any unusual noises from the engine, clutch and gearbox/transmission.
8 Make sure that the engine runs smoothly when idling, and that there is no hesitation when accelerating.
9 Check that, where applicable, the clutch action is smooth and progressive, that the drive is taken up smoothly, and that the pedal travel is not excessive. Also listen for any noises when the clutch pedal is depressed.
10 On manual gearbox models, check that all gears can be engaged smoothly without noise, and that the gear lever action is smooth and not abnormally vague or 'notchy'.
11 On automatic transmission models, make sure that all gearchanges occur smoothly, without snatching, and without an increase in engine speed between changes. Check that all the gear positions can be selected with the vehicle at rest. If any problems are found, they should be referred to a Mercedes-Benz dealer.

Braking system

12 Make sure that the vehicle does not pull to one side when braking, and that the wheels do not lock when braking hard.
13 Check that there is no vibration through the steering when braking.
14 Check that the parking brake operates correctly without excessive movement of the foot pedal, and that it holds the vehicle stationary on a slope.
15 Test the operation of the brake servo unit as follows. With the engine off, depress the footbrake four or five times to exhaust the vacuum. Hold the brake pedal depressed, and then start the engine. As the engine starts, there should be a noticeable 'give' in the brake pedal as vacuum builds-up. Allow the engine to run for at least two minutes, and then switch it off. If the brake pedal is depressed now, it should be possible to detect a hiss from the servo as the pedal is depressed. After about four or five applications, no further hissing should be heard, and the pedal should feel considerably harder.

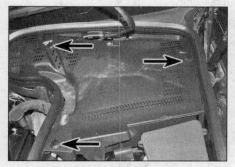
19.1 Pollen filter cover clips

19.2 Pollen filter housing fasteners

19.3 The arrow on the filter element indicates air flow

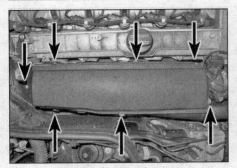

24.2 Air filter cover clips

24.5a Fit the new element into the housing...

24.5b...ensuring the lug engages with the notch

22 Reset the service indicator

Models upto 09/03

1 With the ignition key in position 'I'.
2 Press the 'scroll forward/back' button repeatedly until the service date is displayed in the multi-function display in the instrument cluster.
3 Press and hold the trip reset button for approximately 5 seconds until 'Service Menu' appears on the multi-function display.
4 Use the '+' and '-' button to select 'Confirmation' from the menu.
5 Press the selection button to confirm.
6 The multi-function display should now show the message 'Service Confirmed'.
7 Press the selection button repeatedly until the standard display appears.
8 Turn off the ignition.

Models from 09/03

9 Ignition key in position 'I'
10 Repeatedly press the selection button unit the basic display 'Mile reading or temperature display' is shown in the multi-function display in the instrument cluster.
11 Press the trip reset button 3 times. An acoustic signal will be heard, and the voltage shown in the multi-function display.
12 Press the lower scroll forward/back button. 'Service Menu' should now be shown in the multi-function display.

13 Press the '+' and '-' buttons and select 'Confirmation' menu item.
14 Press the lower selection button to confirm. 'Confirmation' should now appear in the multi-function display, and the menu item 'Complete service' highlighted.
15 Press the lower selection button to confirm.
16 Press the upper selection button repeatedly until 'Service Menu' is displayed.
17 Use the '+' and '-' buttons to select the menu item 'Special work'.
18 Press the lower selection button to confirm.
19 Use the '+' and '-' buttons to select menu choice 'Service 13'.
20 Press the lower selection button to confirm.
21 Press the upper selection button repeatedly until Mile reading or temperature display' is shown in the multi-function display.
22 Switch off the ignition.
23 Switch off the ignition.

23 Roadwheels anti-seize grease

1 Slacken the roadwheel bolts, raise the front and rear of the vehicle and support it securely on axle stands (see *Vehicle jacking and support*). Remove the roadwheels.
2 Check the condition of the wheel hub spigots, and where necessary remove any dirt/rust etc.

3 Apply a little anti-seize grease to the wheel hub spigots.
4 Take this opportunity to examine the wheels/tyres for signs of damage etc.
5 Refit the roadwheels, but do not fully tighten the retaining bolts yet.
6 Lower the vehicle to the ground, and tighten the roadwheel bolts to the specified torque.

24 Air filter element renewal

In-line engines

1 Undo the fasteners and remove the plastic cover from the top of the engine (see illustration 4.2a and 4.2b).
2 Release the retaining clips and remove the air filter cover (see illustration).
3 Lift the filter element at the rear, and manoeuvre it from the housing.
4 Clear any debris from the filter housing.
5 Locate the new filter element into the housing, noting how the lug on the filter engages with the notch in the housing (see illustrations).
6 Remove the cover to the top of the engine.

V6 engines

7 Pull the plastic cover on the top of the engine upwards to release it from the rubber mountings.
8 Remove the left-, and right-hand air filter housings as described in Chapter 4A Section 2.
9 Undo the 4 retaining bolts, and separate the two halves of the filter housing (see illustration).
10 Remove the filter element from the housing, noting its fitted orientation (see illustration).
11 Clear any debris from the filter housing.
12 Insert the new elements into the housings, assemble the two halves, and tighten the retaining bolts securely.
13 Refit the air filter housings as described in Chapter 4A Section 2.

24.9 Undo the screws, separate the housing halves...   **24.10...and lift out the filter element**

25.3 Fuel filter hoses and clamp bolt

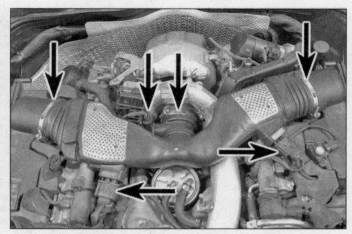

25.12 Slacken the clamps, disconnect the wiring plugs, and move the air intake duct to one side

25 Fuel filter renewal

Note: *Before carrying out the following procedure, read carefully the precautions given in Chapter 4A Section 1.*

In-line engines

1 Undo the fasteners and remove the plastic cover from the top of the engine.
2 The fuel filter is located to the left-hand side of the cylinder head. To minimise fuel spillage, pad the surrounding area with absorbent rags.
3 Release the securing clips and disconnect the fuel hoses from the top of the fuel filter. Note the fitted positions for refitting; one of the fuel hoses has a larger diameter than the other. Plug the ends of the fuel hoses to prevent dirt ingress **(see illustration)**.
4 Slacken the clamp bolt from down the side of the filter, and then withdraw the filter from its mounting bracket.
5 Remove the filter canister from the engine bay, keeping the mating face upwards to minimise fuel spillage.
6 Take the new fuel filter canister and fit it into

the mounting bracket and tighten the retaining bolt.
7 Refit the fuel hoses to the top of the fuel filter in their correct positions (as noted on removal), making sure they are secure.
8 Start and run the engine at idle and check around the fuel filter for fuel leaks. Note that the fuel pump is self-priming, but it may take a few seconds of cranking before the engine starts.
9 Raise the engine speed to about 2000 rpm several times, and then allow the engine to idle again. This should bleed the air bubbles from the filter canister, but if the engine idle is at all rough or hesitant, repeat the action until the fuel system clears itself.
10 Refit the cover to the top of the engine.

V6 engines

11 Pull the plastic cover on the top of the engine upwards from its rubber mountings.
12 Slacken the clamps, disconnect the mass air flow wiring plugs, and remove the air intake duct above the fuel filter **(see illustration)**. The fuel filter is located between the cylinder heads at the top of the engine.
13 Release the clamps and disconnect the hoses from the top of the fuel filter **(see illustration)**. Plug the openings to prevent contamination. Take care not to damage the

hoses, and not allow any debris to enter the fuel system.
14 Where applicable, disconnect the wiring plug from the filter.
15 Slacken the clamp screw and lift the filter from the mounting bracket **(see illustrations)**.
16 Where applicable, transfer the water sensor from the old filter to the new one.
17 Install the new filter into the bracket, ensuring its correctly located, and pushed down fully into the bracket to prevent the engine cover may damage the pipes. Tighten the clamp screw.
18 Refit the hoses, and wiring plug (where applicable) to the filter, and secure with new clamps where necessary.
19 Refit the air intake ducting, tighten the clamps and reconnect the wiring plugs.
20 Start and run the engine at idle and check around the fuel filter for fuel leaks. Note that the fuel pump is self-priming, but it may take a few seconds of cranking before the engine starts.
21 Raise the engine speed to about 2000 rpm several times, and then allow the engine to idle again. This should bleed the air bubbles from the filter canister, but if the engine idle is at all rough or hesitant, repeat the action until the fuel system clears itself.
22 Refit the cover to the top of the engine.

25.13 Release the clamps and disconnect the hoses

25.15a Slacken the clamp screw...

25.15b...and lift the filter from the bracket

26 Brake fluid renewal

⚠️ **Warning: Brake hydraulic fluid can harm your eyes and damage painted surfaces, so use extreme caution when handling and pouring it. Do not use fluid that has been standing open for some time, as it absorbs moisture from the air. Excess moisture can cause a dangerous loss of braking effectiveness.**

1 The procedure is similar to that for the bleeding of the hydraulic system as described in Chapter 9 Section 2, except that the brake fluid reservoir should be emptied by syphoning, using a clean poultry baster or similar before starting, and allowance should be made for the old fluid to be expelled when bleeding a section of the circuit.

2 Working as described in Chapter 9 Section 2, open the first bleed screw in the sequence, and pump the brake pedal gently until nearly all the old fluid has been emptied from the master cylinder reservoir. **Caution: Do not allow the fluid level to drop below the bottom of the reservoir.**

3 Top-up to the MAX level with new fluid, and continue pumping until only the new fluid remains in the reservoir, and new fluid can be seen emerging from the bleed screw. Tighten the screw, and top the reservoir level up to the MAX level line.

4 Work through all the remaining bleed screws in the sequence until new fluid can be seen at all of them. Be careful to keep the master cylinder reservoir topped-up to above the MIN level at all times, or air may enter the system and greatly increase the length of the task.

5 When the operation is complete, check that all bleed screws are securely tightened, and that their dust caps are refitted. Wash off all traces of spilt fluid, and recheck the master cylinder reservoir fluid level.

6 Check the operation of the brakes before taking the car on the road.

27 Manual transmission oil renewal

1 Manual transmission oil renewal is described in Chapter 7A Section 2.

28 Automatic transmission oil renewal

1 Automatic transmission oil renewal is described in Chapter 7B Section 5.

29 Final drive oil renewal

1 Refer to Chapter 8 Section 2.

30 Coolant renewal

⚠️ **Warning: Refer to Chapter 3 Section 1 and observe the warnings given. In particular, never remove the expansion tank filler cap when the engine is running, or has just been switched off, as the cooling system will be hot, and the consequent escaping steam and scalding coolant could cause serious injury. If the engine is hot, the electric cooling fan may start rotating even if the engine is not running, so be careful to keep hands, hair and loose clothing well clear when working in the engine compartment.**

Cooling system draining

⚠️ **Warning: Wait until the engine is cold before starting this procedure.**

1 After allowing the engine to cool completely, cover the pressure cap with a wad of rag, and slowly turn the cap anti-clockwise to relieve the pressure in the cooling system (a hissing sound will normally be heard). Wait until any pressure remaining in the system is released, then continue to turn the cap until it can be removed.

2 Raise the front of the vehicle and support it securely on axle stands (see *Vehicle jacking and support*). Undo the fasteners and remove the engine undershield **(see illustration)**.

3 Push a length of hose onto the radiator drain tap, then open the drain tap and allow the coolant to drain into a suitable container **(see illustration)**. The drain tap is located at the left-hand end of the radiator.

4 Once the coolant has ceased flowing, tighten the drain tap and remove the hose.

5 On in-line engines, if required, push the

30.3 The drain tap is on the left-hand end of the radiator

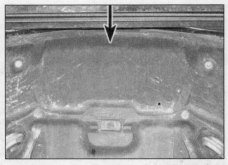

30.2 Remove the front section of the radiator undershield

hose over the cylinder block drain tap, and drain the coolant from the crankcase in a similar manner **(see illustration)**. The drain tap is located on the left-hand side of the cylinder block.

6 Tighten the tap and remove the hose, once the coolant has ceased to flow.

Cooling system flushing

7 If coolant renewal has been neglected, or if the antifreeze mixture has become diluted, then in time, the cooling system may gradually lose efficiency, as the coolant passages become restricted due to rust, scale deposits, and other sediment. The cooling system efficiency can be restored by flushing the system clean.

8 The radiator should be flushed independently of the engine, to avoid unnecessary contamination.

Radiator flushing

9 Disconnect the top and bottom hoses and any other relevant hoses from the radiator, with reference to Chapter 3 Section 2.

10 Insert a garden hose into the radiator top inlet. Direct a flow of clean water through the radiator, and continue flushing until clean water emerges from the radiator bottom outlet.

11 If after a reasonable period, the water still does not run clear, the radiator can be flushed with a good proprietary cleaning agent. It is important that the manufacturer's instructions are followed carefully. If the contamination is particularly bad, remove the radiator, insert

30.5 Cylinder block drain tap

the hose in the radiator bottom outlet, and reverse-flush the radiator.

Engine flushing

12 Remove the thermostat as described in Chapter 3 Section 4 then, if the radiator top hose has been disconnected from the engine, temporarily reconnect the hose.

13 With the top and bottom hoses disconnected from the radiator, insert a garden hose into the radiator top hose. Direct a clean flow of water through the engine, and continue flushing until clean water emerges from the radiator bottom hose.

14 On completion of flushing, refit the thermostat and reconnect the hoses with reference to Chapter 3.

Antifreeze mixture

15 The antifreeze should always be renewed at the specified intervals. This is necessary not only to maintain the antifreeze properties, but also to prevent corrosion, which would otherwise occur as the corrosion inhibitors become progressively less effective.

16 Always use a good quality antifreeze that meets Mercedes specifications. The quantity of antifreeze and levels of protection are indicated in the Specifications.

17 Before adding antifreeze, the cooling system should be completely drained, preferably flushed, and all hoses checked for condition and security.

18 After filling with antifreeze, a label should be attached to the expansion tank or header tank, stating the type and concentration of antifreeze used, and the date installed. Any subsequent topping-up should be made with the same type and concentration of antifreeze.

19 Do not use engine antifreeze in the windscreen/tailgate washer system, as it will cause damage to the vehicle paintwork. A screenwash additive should be added to the washer system in the quantities stated on the bottle.

Cooling system refilling

20 Before attempting to fill the cooling system, make sure that all hoses and clips are in good condition, and that the clips are tight. Note that an antifreeze mixture must be used all year round, to prevent corrosion

of the engine components (see previous sub-Section).

21 Remove the pressure cap, and fill the system by slowly pouring the coolant into the expansion tank to prevent airlocks from forming.

22 If the coolant is being renewed, begin by pouring in a couple of litres of water, followed by the correct quantity of antifreeze, then top-up with more water.

23 Once the level in the expansion tank/header tank starts to rise, squeeze the radiator top and bottom hoses to help expel any trapped air in the system. Once all the air is expelled, top-up the coolant level until the white level indicator is visible in the expansion tank filler neck **(see illustration)**. Refit the pressure cap securely.

24 Start the engine and run it until the thermostat opens – the radiator top hose will begin to heat up as coolant flows through it of the radiator when this happens.

25 Check for leaks, particularly around disturbed components. Check the coolant level in the expansion tank/header tank, and top-up if necessary. Note that the system must be cold before an accurate level is indicated. If the pressure cap is removed while the engine is still warm, cover the cap with a thick cloth, and unscrew the cap slowly to gradually relieve the system pressure (a hissing sound will normally be heard). Wait until any pressure remaining in the system is released, then continue to turn the cap until it can be removed.

Airlocks

26 If, after draining and refilling the system, symptoms of overheating are found which did not occur previously, then the fault is almost certainly due to trapped air at some point in the system, causing an airlock and restricting the flow of coolant; usually, the air is trapped because the system was refilled too quickly.

27 If an airlock is suspected, first try gently squeezing all visible coolant hoses. A coolant hose which is full of air feels quite different to one full of coolant, when squeezed. After refilling the system, most airlocks will clear once the system has cooled, and been topped-up.

30.23 Add coolant until it's level with the indicator in the filler neck

28 While the engine is running at operating temperature, switch on the heater and heater fan, and check for heat output. Provided there is sufficient coolant in the system, any lack of heat output could be due to an airlock in the system.

29 Airlocks can have more serious effects than simply reducing heater output – a severe airlock could reduce coolant flow around the engine. Check that the radiator top hose is hot when the engine is at operating temperature – a top hose which stays cold could be the result of an airlock (or a non-opening thermostat).

30 If the problem persists, stop the engine and allow it to cool down completely, before unscrewing the expansion tank filler cap or loosening the hose clips and squeezing the hoses to bleed out the trapped air. In the worst case, the system will have to be at least partially drained (this time, the coolant can be saved for re-use) and flushed to clear the problem.

Pressure cap check

31 Clean the pressure cap (expansion tank), and inspect the seal inside the cap for damage or deterioration. If there is any sign of damage or deterioration to the seal, fit a new pressure cap. If the cap is old, it is worth considering fitting a new one for peace of mind – they are not expensive. If the pressure cap fails, excess pressure will be allowed into the system, which may result in the failure of hoses, the radiator, or the heater matrix.

Chapter 2 Part A
In-line engine in-car repair procedures

Contents

Degrees of difficulty

Easy, suitable for novice with little experience	**Fairly easy,** suitable for beginner with some experience 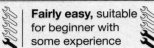	**Fairly difficult,** suitable for competent DIY mechanic	**Difficult,** suitable for experienced DIY mechanic	**Very difficult,** suitable for expert DIY or professional

Specifications

General

Engine type:
    E200 and E220 . . . .   4-cylinder in-line diesel, double overhead camshaft (DOHC)
    E270 . . . .   5-cylinder in-line diesel, double overhead camshaft (DOHC)
    E280 and E320 . . . .   6-cylinder in-line diesel, double overhead camshaft (DOHC)
Engine code:
    4-cylinder engines . . . .   646.821, 646.951 or 646.961
    5-cylinder engines 647.961
    6-cylinder engines 648.961
Bore . . . .   88.0 mm
Stroke . . . .   83.3 mm
Capacity: . . . .
    E200 and E220 . . . .   2148 cc
    E270 . . . .   2685 cc
    E280 and E320 . . . .   3222 cc
Firing order:
    4-cylinder engines   1-3-4-2
    5-cylinder engines   1-2-4-5-3
    6-cylinder engines   1-5-3-6-2-4
Direction of crankshaft rotation . . . .   Clockwise (seen from the front of the vehicle)
Compression ratio 18.0: 1
Compression pressures:
    New compression pressure . . . .   29.0 to 35.0 bar
    Minimum compression pressure . . . .   18.0 bar (approximately)
    Maximum difference between cylinders . . . .   3.0 bar

Cylinder head bolts

Thread diameter M12
Length when new (from under head) . . . .   102.0 mm
Maximum length . . . .   104.0 mm

Lubrication system

Minimum system pressure:

At idle speed. . . . . 0.7 bar

Torque wrench settings

	Nm	lbf ft
Camshaft bearing cap bolts.	9	6
Camshaft cover bolts.	10	7
Centrifuge-to-exhaust camshaft.	36	26
Connecting rod bolts*:		
Stage 1.	5	3
Stage 2.	25	17
Stage 3.	Slacken 180°	
Stage 4.	25	17
Stage 5.	Angle-tighten a further 90°	
Crankshaft pulley bolt*:		
Bolt grade 10.9 (see head of bolt):		
Stage 1.	325	240
Stage 2.	Angle-tighten a further 90°	
Bolt grade 12.9 (see head of bolt):		
Stage 1.	200	147
Stage 2.	Angle-tighten a further 90°	
Stage 3.	Angle-tighten a further 90°	
Crankshaft rear oil seal housing bolts.	10	7
Cylinder head bolts*:		
Stage 1.	15	11
Stage 2.	60	44
Stage 3.	Angle-tighten a further 90°	
Stage 4.	Angle-tighten a further 90°	
Engine/transmission mountings:		
Engine mounting-to-crossmember.	35	26
Bracket to engine mounting.	50	37
Bracket to cylinder block.	20	15
Rear bracket-to-transmission.	50	37
Rear mounting-to-crossmember.	50	37
Rear mounting to transmission bracket.	28	20
Exhaust camshaft sprocket bolts.	18	14
Exhaust manifold-to-turbocharger.	30	22
Flywheel/driveplate bolts*:		
Stage 1.	45	33
Stage 2.	Angle-tighten a further 90°	
Front cover-to-cylinder head.	14	10
Main bearing cap bolts:		
Stage 1.	55	41
Stage 2.	Angle-tighten a further 90°	
Oil pump bolts.	19	14
Oil pump relief valve plug.	50	37
Oil sensor.	14	10
Oil spray jet.	10	7
Sump drain plug.	30	22
Sump:		
To crankcase:		
M6.	10	7
M8.	20	15
To transmission.	40	30
To timing chain cover.	10	7
To rear seal housing.	10	7
Timing chain cover:		
M6.	10	7
M8.	20	15
Timing chain tensioner.	80	60
Turbocharger oil feed pipe:		
To turbocharger.	20	9
To cylinder head.	9	6

*Do not re-use

1 General information

How to use this Chapter

1 This Part of the Chapter describes those repair procedures that can reasonably be carried out on the engine whilst it remains in the vehicle. If the engine has been removed from the vehicle and is being dismantled as described in Part C of this Chapter, any preliminary dismantling procedures can be ignored.

2 Note that whilst it may be possible physically to overhaul items such as the piston/ connecting rod assemblies with the engine in the vehicle, such tasks are not usually carried out as separate operations and usually require the execution of several additional procedures (not to mention the cleaning of components and of oilways). For this reason, all such tasks are classed as major overhaul procedures and are described in Chapter.

Engine description

3 The 4-, 5- and 6-cylinder diesel engines fitted are fundamentally the same, the only significant difference being the number of cylinders.

4 The engines are of in-line double overhead camshaft design, mounted in-line ('north-south') at the front of the vehicle with the transmission mounted on the rear of the engine.

5 On 4-cylinder engines, the crankshaft is supported in five main bearing within the cast iron cylinder block. Crankshaft endfloat is controlled by thrustwashers fitted on either side of No 3 main bearing. On 5-cylinder engines the crankshaft is supported in six main bearings, and the endfloat thrustwashers are fitted either side of No 4 bearing location. On 6-cylinder engines the crankshaft is supported by seven main bearings, and the end float is controlled by thrustwashers fitted either side of No 5 bearing location.

6 The connecting rods are attached to the crankshaft by horizontally-split big-end bearings, and to the pistons by fully-floating gudgeon pins retained by circlips. The alloy pistons are fitted with three piston rings; two compression and one oil control.

7 The exhaust camshaft is driven from the crankshaft sprocket by a double-row chain, and the inlet camshaft is gear-driven from the exhaust camshaft. The camshaft also drives the fuel injection pump.

8 The camshaft is supported in bearings in the cylinder head, and actuates the valves directly, via hydraulic valve lifters.

9 The oil pump is chain-driven from the front of the crankshaft. An oil cooler is located on the oil filter housing at the left-hand front of the cylinder block.

Repair operations possible with the engine in the car

10 The following operations can be carried out with the engine in the car:
a) *Compression pressure – testing*
b) *Camshaft cover – removal and refitting.*
c) *Crankshaft pulley – removal and refitting.*
d) *Camshaft and hydraulic tappets – removal, inspection and refitting.*
e) *Cylinder head – removal and refitting.*
f) *Cylinder head and pistons* – decarbonising.*
g) *Sump – removal and refitting.*
h) *Oil pump – removal and refitting.*
i) *Crankshaft oil seals – renewal.*
j) *Engine mountings – inspection and renewal.*
k) *Flywheel/driveplate – inspection and renewal.*
l) *Timing chain – removal and refitting.*
Note: *Although it is possible to remove these components with the engine in place, for reasons of access and cleanliness it is recommended that the engine be removed.*

2 Compression test – description and interpretation

Compression test

Note: *A compression tester designed for diesel engines must be used for this test.*

1 When engine performance is down, a compression test can provide diagnostic clues as to the engine's condition. If the test is performed regularly, it can give warning of trouble before any other symptoms become apparent.

2 A compression tester specifically intended for diesel engines must be used, because of the higher pressures involved. The tester is connected to an adapter, which screws into the glow plug. It is unlikely to be worthwhile buying such a tester for occasional use, but it may be possible to borrow or hire one – if not, have the test performed by a garage.

3 Unless specific instructions to the contrary are supplied with the tester, observe the following points.
a) *The battery must be in a good state of charge, the air filter must be clean, and the engine should be at normal operating temperature.*
b) *All the glow plugs should be removed before starting the test (see Chapter 5B Section 3).*
c) *The starter should not be operated using the stop/start button, but by a switch/ wiring placed between the battery positive terminal and the positive terminal of the starter solenoid.*

4 There is no need to hold the accelerator pedal down during the test, because the diesel engine air inlet is not throttled.

5 Crank the engine on the starter motor. After one or two revolutions, the compression pressure should build-up to a maximum figure, and then stabilise. Record the highest reading obtained.

6 Repeat the test on the remaining cylinders, recording the pressure in each.

7 The cause of poor compression is less easy to establish on a diesel engine than on a petrol one. The effect of introducing oil into the cylinders ('wet' testing) is not conclusive, because there is a risk that the oil will sit in the swirl chamber or in the recess in the piston crown instead of passing to the rings. However, the following can be used as a rough guide to diagnosis.

8 All cylinders should produce very similar pressures; if there is a large difference, then this indicates a fault. Note that the compression should build-up quickly in a healthy engine; low compression on the first stroke, followed by gradually increasing pressure on successive strokes, indicates worn piston rings. A low compression reading on the first stroke, which does not build-up during successive strokes, indicates leaking valves or a blown head gasket (a cracked head could also be the cause). Deposits on the undersides of the valve heads can also cause low compression.

9 A low reading from two adjacent cylinders is almost certainly due to the head gasket having blown between them; the presence of coolant in the engine oil will confirm this.

10 If the compression reading is unusually high, the combustion chambers are probably coated with carbon deposits. If this is the case, the cylinder head should be removed and decarbonised.

11 On completion of the test, refit the glow plugs.

Leakdown test

12 A leakdown test measures the rate at which compressed air fed into the cylinder is lost. It is an alternative to a compression test, and in many ways is better, since the escaping air provides easy identification of where a pressure loss is occurring (piston rings, valves or head gasket).

13 The equipment needed for leakdown testing is unlikely to be available to the home mechanic. If poor compression is suspected, have the test performed by a suitably-equipped garage.

3 Engine assembly/valve timing settings – general information and usage

 Warning: When turning the engine, do not turn the engine using the camshaft sprocket bolts, and do not turn the engine backwards (ie, anti-clockwise).

1 Top Dead Centre (TDC) is the highest point in the cylinder that each piston reaches as it travels up and down when the crankshaft turns. Each piston reaches TDC at the end

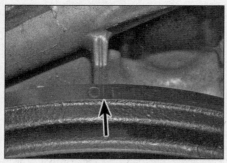

3.4 TDC (O/T) mark on the crankshaft pulley/vibration damper aligned with the pointer on the timing chain cover

of the compression stroke and again at the end of the exhaust stroke, but for valve timing TDC refers to the No 1 piston position on the compression stroke. No 1 piston is at the timing chain end of the engine.

2 Positioning No 1 piston at TDC is an essential part of many procedures, such as timing chain removal and camshaft removal.

3 Remove the camshaft cover as described in Section 4.

4 Using a socket on the crankshaft pulley/vibration damper hub bolt, turn the crankshaft clockwise until the O/T (TDC) mark on the crankshaft pulley/vibration damper is aligned with the pointer on the timing chain cover (see illustration). For access to the bolt, it may be necessary to remove the fan unit and radiator shroud as described in Chapter 3.

5 In this position the alignment indentations (two 1.5 mm dots) on the camshaft gears (timing chain side) should be next to each other and aligned with the centre points of the camshafts (see illustrations). The camshaft lobes on No 1 cylinder should be facing upwards.

6 If necessary, the camshafts can be locked in position. The inlet camshaft gear has a timing hole, which aligns with a hole in the camshaft front bearing cap, and a suitable close-fitting drill should be inserted to lock

the camshaft (see illustration). Note: Do not use this method to lock the engine, while slackening any retaining bolts.

7 With the camshafts aligned as described, No 1 piston is at TDC on its firing stroke.

4 Camshaft cover – removal and refitting

Removal

1 Depending of model variant, two different plastic covers may be fitted to the top of the engine. On some models the covers are retaining by bolts, whilst on others, the cover locates in rubber grommets.

Bolted covers

2 Undo the retaining bolts, and remove the plastic cover from the intake manifold and top of the engine (see illustration).

3.5a Camshaft gear alignment marks...

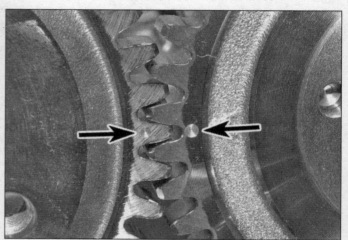

3.5b...aligned through the centre of the camshafts

3.6 Insert a drill bit to lock the camshaft

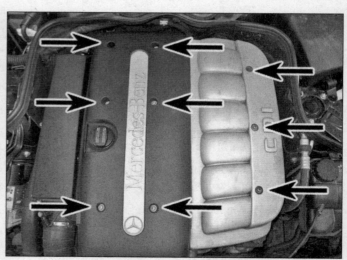

4.2 Engine covers' retaining bolts

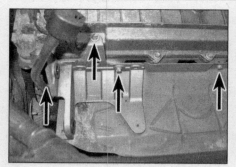

4.5a The heatshield is secured by bolts at the rear...

4.5b...and at the front

4.9 Remove the camshaft cover

Clipped covers

3 Grasp the cover and pull it upwards sharply to release it from the rubber grommets.

All versions

4 Remove the air filter housing as described in Chapter 4A Section 2.

5 Unclip the wiring harness, then undo the retaining bolts and remove the heatshield from above the exhaust manifold **(see illustrations)**.

6 Disconnect the camshaft sensor wiring plug.

7 Unclip the wiring duct from the camshaft cover, and place it to one side.

8 Remove the fuel injectors as described in Chapter 4A Section 11.

9 Gradually, evenly, undo the retaining bolts and remove the camshaft cover **(see illustration)**. Discard the seals – new ones must be fitted.

Refitting

10 Clean the joint surfaces of the cover and cylinder head, then locate the new gaskets in the grooves in the camshaft cover **(see illustrations)**.

11 Position the camshaft cover with gaskets on the cylinder head, then insert the bolts and finger-tighten them progressively. Do not fully tighten at this point as the fuel injectors will need to centralise in the cover.

12 Refit the fuel injectors and fuel lines and tighten the union nuts to the specified torque.

13 Tighten the camshaft cover bolts to their specified torque setting.

4.10a Fit a new camshaft cover gasket...

4.10b...and fuel injector recess gaskets

14 Complete the rest of the installation by reversing the removal procedure, referring to the relevant Chapters. When all components are refitted, start the engine and check carefully around the camshaft cover for any oil leaks.

5 Crankshaft pulley – removal and refitting

Removal

Note: *To gain better access, remove the fan and shroud from the rear of the radiator with reference to Chapter 3 Section 6.*

1 Working under the front of the vehicle, undo the retaining bolts and remove the engine undershield.

2 Remove the auxiliary drivebelt as described in Chapter 1 Section 6.

3 The crankshaft must now be held stationary while the pulley bolt is loosened. The bolt is tightened to a high torque. Mercedes-Benz technicians remove the starter motor (see Chapter 5A Section 9) and use a special tool (No. 602 589 00 40 00) which is bolted to the transmission and locks the flywheel **(see illustrations)**. It may be possible to insert a wide-bladed screwdriver between the starter ring gear teeth to prevent the engine from turning.

4 Unscrew the crankshaft pulley bolt then slide the pulley from the front of the crankshaft. Note the location of the washers under the head of the bolt, as they need to be fitted in the same position on refitting **(see illustration)**. If the pulley is tight on the crankshaft, use a suitable puller to remove

5.3a The Mercedes crankshaft locking tool..

5.3b...slides into the starter motor aperture to engage with the flywheel/driveplate teeth

5.4 Remove the bolt and washer

5.7 Make sure the Woodruff key is located securely

6.9 Protect the radiator with a piece of board

6.12 Timing chain tensioner

it. A two-legged puller, which locates in the pulley holes, is ideal.

5 If necessary, remove the Woodruff key from the groove in the nose of the crankshaft.

6 Examine the oil seal contact surface of the pulley/vibration damper for an excessive wear groove. If evident, it is permissible to position the oil seal slightly further into the timing chain cover so that it runs on the unworn area of the pulley. Alternatively, the pulley should be renewed. The oil seal in the timing cover must be renewed as a matter of course with reference to Section 14.

Refitting

7 Locate the Woodruff key in the groove in the nose of the crankshaft. Make sure that it is firmly pressed into position, and that its outer edge is parallel with the crankshaft so that the pulley/vibration damper will engage with it easily **(see illustration)**.

8 Wipe clean and lightly oil the seal contact surface of the pulley, and then slide it fully onto the crankshaft, engaging it with the Woodruff key.

9 Lightly oil the threads of the crankshaft pulley bolt and the washers, and then locate the washer(s) correctly onto the bolt, as noted on removal. Insert the bolt and tighten it to the specified torque while holding the crankshaft stationary as for removal. If necessary, refit the starter motor

10 Refit the auxiliary drivebelt with reference to Chapter 1 Section 6.

11 Where applicable, refit the fan and shroud to the rear of the radiator with reference to Chapter 3 Section 6.

12 Refit the engine undershield

6.15 Unclip the plastic cover to access the centrifuge

---

6 Timing chain cover – removal and refitting. 🔧

Note: *The timing chain cover is located between the cylinder head and the sump; take care not to damage any of these gaskets.*

Removal

1 Disconnect the battery negative lead as described in Chapter 5A Section 4.

2 Apply the parking brake, then jack up the front of the vehicle and support it on axle stands (see 'Vehicle jacking and support'). Remove the engine compartment undershield.

3 Drain the engine oil from the sump and remove the oil filter as described in Chapter 1 Section 4.

4 Remove the camshaft cover as described in Section 4.

5 Remove the air filter housing as described in Chapter 4A Section 2.

6 Remove the air ducts from between the intercooler and intake manifold.

7 Remove the air ducts from the turbocharger to the air filter housing, and the air intake duct.

8 Remove the cooling fan and shroud from the rear of the radiator as described in Chapter 3 Section 6.

9 Using a piece of thin plywood or similar, cover the radiator/condenser to protect it from any damage **(see illustration)**.

10 Refer to Section 3 and set the engine at TDC compression on No 1 cylinder. Ideally the crankshaft should be locked in this position

6.17 Disconnect the hoses from the coolant pump

during the removal of the timing chain cover. Mercedes-Benz technicians remove the starter motor and use a special tool to lock the teeth of the starter ring gear.

11 Drain the cooling system as described in Chapter 1 Section 30.

12 With the engine set at TDC, slacken and remove the timing chain tensioner from the right-hand front of the engine **(see illustration)**. Discard the sealing washer, as a new one will be required for refitting.

13 Remove the cover plate from the front of the cylinder head as described in Section 15.

14 Remove the high-pressure fuel pump as described in Chapter 4A Section 10. Note that on 6-cylinder engines, this is part of the cylinder head front cover plate procedure.

15 Undo the bolt and remove the centrifuge from the end of the exhaust camshaft **(see illustration)**.

16 Undo the retaining bolt, and remove the charge air pipes to, and from the intercooler.

17 Release the clamps and detach the coolant hoses from the coolant pump **(see illustration)**.

18 Slacken the power steering pump pulley bolts, then remove the auxiliary drivebelt as described in Chapter 1 Section 6.

19 Remove the pulley, then unbolt the power steering pump and position it to one side. Do not disconnect the hydraulic pipes from the pump.

20 Disconnect the wiring plug, then unbolt the air conditioning compressor (where fitted), and position it to one side. Suspend the compressor from the bodywork with cable ties, etc. to prevent any strain on the refrigerant hoses. Do not disconnect the hoses.

21 Release the clamps and disconnect the coolant hoses from the oil cooler assembly.

22 Remove the alternator as described in Chapter 5A Section 6. Note that on 6-cylinder engines, lift the alternator upwards without disconnecting the wiring.

23 Remove the crankshaft pulley/vibration damper as described in Section 5.

24 Unscrew and remove the bolts securing the sump to the bottom of the timing chain cover. Slacken the remaining sump bolts by 2 or 3 turns.

25 Working through the aperture in the top

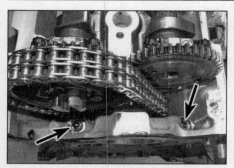

6.25 Timing chain cover upper retaining bolts

of the cylinder head, unscrew the two bolts securing the timing chain cover to the cylinder head **(see illustration)**.

26 Unscrew the bolts and remove the timing chain cover from the front of the engine, taking care not to damage the front parts of the cylinder head gasket and sump gasket. If required, to ensure the bolts are refitted in their correct locations, make a drawing of their positions, or use a dab of paint on them to identify them. If the two location dowels are loose, remove them also.

27 With the timing chain cover removed, it is recommended that the crankshaft front oil seal be renewed with reference to Section 14.

Refitting

28 Commence refitting by thoroughly cleaning away all traces of old sealant from the mating faces of the timing chain cover and cylinder block. Also clean the areas of the cylinder head gasket and sump gasket which contact the timing chain cover.

29 Carefully check the condition of the cylinder head gasket. If the gasket has been damaged during the removal procedure, the cylinder head should be removed in order to renew the gasket, as described in Section 10.

30 Similarly, carefully check the condition of the sump gasket. If the gasket has been damaged during the removal procedure, the sump should be removed in order to renew the gasket, as described in Section 11.

31 Apply sealant (Loctite 5970) to the cylinder block mating face of the timing chain cover. Make sure that the two location dowels are correctly fitted **(see illustration)**.

32 Coat the lips of the crankshaft oil seal with clean engine oil, then slide the cover into position over the crankshaft. Take care not to damage the oil seal lips and the cylinder head and sump gaskets as the cover is fitted.

33 Insert all the retaining bolts, including the two upper ones, in their original positions and hand-tighten them. First, progressively tighten the bolts securing the timing chain cover to the cylinder block to the specified torque, and then tighten the two upper bolts to the specified torque.

34 Insert the bolts securing the sump to the bottom of the timing chain cover.

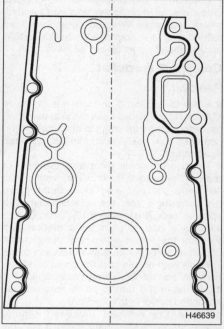

6.31 Apply a 2 mm bead of sealant on the inside of the bolt holes

Progressively tighten all the sump bolts to the specified torque.

35 Complete the rest of the installation by reversing the removal procedure, referring to the relevant Chapters.

36 Refill the engine with the correct grade and quantity of oil, as described in Chapter 1 Section 4.

37 Reconnect the battery negative lead as described in Chapter 5A Section 4.

38 When all components are refitted, start the engine and check carefully around the front of the engine any oil leaks, or coolant leaks.

39 Refit the engine compartment undershield and lower the car to the ground.

7 Timing chain – inspection and renewal

Inspection

1 Remove the camshaft cover as described in Section 4.

2 Using a socket on the crankshaft pulley/vibration damper hub bolt, turn the engine so that the whole length of the chain can be progressively viewed at the camshaft sprocket.

3 The chain should be renewed if the sprocket is worn or if the chain is worn (indicated by excessive lateral play between the links, and excessive noise in operation). Note that the rollers on a very badly worn chain may be slightly grooved. To avoid future problems, if there is any doubt at all about the condition of the chain, renew it.

Renewal

Note: *This following procedure, uses a chain breaker/riveter to renew the chain without removing the front timing chain cover, a second person will be required to assist fitting the timing chain. Ensure that all tools are available, as well as a new chain and new connecting link before proceeding.*

Note: *If the chain needs to be renewed as a complete assembly, then remove the front timing chain cover as described in Section 6.*

4 Disconnect the battery negative lead as described in Chapter 5A Section 4.

5 If not already done, remove the camshaft cover as described in Section 4.

6 Remove the air filter assembly as described in Chapter 4A Section 2.

7 Remove the cover plate from the front of the cylinder head as described in Section 15.

8 Remove the fan and shroud, as described in Chapter 3 Section 6.

9 Using a socket on the crankshaft pulley bolt, turn the engine until the timing marks are aligned, as described in Section 3.

10 Remove the timing chain tensioner as described in Section 8.

11 With the engine still in the TDC position, use a couple of cable-ties to keep the timing chain on the camshaft sprocket. Put some clean rag into the timing chain recess to prevent anything dropping down into the engine.

12 Use the chain breaker to press out one of the timing chain pins and split the timing chain.

13 Connect the new timing chain to the old chain and press the chain link pin back into position. **Note:** Make sure the new chain is connected to the front part of the chain, as the engine has to be turned clockwise, in the direction of rotation to feed the chain around the sprockets.

14 With the new chain connected securely to the old chain, take a firm hold of both ends of the chain and remove the cable-ties from the camshaft sprocket. Remove the clean rag from around the timing chain before turning the engine.

15 With the aid of an assistant, turn the engine in the direction of rotation. Keeping the timing chain taut feed it around the crankshaft sprocket, until the new chain comes all the way around to the camshaft sprocket.

16 Cable-tie both ends of the timing chain back to the camshaft sprocket, and refit the clean rag back into the timing chain recess.

17 Use the chain breaker to press out the timing chain pin and split the old timing chain from the new timing chain. Note: Make sure the chain is pulled tight on the lower section of the engine, and the upper section slack to allow for the fitting of the chain tensioner.

18 Check that the TDC marks on the crankshaft pulley and timing chain cover are aligned, and the marks on the camshaft and camshaft bearing caps are still aligned correctly.

19 Fit the new timing chain link, using the timing chain riveter to connect the two ends of the chain securely. Always read the instructions that come with the chain riveter, as there are many different types available. The link pins need to be riveted securely, to prevent the chain coming apart.

20 Remove the clean rag from the timing chain recess, and fit the timing chain tensioner, with reference to Section 8. With the tensioner now fitted, check the timing marks are still in line.

21 Rotate the engine two complete turns and check the timing marks come back in alignment. Refer to Section 3 to check timing mark alignment is correct.

22 Refit the camshaft cover with reference to Section 4.

23 Refit the air cleaner assembly.

24 Reconnect the battery negative lead as described in Chapter 5A Section 4.

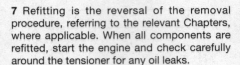

| 8 | Timing chain tensioner, sprockets and guides – removal, inspection and refitting. |

Timing chain tensioner

Removal

1 Set the engine to TDC on No 1 cylinder as described in Section 3.

2 Remove the air filter housing as described in Chapter 4A Section 2.

3 Remove the heat shield above the turbocharger.

4 Unscrew the tensioner from the right-hand side of the timing chain cover **(see illustration)**. Recover the sealing ring and discard; a new one will be required for refitting.

Inspection

5 Do not attempt to dismantle the tensioner assembly. If it is suspected that the tensioner is worn or faulty, the complete unit should be renewed.

Refitting

6 Locate a new sealing ring on the tensioner, then screw it into position in the cylinder head and tighten to the specified torque.

7 Refitting is the reversal of the removal procedure, referring to the relevant Chapters, where applicable. When all components are refitted, start the engine and check carefully around the tensioner for any oil leaks.

Camshaft sprocket

Removal

8 Refer to Section 3 and set the engine to TDC on No 1 cylinder. Lock the inlet camshaft as described by inserting a drill through the camshaft front bearing cap into the gear **(see illustration)**.

9 Remove the cover plate from the front of the cylinder head as described in Section 15.

10 Undo the retaining bolt and remove the centrifuge from the exhaust camshaft sprocket **(see illustration 6.15)**.

11 Use a dab of paint or a marker pen to mark the timing chain and the exhaust camshaft sprocket in relation to each other. This will help ensure that the chain is refitted correctly and the valve timing maintained.

12 Remove the timing chain tensioner as described earlier in this Section.

13 Hold the exhaust camshaft (timing chain) sprocket stationary using a suitable tool located in the sprocket cut-outs, then loosen the bolts securing the sprocket to the camshaft **(see illustration)**. Do not rely only on the drill located in the inlet camshaft sprocket to hold the sprocket.

14 At this stage the crankshaft sprocket will still be at TDC, and the crankshaft must not be turned until the camshaft sprocket has been refitted. Use a length of wire to tie the upper part of the timing chain to the cylinder head to ensure the chain remains on the sprockets.

15 Remove the sprockets from their location dowel on the camshaft flange. Remove the timing chain sprocket from the timing chain, and if required remove the dowel from the flange in the end of the camshaft. Note: The sprocket bolts must be renewed every time they are removed.

Inspection

16 Examine the teeth on the sprockets for wear. Each tooth forms an inverted V. If worn, the side of each tooth under tension will be slightly concave in shape when compared with the other side of the tooth (ie, the teeth

will have a hooked appearance). If the teeth appear worn, the sprocket must be renewed.

Refitting

17 Ensure that the camshaft and crankshaft timing marks are still aligned, as described in Section 3. If a new sprocket is being fitted, transfer the chain alignment mark from the old sprocket to the new.

18 Fit the location dowel to the hole in the exhaust camshaft flange.

19 Engage the sprocket with the chain, aligning the marks made on the chain and sprocket before removal, then locate the sprocket on the camshaft flange and engage it with the dowel.

20 Insert the bolts and tighten them to the specified torque while holding the sprocket stationary using the used tool for removal. Remove the wire used to tie the chain to the cylinder head.

21 Refit the centrifuge to the exhaust camshaft sprocket, and tighten the retaining bolt to the specified torque.

22 Refit the timing chain tensioner as described earlier in this Section.

23 Refit the front plate as described in Section 15.

24 Using a socket on the crankshaft pulley/vibration damper hub bolt, turn the crankshaft through two complete revolutions, and check that the crankshaft and camshaft timing marks are still aligned with No 1 piston at TDC, as described in Section 3.

25 Remove the inlet camshaft locking drill, then refit the camshaft cover with reference to Section 4.

Crankshaft sprocket

Removal

Note: *A puller may be required to remove the sprocket.*

26 Remove the timing chain cover as described in Section 6. This procedure includes removal of the crankshaft pulley/vibration damper and Woodruff key, and the setting of the engine to its TDC position.

27 Remove the sump as described in Section 11.

28 Hold the oil pump sprocket on the oil pump stationary using a suitable tool engaged with the sprocket holes, then unscrew and

8.4 Remove the timing chain tensioner

8.8 Lock the camshaft using a drill bit

8.13 Unbolt the sprocket from the camshaft

remove the mounting bolts. Remove the sprocket from the oil pump drive flange and unhook the drive chain from the crankshaft sprocket on the front of the crankshaft. Note: The oil pump chain drive sprocket is incorporated into the crankshaft sprocket.

29 Remove the camshaft sprocket as described previously in this Section, however, in addition to marking the timing chain in relation to the camshaft sprocket, also mark it in relation to the injection pump sprocket and crankshaft sprocket. This is necessary to ensure the valve timing and injection pump timing is maintained, since it will also be difficult to ascertain the TDC position of the crankshaft with the timing chain cover removed.

30 Unhook the timing chain from the crankshaft sprocket and injection pump sprocket.

31 Slide the crankshaft sprocket from the front of the crankshaft. If it is tight, use a suitable puller, taking care not to damage the sprocket teeth. Alternatively, use two levers against the front of the cylinder block, positioning the levers diagonally opposite each other.

32 Recover the Woodruff key from the groove in the crankshaft.

Inspection

33 Examine the teeth on the sprockets for wear. Each tooth forms an inverted V. If worn, the side of each tooth under tension will be slightly concave in shape when compared with the other side of the tooth (ie, the teeth will have a hooked appearance). If the teeth appear worn, the sprocket must be renewed.

Refitting

34 Locate the Woodruff key in the crankshaft groove, making sure that the upper edge is parallel with the surface of the crankshaft.

35 Slide the crankshaft sprocket onto the front of the crankshaft and engage it with the Woodruff key. If necessary, use a suitable metal tube to tap it into position.

36 Engage the timing chain with the crankshaft sprocket and injection pump sprocket, making sure that the previously-made marks are aligned with each other, then pull the chain up through the aperture at the front of the cylinder head.

37 Refit the camshaft sprocket as described earlier in this Section, making sure that the previously-made marks on the chain and sprocket are aligned with each other. Check that the alignment marks are still correctly aligned.

38 Refit the oil pump drive chain and sprocket with reference to Section 12.

39 Refit the sump as described in Section 11.

40 Refit the timing chain cover and crankshaft pulley/vibration damper as described in Section 6.

Tensioner rail

Removal

41 Remove the cylinder head as described in Section 10.

42 Remove the timing chain cover as described in Section 6.

43 Remove the timing chain tensioner as described earlier in this Section.

44 Remove the tensioner rail from its pin.

Inspection

45 Examine the tensioner rail for signs of excessive wear, damage or cracks, and renew if necessary.

Refitting

46 Locate the tensioner rail on the pin.

47 Refit the timing chain tensioner as described previously in this Section.

48 Refit the timing chain cover as described in Section 6.

49 Refit the cylinder head as described in Section 10.

---

9 Camshafts, camshaft housing and hydraulic tappets – removal, inspection and refitting

Camshafts

Removal

1 Remove the exhaust camshaft sprocket as described in Section 8, making sure that the timing chain remains engaged with the crankshaft sprocket, using wire to tie it to one side.

2 The camshaft bearing caps are numbered from the timing chain end of the engine **(see illustration)**. Check the bearing caps to ensure that marks are present, and if necessary make suitable marks using quick-drying paint or a centre-punch.

3 The camshaft bearing cap bolts must now be slackened according to the following information, and the camshafts removed.

Warning: It is absolutely essential to observe the correct sequence when slackening the camshaft bearing cap bolts, because the camshafts are very sensitive to fracturing.

4-cylinder engine

a) *Progressively slacken and then remove the bolts from bearing caps 1, 3 and 5.*

b) *Lift off bearing caps 1, 3 and 5, keeping them in order* **(see illustration)***. Note that*

the bearing caps locate on dowels – if they are stuck, tap gently using a soft-faced mallet.

c) *Progressively slacken the bearing cap bolts for bearing caps 2 and 4, in one-turn stages until all pressure on the camshaft is relieved. Take care not to allow uneven pressure on the camshaft as the bolts are unscrewed.*

d) *Lift off bearing caps 2 and 4, again keeping them in order.*

e) *Lift the inlet and exhaust camshafts from the camshaft housing and recover the thrustwashers from No 3 bearing location.*

5-cylinder engine

a) *Progressively slacken and then remove the bolts from bearing caps 1, 3, 4 and 6.*

b) *Lift off bearing caps 1, 3, 4 and 6, keeping them in order. Note that the bearing caps locate on dowels – if they are stuck, tap gently using a soft-faced mallet.*

c) *Progressively slacken the bearing cap bolts for bearing caps 2 and 5, in one-turn stages until all pressure on the camshafts is relieved. Take great care not to allow uneven pressure on the camshafts as the bolts are unscrewed.*

d) *Lift off the bearing caps 2 and 5, again keeping them in order.*

e) *Lift the inlet and exhaust camshafts from the camshaft housing and recover the thrustwashers from No 3 bearing location.*

6-cylinder engine

a) *Progressively slacken and then remove the bolts from bearing caps 1, 2, 4, 5 and 7.*

b) *Lift off bearing caps 1, 2, 4, 5 and 7, keeping them in order. Note that the bearing caps locate on dowels – if they are stuck, tap gently using a soft-faced mallet.*

c) *Progressively slacken the bearing cap bolts for bearing caps 3 and 6, in one-turn stages until all pressure on the camshafts is relieved. Take great care not to allow uneven pressure on the camshafts as the bolts are unscrewed.*

d) *Lift off bearing caps 3 and 6, again keeping them in order.*

e) *Lift the inlet and exhaust camshafts from the housing and recover the thrustwashers.*

9.2 Check the marking on the bearing caps

9.3 Note the position of the bearing caps

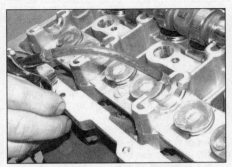

9.7 Lubricate the camshaft bearing housing

9.8a Lower the camshaft into position...

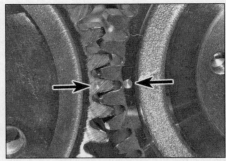

9.8b ...and align the timing marks

Inspection

4 Thoroughly clean the camshafts and the housing/caps.

5 Examine the camshaft journals and cam lobes for any sign of scoring, wear grooves or pitting, and if apparent, renew the relevant camshaft. Any damage of this nature may be attributable to a blocked oil passage in the cylinder head, and careful examination should be carried out to determine the cause.

6 Examine the bearing surfaces in the camshaft housing and bearing caps for excessive wear and scoring. If evident, renew the components together with the camshafts.

Refitting

7 Lubricate the camshaft journals and the bearing locations in the camshaft housing/caps with clean engine oil **(see illustration)**. Also lubricate the hydraulic tappets.

8 Locate the inlet camshaft in the left-hand side of the camshaft housing, and then locate the exhaust camshaft in the right-hand side, at the same time engaging the gears at the fronts of the camshafts so that the timing marks are aligned **(see illustrations)**, see Section 3.

9 Locate the bearing caps in position over the camshafts and tighten the securing bolts according to the following information, ensuring that the bearing caps are fitted to their original locations.

⚠️ *Warning: It is absolutely essential to observe the correct sequence when tightening the camshaft bearing cap bolts, in order to avoid damage to the camshaft.*

4-cylinder engine

a) *Fit bearing caps 2 and 4, then insert the bolts, and tighten them progressively in one-turn stages to the specified torque. Take care not to allow uneven pressure on the camshaft as the bolts are tightened.*

b) *Fit bearing caps 1, 3 and 5, then insert the bolts, and tighten them progressively in one-turn stages to the specified torque.*

5-cylinder engine

a) *Fit bearing caps 2 and 5, then insert the bolts, and tighten them progressively in one-turn stages to the specified torque. Take care not to allow uneven pressure on the camshaft as the bolts are tightened.*

b) *Fit bearing caps 1, 3, 4 and 6, then insert the bolts, and tighten them progressively in one-turn stages to the specified torque.*

6-cylinder engines

a) *Fit bearing caps 3 and 6, then insert the bolts, and tighten them progressively in one-turn stages to the specified torque. Take care not to allow uneven pressure on the camshaft as the bolts are tightened.*

b) *Fit bearing caps 1, 2, 4, 5 and 7, then insert the bolts, and tighten them progressively in one-turn stages to the specified torque.*

10 Refit the exhaust camshaft sprocket as described in Section 8.

Camshaft lower housing and hydraulic tappets

Removal

11 Remove the camshafts as described earlier in this Section. This procedure includes removal of the camshaft cover and cylinder head front cover.

12 Obtain a container with 16, 20 or 24 compartments and number the compartments to indicate the location of the hydraulic tappets. Remove each hydraulic tappet in turn from the camshaft housing and store them in the container **(see illustration)**.

13 Lift the camshaft lower housing from the cylinder head **(see illustration)**.

Inspection

14 Clean the camshaft housing and cylinder head and check for damage and wear.

15 The operation of the removed hydraulic tappets can be checked as follows.

a) *Press down firmly on the top of each tappet, using a blunt instrument such as a wooden hammer handle, for approximately 10 seconds.*

9.12 Remove the hydraulic tappets, noting their fitted positions

9.13 Remove the camshaft lower housing

9.18 Lubricate the hydraulic tappets with clean engine oil

b) Note how far the piston moves when depressed.
c) Repeat the operation for all the tappets in turn.
d) If any one tappet can be depressed more easily than the others, renew it.

16 Check the hydraulic tappets and the bores in the camshaft lower housing for wear and scoring. If any serious damage or wear is evident, the camshaft housing and tappets must be renewed.

Refitting

17 Locate the lower housing back into position on the cylinder head.
18 Lubricate the hydraulic tappet bores in the camshaft housing with clean engine oil, then locate each hydraulic tappet in its original position in the housing (see illustration).
19 Complete the rest of the installation by reversing the removal procedure, referring to the relevant Chapters. When all components are refitted, start the engine and check carefully around the camshaft cover for any oil leaks.

10 Cylinder head – removal, inspection and refitting

Note: New cylinder head bolts may be required – see text.

Removal

1 Ensure that the engine is cold before attempting to remove the cylinder head.

2 Apply the parking brake, then jack up the front of the vehicle and support it on axle stands (see 'Vehicle jacking and support').
3 Disconnect the battery negative lead as described in Chapter 5A Section 4.
4 Raise the bonnet to the fully open position.
5 Drain the engine oil and coolant as described in Chapter 1 Section 4.
6 Remove the glow plugs as described in Chapter 5B Section 3.
7 Remove the camshafts, hydraulic tappets and lower housing, as described in Section 9.
8 Remove the thermostat housing from the right-hand side front of the cylinder head, as described in Chapter 3 Section 4.
9 Remove the inlet manifold as described in Chapter 4A Section 15.
10 Undo the retaining bolts and remove the oil feed pipe to the turbocharger from the cylinder head (see illustration).
11 Undo the retaining bolts from the turbocharger to the exhaust manifold (see illustration).
12 Undo the retaining nut from the exhaust mounting bracket at the rear of the exhaust manifold (see illustration).
13 Using a socket through the cylinder head aperture, unscrew and remove the two bolts securing the timing chain cover to the cylinder head (see illustration 6.25).
14 Make a final check to ensure that all relevant hoses and wires have been disconnected from the cylinder head.
15 Progressively loosen the cylinder head bolts, working in the reverse order to the tightening sequence (see illustration 10.32a or 10.32b). Remove all cylinder head bolts.
16 Release the cylinder head from the cylinder block and locating dowels by rocking it. Do not prise between the mating faces of the cylinder head and block, as this may damage the gasket faces.
17 With the aid of an assistant, carefully lift the cylinder head, complete with exhaust manifold, from the block, and manoeuvre it out from the engine compartment.
18 Recover the cylinder head gasket.
19 If necessary, remove the exhaust manifold from the cylinder head.

Inspection

20 Refer to Chapter 2C Section 6 for

details of the cylinder head dismantling and reassembly.
21 The mating faces of the cylinder head and block must be perfectly clean before refitting the head. Use a scraper to remove all traces of gasket and carbon, and also clean the tops of the pistons. Take particular care with the cylinder head, as the metal is easily damaged. Also make sure that debris is not allowed to enter the oil and water passages. Using adhesive tape and paper, seal the water, oil and bolt holes in the cylinder block. To prevent carbon entering the gap between the pistons and bores, smear a little grease in the gap. After cleaning each piston, rotate the crankshaft so that the piston moves down the bore, and then wipe out the grease and carbon with a cloth rag.
22 Check the block and head for nicks, deep scratches and other damage. If very slight, they may be removed from the cylinder block carefully with a file. More serious damage may be repaired by machining, but this is a specialist job.
23 If warpage of the cylinder head is suspected, use a straight-edge to check it for distortion, with reference to Chapter 2C Section 7.
24 Clean out the bolt holes in the block using a pipe cleaner or thin rag and a screwdriver. Make sure that all oil and water is removed, otherwise there is a possibility of the block being cracked by hydraulic pressure when the bolts are tightened.
25 Examine the bolt threads and the threads in the cylinder block for damage. If necessary, use the correct size tap to chase out the threads in the block.
26 The manufacturers recommend that the cylinder head bolts are measured, to determine whether renewal is necessary; however, some owners may wish to renew all the bolts as a matter of course.
27 Measure the length of each bolt from the base of the head to the end of the shank. If the bolt length is greater than the maximum specified, the bolts should be renewed.
28 Reassemble the cylinder head with reference to Chapter 2C Section 8. Where applicable, refit the exhaust manifold together with a new gasket.

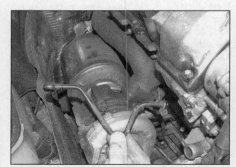

10.10 Remove the turbocharger oil feed pipe

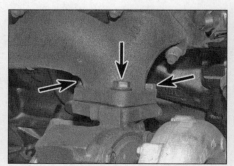

10.11 Turbo-to-manifold retaining bolts

10.12 Exhaust mounting bracket

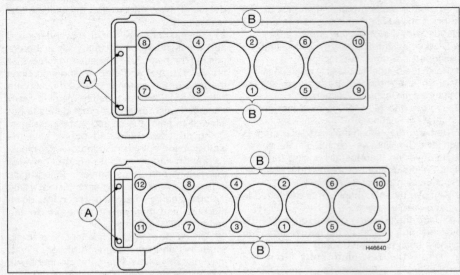

10.32a Cylinder head bolt (B) tightening sequence – 4 and 5 cylinder engines

A bolts securing the cylinder head to the timing chain cover

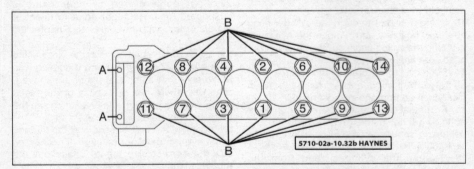

10.32b Cylinder head bolt (B) tightening sequence – 6 cylinder engines

A bolts securing the cylinder head to the timing chain cover

Refitting

29 Locate the new cylinder head gasket on the block, making sure that it is the correct way up and positioned over the location dowels.

30 With the aid of an assistant, lower the cylinder head carefully onto the block.

31 Oil the threads and the cylinder head contact faces of the cylinder head bolts, then insert them and screw them into the cylinder block by hand. Ensure that the bolts are fitted to their correct locations as noted on removal.

32 Tighten the cylinder head bolts in the order shown **(see illustrations)**, and in the stages given in the Specifications – ie, tighten all bolts to the Stage 1 torque, then tighten all bolts to the Stage 2 torque, and so on.

33 Tighten the two bolts securing the timing chain cover to the cylinder head at the front of the engine.

11.9 Disconnect the oil level sensor wiring plug

11.14 Sump-to-transmission bolts

34 The remainder of refitting is a reversal of removal, noting the following points:

a) *Refill the cooling system and refill the engine with oil as described in Chapter 1.*

b) *Reconnect the battery negative lead as described in Chapter 5A Section 4.*

c) *When all components have been refitted, start the engine and check carefully around the engine for any oil or coolant leaks.*

11 Sump – removal and refitting

Removal

Note: *A suitable hoist and lifting tackle will be required for this operation. To carry out this procedure, the front suspension crossmember will need to be lowered, to allow enough room for the sump to be removed. A new sump gasket will be required on refitting.*

1 Remove the engine covers as described in Section 4.

2 Apply the parking brake, then jack up the front of the vehicle and support it on axle stands (see *'Vehicle jacking and support'*). Remove both front road wheels.

3 Drain the engine oil as described in Chapter 1 Section 4. On completion, renew the sealing washer, then refit the drain plug and tighten to the specified torque.

4 Attach a suitable hoist to the engine and take the weight of the engine.

5 Unscrew the bolts from the bottom of the engine mountings at each side of the engine.

6 Lower the front suspension crossmember with reference to Chapter 10 Section 11.

7 Remove the cooling fan and shroud from the rear of the radiator, with reference to Chapter 3 Section 6.

8 Refer to Chapter 4A Section 19 and detach the exhaust downpipe from the turbocharger, then unbolt the exhaust mounting from the transmission and support the exhaust on an axle stand.

9 Disconnect the wiring from the oil level and temperature sensors. If necessary, the sensor may be removed from the sump **(see illustration)**.

10 Undo the bolt and remove the engine oil level dipstick guide tube. Renew the O-ring seal.

11 Remove the charge air pipe from beneath the sump.

12 On automatic transmission models, detach the fluid pipes from the transmission and sump.

13 Where applicable, remove the sump sound insulation material.

14 Unscrew the bolts securing the transmission to the rear of the sump, then unscrew the remaining sump-to-engine bolts and lower the sump from the cylinder block **(see illustration)**. Note the location of the bolts as some are of different lengths. Where applicable, recover the gasket. If the sump is stuck, use a hide or wooden mallet to tap its sides in order to release it. Do not drive a screwdriver between the sump and cylinder block as this may damage the mating surfaces.

15 It is recommended that the oil and oil filter are renewed whenever the sump is removed. Before refitting the sump, it is a good idea to remove the oil filter in order to allow the oil to drain from the cylinder block oil gallery and internal oilways.

Refitting

16 Thoroughly clean the mating surfaces of the sump and cylinder block.

17 Place the gasket onto the sump and align it with the bolt holes in the cylinder block **(see illustrations)**.

18 With the sump in place, insert all of the bolts finger-tight **(see illustration)**. Make sure all bolts are fitted in the correct position as noted on removal.

19 The bolts can now be tightened securing the transmission to the sump to the specified torque. This will ensure the rear of the sump is correctly aligned with the transmission, as if it is not aligned correctly, vibration and noise may occur.

20 Tighten the remaining sump bolts to the specified torque.

21 Complete the rest of the installation by reversing the removal procedure, referring to the relevant Chapters.

22 When all components are refitted, start the engine and check carefully around the sump for any oil leaks.

12 Oil pump – removal, inspection and refitting

Removal

1 Remove the sump as described in Section 11.
2 The sprocket must be disengaged from the chain as the oil pump is being removed.

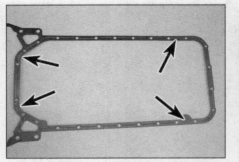

11.17a Note the points where sealant is located on the gasket

11.17b Fit the sump using a new gasket

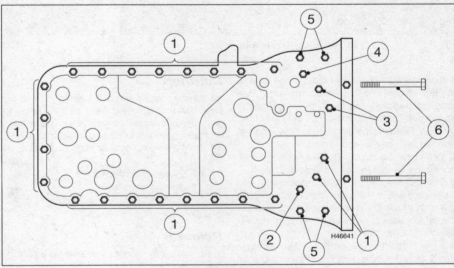

11.18 Sump bolt locations

1 M6x20	2 M6x40	3 M6x80	4 M6x90	5 M8x40	6 M10x40

3 Unscrew the mounting bolts, withdraw the oil pump from the bottom of the crankcase, and recover the O-ring seal **(see illustration)**.
4 Press against the chain tensioner and disengage the sprocket from the chain as the pump is being removed **(see illustration)**.

Inspection

5 With the exception of the oil pressure relief valve components, the oil pump is a sealed unit. To remove the oil pressure relief valve components, proceed as follows.

12.3 Oil pump mounting bolts

12.4 Press against the chain tensioner

12.6 Relief valve retaining plug

13.3 Lock the flywheel in position

6 Unscrew the relief valve plug, in the side of the timing chain cover **(see illustration)**. Take care, as the plug will be pushed out by the spring pressure when it reaches the end of the threads. **Note:** if a sealing ring is present it will need to be renewed on refitting.

7 Withdraw the spring, guide pin and piston, noting the orientation of the piston.

8 Thoroughly clean all components, and examine them for wear and damage. If there is any sign of excessive wear or damage, renew the appropriate component(s) – pay particular attention to the spring.

9 Also clean the oil pump intake strainer thoroughly, however, do not immerse the oil pump in cleaning solvent.

10 Examine the drive chain for wear and damage. If necessary, renew the chain as described later in this Section.

11 Reassemble the oil pressure relief valve using a reversal of the dismantling procedure, lubricating each component with fresh engine oil before fitting. Tighten the relief valve plug to the specified torque.

12 With the oil pump upright, pour fresh engine oil into the upper aperture while turning the pump shaft slowly. This will prime the oil pump so that normal oil pressure will be resumed as soon as possible after starting the engine.

Refitting

13 Check that the sprocket is engaged with the drive chain correctly and then locate the oil pump onto the crankcase. Insert the mounting bolts and tighten the bolts to the specified torque.

14 Refit the sump as described in Section 11.

13 Flywheel/driveplate – removal, inspection and refitting

Removal

1 Remove the manual transmission (Chapter 7A Section 7), or automatic transmission (Chapter 7B Section 6).

2 On manual transmission models, remove the clutch as described in Chapter 6 Section 5.

3 The flywheel/driveplate must be held stationary while the mounting bolts are loosened. To do this, have an assistant insert a wide-bladed screwdriver in the starter ring gear teeth through the access hole in the rear of the sump. Mercedes-Benz technicians use a special tool incorporating serrations which engage with the ring gear teeth **(see illustration 5.3a)**. Alternatively, make up a tool as shown **(see illustration)** and bolt it to a starter motor mounting hole.

4 Unscrew the mounting bolts, then lift the flywheel/driveplate from the rear of the crankshaft **(see illustrations)**. Note that the location dowel ensures the flywheel/driveplate can only be fitted in one position.

5 On automatic transmission models recover the locking plates from each side of the driveplate.

Inspection

6 If the teeth on the flywheel/driveplate starter ring gear are badly worn, it may be possible to fit a new ring gear, however this work should be entrusted to a Mercedes-Benz dealer who will have the necessary equipment to heat the new gear to the critical temperature in order to fit it. Overheating the gear will affect its hardness, resulting in rapid wear. The old gear may be removed by drilling it and using a cold chisel to split it. Take care not to drill into the flywheel/driveplate.

7 On manual transmission models, if the clutch friction face of the flywheel is deeply scored, cracked or otherwise damaged, the flywheel must be renewed. However, it may be possible to have it surface-ground, but seek the advice of an engine reconditioning specialist. Check the condition of the spigot bearing in the centre of the flywheel or in the end of the crankshaft, and renew if necessary **(see illustration)**.

13.4a Remove the flywheel/driveplate

13.4b Location dowel

13.7 The spigot bearing is in the centre of the flywheel

8 It is recommended that the flywheel/driveplate securing bolts are renewed whenever removed.

Refitting

9 Commence refitting by cleaning the mating faces of the crankshaft and flywheel/driveplate.
10 Make sure that the location dowel is in position in the end of the crankshaft. On automatic transmission models, fit the locking plate onto the crankshaft.
11 Locate the flywheel/driveplate onto the crankshaft, then insert the new mounting bolts (and further locking plate on automatic transmission models) and hand-tighten them.
12 Lock the flywheel/driveplate using the method employed during removal, then tighten the securing bolts progressively in a diagonal sequence to the specified torque first, then tighten all the bolts by the specified angle.
13 The remainder of refitting is a reversal of removal.

14 Crankshaft oil seals – renewal
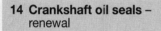

Front oil seal

1 Remove the crankshaft pulley/vibration damper and inspect it as described in Section 5.
2 Measure and note the fitted depth of the oil seal in the timing chain cover.
3 Prise the oil seal from the cover using a hooked instrument. Alternatively, drill a small hole in the oil seal, and use a self-tapping screw and a pair of pliers to remove it.
Caution: Take great care not to damage the crankshaft surface.
4 Clean the seal location in the timing cover, and also clean the oil seal contact surface on the crankshaft pulley/vibration damper. Examine the seal contact surface of the pulley/vibration damper for an excessive wear groove. If evident, refer to Section 5.
5 Press the new seal into the timing chain cover (open end first) to the previously-noted depth, using a suitable tube or socket. Do not apply any lubricant to the seal or the crankshaft.
6 Refit the crankshaft pulley/vibration damper as described in Section 5.

Rear oil seal

Note: The rear oil seal is integral with the oil seal housing and should be renewed whenever it is removed.
7 Remove the flywheel/driveplate as described in Section 13.
8 Unscrew the retaining bolts and remove the oil seal/housing from the cylinder block **(see illustration)**. Take care not to damage the sump gasket.
9 New oil seal/housings are supplied with a

14.8 Rear crankshaft oil seal/housing bolts

plastic sleeve on the inside of the seal to aid refitting of the seal over the end of the crankshaft. DO NOT remove the plastic fitting sleeve until the oil seal housing is in its fitted position.
10 Ensure that the cylinder block mating face of the oil seal housing is free from all traces of old sealant, oil and grease, and then apply a 1.5 to 2.5 mm thick bead of silicone sealant (A 001 898 89 20 10. Loctite 574 or equivalent) to the oil seal housing. Note that the sealant should be run around the inside of the bolt holes in the oil seal housing. It must be fitted within 10 minutes of applying the sealant. Also apply sealant at the area where the sump, oil seal housing and cylinder block meet.
11 Fit the new oil seal housing over the crankshaft and onto the cylinder block, keeping the plastic sleeve in position.
12 Fit the retaining bolts and tighten them to the specified torque setting.
13 Remove the plastic fitting sleeve from the new oil seal housing.
14 Refit the flywheel/driveplate (Section 13).

15 Cylinder head front cover – removal and refitting

Removal

1 Disconnect the battery negative lead as described in Chapter 5A Section 4.
2 Remove the camshaft cover, as described in Section 4.
3 Remove the high-pressure fuel pump as described in Chapter 4A Section 10.
4 Position the engine at TDC for No 1 cylinder as described in Section 3.
5 Remove the chain tensioner as described in Section 8.
6 Clamp the hose leading to the oil separator on the front of the cylinder head, then undo the retaining screws and pull the separator fowards. Renew the gasket.
7 Undo the retaining bolts and pull the front cover forwards from place.

Refitting

8 Ensure the cylinder head and cover mating surfaces are clean.
9 Apply sealant (MB No. A 003 989 98 20,

Loctite 5970 or equivalent) to the area where the front cover contacts the cylinder head.
10 Position the front cover over the locating dowels, insert the retaining bolts and tighten them to the specified torque.
11 The remainder of refitting is a reversal of removal.

16 Engine/transmission mountings – inspection and renewal

Inspection

1 Three engine/transmission mountings are used, one on either side of the engine, and one under the rear of the transmission.
2 For improved access, raise the front of the vehicle and support it securely on axle stands (see *'Vehicle jacking and support'*).
3 Check the condition of the mounting rubber to see if it is cracked, hardened or separated from the metal at any point. Renew the mounting if any such damage or deterioration is evident. The mountings contain hydraulic oil, and must be renewed if oil leakage is evident.
4 Check the mounting bolts are tight.
5 Using a large screwdriver or metal bar, check for wear in the mounting by carefully levering against it to check for free play. Where this is not possible, enlist the aid of an assistant to move the engine/transmission back-and-forth, or from side-to-side, while you observe the mounting. If excessive free play is found, check first that the fasteners are correctly secured, and then renew any worn components as required.

Renewal

Front engine mountings

6 Support the engine, either using a hoist and lifting tackle connected to the engine lifting brackets, or by positioning a jack and interposed block of wood under the sump. Ensure that the engine is adequately supported before proceeding.
7 Depending on which engine mounting requires removal, it may be necessary to remove the alternator or turbocharger to make access easier. See the relevant Chapters to remove any other components.
8 Unscrew the bolts securing the mountings to the engine crossmember.
9 Raise the engine a little, then undo the bolts securing the mounting brackets to the engine.
10 Fit the new mountings, and tighten the fasteners to the specified torque.

Rear engine/transmission mounting

11 Raise the front of the vehicle and support it securely on axle stands (see *'Vehicle jacking and support'*).
12 Support the transmission using a jack and interposed block of wood.
13 Unbolt the mounting bracket from the underbody, then unscrew the bolts securing the mounting rubber to the rear of the transmission.

16.13a Unscrew the rear mounting bolts...

16.13b...and the lower mounting bracket bolts...

16.13c...then manoeuvre it from position

16.15 Earth cable fitted to the rear mounting

Lower the bracket together with the mounting from the underbody **(see illustrations)**.
14 The mounting rubber can then be unbolted from the bracket.

15 Refitting is a reversal of removal, making sure that the earth cable is bolted to the transmission **(see illustration)**.

17 Engine oil sensor – renewal

1 Raise the front of the vehicle and support it securely on axle stands (see *'Vehicle jacking and support'*). Undo the fasteners and remove the engine undershield.
2 Drain the engine oil as described in Chapter 1 Section 4.
3 Disconnect the wiring plug from the oil sensor on the base of the sump **(see illustration 11.9)**.
4 Undo the retaining bolts and withdraw the sensor from the sump. Renew the O-ring seal.
5 Refitting is a reversal of removal, tightening the sensor retaining bolts to the specified torque.

Chapter 2 Part B
V6 engine in-car repair procedures

Contents

Degrees of difficulty

Easy, suitable for novice with little experience	Fairly easy, suitable for beginner with some experience	Fairly difficult, suitable for competent DIY mechanic	Difficult, suitable for experienced DIY mechanic	Very difficult, suitable for expert DIY or professional

Specifications

General

Engine type.	V6 diesel, double overhead camshaft (DOHC)
Engine code:	
E280 CDI	642.920
E320 CDI	642.920
Bore	83.0 mm
Stroke	92.0 mm
Capacity	2987 cc
Firing order.	1-5-3-6-2-4
Direction of crankshaft rotation	Clockwise, viewed from the front of the engine
Compression ratio	18.0: 1
Compression pressure:	
Tolerance	27 to 32 bar
Maximum difference between cylinders.	3.0 bar

Cylinder head bolts

Length when new (from under head)	205 mm
Maximum length.	207 mm

Lubrication system

Minimum system pressure:	
At idle speed.	0.3 bar
At 3000 rpm	3.0 bar

Torque wrench settings

	Nm	lbf ft
Balance shaft:		
Rear retaining bolt:		
Stage 1	20	15
Stage 2	Angle-tighten a further 90°	
Front retaining bolt	9	7
Rear cover bolts	9	7
Camshaft sprocket bolts	18	13
Connecting rod bolts*		
Short side of rod:		
Stage 1	15	11
Stage 2	30	22
Stage 3	40	30
Stage 4	Angle-tighten a further 90°	
Stage 5	Angle-tighten a further 90°	
Long side of rod:		
Stage 1	20	15
Stage 2	40	30
Stage 3	Angle-tighten a further 90°	
Stage 4	Angle-tighten a further 90°	
Crankshaft pulley/vibration damper bolt: *		
Stage 1	200	148
Stage 2	Angle-tighten a further 90°	
Stage 3	Angle-tighten a further 90°	
Cylinder head bolts:		
Stage 1	10	7
Stage 2	60	44
Stage 3	Angle-tighten a further 90°	
Stage 4	Angle-tighten a further 90°	
Stage 5	Angle-tighten a further 90°	
M8 bolt	20	15
Cylinder head covers:		
Stage 1	4	3
Stage 2	6	4
Stage 3	9	7
EGR valve motor bolts	12	9
Engine mountings:		
Front mountings-to-crossmember	35	26
Front mountings-to-support brackets	50	37
Rear mounting-to-transmission	50	37
Rear mounting-to-crossmember	28	21
Exhaust manifold-to-cylinder head	20	15
Flywheel/driveplate bolts: *		
Stage 1	45	33
Stage 2	Angle-tighten a further 90°	
Main bearing bolts: *		
Vertical bolts:		
Stage 1	5	3
Stage 2	35	26
Stage 3	Angle-tighten a further 95°	
Stage 4	Angle-tighten a further 95°	
Lateral bolt:		
Stage 1	53	39
Stage 2	Angle-tighten a further 95°	
Oil filter housing-to-timing chain cover	14	10
Oil pump:		
Oil pump retaining bolts	19	14
Baffle plate with pipe-to-pump	12	8
Bracket-to-pump	10	7
Oil temperature sensor	11	8
Rear oil seal housing:		
Stage 1	8	6
Stage 2	10	7
Sump:		
M6 14	10	
M8 20	15	
Timing chain cover bolts	10	7
Timing chain rail bolts/pins	12	8
Timing chain tensioner	80	59

Do not re-use

1 General information

How to use this Chapter

1 This Part of the Chapter describes those repair procedures that can reasonably be carried out on the engine whilst it remains in the vehicle. If the engine has been removed from the vehicle and is being dismantled as described in Part C of this Chapter, any preliminary dismantling procedures can be ignored.

2 Note that whilst it may be possible physically to overhaul items such as the piston/connecting rod assemblies with the engine in the vehicle, such tasks are not usually carried out as separate operations and usually require the execution of several additional procedures (not to mention the cleaning of components and of oilways). For this reason, all such tasks are classed as major overhaul procedures and are described in Chapter.

Engine description

3 This engine features two banks of 3-cylinders sharing a common crankshaft in a 'V' configuration. A common cylinder head is fitted to each bank, and each is fitted with 2 camshafts (DOHC) – one to operate the intake valves, and one to operate the exhaust valves.

4 The intake camshaft of the right-hand cylinders, and the exhaust camshaft of the left-hand cylinders are driven by a duplex (double-row) timing chain, which is driven from a sprocket on the crankshaft. The timing chain also drives a counter-rotating balance shaft fitted in the 'V' of the cylinder block. The right-hand exhaust, and left-hand inlet camshafts are driven by gears from the neighbouring intake/exhaust camshaft.

5 The aluminium cylinder heads are fitted with hardened steel valve seats. The valves are operated by the camshafts via hydraulic compensation elements (tappets). No maintenance of the valve clearances is required.

6 A single-row chain from a second crankshaft sprocket drives the oil pump, mounted beneath the cylinder block.

7 A single-row chain from a second crankshaft sprocket drives the oil pump, mounted beneath the cylinder block.

8 The one-piece crankshaft is supported by 4 main bearings, with endfloat controlled by thrustwashers fitted each side of the No. 3 main bearing location.

9 The connecting rods are attached to the crankshaft by horizontally-split big-end bearings, and to the pistons by fully-floating gudgeon pins retained by circlips. The alloy pistons are fitted with three piston rings; two compression and one oil control.

Repair operations possible with the engine in the car

10 The following operations can be carried out without having to remove the engine from the vehicle:

a) Removal and refitting of the cylinder heads.
b) Removal and refitting of the timing chain and sprockets.
c) Removal and refitting of the camshafts.
d) Removal and refitting of the sump.
e) Removal and refitting of the connecting rods and pistons*
f) Removal and refitting of the oil pump.
g) Renewal of the engine/transmission mountings.
h) Removal of the flywheel/driveplate.

11 *Although it is possible to remove these components with the engine in place, for reasons of access and cleanliness it is recommended that the engine be removed.

2 Compression and leakdown tests – description and interpretation

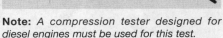

Note: *A compression tester designed for diesel engines must be used for this test.*

1 When engine performance is down, a compression test can provide diagnostic clues as to the engine's condition. If the test is performed regularly, it can give warning of trouble before any other symptoms become apparent.

2 A compression tester specifically intended for diesel engines must be used, because of the higher pressures involved. The tester is connected to an adapter, which screws into the glow plug. It is unlikely to be worthwhile buying such a tester for occasional use, but it may be possible to borrow or hire one – if not, have the test performed by a garage.

3 Unless specific instructions to the contrary are supplied with the tester, observe the following points.

a) *The battery must be in a good state of charge, the air filter must be clean, and the engine should be at normal operating temperature.*
b) *All the glow plugs should be removed as described in Chapter 5B Section 3.*
c) *The starter should not be operated using the stop/start button, but by a switch/wiring placed between the battery positive terminal and the positive terminal of the starter solenoid*

4 Crank the engine on the starter motor. After one or two revolutions, the compression pressure should build-up to a maximum figure, and then stabilise. Record the highest reading obtained.

5 Repeat the test on the remaining cylinders, recording the pressure in each

6 The cause of poor compression is less easy to establish on a diesel engine than on a petrol one. The effect of introducing oil into the cylinders ('wet' testing) is not conclusive, because there is a risk that the oil will sit in the swirl chamber or in the recess in the piston crown instead of passing to the rings.

However, the following can be used as a rough guide to diagnosis.

7 All cylinders should produce very similar pressures; if there is a large difference, then this indicates a fault. Note that the compression should build-up quickly in a healthy engine; low compression on the first stroke, followed by gradually increasing pressure on successive strokes, indicates worn piston rings. A low compression reading on the first stroke, which does not build-up during successive strokes, indicates leaking valves or a blown head gasket (a cracked head could also be the cause). Deposits on the undersides of the valve heads can also cause low compression.

8 A low reading from two adjacent cylinders is almost certainly due to the head gasket having blown between them; the presence of coolant in the engine oil will confirm this.

9 If the compression reading is unusually high, the combustion chambers are probably coated with carbon deposits. If this is the case, the cylinder head should be removed and decarbonised.

10 On completion of the test, refit the injectors or the glow plugs.

Leakdown test

11 A leakdown test measures the rate at which compressed air fed into the cylinder is lost. It is an alternative to a compression test, and in many ways is better, since the escaping air provides easy identification of where a pressure loss is occurring (piston rings, valves or head gasket).

12 The equipment needed for leakdown testing is unlikely to be available to the home mechanic. If poor compression is suspected, have the test performed by a suitably-equipped garage.

3 Engine assembly and valve timing marks – general information and usage

 Warning: When turning the engine, do not turn the engine using the camshaft sprocket bolts, and do not turn the engine backwards (ie, anti-clockwise).

1 Top Dead Centre (TDC) is the highest point in the cylinder that each piston reaches as it travels up and down when the crankshaft turns. Each piston reaches TDC at the end of the compression stroke and again at the end of the exhaust stroke, but for valve timing TDC refers to the No 1 piston position on the compression stroke.

2 Remove the cylinder head covers as described in Section 4.

3 With the cylinder head covers removed, the camshafts must now be clamped to the cylinder heads before the crankshaft/camshafts are rotated. Mercedes Benz technicians use special tools to achieve this (Tool No. 642 589 00 31 00, hold-down device

3.3 Fit the hold-down tools to the centre bearing locations

3.4a The marks on the rear of the camshaft gears are opposite each other...

3.4b...and the holes at the outer edges align with the upper surface of the cylinder head

3.5 The 'O' (TDC) mark on the pulley aligns with the bar on the timing cover

3.6 Lock the camshaft gears using the Mercedes tools or 6 mm diameter pins

4.1 Pull the engine cover upwards from its' mountings

set) **(see illustration)**. These tools are fitted to the centre bearing locations of the camshafts, using some of the cylinder head cover bolts. Tighten the bolts to 8 Nm.

4 Viewed from the front of the engine, use a socket on the crankshaft pulley bolt to rotate the engine clockwise, until the marks on the rear of the camshaft gears are opposite each other, and the holes on the edge of the camshaft gears is aligned with the upper surface of the cylinder head **(see illustrations)**.

5 In this position, the TDC mark on the crankshaft pulley/vibration damper should align with the bar on the timing cover **(see illustration)**.

6 The camshafts gears can be locked in place using Mercedes Benz tools No. 11 589

03 15 00 or equivalent **(see illustration)**. In the absence of the special tools, use 6 mm diameter pins.

7 The marking on the balance shaft sprocket should also be vertical, although this will not be visible at this stage until the timing chain cover has been removed.

---

4 Cylinder head covers – removal and refitting

Removal

1 Pull the plastic engine cover upwards from its' mountings **(see illustration)**.

2 Remove the right-hand air filter housing as described in Chapter 4A Section 2.

3 Disconnect the wiring plugs from the left-, and right-hand mass airflow sensors.

4 Disconnect the wiring plug from the vent line heating element **(see illustration)**.

5 Release the clamp and disconnect the crankcase ventilation hose at the oil separator **(see illustration)**.

6 Release the clamp at the turbocharger, and the clamp at the air filter housings and pull the air intake duct forwards from place.

7 Prise out the wire clip a little, then disconnect the charge air hose upstream of the intercooler.

8 Undo the retaining bolt, and remove the air duct retaining plate **(see illustration)**.

4.4 Disconnect the vent line heater wiring plug

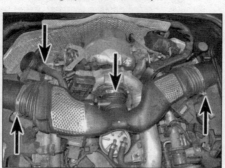

4.5 Ventilation hose and air duct clamps

4.8 Retaining plate bolt and air duct retaining plate bolts

9 Undo the retaining bolts, unclip the coolant hose, and remove the charge air duct upstream of the intercooler.

Left-hand cover

10 Open the coolant expansion tank, and allow any residual pressure to dissipate.
11 Disconnect the wiring plug from the EGR valve motor, then undo the retaining bolts and remove the motor **(see illustration)**. On models with a water-cooled motor, disconnect the coolant hose from the housing as it's withdrawn. Be prepared for coolant spillage. Plug all openings to prevent contamination.
12 Remove the injectors and fuel rail as described in Chapter 4A Sections 11 and 12.
13 Unbolt the power steering fluid reservoir and position it to one side **(see illustration)**.
14 Disconnect the fuel feed and return hoses from the metal pipes to the left-hand side of the cylinder head, then disconnect the fuel return hose from the filter and fuel leak-off pipe, and the fuel feed pipe. Undo the brackets retaining bolts and remove the fuel pipes assembly **(see illustration)**. Be prepared for fuel spillage.
15 Completely remove the upper bolt, slacken the lower bolt, and move oil level dipstick guide the tube gently away from the rear edge cylinder head cover.
16 Unclip the wiring harness from the cylinder head cover.
17 Undo the 2 retaining bolt and remove the oil filter housing bracket at the front of the cylinder head.
18 Gradually and evenly, slacken and remove the cylinder head cover bolts in the reverse of the sequence shown **(see illustration 4.28)**.
19 The cylinder head cover is attached to the cylinder head using sealant. In order to release the cover, ideally attach a threaded stud and slide hammer to the cover and carefully free the cover from the cylinder head. In the absence of a suitable slide hammer, carefully lever the cover from place using the strengthened points provided.

Right-hand cover

20 Remove the injectors and fuel rail as described in Chapter 4A Sections 11 and 12.
21 Undo the retaining bolts and remove the oil separator and connection fitting **(see illustration)**. Renew the O-ring seal.
22 Disconnect the wiring plug from the camshaft position sensor.
23 Unclip the wiring harnesses from the cylinder head cover.
24 Gradually and evenly, slacken and remove the cylinder head cover bolts in the reverse of the sequence shown **(see illustrations 4.28a and b)**.
25 The cylinder head cover is attached to the cylinder head using sealant. In order to release the cover, ideally attach a threaded stud and slide hammer to the cover and

4.11 EGR motor retaining bolts

4.13 Move the power steering pump reservoir to one side

4.14 Disconnect the necessary hoses and remove the pipe assembly

4.21 Undo the bolts and remove the oil separator

carefully free the cover from the cylinder head. In the absence of a suitable slide hammer, carefully lever the cover from place using the strengthened points provided.

Refitting

26 Remove all traces of sealant from the cylinder head and cover, using a suitable sealant removal spray (Eg. Loctite 7063). Don't use any sharp or abrasive tools, as these may damage the sealing surfaces.
27 Apply a 1.5 mm wide bead of suitable sealant (Loctite 5970 or equivalent) to the groove in the cylinder head cover sealing surface **(see illustration)**. Note that the cylinder head cover must be

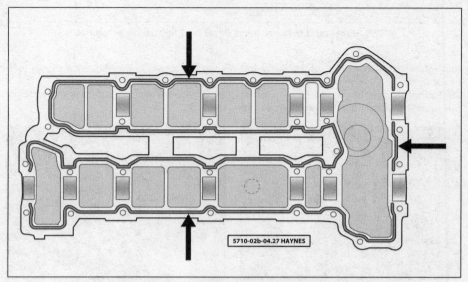

4.27 Apply a 1.5 mm bead of sealant to the cylinder head cover as shown

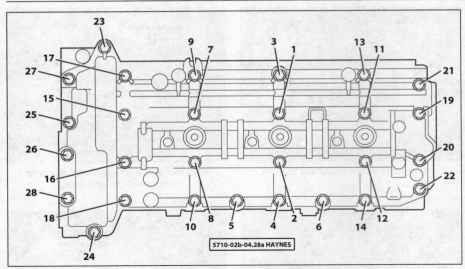

4.28a Left-hand cylinder head cover bolt tightening sequence

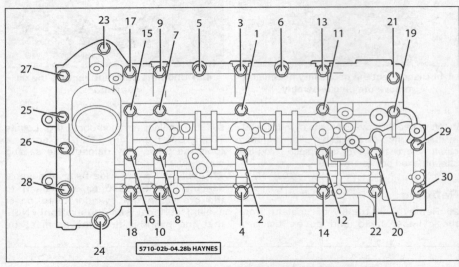

4.28b Right-hand cylinder head cover bolt tightening sequence

refitted within 10 minutes of applying the sealant.

28 Refit the cylinder head cover, insert the retaining bolts and tighten them to the specified torque in the sequence shown **(see illustrations)**.

29 The remainder of refitting is a reversal of removal.

5 Crankshaft pulley/vibration damper – removal and refitting

Removal

1 Remove the auxiliary drivebelt as described in Chapter 1 Section 6.

2 The crankshaft must be locked to prevent rotation whilst the pulley/vibration damper bolt is slackened. Remove the cover plate from the rear, right-hand side of the cylinder block and fit Mercedes Benz tool No. 112 589 03 40 00 (or equivalent) into the recess **(see illustration)**. This tool engages with the starter ring gear around the circumference of the flywheel/driveplate.

3 With the crankshaft locked, slacken and remove the crankshaft pulley/vibration damper retaining bolt **(see illustration)**. Discard the bolt – a new one must be fitted.

4 Slide the pulley/damper from the crankshaft, noting the position of the locating key. If necessary, use a three legged puller to extract the pulley/damper **(see illustration)**.

Refitting

5 Refitting is a reversal of removal, tightening the new pulley/damper retaining bolt to the specified torque.

6 Timing chain cover – removal and refitting

Removal

1 Pull the plastic cover on the top of the engine upwards from its' rubber mountings.

2 Remove the throttle body/mixing chamber as described in Chapter 4A Section 14.

3 Rotate the engine clockwise until the TDC mark on the crankshaft pulley/vibration damper aligns with the bar on the timing chain cover as described in Section 4.

4 Remove the crankshaft pulley/vibration damper as described in Section 5.

5 Undo the retaining bolts and remove the

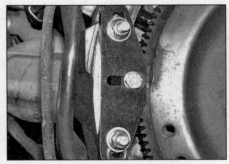

5.2 The tool engages with the starter ring gear

5.3 Remove the retaining bolt and washer

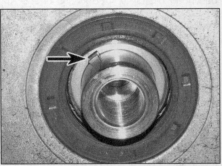

5.4 Note the location of the crankshaft key

6.5 Prise out the plastic caps, undo the idler pulley bolts, then remove the auxiliary drivebelt tensioner

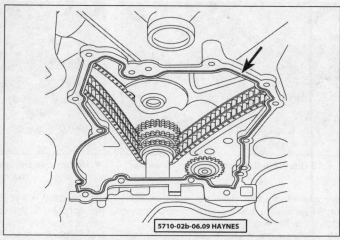

6.9 Apply a 1.5 mm bead of sealant to the cylinder block as shown

auxiliary drivebelt tensioner and idler pulleys **(see illustration)**.

6 Gradually, evenly undo the retaining bolts and remove the timing chain cover. Note that the cover locating dowels must be extracted and discarded – they are only used during engine production, and if left in place, would prevent the sealing compound from functioning correctly, resulting in possible leaks.

Refitting

7 Remove all traces of sealant from the cylinder block and timing chain cover, using a suitable sealant removal spray (Eg. Loctite 7063). Don't use any sharp or abrasive tools, as these may damage the sealing surfaces.

8 As a matter of course, replace the crankshaft oil seal in the cover as described in Section 14.

9 Apply a 1.5 mm wide bead of sealant (Loctite 5970 or equivalent) to the cylinder block as shown **(see illustration)**. Note that the timing chain cover must be refitted within 10 minutes of applying the sealant.

10 Position the timing chain cover on the cylinder block and loosely fit the retaining bolts. Insert Mercedes Benz centring sleeve (Tool No. 642 589 00 14 00 or equivalent) over the end of the crankshaft to ensure the cover is correctly located, then tighten the retaining bolts to the specified torque.

11 The remainder of refitting is a reversal of removal.

7	Timing chain –
	inspection and renewal

Inspection

1 Remove the right-hand cylinder head cover as described in Section 4.

2 In order to retaining camshafts in place on the cylinder head, a special hold-down tool

must be fitted to the camshaft centre bearing location on the cylinder head (Mercedes Benz tool No. 642 589 00 31 00 or equivalent). Fit the hold-down tool and tighten the retaining bolts to 8 Nm **(see illustration 3.3)**.

3 Using a spanner or socket on the crankshaft pulley/vibration damper bolt, rotate the crankshaft clockwise to TDC on No. 1 cylinder as described in Section 3.

4 Lock the right-hand camshafts in position as described in Section 3.

5 The 'stretch' of the timing chain is now checked by gently rotating the crankshaft pulley/vibration damper clockwise with the camshafts locked, and measuring the travel of the pulley/damper in relation to the TDC bar on the timing chain cover. Rotate the pulley/damper clockwise to remove any slack in the chain and hold it in this position. Use a protractor to measure the rotational movement achieved. If the TDC mark on the pulley is more than 11° past the corresponding TDC bar on the timing chain cover, the chain is excessively worn and requires replacement **(see illustration)**.

6 To avoid any future problems, if there is any doubt about the condition of the chain, renew it.

7.5 The bar on the timing cover must not be more than 11° past the 'O' (TDC) mark on the pulley

7 Upon completion, remove the camshaft locking/hold-down tools, and refit the cylinder head cover as described in Section 4.

Renewal

Note: *This following procedure, uses a chain breaker/riveter to renew the chain without removing the front timing chain cover, a second person will be required to assist fitting the timing chain. Ensure that all tools are available, as well as a new chain and new connecting link before proceeding.*

8 Remove the right-hand cylinder head cover as described in Section 4.

9 In order to retain the camshafts in place on the cylinder head, a special hold-down tool must be fitted to the camshaft centre bearing location on the cylinder head (Mercedes Benz tool No. 642 589 00 31 00 or equivalent). Fit the hold-down tool and tighten the retaining bolts to 8 Nm **(see illustration 3.3)**.

10 Unscrew and remove the inlet camshaft sprocket bolt opposite the sprocket locating pin **(see illustration)**.

11 Rotate the crankshaft clockwise to TDC on No. 1 cylinder as described in Section 3.

12 Using a cable tie, secure the old timing chain to the right-hand inlet camshaft

7.10 Remove the bolt opposite the locating pin

7.13 Unscrew the timing chain tensioner

7.15 Remove the holder from each end of the camshaft

sprocket. Put some clean rag into the timing chain recess to prevent anything dropping down into the engine.

13 Unscrew the timing chain tensioner from the right-hand cylinder head **(see illustration)**. Discard the sealing ring – a new one must be fitted.

14 Remove the remaining bolts securing the sprocket to the right-hand inlet camshaft.

15 Remove the camshafts hold-down tool, note its fitted position, remove the holders and lift the intake camshaft from place **(see illustration)**.

16 Use the chain breaker to press out one of the timing chain pins and split the timing chain **(see illustration)**. Mercedes Benz technicians use tools No. 602 589 02 33 00, 602 589 04 63 00 and 602 589 04 63 01 for this task.

17 Refit the right-hand intake camshaft and secure it to the cylinder head using the hold-down tool previously described.

18 Refit the sprocket to the camshaft, then refit and securely tighten just one retaining bolt.

19 In order to prevent the timing chain from jumping the teeth on the camshaft sprocket, fit Mercedes Benz tool No. 642 589 01 40 00 to the corner of the cylinder head **(see illustration)**. In the absence of this tool, we recommend both right-hand camshafts are removed to eliminate the possibilty of accidental piston-to-valve contact whilst the new chain is drawn into place.

20 Connect the new timing chain to the old chain and press the chain link pin back into position. Genuine MB timing chains come with a split-type joining link. This link must

only be used whilst feeding the chain around the sprockets, then removed and replaced with a rivet-type link supplied in the kit. Note: Make sure the new chain is connected to the left-hand part of the chain, as the engine has to be turned clockwise, in the direction of rotation to feed the chain around the sprockets.

21 With the new chain connected securely to the old chain, take a firm hold of both ends of the chain and remove the cable-tie from the camshaft sprocket. Remove the clean rag from around the timing chain before turning the engine.

22 With the aid of an assistant, turn the engine in the direction of rotation. Keeping the timing chain taut, feed it around the crankshaft sprocket, until the new chain comes all the way around to the camshaft sprocket.

23 Remove the timing chain hold down tool from the corner of the cylinder head, keeping the chain engaged with the sprocket teeth.

24 Secure the new timing chain to the inlet camshaft sprocket with a cable tie.

25 Undo the sprocket retaining bolt, remove the hold-down tool, and remove the inlet camshaft. Do not allow the sprocket to fall in the timing chain recess.

26 Put some clean rag into the timing chain recess to prevent anything dropping down into the engine.

27 Fit the new timing chain link, using the timing chain riveter to connect the two ends of the chain securely. Always read the instructions that come with the chain riveter, as there are many different types available. The link pins need to be riveted securely, to prevent the chain coming apart.

28 Refit the camshaft(s), and secure with the hold-down tool. Ensure the camshaft timing marks align as described in Section 3.

29 Refit the sprocket to the camshaft, and tighten all 3 retaining bolts to their specified torque.

30 Refit the chain tensioner, with a new sealing ring, and tighten it to the specified torque.

31 Remove the cable tie securing the timing chain to the camshaft sprocket, then rotate the crankshaft clockwise until the TDC timing marks align as described in Section 3.

32 Refit the cylinder head cover as described in Section 4.

33 Upon completion, check for oil leaks.

8 Timing chain tensioner, sprockets, and guides – removal, inspection and refitting

Timing chain tensioner
Removal

1 Pull the plastic cover on the top of the engine upwards from its' rubber mountings.

2 Remove the right-hand side air filter housing as described in Chapter 4A Section 2.

3 Unscrew the timing chain tensioner from the right-hand cylinder head **(see illustration 7.13)**. Discard the sealing ring – a new one must be fitted.

Inspection

4 Do not attempt to dismantle the tensioner assembly. If it is suspected that the tensioner is worn or faulty, the complete unit should be renewed.

Refitting

5 Locate a new sealing ring on the tensioner, then screw it into position in the cylinder head and tighten to the specified torque.

6 Refitting is the reversal of removal. When all components are refitted, start the engine and check carefully around the tensioner for any oil leaks.

Camshaft sprocket
Removal

7 Remove the relevant cylinder head cover as described in Section 4.

8 In order to retaining camshafts in place on the cylinder head, a special hold-down tool must be fitted to the camshaft centre bearing location on the cylinder head (Mercedes Benz tool No. 642 589 00 31 00 or equivalent). Fit the hold-down tool and tighten the retaining bolts to 8 Nm **(see illustration 3.3)**.

9 Set the crankshaft at TDC on No. 1 cylinder as described in Section 3.

10 Using paint or permanent marker pen, make alignment marks between the timing chain and camshaft sprocket.

11 The camshaft sprocket is secured by 3 bolts. Note the position of the lower bolt, then rotate the crankshaft until the bolt is accessible. Undo and remove the bolt **(see illustration 7.10)**.

7.16 Use a chain breaker to press out one of the chain pins

7.19 The special tool prevents the chain from jumping the sprocket teeth

12 Again set the crankshaft at TDC on No. 1 cylinder as described in Section 3.

13 Slacken, but do not remove the remaining bolts securing the sprocket to the camshaft.

14 Unscrew the timing chain tensioner from the right-hand cylinder head (**see illustration 7.13**). Discard the sealing ring – a new one must be fitted.

15 Remove the camshaft hold-down tool(s) and the camshaft holders (**see illustration 7.15**).

16 Attach a cable tie to the timing chain.

17 Lift the camshaft, complete with sprocket, from the cylinder head.

18 Carefully lay the timing chain into the recess in the timing cover.

19 Undo the bolts and detach the sprocket from the camshaft.

Inspection

20 Examine the teeth on the sprockets for wear. Each tooth forms an inverted V. If worn, the side of each tooth under tension will be slightly concave in shape when compared with the other side of the tooth (ie, the teeth will have a hooked appearance). If the teeth appear worn, the sprocket must be renewed.

Refitting

21 Refitting is a reversal of removal, noting the following points:

a) Fit the sprocket to the camshaft, ensuring the locating pin engages correctly.

b) Tighten all fasteners to their specified torque where given.

Tensioner rail

Removal

22 Remove the left-hand cylinder head cover as described in Section 4.

23 In order to retaining camshafts in place on the cylinder head, a special hold-down tool must be fitted to the camshaft centre bearing location on the cylinder head (Mercedes Benz tool No. 642 589 00 31 00 or equivalent). Fit the hold-down tool and tighten the retaining bolts to 8 Nm (**see illustration 3.3**).

24 Remove the throttle body/mixing chamber as described in Chapter 4A Section 14.

25 Remove the auxiliary drivebelt as described in Chapter 1 Section 6.

26 Unscrew the oil filter housing cap to allow the oil inside to drain into the sump.

27 Undo the bolts from the oil filter housing-to-cylinder head cover bracket.

28 Remove the power steering pump reservoir upper mounting bolt.

29 Undo the retaining bolts and remove the oil filter housing. Replace the gasket. Be prepared for fluid spillage.

30 Remove the high-pressure fuel pump as described in Chapter 4A Section 10.

31 Position the engine at TDC on No. 1 cylinder as described in Section 4.

32 Drain the engine oil as described in Chapter 1 Section 4.

33 Remove the timing chain cover as described in Section 6.

34 Unscrew the timing chain tensioner from the right-hand cylinder head (**see illustration 7.13**). Discard the sealing ring – a new one must be fitted.

35 Remove the 3 side rail bolts from the cylinder heads.

36 Remove the lower bolt from the right-hand side outer rail.

37 Pull the right-hand side outer rail downwards, and out from the timing chain aperture.

38 Use permanent marker or paint to make alignment marks between the timing chain and the exhaust camshaft sprocket.

39 Remove the camshaft hold-down tool, and the camshaft holders, then manoeuvre the camshaft and sprocket from place.

40 Allow the timing chain to sag into the timing case.

41 Undo the lower bolt of the left-hand outer timing chain rail.

42 Compress the oil pump drive chain tensioner piston, then manoeuvre the left-hand outer rail downwards from the timing chain aperture.

43 Unscrew the bolts at the lower ends of the central chain rails, and manoeuvre them downwards from place.

Inspection

44 Examine the tensioner rails for signs of excessive wear, damage or cracks, and renew if necessary.

Refitting

45 Refitting is a reversal of removal, remembering to tighten all fasteners to their specified torque where given.

---

9 Camshafts and hydraulic tappets – removal, inspection and refitting

Removal

Camshafts

1 Removal of the camshafts is described within the camshaft sprocket removal procedure – see Section 8.

Hydraulic tappets

2 Remove the camshafts/sprockets as described in Section 8.

3 Lift out the rocker arms and hydraulic tappets (**see illustration**). Lay the arms out and make a note of their original locations. It's essential that if re-used, they are fitted to their original locations.

4 Obtain a container with 24 compartments, and number the compartments to indicated the location of the tappets. Pull each tappet up in turn from the cylinder head, and store them in the container. **Note:** Do not use a magnet to remove the tappets, as this may magnetise them, causing ferrous metal particles to accumulate on the surface.

Inspection

Camshafts

5 Thoroughly clean the camshafts and cylinder head.

6 Examine the camshaft bearing journals and cam lobes for signs or coring, wear grooves or pitting, and if apparent, renew the camshaft. Any damage of this nature may be attributable to a blocked oil passage in the cylinder head, and careful examination should be carried out to determine the cause.

7 Examine the bearing surfaces of the cylinder head covers and cylinders heads for excessive wear and scoring. If evident, renew these components along with the camshafts.

Hydraulic tappets

8 The operation of the removed hydraulic tappets can be checked as follows:

a) Press down firmly on the top of each tappet, using a blunt instrument such as a wooden hammer handle, for approximately 10 seconds.

b) Note how far the piston moves when depressed.

c) Repeat the operation for all the tappets in turn.

d) If any one tappet can be depressed more easily than the others, renew it.

9 Check the hydraulic tappets and the bores in the cylinder head for wear and scoring. If any serious damage or wear is evident, the cylinder head and tappets must be renewed.

Refitting

Hydraulic tappets

10 Lubricate the hydraulic tappet bores in the cylinder head with clean engine oil, then locate each hydraulic tappet in its original position (**see illustration**).

9.3 Lift the rocker arms and tappet assemblies

9.10 Locate the tappets/rocker arms in their original locations

11 Locate the roller-rocker arms above their original locations and secure them to the tappets with the retaining clips.

Camshafts

12 Lubricate the camshaft journals and the bearing locations in the cylinder head with clean engine oil. Also lubricate the roller-rocker arms.
13 If removed, refit the camshaft sprockets as described in Section 8.
14 Lay the camshafts in position in the cylinder heads. Note that they are marked to indicate their correct orientation:

Left-hand inlet camshaft	A 642 10
Left-hand exhaust camshaft	A 642 12
Right-hand inlet camshaft	A 642 09
Right-hand exhaust camshaft	A 642 11

15 The camshafts are correctly positioned when the crankshaft is at TDC on No.1 cylinder, and the markings on the rear face of the camshaft gears are directly opposite each other, the the mark on the edge of the gear is aligned with the upper level of the cylinder heads – see Section 3.
16 The remainder of refitting is a reversal of removal.

---

10 Cylinder head – removal, inspection and refitting

Removal

Note: *New cylinder head bolts may be required – see text.*
1 Disconnect the battery negative lead as described in Chapter 5A Section 4.
2 Drain the coolant and engine oil, then remove the oil filter as described in Chapter 1.

3 Remove the intake manifold and catalytic converter as described in Chapter 4A.
4 Remove the cylinder head covers as described in Section 4.
5 Remove the glow plugs as described in Chapter 5B Section 3.
6 Remove the auxiliary drivebelt as described in Chapter 1 Section 6.
7 Remove the upper bolt securing the power steering pump reservoir.
8 Undo the retaining bolts and remove the oil filter housing.
9 Remove the high-pressure fuel injection pump as described in Chapter 4A Section 10.
10 Remove the camshafts and hydraulic tappets as described in Section 9.
11 Undo the retaining bolts and remove the heat shields above the exhaust manifolds **(see illustration)**.
12 Undo and extract the timing chain guide rail pins from the cylinder heads **(see illustration)**.
13 Make a final check to ensure that all relevant hoses and wires have been disconnected from the cylinder head(s)
14 Progressively loosen the cylinder head bolts, working in the reverse order to the tightening sequence **(see illustration 10.31)**. Remove all cylinder head bolts.
15 Release the cylinder head from the cylinder block and locating dowels by rocking it. Do not prise between the mating faces of the cylinder head and block, as this may damage the gasket faces.
16 With the aid of an assistant, carefully lift the cylinder head, complete with exhaust manifold, from the block, and manoeuvre it out from the engine compartment.
17 Recover the cylinder head gasket.
18 If necessary, remove the exhaust manifold from the cylinder head.

Inspection

19 Refer to Chapter 2C for details of cylinder head dismantling and reassembly.

20 The mating faces of the cylinder heads and block must be perfectly clean before refitting the heads. Use a scraper to remove all traces of gasket and carbon, and also clean the tops of the pistons. Take particular care with the cylinder heads, as the metal is easily damaged. Also make sure that debris is not allowed to enter the oil and water passages. Using adhesive tape and paper, seal the water, oil and bolt holes in the cylinder block. To prevent carbon entering the gap between the pistons and bores, smear a little grease in the gap. After cleaning each piston, rotate the crankshaft so that the piston moves down the bore, and then wipe out the grease and carbon with a cloth rag.
21 Check the block and head for nicks, deep scratches and other damage. If very slight, they may be removed from the cylinder block carefully with a file. More serious damage may be repaired by machining, but this is a specialist job.
22 If warpage of the cylinder heads is suspected, use a straight-edge to check them for distortion, with reference to Chapter 2C Section 7.
23 Clean out the bolt holes in the block using a pipe cleaner or thin rag and a screwdriver. Make sure that all oil and water is removed, otherwise there is a possibility of the block being cracked by hydraulic pressure when the bolts are tightened.
24 Examine the bolt threads and the threads in the cylinder block for damage. If necessary, use the correct size tap to chase out the threads in the block.
25 The manufacturers recommend that the cylinder head bolts are measured, to determine whether renewal is necessary; however, some owners may wish to renew all the bolts as a matter of course.
26 Measure the length of each bolt from the base of the head to the end of the shank **(see**

10.11 Remove the heatshield above the exhaust manifolds

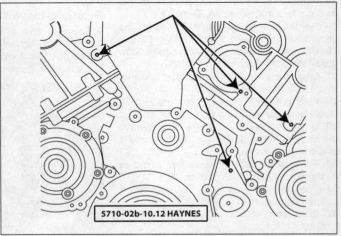

10.12 Extract the timing chain guide rail pins

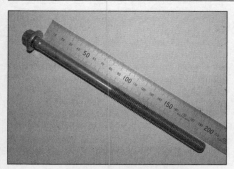

10.26 Measure from the base of the head to the end of the shank

illustration). If the bolt length is greater than the maximum specified, the bolts should be renewed.

27 Reassemble the cylinder heads with reference to Chapter 2C. Where applicable, refit the exhaust manifold together with a new gasket.

Refitting

28 Locate the new cylinder head gasket on the block, making sure that it is the correct way up and positioned over the location dowels.

29 With the aid of an assistant, lower the cylinder head(s) carefully onto the block.

30 Oil the threads and the cylinder head contact faces of the cylinder head bolts, then insert them and screw them into the cylinder block by hand. Ensure that the bolts are fitted to their correct locations as noted on removal.

31 Tighten the cylinder head bolts in the order shown (see illustration), and in the stages given in the Specifications – ie, tighten all bolts to the Stage 1 torque, then tighten all bolts to the Stage 2 torque, and so on. Note: After each stage, tighten the two M8 bolts at the front of the cylinder heads to their specified torque.

32 The remainder of refitting is a reversal of removal, noting the following points:

a) Tighten all fasteners to their specified torque where given.

b) Refill the cooling system, fit a new oil filter and top-up the engine oil as described in Chapter 1.

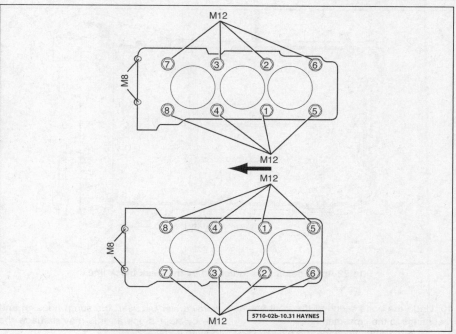

10.31 Cylinder head bolt tightening sequence

c) Reconnect the battery negative lead as described in Chapter 5A Section 4.

d) When all components are refitted, start the engine and check carefully for any oil or coolant leaks.

11 Sump – removal and refitting

Removal

Lower pan

1 Drain the engine oil as described in Chapter 1 Section 4.

2 Undo the bolts and carefully detach the lower pan from the upper sump housing (see illustration). If the sump is stuck, use a hide or wooden hammer to tap its sides in order to release it. Do not drive a screwdriver between the pan and sump housing as this may

damage the mating surfaces. Disconnect the temperature sensor wiring plug as the pan is removed.

3 Note that Mercedes Benz state that the lower pan is always distorted during removal, and should therefore be renewed.

Upper sump housing

4 Drain the engine oil as described in Chapter 1 Section 4.

5 Pull the plastic cover on the top of the engine upwards from its' rubber mountings.

6 Undo the bolts securing the engine oil dipstick guide tube, and pull the tube upwards from place (see illustrations). Discard the O-ring seals – a new one must be fitted.

7 Attach a lifting hoist to the engine.

8 Remove the transmission as described in Chapter 7A Section 7 or Chapter 7B Section 6 as applicable.

9 Remove the crankshaft rear seal housing as described in Section 14.

11.2 Undo the lower sump pan retaining bolts

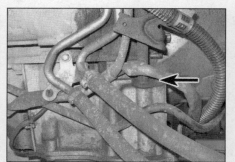

11.6a Oil dipstick guide tube lower bolt location...

11.6b...and upper bolt location

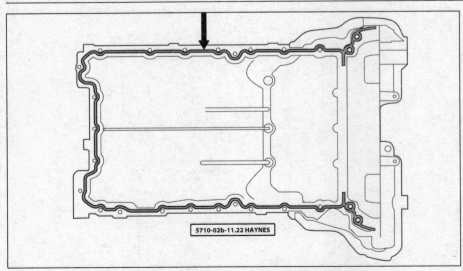

11.22 Apply sealant as indicated by the thick black line

10 Undo the bolts securing the front engine mountings to the crossmember.
11 Undo the bolts securing the pipe bracket to the sump.
12 Undo the bolts and remove the lower sump pan as described earlier in this Section.
13 Disconnect the oil sensor wiring plug.
14 Undo the bolt securing the air conditioning compressor to the upper sump housing.
15 Note their fitted positions, then undo the bolts securing the upper sump housing to the cylinder block.
16 Carefully release the upper sump housing from the cylinder block. If the sump is stuck, use a hide or wooden hammer to tap its sides in order to release it. Do not drive a screwdriver between the sump housing and the cylinder block as this may damage the mating surfaces.

Refitting

Lower pan

17 Clean all traces of sealant from the upper sump housing mating surface, using non-abrasive tools, or sealant removal spray (Eg. Loctite 7063).
18 Apply a 1.5 mm bead of sealant (Loctite 5970 or equivalent) to the new lower pan mating surface, ensuring the seal path is around the inside of the bolt holes. Note that the lower pan must be refitted to the upper sump housing within 7 minutes of the sealant being applied.
19 Position the lower pan, insert the retaining bolts and tighten them gradually, evenly, to the specified torque.
20 The remainder of refitting is a reversal of removal.

Upper sump housing

21 Clean all traces of sealant from the upper sump housing and cylinder block mating surfaces, using non-abrasive tools, or sealant removal spray (Eg. Loctite 7063).
22 Apply a 1.5 mm wide bead of sealant (Loctite 5970 or equivalent) to the upper sump housing mating surface as shown **(see illustration)**. Note that the sump housing must be refitted within 7 minutes of the sealant being applied.
23 Position the upper sump housing, insert the engine oil level dipstick guide tube (with a new O-ring seal) in the sump, then refit the retaining bolts to their original locations, and tighten them to the specified torque **(see illustration)**.
24 The remainder of refitting is a reversal of removal.

12 Oil pump – removal, inspection and refitting

Removal

1 Remove the upper sump housing as described in Section 11.
2 Undo the retaining bolts and remove the baffle plate along with the oil pump pick-up tube **(see illustration)**. Discard the sealing ring – a new one must be fitted.
3 Undo the bolts securing the oil pump to the cylinder block, then depress the drive chain tensioner, and disengage the chain from the sprocket as the pump is withdrawn **(see illustrations)**.

Inspection

4 The oil pump is a sealed unit. If faulty, a complete new unit must be fitted.
5 Clean the oil pump intake strainer thoroughly, however, do not immerse the oil pump in cleaning solvent.

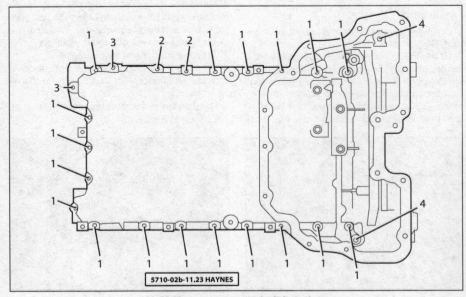

11.23 Upper sump pan bolt locations
1 M6 x 30   2 M6 x 40   3 M6 x 60   4 M8 x 25

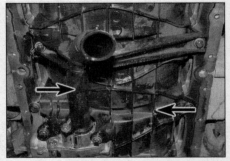

12.2 Remove the pick-up tube and baffle plate

12.3a Oil pump retaining bolts

12.3b Move the chain tensioner away from the chain

6 With the oil pump upright, pour fresh engine oil into the upper aperture while turning the pump shaft slowly. This will prime the oil pump so that normal oil pressure will be resumed as soon as possible after starting the engine.

Refitting

7 Depress the chain tensioner, check that the sprocket is engaged with the drive chain correctly and then locate the oil pump onto the crankcase. Insert the mounting bolts and tighten the bolts to the specified torque.
8 Refit the baffle plate and pick-up tube (with a new sealing ring) and tighten the retaining bolts to their specified torque **(see illustration)**.
9 Refit the upper sump housing as described in Section 11.

13 Flywheel/driveplate – removal, inspection and refitting

Removal

1 Remove the transmission as described in Chapter 7A Section 7 or Chapter 7B Section 6.

2 On manual transmission models, remove the clutch assembly as described in Chapter 6 Section 5.
3 The flywheel/driveplate must be held stationary while the mounting bolts are loosened. To do this, have an assistant insert a wide-bladed screwdriver in the starter ring gear teeth through the access hole in the rear of the sump. Mercedes-Benz technicians use a special tool bolted to the sump incorporating serrations which engage with the ring gear teeth. Alternatively, after-market flywheel locking tools are available **(see illustration)**.
4 Unscrew the mounting bolts, then lift the flywheel/driveplate from the rear of the crankshaft **(see illustration)**. Note that the location dowel ensures the flywheel/driveplate can only be fitted in one position. Discard the bolts – new ones must be fitted.

Inspection

5 If the teeth on the flywheel/driveplate starter ring gear are badly worn, it may be possible to fit a new ring gear, however this work should be entrusted to a Mercedes-Benz dealer who will have the necessary equipment to heat the new gear to the critical temperature in order to fit it. Overheating the gear will affect its hardness, resulting in rapid wear. The old gear

may be removed by drilling it and using a cold chisel to split it. Take care not to drill into the flywheel/driveplate.
6 On manual transmission models, if the clutch friction face of the flywheel is deeply scored, cracked or otherwise damaged, the flywheel must be renewed. However, it may be possible to have it surface-ground, but seek the advice of an engine reconditioning specialist. Check the condition of the spigot bearing in the centre of the flywheel or in the end of the crankshaft, and renew if necessary.
7 Some of these vehicles are fitted with dual mass flywheels. Whilst Mercedes Benz do not publish any checking procedures, some clutch and flywheel manufacturers do publish some information concerning rotational and lateral movement.
8 In order to check the rotational movement, lock the flywheel in place as previously described. Rotate the flywheel secondary element (drive surface) by hand anti-clockwise, mark its position in relation to the primary flywheel element (bolted to the crankshaft), then rotate it by hand clockwise and mark its position. Bear in mind, that the free rotational movement is being measured here – do not use excessive force to rotate the secondary element. Mark the limits of

12.8 Renew the pick-up tube sealing ring

13.3 This after-market locking tool engages with the starter teeth on the flywheel/driveplate

13.4 Note the position of the locating dowel

13.8a Turn the flywheel secondary element anti-clockwise and mark the limit of its travel on the starter ring gear...

13.8b...then turn the secondary element clockwise, and mark its travel limit again

the rotational movement is relation to the number of flywheel starter ring gear teeth **(see illustrations)**.

9 The number of starter ring gear teeth travelled by the flywheel secondary element, should be noted and compared to the flywheel manufacturers specification. The permissible travel varies enormously, and differs from one flywheel part number to the next. If in any doubt, consult a Mercedes Benz dealer or transmission specialist as to whether a replacement unit is needed.

10 In order to check the lateral movement of the flywheel, attach a length of steel strip to the flywheel secondary element (drive surface), and mount a DTI gauge so that it measures in-line with the edge of the secondary flywheel element **(see illustrations)**. Pull the steel strip away from the flywheel, zero the DTI gauge, then push the strip towards the flywheel

and read off the measurement. Again, the permissible amount of lateral movement varies from one flywheel part number to the next. Compare the measurement taken with the manufacturers specification. If in any doubt, consult a Mercedes Benz dealer or transmission specialist as to whether a replacement unit is needed.

Refitting

11 Commence refitting by cleaning the mating faces of the crankshaft and flywheel/driveplate.

12 Make sure that the location dowel is in position in the end of the crankshaft.

13 Locate the flywheel/driveplate onto the crankshaft, then insert the new mounting bolts and hand-tighten them.

14 Lock the flywheel/driveplate using the method employed during removal, then

tighten the securing bolts progressively in a diagonal sequence to the specified torque first, then tighten all the bolts by the specified angle.

15 Refit the clutch, and/or transmission as described in Chapter 6 Section 5 or Chapter 7B Section 6.

14 Crankshaft oil seals – renewal

Crankshaft front oil seal

1 Remove the crankshaft pulley/vibration damper as described in Section 5.

2 Measure and note the fitted depth of the oil seal in the timing chain cover.

3 Prise the oil seal from the cover using

13.10a Attach a length of steel strip to the flywheel secondary element (drive surface)...

13.10b...and mount a DTI gauge in line with the edge of the secondary element

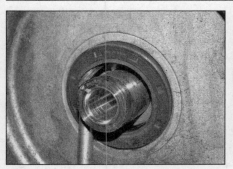

14.3 Carefully prise the oil seal from the timing cover

14.5a Use a socket (or similar)...

14.5b...to drive the seal to its original depth

a hooked instrument **(see illustration)**. Alternatively, drill a small hole in the oil seal, and use a self-tapping screw and a pair of pliers to remove it.

4 Clean the seal location in the timing cover, and also clean the oil seal contact surface on the crankshaft pulley/vibration damper. Examine the seal contact surface of the pulley/vibration damper for an excessive wear groove. If evident, refer to Section 5.

5 Press the new seal into the timing chain cover (open end first) to the previously-noted depth, using a suitable tube or socket. Do not apply any lubricant to the seal or the crankshaft **(see illustrations)**.

6 Refit the crankshaft pulley/vibration damper as described in Section 5.

Crankshaft rear oil seal

Note: *The rear oil seal is integral with the oil seal housing and should be renewed whenever it is removed.*

7 Remove the flywheel/driveplate as described in Section 13.

8 Unscrew the retaining bolts and remove the oil seal/housing from the cylinder block **(see illustration)**.

9 New oil seal/housings are supplied with a plastic sleeve on the inside of the seal to aid refitting of the seal over the end of the crankshaft. DO NOT remove the plastic fitting sleeve until the oil seal housing is in its fitted position. Do not touch the sealing lips of the seal with bare fingers.

10 Ensure that the cylinder block mating face is free from all traces of old sealant, oil and grease, and then apply a 1.5 to 2.5 mm thick bead of silicone sealant (Loctite 5970 or equivalent) to the oil seal housing. Note that the sealant should be run around the inside of the bolt holes in the oil seal housing. It must be fitted within 7 minutes of applying the sealant.

11 Fit the new oil seal housing over the crankshaft and onto the cylinder block, keeping the fitting sleeve in position **(see illustration)**.

12 Carefully pull the fitting sleeve from place. Examine the seal lips and confirm that the outer lips point towards the transmission all around it's circumference.

13 Fit the retaining bolts and tighten them to the specified torque.

14 Refit the flywheel/driveplate as described in Section 13.

15 Engine and transmission mountings – inspection and renewal

Inspection

1 Three engine/transmission mountings are used, one on either side of the engine, and one under the rear of the transmission.

2 For improved access, raise the front of the vehicle and support it securely on axle stands (see *'Vehicle jacking and support'*). Undo the fasteners and remove the engine undershield.

3 Check the condition of the mounting rubber to see if it is cracked, hardened or separated from the metal at any point. Renew the mounting if any such damage or deterioration is evident. The mountings contain hydraulic oil, and must be renewed if oil leakage is evident.

4 Check that all the mounting bolts are securely tightened.

5 Using a large screwdriver or metal bar, check for wear in the mounting by carefully levering against it to check for free play. Where this is not possible, enlist the aid of

14.8 Rear oil seal/housing retaining bolts

14.11 Locate the fitting sleeve over the end of the crankshaft

15.14 Detach the mounting from the support arm

16.8 Unscrew the temperature sensor from the sump pan

an assistant to move the engine/transmission back-and-forth, or from side-to-side, while you observe the mounting. If excessive free play is found, check first that the fasteners are correctly secured, and then renew any worn components as required.

Renewal

Front engine mountings

6 Support the engine, either using a hoist and lifting tackle connected to the engine lifting brackets, or by positioning a jack and interposed block of wood under the sump. Ensure that the engine is adequately supported before proceeding.
7 Remove the air filter housing as described in Chapter 4A Section 2.
8 Undo the bolt securing the bracket to the mounting.
9 Remove the catalytic converter as described in Chapter 4A Section 19.

10 Undo the bolt securing the mounting to the crossmember.
11 Raise the engine, ensuring the various hydraulic/coolant/fuel pipes are not placed under tension.
12 Undo the bolt securing the mounting to the support bracket.
13 Unclip the oxygen sensor from the left-hand mounting heatshield.
14 Remove the heatshields (where applicable) and detach the mountings from the support arms **(see illustration)**. Note how the locating lugs on the mountings engage with the slots in the support brackets.
15 Refitting is a reversal of removal. Tighten the retaining bolts to their specified torque.

Rear engine/transmission mounting

16 Raise the front of the vehicle and support it securely on axle stands (see 'Vehicle jacking and support').

17 Support the transmission using a jack and interposed block of wood.
18 Undo the bolts securing the mounting to the rear crossmember.
19 Undo the bolts securing the mounting to the transmission.
20 Manoeuvre the mounting from place.
21 Refitting is a reversal of removal. Tighten the fasteners to their specified torque.

16 Oil sensors – renewal

1 Raise the front of the vehicle and support it securely on axle stands (see 'Vehicle jacking and support'). Undo the fasteners and remove the engine undershield.
2 Drain the engine oil as described in Chapter 1 Section 4.

Oil level sensor

3 Remove the lower section of the sump as described in Section 11.
4 Disconnect the wiring plug, and release the wiring harness clamp.
5 Undo the retaining bolts and remove the sensor. Renew the gasket.
6 Refitting is a reversal of removal.

Oil temperature sensor

7 The sensor is located on the sump pan. Disconnect the sensor wiring plug.
8 Unscrew the sensor from the sump pan **(see illustration)**. Renew the sealing ring.
9 Refitting is a reversal of removal. Tighten the sensor to the specified torque.

Chapter 2 Part C
General engine removal and overhaul procedures

Contents

Degrees of difficulty

Easy, suitable for novice with little experience	**Fairly easy,** suitable for beginner with some experience	**Fairly difficult,** suitable for competent DIY mechanic	**Difficult,** suitable for experienced DIY mechanic	**Very difficult,** suitable for expert DIY or professional

Specifications

Note: *At the time of writing, some specifications for certain engines were not available. Where the relevant specifications are not given here, refer to your Mercedes dealer for further information.*

Cylinder head

Maximum gasket face distortion	0.08 mm
Cylinder head height:	
In-line engines	126.85 to 127.15 mm
V6 engines	128.35 to 128.65 mm
Wear limit after machining:	
In-line engines	126.65 mm
V6 engines	N/A

Valves

	Intake	Exhaust
Valve stem diameter:		
In-line engines	6.960 to 6.975 mm	6.955 to 6.970 mm
V6 engines	5.960 to 5.975 mm	5.945 to 5.975 mm

Crankshaft

Endfloat:	
All engines	0.10 to 0.30 mm

Pistons

	In-line engines	V6 engines
Ring end gap:		
1st compression ring	0.22 to 0.37 mm	N/A
2nd compression ring	0.80 to 1.00 mm	N/A
Oil control ring	0.20 to 0.40 mm	N/A

1 General information

1 Included in this Part of Chapter 2 are details of removing the engine from the car and general overhaul procedures for the cylinder head, cylinder block/crankcase and all other engine internal components.
2 The information given ranges from advice concerning preparation for an overhaul and the purchase of parts, to detailed step-by-step procedures covering removal, inspection, renovation and refitting of engine internal components.
3 After Section 9, all instructions are based on the assumption that the engine has been removed from the car. For information concerning in-car engine repair, as well as the removal and refitting of those external components necessary for full overhaul, refer to Part A or B of this Chapter, as applicable, and to Section 6. Ignore any preliminary dismantling operations described in Parts A or B that are no longer relevant once the engine has been removed from the car.

2 Engine overhaul – general information

1 It is not always easy to determine when, or if, an engine should be completely overhauled, as a number of factors must be considered.
2 High mileage is not necessarily an indication that an overhaul is needed, while low mileage does not preclude the need for an overhaul. Frequency of servicing is probably the most important consideration. An engine which has had regular and frequent oil and filter changes, as well as other required maintenance, should give many thousands of miles of reliable service. Conversely, a neglected engine may require an overhaul very early in its life.
3 Excessive oil consumption is an indication that piston rings, valve seals and/or valve guides are in need of attention. Make sure that oil leaks are not responsible before deciding that the rings and/or guides are worn. Perform a compression test, as described in Part A or B of this Chapter (as applicable), to determine the likely cause of the problem.
4 Check the oil pressure with a gauge fitted in place of the oil pressure switch, and compare it with that specified in Part A or B. If it is extremely low, the main and big-end bearings, and/or the oil pump, are probably worn out.
5 Loss of power, rough running, knocking or metallic engine noises, excessive valve gear noise, and high fuel consumption may also point to the need for an overhaul, especially if they are all present at the same time. If a complete service does not remedy the

situation, major mechanical work is the only solution.
6 A full engine overhaul involves restoring all internal parts to the specification of a new engine. During a complete overhaul, the pistons and the piston rings are renewed, and the cylinder bores are reconditioned. New main and big-end bearings are generally fitted; if necessary, the crankshaft may be reground, to compensate for wear in the journals. The valves are also serviced as well, since they are usually in less-than-perfect condition at this point. Always pay careful attention to the condition of the oil pump when overhauling the engine, and renew it if there is any doubt as to its serviceability. The end result should be an as-new engine that will give many trouble-free miles.
Note: *Critical cooling system components such as the hoses, thermostat and coolant pump should be renewed when an engine is overhauled. The radiator should be checked carefully, to ensure that it is not clogged or leaking. Also, it is a good idea to renew the oil pump whenever the engine is overhauled.*
7 Before beginning the engine overhaul, read through the entire procedure, to familiarise yourself with the scope and requirements of the job. Overhauling an engine is not difficult if you follow carefully all of the instructions, have the necessary tools and equipment, and pay close attention to all specifications. It can, however, be time-consuming. Plan on the car being off the road for a minimum of two weeks, especially if parts must be taken to an engineering works for repair or reconditioning. Check on the availability of parts and make sure that any necessary special tools and equipment are obtained in advance. Most work can be done with typical hand tools, although a number of precision measuring tools are required for inspecting parts to determine if they must be renewed. Often the engineering works will handle the inspection of parts and offer advice concerning reconditioning and renewal.
Note: *Always wait until the engine has been completely dismantled, and until all components (especially the cylinder block/ crankcase and the crankshaft) have been inspected, before deciding what service and repair operations must be performed by an engineering works. The condition of these components will be the major factor to consider when determining whether to overhaul the original engine, or to buy a reconditioned unit. Do not, therefore, purchase parts or have overhaul work done on other components until they have been thoroughly inspected. As a general rule, time is the primary cost of an overhaul, so it does not pay to fit worn or sub-standard parts.*
8 As a final note, to ensure maximum life and minimum trouble from a reconditioned engine, everything must be assembled with care, in a spotlessly-clean environment.

3 Engine removal – methods and precautions

1 If you have decided that the engine must be removed for overhaul or major repair work, several preliminary steps should be taken.
2 Locating a suitable place to work is extremely important. Adequate workspace, along with storage space for the car, will be needed. If a workshop or garage is not available, at the very least, a flat, level, clean work surface is required.
3 Cleaning the engine compartment and engine/transmission before beginning the removal procedure will help keep tools clean and organised.
4 An engine hoist will also be necessary. Make sure the equipment is rated in excess of the weight of the engine (and transmission if both are being removed). Safety is of primary importance, considering the potential hazards involved in lifting the engine out of the car.
5 If this is the first time you have removed an engine, an assistant should ideally be available. Advice and aid from someone more experienced would also be helpful. There are many instances when one person cannot simultaneously perform all of the operations required when lifting the engine out of the vehicle.
6 Plan the operation ahead of time. Before starting work, arrange for the hire of or obtain all of the tools and equipment you will need. Some of the equipment necessary to perform engine removal and installation safely and with relative ease (in addition to an engine hoist) is as follows: a heavy duty trolley jack, complete sets of spanners and sockets (see *Tools and working facilities* in the Reference section), wooden blocks, and plenty of rags and cleaning solvent for mopping-up spilled oil, coolant and fuel. If the hoist must be hired, make sure that you arrange for it in advance, and perform all of the operations possible without it beforehand. This will save you money and time.
7 Plan for the car to be out of use for quite a while. An engineering works will be required to perform some of the work, which the do-it-yourselfer cannot accomplish without special equipment. These places often have a busy schedule, so it would be a good idea to consult them before removing the engine, in order to accurately estimate the amount of time required to rebuild or repair components that may need work.
8 Always be extremely careful when removing and refitting the engine. Serious injury can result from careless actions. Plan ahead and take your time, and a job of this nature, although major, can be accomplished successfully.

3.9 The engine and transmission is lifted out from above

4.5 Remove the power steering fluid reservoir

4.10 Coolant expansion tank retaining bolt

9 On all models, the engine is removed by lifting the assembly out from above the vehicle **(see illustration)**.

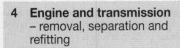

4 Engine and transmission – removal, separation and refitting

Removal

1 Disconnect the battery negative lead as described in Chapter 5A Section 4.
2 Remove the plastic trim panel(s) from the top of the engine.
3 Remove the air filter assembly and intake ducts as described in Chapter 4A Section 2.
4 Undo the bolts and remove the heatshield above the turbocharger.
5 Syphon out the fluid, then disconnect the hoses, undo the bolts and remove the power steering pump fluid reservoir **(see illustration)**. Release the wiring harness retaining clip where applicable.
6 Disconnect the fluid hoses from the power steering pump.
7 Raise the front of the vehicle and support it securely on axle stands (see 'Vehicle jacking and support'). Undo the fasteners and remove the engine undershields.
8 Drain the engine oil and coolant as described in Chapter 1 Sections 4 and 30.
9 Release the clamps and disconnect the coolant hoses from the radiator, thermostat

housing and electric circulation pump (where applicable).
10 Disconnect the hoses, undo the retaining bolt(s) and remove the coolant expansion tank **(see illustration)**. Disconnect the sensor wiring plug as the tank is withdrawn.
11 Release the clamps and disconnect the air ducts to and from the intercooler **(see illustration)**.
12 Remove the auxiliary drivebelt as described in Chapter 1 Section 6.
13 Disconnect the following wiring plugs, noting their locations and harness routing **(see illustrations)**:
a) ECM wiring plug as described in Chapter 4A Section 13.
b) SAM unit.

c) Earth connection – right-hand engine compartment fusebox.
d) Remove the rubber seal and pull the harness from the bulkhead.
e) Earth connection on the transmission.
f) Reversing light switch.
g) Transmission control module (TCM) – automatic transmission only.
14 Undo the bolt securing the air conditioning pipe to the oil filter housing.
15 Disconnect the heater hose at the engine compartment bulkhead.
16 Where applicable, disconnect the fluid pipes from the automatic transmission cooler **(see illustration)**. Be prepared for fluid spillage.
17 Mark the fuel supply and return pipes to aid refitting, then disconnect them **(see**

4.11 Prise out the clip and disconnect the air ducts from the intercooler

4.13a Disconnect the engine wiring harness plugs from the SAM unit, ECM, TCM...

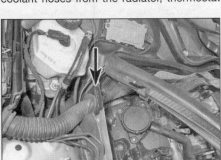

4.13b...and pull the harness from the bulkhead

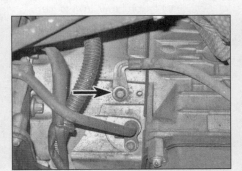

4.13c Disconnect the earth lead from the transmission

4.16 Prise out the clip and disconnect the transmission cooler pipe each side of the radiator

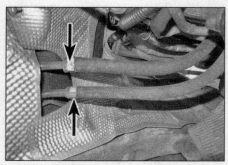

4.17 Disconnect the fuel feed and return pipes underneath the engine compartment

4.18 Prise open the cap and disconnect the auxiliary heating element connection

illustration). Plug the openings to prevent contamination.

18 On models with an auxiliary heating element, remove the shield, prise open the cap, and disconnect the wiring lead from the underisde of the transmission tunnel (see illustration).

19 Remove the air conditioning compressor as described in Chapter 3 Section 10.

20 Undo the bolt securing the power steering pipe to the engine sump (where applicable).

21 Remove the catalytic converter or particulate filter (as applicable) as described in Chapter 4A.

22 Remove the exhaust pipe bracket from the transmission (see illustration).

23 Disconnect the gear change/selector rod/cable from the transmission as described in Chapter 7A Section 3 or Chapter 7B Section 3.

24 On manual transmission models, disconnect the fluid pipe from the clutch slave cylinder as described in Chapter 6 Section 3.

25 Position a trolley jack under the rear of the transmission with a block of wood interposed at the jack head.

26 Undo the bolts and remove the crossmember from the rear of the transmission (see illustration).

27 With reference to Chapter 8 Section 7, disconnect the propeller shaft from the transmission. Support the free end of the shaft to prevent damage to the joints.

28 Attach a hoist to the engine lifting eyes, and take the weight of the engine.

29 Unscrew the lower bolts from the engine front mountings.

30 With the help of an assistant, lift and tilt the engine and transmission to withdraw it from the engine compartment, taking care not to damage the surrounding components and wiring. It will be necessary to move the hoist forwards and guide the engine and transmission up through the engine compartment, taking care not to damage the surrounding components. Move the hoist forwards and lower the engine/transmission assembly to the ground.

31 To remove the transmission from the engine, refer to Chapter 7A Section 7 or Chapter 7B Section 6 as necessary.

Refitting

32 Before refitting the engine and transmission, check the condition of the engine/transmission mountings. In particular, check if they are compressed, are damaged or split, or have signs of oil leakage. If necessary, renew them with reference to Chapter 2A Section 16 or Chapter 2B Section 15.

33 The reconnection and refitting procedures are a reversal of removal, noting the following additional information.

a) Tighten all nuts and bolts to the specified torque wrench settings, where given.

b) On automatic transmission models, adjust the selector rod as described in Chapter 7B Section 3.

c) On manual transmission models, bleed the clutch hydraulic system as described in Chapter 6 Section 4.

d) Reconnect the propeller shaft to the

flange on the rear of the transmission with reference to Chapter 8 Section 7.

e) Refill the power steering fluid reservoir with fresh fluid and bleed the system as described in Chapter 10 Section 27.

f) Ensure that all wiring, hoses and brackets are positioned and routed as noted before removal.

g) On completion, refill the engine with oil, and refill the cooling system as described in Chapter 1.

5 Engine overhaul – dismantling sequence

1 It is much easier to dismantle and work on the engine if it is mounted on a portable engine stand. These stands can often be hired from a tool hire shop. Before the engine is mounted on a stand, the flywheel/driveplate should be removed, so that the stand bolts can be tightened into the end of the cylinder block/crankcase.

2 If a stand is not available, it is possible to dismantle the engine with it blocked up on a sturdy workbench, or on the floor. Be extra careful not to tip or drop the engine when working without a stand.

3 If you are going to obtain a reconditioned engine, all the external components around the engine must be removed first, so that they can be transferred to the new engine (just as they will if you are doing a complete engine overhaul yourself). These components include the following.

a) Ancillary unit mounting brackets (oil filter, alternator, power steering pump, engine mountings, crankcase breather housing, etc).

b) Thermostat and housing (Chapter 3 Section 4).

c) Dipstick tube.

d) All electrical switches and sensors.

e) Inlet and exhaust manifolds (Chapter 4A Section 15).

f) Injectors and fuel pipes (Chapter 4A Section 11).

Note: When removing the external components from the engine, pay close attention to details that may be helpful or important during refitting. Note the fitted position of gaskets, seals, spacers, pins, washers, bolts, and other small items.

4 If you are obtaining a 'short' engine (which consists of the engine cylinder block/crankcase, crankshaft, pistons and connecting rods all assembled), then the cylinder head(s), sump, oil pump, and timing chain will have to be removed also.

5 If you are planning a complete overhaul, the engine can be dismantled, and the internal components removed, in the order given below, referring to Part A or B of this Chapter unless otherwise stated.

a) Inlet and exhaust manifolds (Chapter 4A Section 15).

b) Timing chain, sprockets and tensioner.

c) Cylinder head(s).

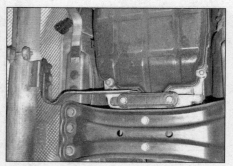

4.22 Remove the exhaust pipe bracket

4.26 Remove the crossmember from under the transmission

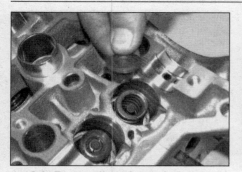
6.4a Remove the valve spring cap...

6.4b ...and spring

6.5 Lift off the spring seat

d) *Flywheel/driveplate.*
e) *Sump.*
f) *Oil pump.*
g) *Piston/connecting rod assemblies.*
h) *Balance shaft assembly – V6 engines only.*
i) *Crankshaft.*

6 Before beginning the dismantling and overhaul procedures, make sure that you have all of the correct tools necessary. Refer to Tools and working facilities for further information.

6 Cylinder head – dismantling

Note: *New and reconditioned cylinder heads are available from the manufacturer, and from engine overhaul specialists. Be aware that some specialist tools are required for the dismantling and inspection procedures, and new components may not be readily available. It may therefore be more practical and economical for the home mechanic to purchase a reconditioned head, rather than dismantle, inspect and recondition the original head. A valve spring compressor tool will be required for this operation.*

1 Remove the cylinder head(s) as described in Chapter 2A Section 10 or Chapter 2B Section 10.
2 Remove the exhaust manifold as described in Chapter 4A Section 15.
3 Remove the glow plugs as described in Chapter 5B Section 3.

4 Using a valve spring compressor, compress the spring on each valve in turn until the split collets can be removed. Release the compressor, and lift off the spring cap and spring **(see illustrations)**. If, when the valve spring compressor is screwed down, the spring cap refuses to free and expose the split collets, gently tap the top of the tool, directly over the spring cap, with a light hammer. This will free the retainer.
5 Using a pair of pliers or special removal tool, carefully extract the valve stem oil seal from the top of the guide, then lift off the spring seat **(see illustration)**.
6 Withdraw the valve through the combustion chamber **(see illustration)**.
7 It is essential that each valve is stored with its collets, cap, spring, and spring seat. The valves should also be kept in their correct sequence, unless they are so badly worn that they are to be renewed. If they are going to be kept and used again, place each valve assembly in a labelled polythene bag or similar small container **(see illustration)**. Label each bag No 1 inlet, No 1 exhaust, No 2 inlet, No 2 exhaust, etc, noting that No 1 valve is nearest to the timing chain end of the engine.

7 Cylinder head and valves – cleaning and inspection

1 Thorough cleaning of the cylinder head and valve components, followed by a detailed inspection, will enable you to decide how much valve service work must be carried out during the engine overhaul. **Note:** If the engine has been severely overheated, it is best to assume that the cylinder head is warped – check carefully for signs of this.

Cleaning

2 Scrape away all traces of old gasket material from the cylinder head.
3 Scrape away the carbon from the combustion chambers and ports, then wash the cylinder head thoroughly with paraffin or a suitable solvent.
4 Scrape off any heavy carbon deposits that may have formed on the valves, then use a power-operated wire brush to remove deposits from the valve heads and stems.

Inspection

Note: *Be sure to perform all the following inspection procedures before concluding that the services of a machine shop or engine overhaul specialist are required. Make a list of all items that require attention.*

Cylinder head

5 Inspect the head very carefully for cracks, evidence of coolant leakage, and other damage. If cracks are found, a new cylinder head should be obtained.
6 Use a straight-edge and feeler blade to check that the cylinder head gasket surface is not distorted **(see illustration)**. If it is, it may be possible to have it machined, provided that the cylinder head is not reduced to less than the specified height.

6.6 Remove the valves from the combustion chamber

6.7 Store the valve components in a labelled bag

7.6 Use a straight-edge and feeler blade to check the cylinder head gasket face for distortion

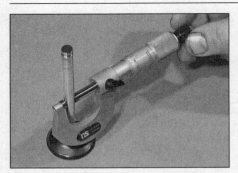

7.12 Measure the valve stem diameter with a micrometer

7 Examine the valve seats in each of the combustion chambers. If they are severely pitted, cracked, or burned, they will need to be renewed or recut by an engine overhaul specialist. If they are only slightly pitted, this can be removed by grinding-in the valve heads and seats with fine valve-grinding compound, as described later in this Section.

8 Check the valve guides for wear by inserting the relevant valve, and checking for side-to-side motion of the valve. A very small amount of movement is acceptable. If the movement seems excessive, remove the valve. Measure the valve stem diameter (see later in this Section), and renew the valve if it is worn. If the valve stem is not worn, the wear must be in the valve guide, and the guide must be renewed. The renewal of new valve guides should be entrusted to a Mercedes-Benz dealer or engine overhaul specialist, who will have the necessary tools available.

9 If renewing the valve guides, the valve seats should be recut or reground only after the guides have been fitted.

10 Examine the camshaft bearing surfaces in the cylinder head and the bearing caps for signs of wear or damage. If the bearings are excessively worn, consult a Mercedes-Benz dealer, or an engine overhaul specialist for further advice.

Valves

 Warning: The exhaust valves on most petrol and diesel engines are filled with sodium to improve their heat transfer. Sodium is a highly

reactive substance, and will ignite or explode spontaneously on contact with water (including water vapour in the air). These valves must NOT be disposed of as ordinary scrap. Seek advice from a Mercedes-Benz dealer when disposing of the valves.

11 Examine the head of each valve for pitting, burning, cracks, and general wear. Check the valve stem for scoring and wear ridges. Rotate the valve, and check for any obvious indication that it is bent. Look for pits or excessive wear on the tip of each valve stem. Renew any valve that shows any such signs of wear or damage.

12 If the valve appears satisfactory at this stage, measure the valve stem diameter at several points using a micrometer **(see illustration)**. Any significant difference in the readings obtained indicates wear of the valve stem. Should any of these conditions be apparent, the valve(s) must be renewed.

13 If the valves are in satisfactory condition, they should be ground (lapped) into their respective seats, to ensure a smooth, gas-tight seal. If the seat is only lightly pitted, or if it has been recut, fine grinding compound should be used to produce the required finish. Coarse valve-grinding compound should not be used, unless a seat is badly burned or deeply pitted. If this is the case, the cylinder head and valves should be inspected, to decide whether seat recutting, or even the renewal of the valve or seat insert (where possible) is required.

14 Valve grinding is carried out as follows. Place the cylinder head upside-down on a bench.

15 Smear a trace of (the appropriate grade of) valve-grinding compound on the seat face, and press a suction grinding tool onto the valve head. With a semi-rotary action, grind the valve head to its seat, lifting the valve occasionally to redistribute the grinding compound. A light spring placed under the valve head will greatly ease this operation.

16 If coarse grinding compound is being used, work only until a dull, matt even surface is produced on both the valve seat and the valve, then wipe off the used compound, and repeat the process with fine compound. When a smooth unbroken ring of light grey matt finish is produced on both the valve and seat,

the grinding operation is complete. Do not grind-in the valves any further than absolutely necessary, or the seat will be prematurely sunk into the cylinder head.

17 When all the valves have been ground-in, carefully wash off all traces of grinding compound using paraffin or a suitable solvent, before reassembling the cylinder head.

Valve components

18 Examine the valve springs for signs of damage and discoloration. Compare the length of the valve springs with that of a new component, where possible, and if necessary renew the springs.

19 Stand each spring on a flat surface, and check it for squareness. If any of the springs are damaged, distorted or have lost their tension, obtain a complete new set of springs. It is normal to renew the valve springs as a matter of course if a major overhaul is being carried out.

20 Renew the valve stem oil seals regardless of their apparent condition.

Hydraulic tappets

21 Refer to Chapter 2A Section 9 or Chapter 2B Section 9 for further details.

8 Cylinder head – reassembly

1 Lubricate the stems of the valves, and insert the valves into their original locations **(see illustration)**. If new valves are being fitted, insert them into the locations to which they have been ground.

2 Refit the spring seat.

3 Working on the first valve, dip the new valve stem seal in fresh engine oil. New seals are normally supplied with protective sleeves, which should be fitted to the tops of the valve stems to prevent the collet grooves from damaging the oil seals. If no sleeves are supplied, wind a little thin tape round the top of the valve stems to protect the seals. Carefully locate the seal over the valve and onto the guide. Take care not to damage the seal as it is passed over the valve stem. Use a suitable socket or tube to press the seal firmly onto the guide **(see illustrations)**. Remove the sleeve from the valve stem.

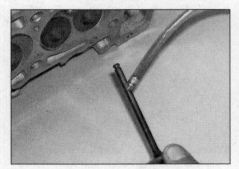

8.1 Lubricate the stems of the valves before inserting them

8.3a Locate the protective sleeve on the valve stem...

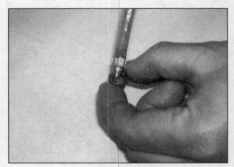

8.3b...then oil the new valve stem seal...

8.3c ...and press it onto the valve guide

8.5 Fit the split collets

4 Locate the valve spring on top of the seat, then refit the spring cap. On engines where the spring is tapered, make sure that the large diameter end of the spring locates on the seat.

5 Fit the compressor tool, then compress the valve spring and locate the split collets in the recess in the valve stem **(see illustration)**. Release the compressor, then repeat the procedure on the remaining valves.

6 With all the valves installed, support the cylinder head on blocks of wood and, using a hammer and interposed block of wood, tap the end of each valve stem to settle the components.

7 Refit the glow plugs as described in Chapter 5B Section 3.

8 Refit the exhaust manifold as described in Chapter 4A Section 15.

9 Refit the cylinder head(s) as described in Part A or Part B of this Chapter.

9 Piston/connecting rod assembly – removal

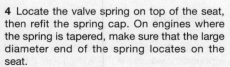

Note: *On V6 engines, Mercedes Benz insist that the connecting rods must not be re-used due to the 'fracture-alignment' production technique used. Consult a Mercedes Benz dealer or specialist. Only remove the pistons/ connecting rods if absolutely necessary.*

1 Remove the cylinder head(s), sump and oil pump as described in Chapter 2A or Chapter 2B as applicable. Where fitted, remove the baffle plate from the base of the crankcase.

2 If there is a pronounced wear ridge at the top of any bore, it may be necessary to remove it with a scraper or ridge reamer, to avoid piston damage during removal. Such a ridge indicates excessive wear of the cylinder bore.

3 Check the connecting rods and big-end caps for identification marks. Both rods and caps should be marked with the cylinder number on the inlet manifold side of each assembly. Note that No 1 cylinder is at the timing chain end of the engine. If no marks are present, using a hammer and centre-punch, paint or similar, mark each connecting rod and big-end bearing cap with its respective

cylinder number on the flat-machined surface provided – note on which side of the connecting rods the marks are made.

4 Similarly, check the piston crowns for a direction marking. An arrow on each piston crown should point towards the timing chain end of the engine. On some engines, this mark may be obscured by carbon build-up, in which case the piston crown should be cleaned to check for a mark. In some cases, the direction arrow may have worn off, in which case a suitable mark should be made on the piston crown using a scriber – do not deeply score the piston crown, but ensure that the mark is easily visible.

5 Turn the crankshaft to bring piston No 1 to BDC (bottom dead centre).

6 Unscrew the bolts from No 1 piston big-end bearing cap. Take off the cap, and recover the bottom half bearing shell. If the bearing shells are to be re-used, tape the cap and the shell together.

7 Using a hammer handle, push the piston up through the bore, and remove it from the top of the cylinder block. Take care not to damage the piston cooling oil spay jets in the cylinder block as the piston/connecting rod assembly is removed. Recover the bearing shell, and tape it to the connecting rod for safekeeping.

8 Loosely refit the big-end cap to the connecting rod, and secure with the bolts – this will help to keep the components in their correct order.

9 On 4-cylinder engines, remove No 4 piston assembly in the same way before turning the crankshaft.

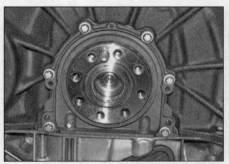

10.2 Crankshaft rear oil seal housing

10 Turn the crankshaft as necessary to bring the remaining pistons to BDC, and remove them in the same manner.

10 Crankshaft – removal

1 Remove the sump, the timing chain cover, timing chain, crankshaft sprocket, and the flywheel/driveplate, as described in Part A or B of this Chapter.

2 Unbolt the crankshaft rear oil seal housing from the cylinder block **(see illustration)**.

3 Remove the pistons and connecting rods, as described in Section 9. If no work is to be done on the pistons and connecting rods, there is no need to remove the cylinder head, or to push the pistons out of the cylinder bores. The pistons should just be pushed far enough up the bores so that they are positioned clear of the crankshaft journals.

4 Check the crankshaft endfloat as described in Section, then proceed as follows.

5 The crankshaft main bearing caps should be numbered from 1, starting from the timing chain end of the engine. If the bearing caps are not marked, mark them accordingly using a centre-punch. Note the orientation of the markings to ensure correct refitting.

6 Unscrew and remove the main bearing cap retaining bolts, and lift off each bearing cap **(see illustration)**. Recover the lower bearing shells, and tape them to their respective caps for safe-keeping.

7 Recover the lower endfloat control thrustwasher halves from either side of the appropriate bearing cap, noting their positions, as follows.

● 4-cylinder engine – centre (No.3) main bearing.

● 5-cylinder engine – No.4 main bearing.

● 6-cylinder in-line engine – centre (No.3) main bearing.

● V6 engine – No.3 main bearing.

8 Lift the crankshaft from the crankcase.

9 Recover the upper bearing shells from the cylinder block, and tape them to their respective caps for safe-keeping. Similarly, recover the upper thrustwasher halves, noting their orientation.

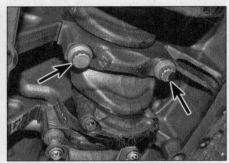

10.6 Main bearing cap bolts

11.2 Remove the balance shaft rear cover

12.7 Piston oil spray jet

12.8 Clean damaged threads using a tap

11 Balance shaft – removal

Note: *A balance shaft assembly is only fitted to V6 engines.*

1 With the engine removed, remove the right-hand intake camshaft sprocket and timing chain cover as described in Chapter 2B.

2 Undo the retaining bolts and remove the balance shaft cover at the rear of the crankcase **(see illustration)**.

3 Insert an 8.5 mm drill bit into the hole in the rear flange of the balance shaft to prevent rotation, then undo the retaining bolt in the centre of the shaft and remove the counterweight.

4 Undo the retaining bolt at the front, and pull the shaft from place.

12 Cylinder block/crankcase – cleaning and inspection

Cleaning

1 Remove all external components, brackets and electrical switches/sensors from the block. Note the position of any mounting brackets before removal. For complete cleaning, the core plugs should ideally be removed. Drill a small hole in the plugs, and then insert a self-tapping screw into the hole. Pull out the plugs by pulling on the screw with a pair of grips, or by using a slide hammer.

2 Scrape all traces of gasket from the cylinder block/crankcase, taking care not to damage the gasket/sealing surfaces.

3 Where applicable, remove the oil gallery plugs, and use new plugs when the engine is reassembled.

4 If the castings are extremely dirty, they should be steam-cleaned.

5 After the castings have been steam-cleaned, clean all oil holes and oil galleries one more time. Flush all internal passages with warm water until the water runs clear. Dry thoroughly, and apply a light film of oil to

all mating surfaces, to prevent rusting. Also oil the cylinder bores. If you have access to compressed air, use it to speed up the drying process, and to blow out all the oil holes and galleries.

⚠️ *Warning: Wear eye protection when using compressed air.*

6 If the castings are not very dirty, you can do an adequate cleaning job with hot (as hot as you can stand!), soapy water and a stiff brush. Take plenty of time, and do a thorough job. Regardless of the cleaning method used, be sure to clean all oil holes and galleries very thoroughly, and to dry all components well. Protect the cylinder bores as described above, to prevent rusting.

7 Where applicable, the piston oil spray jets can be removed from the cylinder block for cleaning, however a special tool is required and it is recommended that an engine overhaul specialist carry out the work **(see illustration)**. The tool for removing the jets consists of an adapter, which engages the base of the jet, and a slide hammer screwed into the adapter. Renew any jets which show signs of damage. Check the oil spray hole and oil passages for blockage.

8 All threaded holes must be clean, to ensure accurate torque readings during reassembly. To clean the threads, run the correct-size tap into each of the holes to remove rust, corrosion, thread sealant or sludge, and to restore damaged threads **(see illustration)**. If possible, use compressed air to clear the holes of debris produced by this operation.

9 Ensure that all threaded holes in the cylinder block are dry.

10 After coating the mating surfaces of the new core plugs with suitable sealant, fit them to the cylinder block. Make sure that they are driven in straight and seated correctly, or leakage could result.

11 Where applicable, fit the new oil gallery plugs.

12 If the engine is not going to be reassembled right away, cover it with a large plastic bag to keep it clean; protect all mating surfaces and the cylinder bores as described above, to prevent rusting.

Inspection

13 Visually check the cylinder block/crankcase for cracks and corrosion. Look for stripped threads in the threaded holes. If there has been any history of internal water leakage, it may be worthwhile having an engine overhaul specialist check the cylinder block/crankcase with special equipment. If defects are found, have them repaired if possible, or renew the assembly.

14 Check each cylinder bore for scuffing and scoring. Check for signs of a wear ridge at the top of the cylinder, indicating that the bore is excessively worn.

15 If the cylinder walls are badly scored or scuffed, then the cylinders will have to be rebored by a suitably qualified specialist, and new oversize pistons will have to be fitted. A Mercedes-Benz dealer or engineering workshop will normally be able to supply suitable oversize pistons when carrying out the reboring work.

16 Inspect the upper surface of the cylinder block for damage. Use a straight-edge and feeler blade to check that the cylinder head gasket surface is not distorted. Note also that on in-line diesel engines, the piston protrusion must be checked whenever the cylinder head surface is machined.

17 After checking the cylinder block/crankcase, refit the items removed.

Piston protrusion – in-line engines

18 When inspecting the cylinder block, the piston protrusion should be checked – this is particularly important if the cylinder head face has been machined. If the piston protrusion is too great, the pistons may hit the swirl chambers when the engine is running, causing expensive damage.

19 Measure the protrusion of the piston from the sealing face of the cylinder head (a dial gauge should be used if possible). If the protrusion is greater than the specified maximum, consult a Mercedes-Benz dealer or an engine-reconditioning specialist for advice – it is likely that the cylinder block will have to be renewed.

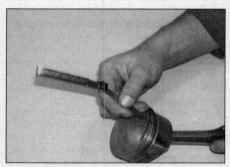

13.2 Use an old feeler gauge blade to help remove the piston rings

13.13a Prise out the circlips...

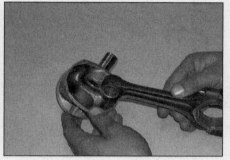

13.13b...then press out the gudgeon pin and separate the connecting rod

13 Piston/connecting rod assembly – cleaning and inspection

Cleaning

1 Before the inspection process can begin, the piston/connecting rod assemblies must be cleaned, and the original piston rings removed from the pistons.

2 Carefully expand the old rings over the top of the pistons. The use of two or three old feeler blades will be helpful in preventing the rings dropping into empty grooves **(see illustration)**. Be careful not to scratch the piston with the ends of the ring. The rings are brittle, and will snap if they are spread too far. They are also very sharp – protect your hands and fingers. Note that the third ring incorporates an expander. Always remove the rings from the top of the piston. Keep each set of rings with its piston if the old rings are to be re-used. Note which way up each ring is fitted to ensure correct refitting.

3 Scrape away all traces of carbon from the top of the piston. A hand-held wire brush (or a piece of fine emery cloth) can be used, once the majority of the deposits have been scraped away.

4 Remove the carbon from the ring grooves in the piston, using an old ring. Break the ring in half to do this (be careful not to cut your fingers – piston rings are sharp). Be careful to remove only the carbon deposits – do not remove any metal, and do not nick or scratch the sides of the ring grooves.

5 Once the deposits have been removed, clean the piston/connecting rod assembly with paraffin or a suitable solvent, and dry thoroughly. Make sure that the oil return holes in the ring grooves are clear.

Inspection

6 If the pistons and cylinder bores are not damaged or worn excessively, and if the cylinder block does not need to be rebored, the original pistons can be refitted. Measure the piston diameters, and check that they are within limits for the corresponding bore diameters. If the piston-to-bore clearance is excessive, the block will have to be rebored, and new pistons and rings fitted. Normal piston wear shows up as even vertical wear on the piston thrust surfaces, and slight looseness of the top ring in its groove. New piston rings should always be used when the engine is reassembled. Note that the piston and bore size grades are stamped on the piston crowns, and on the adjacent cylinder head mating face of the cylinder block.

7 Carefully inspect each piston for cracks around the skirt, around the gudgeon pin holes, and at the piston ring 'lands' (between the ring grooves).

8 Look for scoring and scuffing on the piston skirt, holes in the piston crown, and burned areas at the edge of the crown. If the skirt is scored or scuffed, the engine may have been suffering from overheating, and/or abnormal combustion, which caused excessively high operating temperatures. The cooling and lubrication systems should be checked thoroughly. Scorch marks on the sides of the pistons show that blow-by has occurred. A hole in the piston crown, or burned areas at the edge of the piston crown, indicates that abnormal combustion (pre-ignition, knocking or detonation) has been occurring. If any of the above problems exist, the causes must be investigated and corrected, or the damage will occur again. The causes may include a faulty fuel injector.

9 Corrosion of the piston, in the form of pitting, indicates that coolant has been leaking into the combustion chamber and/or the crankcase. Again, the cause must be corrected, or the problem may persist in the rebuilt engine.

10 New pistons can be purchased from a Mercedes-Benz dealer or motor factor.

11 Examine each connecting rod carefully for signs of damage, such as cracks around the big-end and small-end bearings. Check that the rod is not bent or distorted. Damage is highly unlikely, unless the engine has been seized or badly overheated. Detailed checking of the connecting rod assembly can only be carried out by a Mercedes-Benz dealer or engine repair specialist with the necessary equipment.

12 The gudgeon pins are of the floating type, secured in position by two circlips. The pistons and connecting rods can be separated as follows.

13 Using a small screwdriver, prise out the circlips, and push out the gudgeon pin **(see illustrations)**. Hand pressure should be sufficient to remove the pin. Identify the piston and rod to ensure correct reassembly. Discard the circlips – new ones must be used on refitting.

14 Examine the gudgeon pin and connecting rod small-end bearing for signs of wear or damage. It should be possible to push the gudgeon pin through the connecting rod bush by hand, without noticeable play. Wear can be cured by renewing both the pin and bush. Bush renewal, however, is a specialist job – press facilities are required, and the new bush must be reamed accurately.

15 The connecting rods themselves should not be in need of renewal, unless seizure or some other major mechanical failure has occurred. Check the alignment of the connecting rods visually, and if the rods are not straight, take them to an engine overhaul specialist for a more detailed check. **Note:** On V6 engines, Mercedes Benz insist that the connecting rods must not be re-used due to the 'fracture-alignment' production technique used. Consult a Mercedes Benz dealer or specialist.

16 Examine all components, and obtain any new parts from your Mercedes-Benz dealer. If new pistons are purchased, they will be supplied complete with gudgeon pins and circlips. Circlips can also be purchased individually.

17 Position the piston in relation to the connecting rod as noted on removal.

18 Apply a smear of clean engine oil to the gudgeon pin. Slide it into the piston and through the connecting rod small-end. Check that the piston pivots freely on the rod, then secure the gudgeon pin in position with two new circlips. Ensure that each circlip is correctly located in its groove in the piston.

14.2 Check the crankshaft end float using a dial test indicator (DTI)

14 Crankshaft – inspection

Checking crankshaft endfloat

1 If the crankshaft endfloat is to be checked, this must be done when the crankshaft is still installed in the cylinder block/crankcase, but is free to move.

2 Check the endfloat using a dial gauge in contact with the end of the crankshaft. Push the crankshaft fully one way, and then zero the gauge. Push the crankshaft fully the other way, and check the endfloat. The result can be compared with the specified amount, and will give an indication as to whether new thrustwasher halves are required **(see illustration)**. Note that all thrustwashers must be of the same thickness.

3 If a dial gauge is not available, feeler blades can be used. First push the crankshaft fully towards the flywheel/driveplate end of the engine, and then use feeler blades to measure the gap between the web of No 3 crankpin and the thrustwasher halves on 4-cylinder and 6 engines, or between the web of No 4 crankpin and the thrustwasher halves on the 5-cylinder engine.

Inspection

4 Clean the crankshaft using paraffin or a suitable solvent, and dry it, preferably with compressed air if available. Be sure to clean the oil holes with a pipe cleaner or similar probe, to ensure that they are not obstructed.

5 Check the main and big-end bearing journals for uneven wear, scoring, pitting and cracking.

6 Big-end bearing wear is accompanied by distinct metallic knocking when the engine is running (particularly noticeable when the engine is pulling from low speed) and some loss of oil pressure.

7 Main bearing wear is accompanied by severe engine vibration and rumble – getting progressively worse as engine speed increases – and again by loss of oil pressure.

8 Check the bearing journal for roughness by running a finger lightly over the bearing surface. Any roughness (which will be accompanied by obvious bearing wear) indicates that the crankshaft requires regrinding (where possible) or renewal.

9 If the crankshaft has been reground, check for burrs around the crankshaft oil holes (the holes are usually chamfered, so burrs should not be a problem unless regrinding has been carried out carelessly). Remove any burrs with a fine file or scraper, and thoroughly clean the oil holes.

10 Have the crankshaft inspected and measured by a Mercedes Benz dealer or engine reconditioning specialist. They will be able to advise of any reconditioning work needed, and supply the appropriate replacement bearings etc.

15 Main and big-end bearings, and bearing cap bolts – inspection

Bearings

1 Even though the main and big-end bearings should be renewed during the engine overhaul, the old bearings should be retained for close examination, as they may reveal valuable information about the condition of the engine. The bearing shells are graded by thickness.

2 Bearing failure can occur due to lack of lubrication, the presence of dirt or other foreign particles, overloading the engine, or corrosion. Regardless of the cause of bearing failure, the cause must be corrected before the engine is reassembled to prevent it from happening again.

3 When examining the bearing shells, remove them from the cylinder block/crankcase, the connecting rods and the connecting rod big-end bearing caps. Lay them out on a clean surface in the same general position as their location in the engine. This will enable you to match any bearing problems with the corresponding crankshaft journal. Do not touch any shell's bearing surface with your fingers while checking it, or the delicate surface may be scratched.

4 Dirt and other foreign matter get into the engine in a variety of ways. It may be left in the engine during assembly, or it may pass through filters or the crankcase ventilation system. It may get into the oil, and from there into the bearings. Metal chips from machining operations and normal engine wear are often present. Abrasives are sometimes left in engine components after reconditioning, especially when parts are not thoroughly cleaned using the proper cleaning methods. Whatever the source, these foreign objects often end up embedded in the soft bearing material, and are easily recognised. Large particles will not embed in the bearing, and will score or gouge the bearing and journal. The best prevention for this cause of bearing failure is to clean all parts thoroughly, and keep everything spotlessly clean during engine assembly. Frequent and regular engine oil and filter changes are also recommended.

5 Lack of lubrication (or lubrication breakdown) has a number of interrelated causes. Excessive heat (which thins the oil), overloading (which squeezes the oil from the bearing face) and oil leakage (from excessive bearing clearances, worn oil pump or high engine speeds) all contribute to lubrication breakdown. Blocked oil passages, which may be the result of misaligned oil holes in a bearing shell, will also oil-starve a bearing, and destroy it. When lack of lubrication is the cause of bearing failure, the bearing material is wiped or extruded from the steel backing of the bearing. Temperatures may increase to the point where the steel backing turns blue from overheating.

6 Driving habits can have a definite effect on bearing life. Full-throttle, low-speed operation (labouring the engine) puts very high loads on bearings, tending to squeeze out the oil film. These loads cause the bearings to flex, which produces fine cracks in the bearing face (fatigue failure). Eventually, the bearing material will loosen in pieces, and tear away from the steel backing.

7 Short-distance driving leads to corrosion of bearings, because insufficient engine heat is produced to drive off the condensed water and corrosive gases. These products collect in the engine oil, forming acid and sludge. As the oil is carried to the engine bearings, the acid attacks and corrodes the bearing material.

8 Incorrect bearing installation during engine assembly will lead to bearing failure as well. Tight-fitting bearings leave insufficient bearing running clearance, and will result in oil starvation. Dirt or foreign particles trapped behind a bearing shell result in high spots on the bearing, which lead to failure.

9 Do not touch any shell's bearing surface with your fingers during reassembly; there is a risk of scratching the delicate surface, or of depositing particles of dirt on it.

10 As mentioned at the beginning of this Section, the bearing shells should be renewed as a matter of course during engine overhaul; to do otherwise is false economy.

Bolts

11 It's strongly recommended that the main, and big-end bearing cap bolts are renewed regardless of their apparent condition.

16 Engine overhaul – reassembly sequence

1 Before reassembly begins, ensure that all new parts have been obtained, and that all necessary tools are available. Read through the entire procedure to familiarise yourself with the work involved, and to ensure that all items necessary for reassembly of the engine are at hand. In addition to all normal tools and materials, thread-locking compound will be needed. A suitable tube of liquid sealant (Loctite 5970 or equivalent) will also be required for the joint faces that are fitted without gaskets.

2 In order to save time and avoid problems, engine reassembly can be carried out in the following order, referring to Part A or B of this Chapter unless otherwise stated. Where applicable, use new gaskets and seals when refitting the various components.

a) Crankshaft.
b) Balance shaft assembly – V6 engines.
c) Piston/connecting rods.
d) Oil pump.
e) Sump.
f) Flywheel/driveplate.
g) Cylinder head(s).
h) Timing chain, tensioner and sprockets.
i) Engine external components.

3 At this stage, all engine components should be absolutely clean and dry, with all faults repaired. The components should be laid out (or in individual containers) on a completely clean work surface.

17 Piston rings – refitting

1 Before fitting new piston rings, the ring end gaps must be checked as follows.

2 Lay out the piston/connecting rod assemblies and the new piston ring sets, so that the ring sets will be matched with the same piston and cylinder during the end gap measurement and subsequent engine reassembly.

3 Insert the top ring into the first cylinder, and push it down the bore using the top of the piston. This will ensure that the ring remains square with the cylinder walls. Position the ring near the bottom of the cylinder bore, at the lower limit of ring travel. Note that the top and second compression rings are different. The second ring is easily identified by the step on its lower surface.

4 Measure the end gap using feeler blades.

5 Repeat the procedure with the ring at the top of the cylinder bore, at the upper limit of its travel **(see illustration)**, and compare the

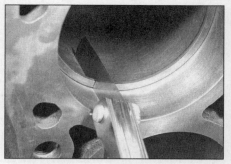

17.5 Measure the piston ring end-gaps

measurements with the figures given in the Specifications.

6 If the gap is too small (unlikely if genuine Mercedes-Benz parts are used), it must be enlarged, or the ring ends may contact each other during engine operation, causing serious damage. Ideally, new piston rings providing the correct end gap should be fitted. As a last resort, the end gap can be increased by filing the ring ends very carefully with a fine file. Mount the file in a vice equipped with soft jaws, slip the ring over the file with the ends contacting the file face, and slowly move the ring to remove material from the ends. Take care, as piston rings are sharp, and are easily broken.

7 With new piston rings, it is unlikely that the end gap will be too large. If the gaps are too large, check that you have the correct rings for your engine and for the particular cylinder bore size.

8 Repeat the checking procedure for each ring in the first cylinder, and then for the rings in the remaining cylinders. Remember to keep rings, pistons and cylinders matched up.

9 Once the ring end gaps have been checked and if necessary corrected, the rings can be fitted to the pistons.

10 Fit the piston rings using the same technique as for removal. Fit the bottom (oil control) ring first, and work up. When fitting the oil control ring, first insert the wire expander, then fit the ring with its gap positioned 180° from the protruding wire ends of the expander. Ensure that the rings are fitted the correct way up – the top surface

17.10 Fit the oil control ring expander

of the rings is normally marked TOP **(see illustration)**. Arrange the gaps of the top and second compression rings 120° either side of the oil control ring gap, but make sure that none of the rings gaps are positioned over the gudgeon pin hole. Note: Always follow any instructions supplied with the new piston ring sets – different manufacturers may specify different procedures. Do not mix up the top and second compression rings, as they have different cross-sections.

18 Crankshaft – refitting

1 If the original crankshaft is in good condition and is being refitted, new main bearing shells, which are the same size as the removed shells, should be fitted.

2 If the crankshaft has been reground, undersize bearing shells must be fitted. The engine-reconditioning specialist normally supplies the appropriate shells.

3 Clean the backs of the bearing shells, and the bearing locations in both the cylinder block/crankcase and the main bearing caps.

4 Press the bearing shells into their locations, ensuring that the tab on each shell engages in the notch in the cylinder block/crankcase or bearing cap **(see illustration)**. Take care not to touch any shell's bearing surface with your fingers. If the original bearing shells are being used for the check, ensure that they are refitted in their original locations. Note that the bearings shells with oil grooves fit in the cylinder block, and the plain bearing shells fit in the bearing caps.

5 Where applicable, ensure that the oil spray jets are fitted to the cylinder block.

6 Liberally lubricate each bearing shell in the cylinder block/crankcase and cap with clean engine oil.

7 Fit the upper thrustwasher halves to the appropriate bearing location in the cylinder block as follows **(see illustration)**.

● 4 and 6 cylinder engines – No.3 main bearing.
● 5 cylinder engines – No.4 main bearing.

8 Ensure that the oil grooves in the thrustwasher halves face out towards the crankshaft journals.

18.4 Ensure that the tab on each bearing shell engages with the notch in the cap

18.7 Fit the upper thrustwasher halves

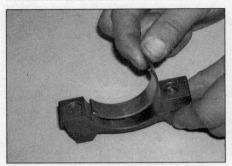

18.10a Locate the main bearing shells in the caps...

18.10b...and lubricate them with clean engine oil

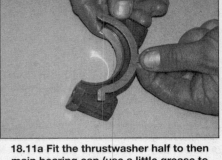

18.11a Fit the thrustwasher half to then main bearing cap (use a little grease to hold the washer in place)

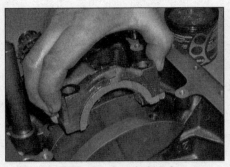

18.11b Fit the No 3 main bearing cap

18.13 Use an angle-tightening gauge

9 The crankshaft can now be lowered into position.

10 Lubricate the lower bearing shells in the main bearing caps with clean engine oil. Make sure that the locating lugs on the shells engage with the corresponding recesses in the caps (see illustrations).

11 Fit the main bearing caps to their correct locations, ensuring that they are fitted the correct way round. Ensure that the thrustwasher halves are in place on the appropriate bearing cap (see illustrations).

12 Lightly lubricate the bolt threads, then fit the main bearing cap bolts. Where applicable, ensure that the oil pick-up pipe support bracket is in place on the relevant bolts, as noted before removal. Tighten the bolts by hand only at this stage.

13 Progressively tighten the main bearing

cap bolts to the specified torque, starting with the centre bearing cap and working outwards. Observe the tightening stages given in the Specifications (see illustration). If the bolts are angle-tightened, it is recommended that an angle-measuring gauge be used during this stage of the tightening, to ensure accuracy. If a gauge is not available, use a dab of white paint to make alignment marks between the bolt and bearing cap prior to tightening; the marks can then be used to check that the bolt has been rotated sufficiently during tightening.

14 Check that the crankshaft rotates freely.

15 Fit a new crankshaft rear oil seal to the housing, then refit the housing, using a new gasket, or suitable sealant, as applicable.

16 Refit the balance shaft assembly (where applicable) and piston/connecting rod assemblies.

19 Balance shaft assembly – refitting

1 Lubricate the bearing surfaces of the balance shaft, then insert it into the crankcase.

2 Tighten the front retaining bolt to the specified torque.

3 Refit the counterweight and tighten the retaining bolt to the specified torque.

4 Apply a little sealant (Loctite 5970 or equivalent) to the mating surfaces, then refit the balance shaft rear cover and tighten the retaining bolts to the specified torque.

5 With the engine set at TDC for No.1 cylinder as described in Chapter 2B Section 3, the mark on the edge of the balance shaft front counterweight must be in the 12 o'clock position.

6 Refit the camshaft sprocket and timing chain cover as described in Chapter 2B.

20 Piston/connecting rod assemblies – refitting

Note: A piston ring compressor tool will be required for this operation. Note that the following procedure assumes that the main bearing caps are in place.

1 If the big-end journals on the crankshaft are in good condition, new big-end bearing shells, which are the same size as the removed shells, should be fitted.

2 If the crankshaft has been reground, undersize bearing shells must be fitted. The engine-reconditioning specialist normally supplies the appropriate shells.

3 Clean the backs of the bearing shells, and the bearing locations in both the connecting rod and bearing cap.

4 Press the bearing shells into their locations, ensuring that the tab on each shell engages in the notch in the connecting rod and cap (see illustrations). Take care not to touch the bearing surface of the shell with your fingers.

5 Lubricate the cylinder bores, the pistons, and piston rings, then lay out each piston/

20.4a Insert the bearing shells in the conrod...

20.4b...and big-end cap

20.5a Lubricate the pistons, rings...

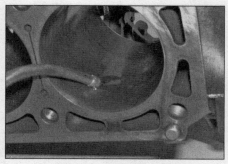

20.5b...and cylinder bores

20.6 Fit a piston ring compressor

connecting rod assembly in its respective position **(see illustrations)**.

6 Start with assembly No 1. Make sure that the piston rings are still spaced as described in Section 17, and then clamp them in position with a piston ring compressor **(see illustration)**.

7 Insert the piston/connecting rod assembly into the top of cylinder No 1. Ensure that the arrow on the piston crown points towards the timing chain end of the engine, and that the identifying marks on the connecting rods and big-end caps are positioned as noted before removal. Using a block of wood or hammer handle against the piston crown, tap the assembly into the cylinder until the piston crown is flush with the top of the cylinder **(see illustration)**. Where applicable, take care not to damage the piston cooling oil spray jets as the piston/connecting rod assemblies are refitted.

8 Ensure that the bearing shell is still correctly installed. Liberally lubricate the crankpin and both bearing shells. Taking care not to mark the cylinder bores or damage the piston oil jets (where fitted), pull the piston /connecting rod assembly down the bore and onto the crankpin. Refit the big-end bearing cap **(see illustration)**. Note that the bearing shell locating tabs must abut each other. On some engines, the caps and rods are 'fractured' to

ensure improved component location. Ensure the matching pair (cap and rod) are fitted together.

9 Lightly lubricate the bolt threads, then screw the big-end bearing cap bolts by hand into position in the connecting rods.

10 Progressively tighten the bolts to the specified torque and angle, observing the two tightening stages given in the Specifications. It is recommended that an angle-measuring gauge is used to angle- tighten the bolts. If a gauge is not available, use a dab of white paint to make alignment marks between the bolt and bearing cap prior to tightening; the marks can then be used to check that the bolt has been rotated sufficiently during tightening.

11 Once the bearing cap bolts have been correctly tightened, rotate the crankshaft and check that it turns freely. Some stiffness is to be expected if new components have been fitted, but there should be no signs of binding or tight spots.

12 Refit the remaining piston/connecting rod assemblies in the same way.

21 Engine – initial start-up after overhaul

1 Refit the remainder of the engine components in the correct order listed in

this Chapter. Refit the engine to the vehicle as described in the relevant Section of this Chapter. Double-check the engine oil and coolant levels, and make a final check that everything has been reconnected. Make sure that there are no tools or rags left in the engine compartment.

2 Reconnect the battery negative lead as described in Chapter 5A Section 4.

3 Disconnect the injector harness wiring plug at the right-hand rear of the engine compartment.

4 Turn the engine using the starter motor until the oil pressure warning lamp goes out.

5 If the lamp fails to extinguish after several seconds of cranking, check the engine oil level and oil filter security. Assuming these are correct, check the security of the oil pressure switch cabling – do not progress any further until you are satisfied that oil is being pumped around the engine at sufficient pressure.

6 Reconnect the injector wiring plug.

7 Start the engine, but be aware that as fuel system components have been disturbed, the cranking time may be a little longer than usual.

8 While the engine is idling, check for fuel, water and oil leaks. Don't be alarmed if there are some odd smells and the occasional plume of smoke as components heat up and burn off oil deposits.

9 Assuming all is well; keep the engine idling until hot water is felt circulating through the top hose.

10 After a few minutes, recheck the oil and coolant levels, and top-up as necessary.

11 There is no need to retighten the cylinder head bolts once the engine has been run following reassembly.

12 If new pistons, rings or crankshaft bearings have been fitted, the engine must be treated as new, and run-in for the first 600 miles. Do not operate the engine at full-throttle, or allow it to labour at low engine speeds in any gear. It is recommended that the engine oil and filter are changed at the end of this period.

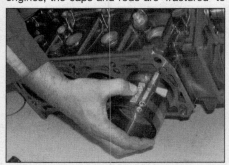

20.7 Insert the piston into the cylinder bore

20.8 Refit the big-end bearing caps

Chapter 3
Cooling, heating and ventilation systems

Contents

Degrees of difficulty

Easy, suitable for novice with little experience		Fairly easy, suitable for beginner with some experience	Fairly difficult, suitable for competent DIY mechanic	Difficult, suitable for experienced DIY mechanic	Very difficult, suitable for expert DIY or professional	

Specifications

System
Type .... Pressurised, pump-assisted with front mounted radiator and ECM controlled cooling fan

Thermostat
Type	Wax	
Operating temperatures	Starts to open	Fully open
All engines	80° C	100° C

Expansion tank
Cap pressure .... 1.4 bar

Air conditioning system
Refrigerant R134a
Refrigerant charge quantity .... 950 ± 10g
Lubricating oil.................................... MB 362.0 A 001 989 08 03

Torque wrench settings

	Nm	lbf ft
Coolant pump:		
In-line engines:		
Pump-to-timing case:		
M6..	14	11
M8..	20	15
V6 engines	10	7
Coolant pump pulley bolts........................	10	7
Facia crossmember to vehicle body	25	18
Thermostat housing bolts........................	8	5
Compressor mounting bolts......................	20	15
Compressor refrigerant pipe connections	24	18
Condenser mounting bolts.......................	10	7
Pressure sensor	8	5

1 General information and precautions

General information

1 The cooling system is of pressurised type, comprising a pump, an aluminium crossflow radiator, an electric cooling fan, and a thermostat. The system functions as follows. Cold coolant from the radiator passes through the hose to the coolant pump, where it is pumped around the cylinder block and head passages. After cooling the cylinder bores, combustion surfaces and valve seats, the coolant reaches the underside of the thermostat, which is initially closed. The coolant passes through the heater and is returned through the cylinder block to the coolant pump.

2 When the engine is cold, the coolant circulates only through the cylinder block, cylinder head(s), expansion tank and heater. When the coolant reaches a predetermined temperature, the thermostat opens and the coolant passes through to the radiator. As the coolant circulates through the radiator, it is cooled by the inrush of air when the car is in forward motion. Airflow is supplemented by the action of the electric fan as necessary. Upon reaching the bottom of the radiator, the coolant is now cooled and the cycle is repeated.

3 The coolant pump is mounted externally on the front of the engine, and is driven by the auxiliary drivebelt.

4 Coolant temperature information for the gauge mounted in the instrument panel, and for the fuel system, is provided by temperature sensors mounted in the thermostat housing, left-hand coolant passage or in the cylinder head, depending on model. A coolant level switch is fitted to bottom of the radiator expansion tank.

5 An electric cooling fan is fitted and serves a dual purpose, regulating both the engine coolant temperature and that of the air conditioning refrigerant in the condenser (which is mounted in front of the radiator). Partly because of these two roles, the fan is controlled via an electronic unit.

6 All models have a remote-mounted coolant expansion tank, which is located on the left-hand side of the engine compartment and collects the coolant, which is displaced from the system as it expands due to the rise in temperature. The displaced coolant is returned to the radiator as the system cools.

7 The vehicle interior heater operates by means of coolant from the engine cooling system. Coolant flow through the heater matrix is regulated by solenoid valves, which are controlled by a temperature sensor at the front of the heater unit. Unusually, the heater matrix is divided into two separate sections, for the driver and front seat passenger. Accordingly, two solenoid valves are fitted into the coolant pipes which lead to the heater, providing independent control of coolant flow through the matrix halves (a further main supply valve is fitted on air conditioning models). Temperature control is further achieved by blending cool air from outside the vehicle (or from the air conditioning system) with the warm air from the heater matrix, in the desired ratio.

Precautions

⚠️ **Warning: Do not attempt to remove the pressure cap, or disturb any part of the cooling system, while the engine is hot, as there is a high risk of scalding. If the pressure cap must be removed before the engine and radiator have fully cooled (even though this is not recommended), the pressure in the cooling system must first be relieved. Cover the cap with a thick layer of cloth, to avoid scalding, and slowly unscrew the pressure cap until a hissing sound is heard (be prepared to refit the cap quickly if bubbling noises are heard and hot coolant starts to come out). When the hissing stops, indicating that the pressure has reduced, slowly unscrew the pressure cap until it can be removed; if more hissing sounds are heard, wait until they have stopped before unscrewing the cap completely. At all times, keep your face well away from the pressure cap opening, and protect your hands.**

⚠️ **Warning: Do not allow antifreeze to come into contact with your skin, or with the painted surfaces of the vehicle. Rinse off spills immediately with plenty of water. Never leave antifreeze lying around in an open container, or in a puddle in the driveway or on the garage floor. Children and pets are attracted by its sweet smell, but antifreeze can be fatal if ingested.**

⚠️ **Warning: The cooling fan could cut in even if the engine is not running (if the ignition is on). Be careful to keep your hands, hair, and any loose clothing well clear when working in the engine compartments.**

2 Cooling system hoses – disconnection and renewal

⚠️ **Warning: Never work on the cooling system when it is hot. Release any pressure from the system by loosening the expansion tank cap, having first covered it with a cloth to avoid any possibility of scalding.**

1 The number, routing and pattern of hoses will vary according to model, but the same basic procedure applies. Before commencing work, make sure that the new hoses are to hand, along with new hose clips if needed. It is good practice to renew the hose clips at the same time as the hoses.

2 Drain the cooling system as described in Chapter 1 Section 30, saving the coolant if it is fit for re-use. Squirt a little penetrating oil onto the hose clips if they are corroded.

3 Release the hose clips from the hose concerned. The clip most commonly used on the Mercedes-Benz is the spring clip, which is released by squeezing its tags together with pliers, at the same time working the clip away from the hose stub **(see illustration)**. The worm-drive clip is released by turning its screw anti-clockwise **(see illustration)**. The 'sardine-can' clips are not re-usable, and are best cut off with snips or side cutters.

4 Unclip any wires, cables or other hoses, which may be attached to the hose being removed. Make notes for reference when reassembling, if necessary.

5 Release the hose from its stubs with a twisting motion. Be careful not to damage the stubs on delicate components such as the radiator, or thermostat housings. If the hose is stuck fast, the best course is often to cut it off using a sharp knife, but again be careful not to damage the stubs.

6 Before fitting the new hose, smear the stubs with washing-up liquid or a suitable rubber lubricant to aid fitting. Do not use oil or grease, which may attack the rubber.

7 Fit the hose clips over the ends of the hose, and then fit the hose over its stubs. Work the hose into position. When satisfied, locate and tighten the hose clips.

8 Refill the cooling system as described in Chapter 1 Section 30. Run the engine, and check that there are no leaks.

9 Recheck the tightness of the hose clips on any new hoses after a few hundred miles.

10 Top-up the coolant level if necessary (see 'Weekly checks').

2.3a Spring type hose clips...   **2.3b...and worm-drive hose clips**

3.3 Pull up the weatherstrip from the slam panel

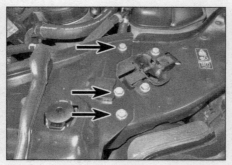

3.4 Remove the slam panel retaining bolts each side

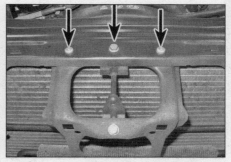

3.5 Undo the catch hook reinforcement bolts

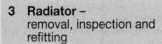

3 Radiator –
removal, inspection and refitting

Removal

1 Drain the cooling system as described in Chapter 1 Section 30.
2 Remove the plastic cover from the top of the engine.
3 Pull up the rubber weatherstrip from the bonnet slam panel **(see illustration)**.
4 Undo the 3 bolts at each end of the bonnet slam panel **(see illustration)**.
5 Undo the bolts securing the catch hook reinforcement in the centre of the bonnet slam panel **(see illustration)**.
6 Remove the expansion clips securing the rubber mouldings each side **(see illustration)**.
7 Lift the bonnet slam panel a little, and unclip the release cable.
8 Move the bonnet slam panel to one side.
9 Remove the air intake duct upstream of the air filter on the left-, and right-hand sides.
10 Remove the front bumper as described in Chapter 11 Section 16.
11 Remove the radiator cooling fan assembly as described in Section 6.
12 Remove the intercooler as described in Chapter 4A Section 18.
13 Carefully unclip and remove the air ducting surrounding the front of the radiator. Where necessary, remove the horn to enable removal of the ducting.

3.6 Prise up the centre pins, then lever out the expansion clips

14 Where applicable, disconnect the fluid cooler pipes from the radiator **(see illustration)**. Be prepared for fluid spillage. Plug the openings to prevent contamination. Renew the seals.
15 Unclip the power steering cooling loop from the radiator, and secure it to the crossmember.
16 Unclip the air conditioning condenser from the radiator and secure it to the crossmember.
17 Disconnect the coolant hoses from the radiator **(see illustrations)**.
18 Lift the radiator upwards from place, and recover the rubber mountings from the base **(see illustration)**.

Inspection

19 If the radiator was removed because

3.14 Prise out the clip and pull the transmission fluid pipe each side from the radiator

of clogging (causing overheating) then try reverse flushing using a garden hose or, in severe cases, use a radiator cleanser strictly in accordance with the manufacturer's instructions.
20 Use a soft brush and an air line or garden hose to clear the radiator matrix of leaves, insects etc.
21 Major leaks or extensive damage should be repaired by a specialist, or the radiator should be renewed or exchanged for a reconditioned unit.
22 Examine the mounting rubbers for signs of damage or deterioration and renew if necessary.

Refitting

23 Refitting the radiator is the reverse

3.17a Disconnect the small diameter hose at the top, then prise out the clip, disconnect the hose at the left-hand side...

3.17b ...and the right-hand side

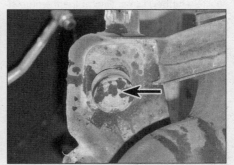

3.18 Radiator rubber mountings

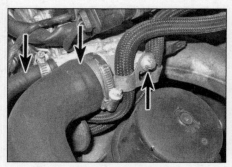
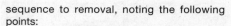

4.4 Thermostat housing fuel pipe clamp and coolant hoses

4.6 Remove the thermostat

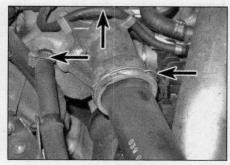

4.7 Unclip the hose at the top, and disconnect the coolant hoses

sequence to removal, noting the following points:
a) *Ensure that the lower mounting lugs properly engage with the rubber mountings, and that (where applicable) the locating studs are pressed fully home.*
b) *Make sure that the radiator and fan shroud retaining clips are a secure fit.*
c) *After fitting, fill the cooling system as described in Chapter 1 Section 30.*
d) *On automatic transmission models, check the transmission fluid level as described in Chapter 7B Section 5.*
e)

4 Thermostat – removal, testing and refitting

Removal

1 Drain the coolant as described in Chapter 1 Section 30.
2 Remove the plastic cover from the top of the engine.

In-line engines

3 Disconnect the temperature sensor wiring plug.
4 Undo the bolt securing the fuel pipe bracket to the thermostat housing **(see illustration)**.
5 Release the clamps and disconnect the coolant hoses from the thermostat housing.
6 Undo the retaining bolt and remove the thermostat **(see illustration)**. Renew the seal. No further dismantling of the thermostat

is recommended. If faulty, the complete unit must be replaced.

V6-engines

7 Unclip the hose from the top of the thermostat housing **(see illustration)**.
8 Disconnect the wiring plug from the thermostat heating element (where fitted).
9 Disconnect the coolant hoses from the thermostat housing.
10 Undo the retaining bolts and remove the thermostat housing. Renew the sealing ring **(see illustration)**.

Testing

11 If the thermostat remains in the open position at room temperature, then it is faulty and the complete housing assembly must be renewed.
12 To test it fully, suspend the (closed) thermostat housing on a length of string in a container of cold water, with a thermometer beside it.
13 Heat the water and check the temperature at which the thermostat begins to open. Compare this value with that specified. Continue to heat the water until the thermostat is fully open. Allow the thermostat to cool down and check that it closes fully.
14 If the thermostat does not open and close as described, if it sticks in either position, or if it does not open at the specified temperature, then it must be renewed.

Refitting

15 Refitting is a reversal of removal, but note the following additional points:

a) *Clean all mating surfaces thoroughly before reassembly.*
b) *Renew the thermostat housing seal/gasket regardless of condition.*
c) *Renew the hose O-ring seals if they show signs of deterioration.*
d) *Tighten all bolts to their specified torque wrench settings (where given).*
e) *Ensure the coolant hose clips are positioned so that they do not foul any other component, then tighten them securely.*
f) *Refill the cooling system as described in Chapter 1 Section 30.*

5 Coolant pump – removal and refitting

Removal

1 Drain the cooling system as described in Chapter 1 Section 30.

In-line engines

2 Remove the auxiliary drivebelt as described in Chapter 1 Section 6.
3 On 5-, or 6-cylinder engines, remove the cooling fan assembly as described in Section 6.
4 Remove the plastic cap and remove the guide pulley from the oil filter lower housing **(see illustrations)**. Note: One of the coolant pump retaining bolts is positioned behind the guide pulley.
5 Remove the plastic cap and remove the guide

4.10 V6 thermostat housing retaining bolts

5.4a Prise out the plastic cap...

5.4b...and remove the guide pulley

5.8 Note the different sizes of the coolant pump retaining bolts

5.9 Renew the coolant pump gasket

5.12 Coolant pump retaining bolts – V6 engines

pulley from the top of the coolant pump housing. Note: One of the coolant pump retaining bolts is positioned behind the guide pulley.

6 Release the clamps and disconnect the coolant hoses from the pump.

7 Undo the retaining bolts and remove the heat shield adjacent to the pump.

8 Loosen and remove the bolts securing the coolant pump, noting their locations, as they are of different lengths and sizes (see illustration).

9 Withdraw the pump, and recover the gasket (see illustration). Discard the gasket, as a new one will be required when refitting.

V-6 engines

10 Pull the plastic cover on the top of the engine upwards from the rubber mountings.

11 Remove the auxiliary drivebelt as described in Chapter 1 Section 6. Note that it's only necessary to disengage the belt from the coolant pump pulley – no need to completely remove it.

12 Undo the retaining bolts and remove the coolant pump (see illustration). Renew the gasket.

Refitting

13 Carefully clean the coolant pump and cylinder block mating surfaces, removing all traces of the old gasket or sealant. Take care to avoid scoring the surfaces, as this will cause leakage.

14 Refit the coolant pump by following the removal procedure in reverse, noting these points:

a) Fit a new gasket when refitting the pump.
b) Tighten the pump bolts in a diagonal sequence to the correct torque, noting the different figures for the different size bolts used.
c) Refit the auxiliary drivebelt as described in Chapter 1 Section 6.
d) On completion, refill the cooling system as described in Chapter 1 Section 30.

6 Electric cooling fan assembly – removal and refitting

Removal

1 Remove the plastic cover from the top of the engine.
2 Remove the air intake duct(s) upstream or the air filter.
3 Pull up the rubber sealing strip from the bonnet slam panel (see illustration 3.3).
4 Undo the bolts securing the bonnet catch bracket in the centre, and remove the expansion rivets each side securing the rubber mouldings each side (see illustrations 3.4 and 3.6).
5 Undo the 3 bolts at each end, and move the bonnet slam panel upwards, then forwards a little (see illustration 3.5).
6 Release the retaining clips each side of the cooling fan shroud (see illustration).
7 Unclip the coolant hose from the brackets on the fan shroud.
8 Disconnect the fan motor wiring plug (see

illustration). On in-line engines, the plug is on the left-hand side, and on V6-engines, it's on the right.
9 Manoeuvre the fan shroud upwards from place (see illustration). Take great care not to damage the radiator during this procedure.
10 If required, release the wiring harness, disconnect the wiring plug, undo the screws and remove the fan motor.

Refitting

11 Refitting is a reversal of removal. Note the locating lug at the top, centre of the shroud.

7 Cooling system sensors – testing, removal and refitting

Engine coolant temperature sensor (ECT)

Testing

1 The engine coolant temperature sensor monitors the temperature of the coolant as it leaves the engine. The sensor is a 'thermistor', i.e. the resistance of the sensor changes as the temperature changes. The signal from the sensor is used by the engine management ECM (electronic control module) to regulate fuel injection quantity and timing, glow plugs, cooling fan operation, and the temperature gauge in the instrument cluster. Should the sensor fail, the ECM will adopt a pre-determined substitute value, and illuminate the MIL (malfunction indicator lamp) on the

6.6 Prise up the clip each side

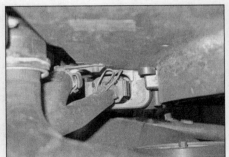

6.8 Fan motor wiring plug

6.9 Manoeuvre the fan shroud upwards

7.5a Coolant temperature sensor on the thermostat housing – in-line engines

7.5b On V6-engines, the coolant temperature sensor is located on the left-hand cylinder head

instrument cluster. No specific test values are available for the sensor. Consequently, testing is limited to inspecting the wiring and connectors to the sensor. Further investigation can only be carried out by the use of dedicated test equipment. Consult your Land Rover dealer or fuel injection specialist. Testing by any other means could result in ECM damage.

Removal

2 Drain the cooling system as described in Chapter 1 Section 30.

3 Remove the plastic cover from the top of the engine.

4 On V-6 engines, remove the air intake duct down stream of the air filter on the left-hand side.

5 Disconnect the coolant temperature sensor wiring plug (see illustrations).

6 Pull out the retaining clip and withdraw the sensor. Discard the sealing ring – a new one must be fitted.

Refitting

7 Refit the sensor with a new O-ring seal, and secure it with the retaining clip.

8 The remainder of refitting is a reversal of removal. Top up the coolant as described in Chapter 1 Section 30.

Coolant level sensor

Testing

9 The level sensor is fitted to the base of the coolant expansion tank. Should a sensor fail, testing is only possible using Mercedes test equipment.

Removal

10 On V-6 engines, remove the left-hand air intake duct.

11 On all engines, rotate the level sensor 90° anti-clockwise and pull it from the coolant expansion tank. Disconnect the wiring plug as the sensor is withdrawn. Be prepared for coolant spillage.

Refitting

12 Refitting is a reversal of removal, renewing the sensor O-ring seal as necessary. Top up the cooling system as described in 'Weekly checks'.

---

8 Heating and ventilation system components – removal and refitting

Heater control panel

Removal

1 Disconnect the battery negative lead as described in Chapter 5A Section 4.

2 Remove the facia loudspeaker as described in Chapter 12 Section 17.

3 Using a blunt, flat-bladed tool, carefully prise the right-hand end of the decorative trim strip from the passengers side of the facia, then slide it to the left and remove it (see illustrations).

4 Remove the 2 bolts beneath and above the heater control panel (see illustration).

5 Manoeuvre the heater control panel rearwards, disconnecting the wiring plugs as they become accessible.

6 If required, undo the screws and detach the control unit from the panel.

Refitting

7 Refitting is a reversal of removal.

Heater blower motor

Removal

8 Move the passengers sear fully rearwards.

9 Disconnect the battery negative lead as described in Chapter 5A Section 4.

10 Undo the 2 retaining screws and remove the passengers side lower facia panel (see illustration). Disconnect any wiring plugs as the panel is withdrawn.

11 Undo the screws, and remove the blower base (see illustration). Disconnect any wiring plugs as the base is withdrawn.

8.3a Prise the right-hand end of the trim strip rearwards...

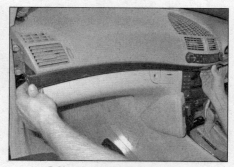

8.3b...then slide it to the left

8.4 Heater control panel retaining screws

8.10 Passengers side lower facia panel retaining screws

8.11 Undo the screws and remove the blower base

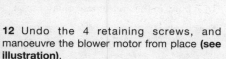

8.12 Blower motor retaining screws

8.13 Blower motor control unit retaining screws

8.16 Undo the screws and remove the bracket each side

12 Undo the 4 retaining screws, and manoeuvre the blower motor from place **(see illustration)**.

13 If required, disconnect the wiring plug, undo the 2 screws, and detach the blower motor control unit **(see illustration)**.

Refitting

14 Refitting is a reversal of removal.

Heater matrix

Removal

15 Remove the heater/air conditioning housing as described in this Section.

16 Remove the bracket each side of the heater/air conditioning housing **(see illustration)**.

17 Remove the left-hand, centre air outlet flap actuator motor **(see illustration)**.

18 On models with an auxiliary heating element, disconnect the wiring plug.

19 Carefully remove the seal around the expansion valve/heater pipes connection **(see illustration)**.

20 Undo the screws and remove the clamping bracket around the pipes **(see illustration)**.

21 Remove the clips around the circumference of the housing **(see illustration)**.

22 Lift away the air distributor housing.

23 Lift out the heater matrix, taking care not to damage the sealing tape **(see illustration)**.

Refitting

24 Refitting is a reversal of removal. Top up the cooling system as described in Chapter 1 Section 30.

Heater/air conditioning housing

25 On models with air conditioning, have the refrigerant circuit evacuated by a Mercedes Benz dealer or suitably equipped specialist.

26 Remove the wiper motor linkage assembly Chapter 12 Section 14.

27 Drain the cooling system as described in Chapter 1 Section 30, or apply clamps to the coolant hoses at the engine compartment bulkhead.

28 Working at the rear of the engine compartment, lift out the insulation mat, and undo the retaining nut, and pull the refrigerant pipe from the connection at the bulkhead **(see illustration)**. Plug the openings to prevent contamination. Renew the pipe seals.

29 Prise up the wire clips a little, and detach the heater matrix shut-off valve from

8.17 The left-hand, centre air outlet flap motor is retained by 3 screws

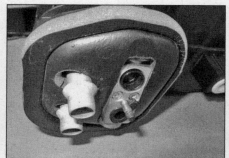

8.19 Remove the foam seal...

8.20...then undo the screws and remove the clamping bracket

8.21 Prise away the clips around the circumference of the housing

8.23 Lift the heater matrix from the housing

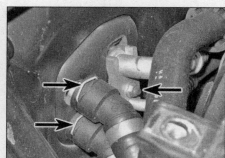

8.28 Refrigerant pipe connection retaining nut, and heater/coolant hose retaining clips

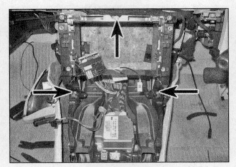

8.32 Centre air duct mounting retaining screw

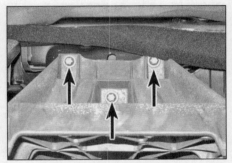

8.33 Centre crossmember frame retaining bolts

8.39a The facia crossmember is secured by 3 bolts in the instrument cluster area...

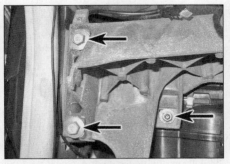

8.39b...a bolt/nut each side of the centre console area...

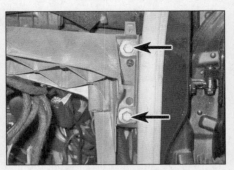

8.39c...2 bolts and a nut at the passengers end...

8.39d...and 2 bolts at the drivers end

the connection at the engine compartment bulkhead. Plug the openings to prevent contamination.

30 Remove the entire facia as described in Chapter 11 Section 36.

31 Remove the passengers air bag as described in Chapter 12 Section 20.

32 Undo the retaining screw and remove the centre air duct mounting **(see illustration)**.

33 Undo the 3 bolts and remove the centre facia crossmember frame, and the insulation mat in front of the frame **(see illustration)**.

34 Remove the rear air duct from the heater/air conditioning housing. Release the wiring as the duct is removed.

35 Remove the steering column combination switch as described in Chapter 12 Section 5.

36 Remove the steering column as described in Chapter 10 Section 22.

37 Make a note of the routing, then release the facia crossmember wiring harness from the various retaining clips.

38 Fold back the carpet, undo the nut/bolt and lower the parking brake pedal assembly from the crossmember.

39 Make alignment marks between the facia crossmember and the A-pillars, and centre console bracket, then undo the bolts/nuts and move the crossmember rearwards a little **(see illustrations)**.

40 Make alignement marks, undo the 3 bolts, dismantle the crossmember and manoeuvre it from place **(see illustration)**.

41 Fold back the carpet on the passengers side.

42 Pull the heater/air conditioning housing rearwards/upwards a little, remove the covers, then disconnect the positive and negative leads from the heater booster (where fitted) **(see illustration)**.

43 Lift and pull the heater/air conditioning

housing from place, unclipling the wiring harness as the housing is withdrawn. Note the location of the drain hose each side **(see illustrations)**.

Refitting

44 Check the condition of the seals between the heater/air conditioning housing and the vehicle body. Renew where necessary.

45 Refitting is a reversal of removal, noting the following points:

a) *Tighten all fasteners to their specified torque where given.*

b) *Align the facia crossmember with previously made marks.*

c) *Top up the cooling system as described in Chapter 1 Section 30.*

d) *Have the air conditioning refrigerant circuit recharged by a Mercedes Benz dealer or suitably equipped specialist.*

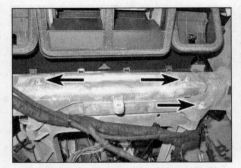

8.40 Undo the 3 bolts and dismantle the crossmember

8.42 Disconnect the leads from the heater booster

8.43 Note the evaporator drain hose each side

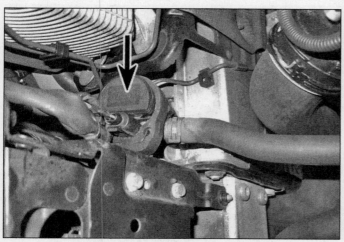

8.47 The heating water circulation pump is located on the right-hand side of the engine compartment

8.54 Auxiliary electrical heater retaining screws

Heating water circulation pump

Removal

46 Disconnect the battery negative lead as described in Chapter 5A Section 4.
47 Apply clamps to the pump coolant hoses **(see illustration)**.
48 Disconnect the pump wiring plug.
49 Pull the pump out of the holder, and disconnect the hoses.

Refitting

50 Refitting is a reversal of removal.

Auxiliary electrical heater (booster)

Removal

51 Remove the heater/air conditioning housing as described previously in this Section.
52 Disconnect the booster heater wiring connections **(see illustration 8.42)**.
53 Undo the bolts, then place the right-rear, and the left-rear blending air flap motors to one side, without disconnecting the wiring plugs.
54 Undo the 3 retaining screws and pull the booster heater from the housing **(see illustration)**.

Refitting

55 Refitting is a reversal of removal.

9 Air conditioning system – general information and precautions

1 An air conditioning system is fitted as standard equipment on high-specification models, and was available as an optional extra on lower-specification models. In conjunction with the heater, the system enables any reasonable air temperature to be achieved inside the car, it also reduces the humidity of the incoming air, aiding demisting even when cooling is not required.

2 The refrigeration circuit of the air conditioning system functions in a similar way to a domestic refrigerator. A compressor, belt-driven from the crankshaft pulley, draws refrigerant in its gaseous state from an evaporator. The refrigerant heats up as a result of being compressed, but is then passed through a condenser (mounted in front of the engine radiator) where it loses heat and enters its liquid state. After dehydration, the refrigerant is passed through an evaporator (mounted alongside the heater/ventilation unit) where it is allowed to expand and reverts to being gas. This change of state has the effect of absorbing heat from the air passing over the evaporator fins, reducing its temperature. This cool air is mixed with warm air from the heater unit to achieve the desired cabin temperature. The refrigerant is directed back to the compressor and the cycle is then repeated.

3 Various subsidiary controls and sensors protect the system against excessive temperature and pressures. Additionally, engine idle speed is increased when the system is in use to compensate for the additional load imposed by the compressor. Electronic sensors detect the rotational speed differential between the engine and the compressor – if this becomes too great

9.4 Refrigerant circuit service ports

(due to a malfunctioning compressor), the compressor clutch is disengaged, to preserve the drivebelt.
4 The refrigerant circuit service ports are located on the left-hand side of the engine compartment **(see illustration)**.
Note: *The air conditioning electronic control system can only be tested using dedicated equipment. For this reason, it is recommended that problems with the operation of the air conditioning system are referred to a Mercedes-Benz dealer for diagnosis.*

⚠ **Warning: The refrigeration circuit contains pressurised liquid refrigerant. The refrigerant is potentially dangerous, and should only be handled by qualified persons. Refrigerant that is allowed to come into contact with the skin will cause severe frostbite. It is not itself poisonous, but in the presence of a naked flame (including inhalation through a lighted cigarette), it forms a poisonous gas. Uncontrolled discharging of the refrigerant is dangerous and is also extremely damaging to the environment. For these reasons, disconnection of any part of the system without specialised knowledge and equipment is not recommended.**
Caution: Do not allow refrigerant lines to be exposed to temperatures in excess of 110°C, for example during welding or paint-drying operations.
Caution: Do not operate the air conditioning system if it is known to be short of refrigerant, or component damage may result.

10 Air conditioning system components – removal and refitting

⚠ *Warning: Refer to the previous Section before proceeding. Before carrying out any of the procedures detailed below,*

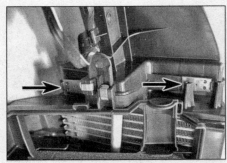

10.2 These blower housing clips slide out

10.3 Release the clips securing the housing cover

10.4 Expansion valve retaining screws

10.6 Separate the halves of the housing and lift the evaporator from place

10.9 Undo the retaining plate bolt

c) *Have the refrigerant circuit recharged and leak tested by a Mercedes Benz dealer or suitably equipped specialist.*

Receiver/drier

Removal

8 Raise the front of the vehicle and support it securely on axle stands (see *'Vehicle jacking and support'*). Undo the fasteners and remove the engine undershield.

9 Undo the bolt and remove the refrigerant pipe retaining plate **(see illustration)**.

10 Undo the 2 retaining bolts and detach the receiver/drier from the condenser **(see illustration)**. Plug the openings to prevent contamination.

Refitting

11 Refitting is a reversal of removal, noting the following points:

a) *Renew the refrigerant circuit O-ring seals.*
b) *Apply a little refrigerant oil to the seals prior to reassembly.*
c) *Have the refrigerant circuit recharged and leak tested by a Mercedes Benz dealer or suitably equipped specialist.*

Condenser

Removal

12 Raise the front of the vehicle and support it securely on axle stands (see *'Vehicle jacking and support'*). Undo the fasteners and remove the engine undershield.

13 Remove the intercooler as described in Chapter 4A Section 18.

14 Undo the retaining bolts, and remove the bonnet hook reinforcement bracket above the condenser.

15 Release the retaining clips and remove the top of the radiator air ducting, with the intake fittings.

16 Unclip the oil pipe on the right-, and left-hand sides of the radiator.

17 Release the clips, unhook the radiator lower air ducting and lower it from place.

18 Release the clips each side of the condenser, and tilt it forwards a little **(see illustration)**.

19 Undo the nut and detach the refrigerant pipes from the condenser **(see illustration)**. Plug the openings to prevent contamination. Renew the pipe O-ring seals.

the air conditioning system MUST be professionally discharged by a garage or air conditioning specialist.

Note: *The car may be driven once the system has been discharged, but the air conditioning system should NOT be switched on, as this will cause damage to the compressor. The safest option is to have the system discharged where the car is to be worked on, and not move the car until the system has been recharged. With air conditioning becoming an increasingly common fitment, mobile air conditioning specialists are becoming more widespread.*

Evaporator

Removal

1 Remove the heater matrix as described in Section 8.

2 Release the clips and detach the blower housing from the side of the evaporator housing **(see illustration)**.

3 Undo the retaining bolt, release the clips and lift off the evaporator housing cover **(see illustration)**.

4 Undo the retaining screws and remove the expansion valve **(see illustration)**. Renew the O-ring seal.

5 Remove the retaining plate and seal boot from the refrigerant pipes.

6 Lift the evaporator from the housing **(see illustration)**.

Refitting

7 Refitting is a reversal of removal, noting the following points:

a) *Renew the refrigerant circuit O-ring seals.*
b) *Apply a little refrigerant oil to the seals prior to reassembly.*

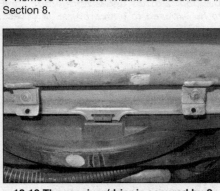

10.10 The receiver/drier is secured by 2 bolts on the underside

10.18 Squeeze together the clips to release the condenser

20 Lower the condenser and manoeuvre it from under the vehicle.

Refitting

21 Refitting is a reversal of removal, noting the following points:
a) Renew the refrigerant circuit O-ring seals.
b) Apply a little refrigerant oil to the seals prior to reassembly.
c) If a new condenser is to be fitted, renew the receiver/drier as described in this Section.
d) Upon completion, have the refrigerant circuit recharged and leak tested by a Mercedes Benz dealer or suitably equipped specialist.

Compressor

Removal

22 Raise the front of the vehicle and support it securely on axle stands (see 'Vehicle jacking and support'). Undo the fasteners and remove the engine undershield.
23 Disconnect the battery negative lead as described in Chapter 5A Section 4.
24 Remove the auxiliary drivebelt as described in Chapter 1 Section 6.
25 Undo the retaining bolt and disconnect the refrigerant line bracket from the oil filter housing.
26 Support the compressor (it is a heavy unit) and remove the mounting bolts. Depending on the exact type of compressor, and on the engine to which it is fitted, there will be either three or four mounting bolts. Lift the compressor and move it forward to access the refrigerant lines and wiring connector.
27 If the compressor is being removed as part of another procedure (such as engine removal), it is sufficient to remove the mounting bolts and tie the compressor up to one side without disconnecting the refrigerant lines. If the compressor is being removed completely, proceed as follows.
28 Unscrew the unions on the two pipes on the compressor, and disconnect them. Recover the O-ring seals – new ones must be used when refitting. Cover the pipe ends, to prevent the entry of foreign matter.

10.19 Condenser refrigerant pipe connection retaining nut

29 Disconnect the wiring plug from the top of the compressor.
30 It is advisable to cover the openings on the compressor while it is removed, to reduce oil loss and to prevent foreign matter from entering.

Refitting

31 Refitting is a reversal of removal, noting the following points:
a) Renew the refrigerant circuit O-ring seals.
b) Apply a little refrigerant oil to the seals prior to reassembly.
c) Upon completion, have the refrigerant circuit recharged and leak tested by a Mercedes Benz dealer or suitably equipped specialist.

Sunlight sensor

32 Open the bonnet, release the clips and remove the cover from the bonnet underside.
33 Disconnect the wiring plug, then unclip the sensor from the vent.
34 Refitting is a reversal of removal, noting that the arrow on the sensor must point in the direction of travel.

Expansion valve

Removal

35 Remove the wiper motor and linkage as described in Chapter 12 Section 14.
36 Undo the retaining nut and disconnect the refrigerant pipes from the bulkhead

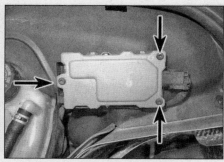

10.41 Multi-function sensor retaining bolts

connection (see illustration 8.28). Renew the O-ring seals. Plug the openings to prevent contamination.
37 Undo the 2 retaining bolts and remove the expansion valve (see illustration 10.4). Renew the O-ring seals. Plug the openings to prevent contamination.

Refitting

38 Refitting is a reversal of removal, noting the following points:
a) Renew the refrigerant circuit O-ring seals.
b) Apply a little refrigerant oil to the seals and valve retaining bolts prior to reassembly.
c) Have the refrigerant circuit recharged and leak tested by a Mercedes Benz dealer or suitably equipped specialist.

Multi-function sensor

39 On models with automatic air conditioning, the multi-function sensor records the ambient temperature, humidity, and pollution concentration, then transmits this information to the air conditioning control unit.
40 The multi-function sensor is located on the scuttle trim panel. Undo the fasteners and remove the cover (where fitted) over the fusebox in the right-hand corner of the engine compartment.
41 Undo the 3 bolts and remove the sensor (see illustration). Disconnect the wiring plug as the sensor is withdrawn.
42 Refitting is a reversal of removal.

Chapter 4 Part A
Fuel and exhaust systems

Contents

Degrees of difficulty

Easy, suitable for novice with little experience	Fairly easy, suitable for beginner with some experience	Fairly difficult, suitable for competent DIY mechanic	Difficult, suitable for experienced DIY mechanic	Very difficult, suitable for expert DIY or professional

Specifications

System type.. Direct injection common rail with high-pressure delivery pump and Electronic Diesel Control
Fuel injection pump pressure............................... upto 1600 bar
Turbocharger type .... Variable vane geometry

Torque wrench settings	Nm	lbf ft
Camshaft position sensor	11	8
Common rail:		
Mounting bolts..................................	14	10
Fuel return banjo bolt (in-line engines)	20	15
Crankshaft position sensor	8	6
Engine oil level dipstick guide tube	10	7
EGR pipe-to-exhaust collector (V6 engines):		
Stage 1......................................	10	7
Stage 2......................................	Angle-tighten a further 90°	
Exhaust manifold-to-cylinder head: *		
In-line engines	30	22
V6 engines	25	18
Exhaust collector (V6 engines)*:		
Stage 1......................................	20	15
Stage 2......................................	Angle-tighten a further 90°	
Exhaust collector support bracket-to-cylinder block (V6 engines)	20	15
Fuel injector clamp bolts*:		
Stage 1......................................	7	5
Stage 2......................................	Angle-tighten a further 90°	
Stage 3......................................	Angle-tighten a further 90°	
Fuel injection pump	15	10
Fuel pump drive gear (V6 engines).....................	70	52
Fuel tank level sensor/pump cover retaining rings.............	80	60
Fuel temperature sensor	23	17

Torque wrench settings (continued)

	Nm	lbf ft
Intake manifold:		
In-line engines	16	11
High-pressure fuel pipe unions:		
In-line engines:		
Stage 1	7	5
Stage 2	33	25
V6 engines:		
High pressure pump union nuts	33	25
Common fuel rail union nuts	27	19
Injector union nuts	33	25
Knock sensor	20	15
Rear crossmember-to-body	25	18
Steering shaft-to-pinion pinch bolt nut*	24	18
Throttle body bolts:		
In-line engines	10	7
V6 engines	5	3
Turbocharger-to-charge air manifold (V6 engines)	10	7
Turbocharger-to-exhaust collector (V6 engines):		
Stage 1	20	15
Stage 2	Angle-tighten a further 90°	
Turbocharger-to-exhaust manifold (In-line engines):		
Stage 1	20	15
Stage 2	Angle-tighten a further 90°	
Turbocharger-to-exhaust pipe (V6 engines)	20	15
Turbocharger oil feed banjo bolt (In-line engines):		
To-turbocharger	18	14
To-cylinder head	10	7
Turbocharger oil feed fitting V6 engines:		
To-cylinder block	20	15
To-turbocharger:		
Stage 1	20	15
Stage 2	Angle-tighten a further 60°	
Turbocharger oil return (in-line engines)	10	7
Turbocharger support bracket:		
In-line engines:		
To-turbocharger	30	22
To-cylinder block	20	15

*Do not re-use

1 General information and precautions

General information

1 The operation of the fuel injection system is described in more detail in Section 6.

2 Fuel is drawn from a tank under the rear of the vehicle, by a tank-mounted pump, through the pipework, and through fuel filter/water separator/heater into the high-pressure injection pump. The high-pressure injection pump is driven by timing chain end of the inlet camshaft (left-hand camshaft on V6 engines), and supplies very high pressure fuel to the common fuel rail, which is connected to each individual injector. The injectors are operated by solenoids controlled by the ECM, based on information supplied by various sensors. The multi-hole injectors are capable of multiple pre-, and post-injections per stroke. The engine ECM also controls the pre-heating side of the system – refer to Chapter 5B for more details.

3 The EDC (electronic diesel control) system fitted, incorporates a 'drive by wire' system, where the traditional accelerator cable is replaced by an accelerator pedal position sensor. The position and rate-of-change of the accelerator pedal is reported by the position sensor to the ECM, which then adjusts the fuel injectors to deliver the required amount of fuel, and optimum combustion efficiency.

4 Fuel level in the tank is determined by 2 level sensors – on each side of the saddle tank. The right-hand side sensor is fitted to in the in-tank pump module.

5 The exhaust system incorporates a turbocharger, EGR and on some models, a diesel particulate filter. Further detail of the emission control systems can be found in Chapter 4B.

Precautions

6 When working on diesel fuel system components, scrupulous cleanliness must be observed, and care must be taken not to introduce any foreign matter into fuel lines or components.

7 After carrying out any work involving disconnection of fuel lines, it is advisable to check the connections for leaks; pressurise the system by cranking the engine several times.

8 Electronic control units are very sensitive components, and certain precautions must be taken to avoid damage to these units as follows.

9 When carrying out welding operations on the vehicle using electric welding equipment, the battery and alternator should be disconnected.

10 Although the underbonnet-mounted modules will tolerate normal underbonnet conditions, they can be adversely affected by excess heat or moisture. If using welding equipment or pressure-washing equipment in the vicinity of an electronic module, take care not to direct heat, or jets of water or steam, at the module. If this cannot be avoided, remove the module from the vehicle, and protect its wiring plug with a plastic bag.

11 Before disconnecting any wiring, or removing components, always ensure that the ignition is switched off.

12 Do not attempt to improvise ECM fault diagnosis procedures using a test lamp or multi-meter, as irreparable damage could be caused to the module.

13 After working on fuel injection/engine management system components, ensure that all wiring is correctly reconnected before reconnecting the battery or switching on the ignition.

2 Air cleaner assembly – removal and refitting

Removal

In-line engines

1 Undo the fasteners and remove the plastic cover on the top of the engine (see illustration).

2 Remove the intake hose upstream of the air filter housing (see illustration).

3 Where applicable, disconnect the breather hose from the oil separator on the cylinder head cover.

4 Disconnect the wiring plugs from the breather hose heater element (where fitted), hot film mass air flow sensor, and air pressure sensor (see illustration).

5 Release the clamps and remove the air outlet pipe from the air filter housing (see illustration).

6 Pull the air filter housing upwards from its rubber mountings (see illustration).

V6-engines

7 Pull the plastic cover on the top of the engine upwards from its rubber mountings (see illustration).

8 Disconnect the wiring plug from the air pressure sensor on the left-hand air filter housing (see illustration).

9 Remove the air intake ducts upstream of the air filter housings (see illustration).

10 Disconnect the mass airflow sensors, release the clamps securing the air duct downstream of the air filter housings (see illustration).

11 Undo the 2 bolts securing each air filter

2.1 Engine cover retaining screws

2.2 Unclip the air intake hose

2.4 Mass airflow sensor and air pressure sensor wiring plugs

2.5 Release the clamp and disconnect the air outlet pipe

2.6 Note the locating lug at the rear of the air filter housing

2.7 Pull the engine cover upwards from its' mountings

2.8 Disconnect the wiring plug from the pressure sensor on the left-hand filter housing

2.9 Unclip the air intake duct each side

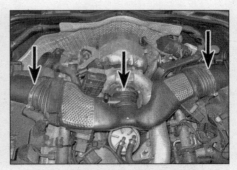
2.10 Release the clamps securing the downstream air duct

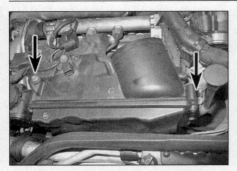

2.11 Each air filter housing is secured by a bolt at the front and rear

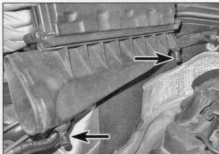

2.12 Note the locating lugs at the base of the housing

9 Release the fasteners and remove both sections of the rear underfloor panelling.
10 Remove the complete exhaust system as described in Section 19.
11 Undo the fasteners and remove the heatshields above the exhaust system location.
12 Remove the propeller shaft as described in Chapter 8 Section 7.
13 Release the fasteners and remove the heatshield from beneath the fuel tank.
14 With reference to Chapter 9 Section 16, unhook the parking brake cables from the automatic slack adjuster.
15 Release the clamp securing the filler hose to the fuel tank (see illustration).
16 Release the clamps and detach the fuel feed and return pipes at the front of the tank (see illustration). Plug the openings to prevent contamination. Be prepared for fuel spillage.
17 Support the fuel tank with a suitable jack. Use a sheet of plywood (or similar) interposed between the jack head and tank to prevent damage.
18 Undo the bolts and detach the fuel tank retaining straps (see illustration).
19 With the help of an assistant, lower the fuel tank slightly, then disconnect the tank breather hose(s) as they become accessible.
20 Lower the tank completely, and manoeuvre it from under the vehicle.

Refitting

21 Refitting is a reversal of removal.

housing to the cylinder head covers (see illustration).
12 Pull the air filter upwards from its mountings, detaching it from the air outlet duct as it's withdrawn (see illustration).

Refitting

13 Refitting is a reversal of removal.

3 Fuel tank – removal and refitting

Removal

1 The fuel tank must be emptied before the operation can be started. This is best

achieved by waiting until the tank is almost empty through the course of normal driving.
2 Raise the rear of the vehicle and support it securely on axle stands (see 'Vehicle jacking and support').
3 Disconnect the battery negative lead as described in Chapter 5A Section 4.
4 Remove the rear seat cushion as described in Chapter 11 Section 30.
5 Fold back the insulation, undo the screws and remove the left-hand access cover above the fuel tank (see illustration 4.2).
6 Disconnect the wiring plug from the left-hand sensor cover.
7 Undo the fuel tank centre mounting nut, between the access covers (see illustration).
8 Undo the bolts and remove the crossmember beneath the propeller shaft.

4 Fuel level sensors/pump – removal and refitting

Removal

1 Remove the rear seat cushion as described in Chapter 11 Section 30.
2 Fold back the insulation material, undo the retaining screws and remove both the left- and right-hand tank access covers (see illustration).
3 Note their fitted positions, then disconnect

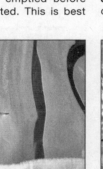

3.7 Undo the mounting nut between the access covers, under the rear seat cushion

3.15 Slacken the clamp and disconnect the fuel filler hose

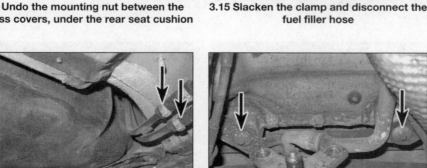

3.16 Fuel feed/return hose connections, and tank retaining strap outer bolt

3.18 Fuel tank retaining straps centre bolts

4.2 Undo the fasteners and remove both access covers

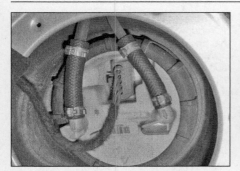

4.3 Disconnect the hoses and wiring plug from the left-hand cover

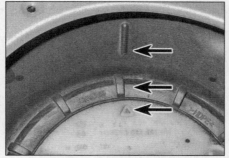

4.4a Make alignment marks between the cover, ring and tank...

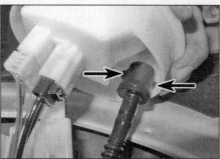

4.4b...then slacken and remove the retaining ring – note that the ring maybe very tight!

the wiring plug and hoses from the left-hand sensor/pump cover **(see illustration)**.

4 The retaining rings must now be loosened and removed. To do this, Mercedes-Benz technicians use a special tool, which engages the holes in the ring **(see illustrations)**. Alternative after-market fuel tank cap removal tools are readily available. Make alignment marks between the cover, retaining ring and tank to aid reassembly.

5 Lift the left-hand sensor cover, and disconnect the wiring plugs and fuel pipe from the underside **(see illustration)**.

6 Prise down the retaining tab, and pull the fuel pipe connection from the base of the unit **(see illustrations)**.

7 Release the retaining clip and detach the level sensor from the assembly **(see illustration)**.

8 Lift the right-hand sensor/pump cover, and withdraw the sensor/pump from the tank **(see illustration)**. Note the alignment marks on the cover and tank.

9 If required, the resistance of the fuel level sensor can be checked using a multi-meter. On full deflection (full tank) we recorded approximately 50 ohms, and on zero deflection (empty tank) we recorded approximately 870 ohms **(see illustration)**. If the resistance of the sensor(s) varies significantly from these measurements, it may be faulty.

Refitting

10 Refitting is a reversal of removal, noting the following points:

a) *Renew the sensor/pump cover seals* **(see illustration)**.

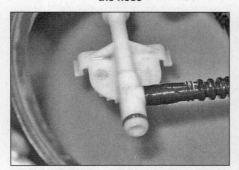

4.5 Disconnect the wiring plugs, then squeeze together the clips and disconnect the hose

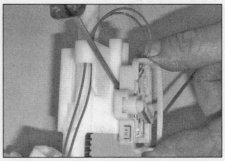

4.6a Prise down the tab...

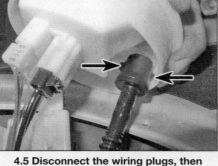

4.6b...and slide the pipe connection from place

b) *Tighten the retaining rings to their specified torque.*

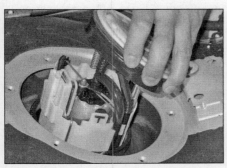

4.7 Use a small screwdriver to release the sensor retaining clip

c) *Align the marks between the covers and the tank.*

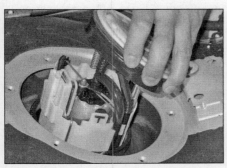

4.8 Lift the sensor/pump from the right-hand fuel tank aperture

4.9 Measure the fuel tank level sensor resistance with a multi-meter

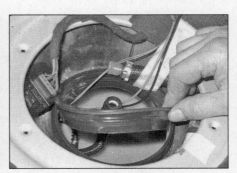

4.10 Renew the cover seals

5 Accelerator pedal – removal and refitting

Removal

1 Prise up the plastic cap, undo the retaining nut and pull the accelerator pedal assembly upwards from place **(see illustration)**. Disconnect the wiring plug as the assemby is withdrawn.

Refitting

2 Refitting is a reversal of removal.

6 Fuel injection system – general information

1 The system is under the overall control of the Common rail Diesel Injection (CDI) system, which also controls the pre-heating system (see Chapter 5B).
2 Fuel is supplied from the rear-mounted fuel tank, via an electrically powered lift pump, and fuel filter, to the fuel injection pump. The fuel injection pump supplies fuel under high pressure to the common fuel rail. The fuel rail provides a reservoir of fuel under pressure ready for the injectors to deliver direct to the combustion chamber. The individual fuel injectors incorporate solenoids, which when operated, allow the high pressure fuel to be injected. The solenoids are controlled by the ECM. The fuel injection pump purely provides high pressure fuel. The timing and duration of the injection is controlled by the ECM based, on the information received from the various sensors. In order to increase combustion efficiency and reduce combustion noise (diesel 'knock'), a small amount of fuel can be injected before, and after the main injection takes place – this is known as Pre-, Pilot-, or Post-injection.
3 Additionally, the control module activates the pre-heating system, and the exhaust gas recirculation (EGR) system (see Chapter 5B).
4 The system uses the following sensors:
a) *Crankshaft sensor – informs the ECM of the crankshaft speed and position.*
b) *Coolant temperature sensor – informs the ECM of engine temperature.*
c) *Mass airflow sensor(s) – informs the*

ECM of the mass and temperature of air entering the intake tract.
d) *Air intake sensor(s) - informs the ECM of the intake air temperature.*
e) *Wheel speed sensors – informs the ECM of the vehicle speed.*
f) *Accelerator pedal position sensor - informs the ECM of throttle position, and the rate of throttle opening/closing.*
g) *Fuel high-pressure sensor – informs the ECM of the pressure of the fuel in the common rail.*
h) *Manifold absolute pressure sensor – informs the ECM of the pressure in the intake manifold.*
i) *Fuel temperature sensor – informs the ECM of the fuel supply temperature.*
j) *Camshaft position sensor(s) – informs the ECM of the camshaft position so that the engine firing sequence can be established.*
k) *Stop-light switch – informs the ECM when the brakes are being applied.*
l) *Exhaust gas temperature sensor – informs the ECM of the temperature of the exhaust gases.*
m) *Exhaust gas pressure sensor – informs the ECM of the back pressure in the exhaust system.*
n) *O2 sensors - informs the ECM of the oxygen content in the exhaust gases - fitted upstream, and downstream of the catalytic converter.*
5 On all models, a "drive-by-wire" throttle control system is used. No traditional cable is fitted, instead an accelerator pedal position sensor informs the ECM of the pedal position and rate of change.
6 The signals from the various sensors are processed by the ECM, and the optimum fuel quantity and injection timing settings are selected for the prevailing engine operating conditions.
7 A catalytic converter and an exhaust gas recirculation (EGR), and on some models, a diesel particulate filter system is fitted, to reduce harmful exhaust gas emissions. Details of this and other emissions control system equipment are given in Chapter 4B.
8 If there is an abnormality in any of the readings obtained from any sensor, the ECM enters its back-up mode. In this event, the ECM ignores the abnormal sensor signal, and assumes a pre-programmed value which will

allow the engine to continue running (albeit at reduced efficiency). If the ECM enters this back-up mode, the warning light on the instrument panel will come on, and the relevant fault code will be stored in the ECM memory.
9 If the warning light comes on, the vehicle should be taken to a Mercedes dealer or specialist at the earliest opportunity. A complete test of the CDI system can then be carried out, using a special electronic test unit which is simply plugged into the system's diagnostic connector **(see illustration)**. The connector is located under the driver's side of the facia.

7 Fuel system – priming and bleeding

1 The fuel system fitted to the diesel engines in the range, is designed to be self-priming. After disturbing an element of the fuel system, operate the starter and attempt to start the engine. Only operate the starter for a maximum of 10 seconds at a time to prevent overheating. It may take several attempts before the engine starts.

8 Fuel pipes and fittings – general information and disconnection

1 Disconnect the cable from the negative battery terminal (see Chapter 5A Section 4) before proceeding.
2 The fuel supply pipe connects the fuel pump in the fuel tank to the fuel filter on the engine.
3 Whenever you're working under the vehicle, be sure to inspect all fuel and evaporative emission pipes for leaks, kinks, dents and other damage. Always replace a damaged fuel pipe immediately.
4 If you find signs of dirt in the pipes during disassembly, disconnect all pipes and blow them out with compressed air. Inspect the fuel strainer on the fuel pump pick-up unit for damage and deterioration.

Steel tubing

5 It is critical that the fuel pipes be replaced with pipes of equivalent type and specification.
6 Some steel fuel pipes have threaded fittings. When loosening these fittings, hold the stationary fitting with a spanner while turning the union nut.

Plastic tubing

⚠ *Warning: When removing or installing plastic fuel tubing, be careful not to bend or twist it too much, which can damage it. Also, plastic fuel tubing is NOT heat resistant, so keep it away from excessive heat.*

7 When replacing fuel system plastic tubing, use only original equipment replacement plastic tubing.

Flexible hoses

8 When replacing fuel system flexible hoses,

5.1 Prise up the cap and undo the accelerator pedal retaining nut

6.9 Pull down the flap to access the 16-pin diagnostic plug

use original equipment replacements, or hose to the same specification.

9 Don't route fuel hoses (or metal pipes) within 100 mm of the exhaust system or within 280 mm of the catalytic converter. Make sure that no rubber hoses are installed directly against the vehicle, particularly in places where there is any vibration. If allowed to touch some vibrating part of the vehicle, a hose can easily become chafed and it might start leaking. A good rule of thumb is to maintain a minimum of 8.0 mm clearance around a hose (or metal pipe) to prevent contact with the vehicle underbody.

Disconnecting Fuel pipe Fittings

10 Typical fuel pipe fittings:

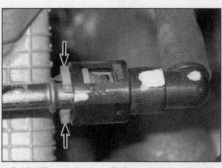

8.10a Two-tab type fitting; depress both tabs with your fingers, then pull the fuel pipe and the fitting apart

8.10b On this type of fitting, depress the two buttons on opposite sides of the fitting, then pull it off the fuel pipe

8.10c Threaded fuel pipe fitting; hold the stationary portion of the pipe or component (A) while loosening the union nut (B) with a flare-nut spanner

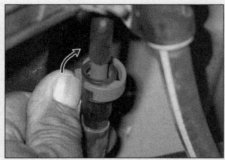

8.10d Plastic collar-type fitting; rotate the outer part of the fitting

8.10e Metal collar quick-connect fitting; pull the end of the retainer off the fuel pipe and disengage the other end from the female side of the fitting...

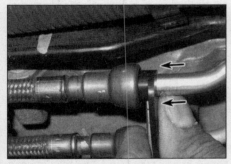

8.10f... insert a fuel pipe separator tool into the female side of the fitting, push it into the fitting and pull the fuel pipe off the pipe

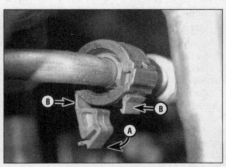

8.10g Some fittings are secured by lock tabs. Release the lock tab (A) and rotate it to the fully-opened position, squeeze the two smaller lock tabs (B)...

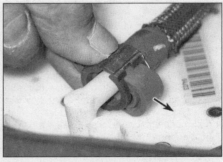

8.10h... then push the retainer out and pull the fuel pipe off the pipe

8.10i Spring-lock coupling; remove the safety cover, install a coupling release tool and close the tool around the coupling...

8.10j... push the tool into the fitting, then pull the two pipes apart

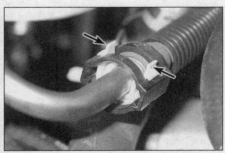

8.10k Hairpin clip type fitting: push the legs of the retainer clip together, then push the clip down all the way until it stops and pull the fuel pipe off the pipe

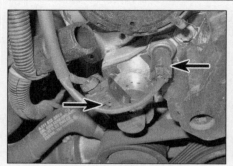

10.4 Disconnect the fuel temperature sensor and quantity control valve wiring plugs

10.6 Fuel pump retaining bolts and high-pressure fuel pipe union

10.10 Undo the high-pressure pipe union at the pump

9 Fuel injection system – testing and adjustment

Testing

1 If a fault appears in the fuel injection system, first ensure that all the system wiring connectors are securely connected and free from corrosion. Ensure that the fault is not due to poor maintenance; ie, check that the air cleaner filter element is clean, that the cylinder compression pressures are correct (see Chapter 2A Section 2 or Chapter 2B Section 2), and that the engine breather hoses are clear and undamaged (see Chapter 4B).

2 If the engine will not start, check the condition of the glow plugs (see Chapter 5B Section 2).

3 If these checks fail to reveal the cause of the problem, the vehicle should be taken to a Mercedes Benz dealer or specialist for testing using special electronic equipment which is plugged into the diagnostic connector (see Section 6). The tester should locate the fault quickly and simply, avoiding the need to test all the system components individually, which is time-consuming, and also carries a risk of damaging the ECM.

Adjustment

4 The engine idle speed, and maximum speed are all controlled by the ECM. Whilst in

theory it is possible to check the settings, if they are found to be in need of adjustment, the car will have to be taken to a suitably-equipped Mercedes Benz dealer or specialist. They will have access to the necessary diagnostic equipment required to test and (where possible) adjust the settings.

10 Fuel injection pump – removal and refitting

⚠️ **Warning: Observe the precautions in Section 1 before working on any component in the fuel system.**

Removal

1 Remove the plastic cover from the top of the engine.

In-line engines

2 To improve access remove the cooling fan shroud as described in Chapter 3 Section 6.

3 Undo the bolts and remove the heatshield (where fitted) adjacent to the injection pump.

4 Disconnect the wiring plugs from the fuel temperature sensor and the quantity control valve (see illustration).

5 Release the clamp and disconnect the fuel supply/return hoses from left-hand side of the pump. Be prepared for fuel spillage. Plug the openings to prevent contamination.

6 Remove the support bracket bolt, then undo the unions securing the high-pressure

fuel pipe to the pump and the common rail (see illustration). Take care not to bend or squeeze the pipe. Plug the openings to prevent contamination.

7 Undo the 3 retaining bolts, and remove the high-pressure fuel pump from the front of the cylinder head. As the pump is removed, retrieve the drivegear from the end of the shaft.

8 Recover the O-ring seal from the rear of the injection pump and discard it – a new one must be used on refitting.

9 Mercedes Benz insist that no further dismantling of the pump is to be carried out. If a fault is suspected, have the pump inspected by a Mercedes Benz dealer or specialist.

V6 engines

10 Using a second spanner to counterhold, undo the union nut securing the high-pressure fuel pipe to the pump (see illustration). Be prepared for fuel spillage. Plug the openings as they become accessible.

11 Disconnect the remaining fuel hose(s) from the pump (see illustration). Plug the openings to prevent contamination. Be prepared for fuel spillage.

12 Disconnect the wiring plugs from the fuel quantity control valve, and fuel temperature sensor (see illustration).

13 Undo the 3 retaining bolts and detach the high-pressure pump from the cylinder head (see illustration). Note that the retaining bolts and the O-ring seal must be renewed.

10.11 Disconnect the fuel feed and return hoses from the pump

10.12 Disconnect the fuel quantity control valve and temperature sensor wiring plugs

10.13 Fuel pump retaining bolts

11.2 Undo the unions of the common rail-to-injector pipes

11.4a Prise out the clips...

14 With the exception of drive gear removal, Mercedes Benz insist that no further dismantling of the pump is to be carried out. If a fault is suspected, have the pump inspected by a Mercedes Benz dealer or specialist.

Refitting

15 Refitting is a reversal of removal, noting the following points:
a) *Ensure the mating surfaces of the pump and cylinder head are clean.*
b) *Apply a little clean engine oil to the new pump O-ring seal prior to refitting.*
c) *All high-pressure fuel pipes must be fitted 'without tension'.*
d) *Tighten all fasteners to their specified torque, where given.*
e) *Upon completion, switch the ignition on for at least 15 seconds to circulate fuel through the pump. Failure to do so may damage the pump.*

11 Fuel injectors – removal and refitting

⚠ *Warning: Exercise extreme caution when working on the fuel injectors. Never expose the hands or any part of the body to injector spray, as the high working pressure can cause the fuel to penetrate the skin, with possibly fatal results. You are strongly advised to have any work which involves testing the*

injectors under pressure carried out by a dealer or fuel injection specialist. Refer to the precautions given in Section 1 of this Chapter before proceeding. **Note:** *Take care not to allow dirt into the fuel rail, injectors or fuel pipes during this procedure. Keep the fuel pipes and injectors identified for position to ensure correct refitting. As the fuel pipes are removed, plug the ends of the pipes, injectors and fuel rail to prevent dirt ingress.*

Removal

In-line engines

1 Undo the fasteners and remove the plastic cover from the top of the engine.
2 Using a second spanner to counterhold, undo the unions securing the high-pressure fuel pipes to the injectors and common fuel rail **(see illustration)**.
3 Undo any nuts/bolts securing the pipe retaining brackets and manoeuvre the pipes from place. Take care not to bend or squeeze the pipes. Plug all openings to prevent contamination.
4 Release the catches and disconnect the fuel return hoses from the top of each injector **(see illustrations)**.
5 Squeeze together the retaining clips and disconnect the wiring plugs from each injector.
6 Slacken and remove the injector clamp mounting bracket retaining bolts from between the injectors **(see illustrations)**. Discard the mounting bolts, as new ones will be required when refitting.

11.4b...and pull the return pipes upwards

7 If required use a slide hammer/puller to withdraw the injectors from the cylinder head, making sure it is in the vertical position **(see illustration)**. Recover the sealing rings/washers and discard. New ones must be used for refitting. **Note:** If the injectors are to be refitted, it's essential that they're refitted to their original locations. Mark the injectors with permanent marker (or similar) to indicate the cylinder number.

V6 engines

8 Remove the air cleaner housing as described in Section 2.
9 Release the clamps and remove the air intake duct downstream of the air filter.
10 Remove the soundproofing material above the injectors.
11 Pull the retaining clips upwards and disconnect the fuel return hoses from the

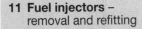

11.6a Undo the retaining bolts...

11.6b...and remove the clamp brackets

11.7 Withdraw each injector from the cylinder head

11.11a Pull the retaining collars upwards...

11.11b...and disconnect the fuel return hoses

11.12 Remove the wiring harness bracket

top of the injectors **(see illustrations)**. Be prepared for fuel spillage. Plug the openings to prevent contamination.

12 Undo the bolt securing the wiring harness bracket (where applicable) **(see illustration)**.

13 Undo the union nuts and remove the high-pressure fuel injection pipes between the common fuel rail and the injectors. Take care not to bend or squeeze the pipes. Plug all openings as they become accessible. Mark the pipes with paint (or similar) to indicate their fitted positions.

14 Disconnect the wiring plugs from the top of each injector **(see illustration)**.

15 Slacken and remove the injector clamp mounting bracket retaining bolts from each injector **(see illustration)**. Discard the mounting bolts, as new ones will be required when refitting.

16 If required use a slide hammer/puller

11.14 Depress the catch and pull the wiring plug from the injector

11.16 Withdrawn the injector from the cylinder head

to withdraw the injectors from the cylinder head, making sure it is in the vertical position **(see illustration)**. Recover the sealing rings/ washers and discard. New ones must be used for refitting. Note: If the injectors are to be refitted, it's essential that they're refitted to their original locations. Mark the injectors with permanent marker (or similar) to indicate the cylinder number.

Refitting

17 Thoroughly clean the injectors and their locating holes in the cylinder head. Use a bottle brush (or similar) and and vacuum cleaner to remove all traces of carbon/debris from the area.

18 Renew the sealing washers at the base of each injector **(see illustration)**.

19 Apply special grease (Mercedes No. A 001 898 42 51 10) to the injector bodies to prevent them seizing in place.

11.15 Remove the injector clamp retaining bolt

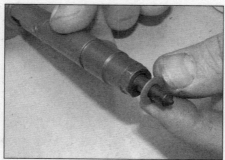

11.18 Renew the injector sealing washers

20 Make a note of any numbers on the injectors. If new injectors are being fitted, a control unit adaption must be carried out using Mercedes Benz diagnostic equipment (or equivalent). These numbers will be needed during the adaption process.

21 Fit the injectors in to the holes in the cylinder heads. If the original injectors are being refitted, they must be fitted into their original locations.

22 Refit the retaining brackets and tighten the new retaining bolts to their specified torque.

23 The remainder of refitting is a reversal of removal, noting the following points:

a) *Tighten all fasteners to their specified torque where given.*

b) *When refitting the high-pressure fuel pipes, slacken the common rail mounting bolts prior to tightening the pipe union nuts. The pipes must be fitted 'without tension'.*

c) *If new injectors have been fitted, carry out the control unit adaption using Mercedes Benz diagnostic equipment (or similar). Entrust this task to a dealer or suitably equipped specialist.*

d)

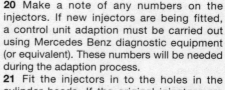

12 Common fuel rail – removal and refitting

Removal

1 Remove the plastic cover from the top of the engine.

In-line engines

2 Using a second spanner to counterhold, undo the unions securing the high-pressure fuel pipes to the injectors and common fuel rail, and from the common rail to the injection pump.

3 Undo the retaining bolts and detach the wiring harness cable duct.

4 Release the cable ties, and disconnect the wiring plugs from the common rail pressure sensor and pressure regulator valve.

5 Remove the exhaust back pressure sensor as described in Section 13.

6 Undo the retaining bolts and withdraw

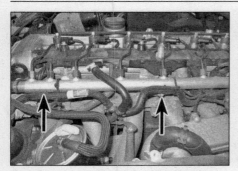

12.6 Common rail retaining bolt locations – in-line engines

12.14 Common rail mounting bolts – V6 engines

12.15 Disconnect the fuel return hose from the left-hand common rail

the fuel rail from the top of the engine **(see illustration)**.

V6 engines

7 Remove the air filter housing as described in Section 2.

8 Release the clamps and remove the air intake duct downstream of the air filter.

9 Undo the retaining nut/bolt, and remove the turbocharger air outlet metal pipe.

10 Remove the soundproofing material above the injectors.

11 Pull the retaining clips upwards and disconnect the fuel return hoses from the top of the injectors **(see illustrations 11.11a and 11.11b)**. Be prepared for fuel spillage. Plug the openings to prevent contamination.

12 Undo the bolt securing the wiring harness bracket **(see illustration 11.12)**.

13 Undo the union nuts and remove the high-pressure fuel injection pipes between the common fuel rail and the injectors. Take care not to bend or squeeze the pipes. Plug all openings as they become accessible. Mark the pipes with paint (or similar) to indicate their fitted positions.

14 Slacken the common rail mounting bolts, then undo the union securing the high-pressure pipe from the pump to the rail, and the unions securing the pipe between the common rails **(see illustration)**.

15 If removing the left-hand common rail, release the clamp securing the fuel return hose to the common rail **(see illustration)**.

16 Disconnect any wiring plugs from the common rail.

17 Completely remove the mounting bolts, and withdraw the common rail(s). Disconnect the fuel return hose as the common rail is removed (where applicable).

Refitting

18 Refitting is a reversal of removal, noting the following points:

a) *Examine the condition of the rigid, high-pressure fuel pipes. If they show any sign of wear or damage, particularly at the tapered seats at each end, renew them. It may be prudent to renew them regardless of condition.*

b) *Tighten all fasteners to their specified torque where given.*

c) *Check the fuel system for leaks prior to refitting the engine cover.*

---

13 Engine management control system components – removal and refitting

1 Disconnect the battery negative lead, as described in Chapter 5A Section 4, then wait at least 5 minutes for any residual electrical energy to dissipate.

Crankshaft sensor

2 Remove the plastic cover from the top of the engine.

3 Raise the front of the vehicle and support it securely on axle stands (see *'Vehicle jacking and support'*). Release the fasteners

and remove the engine undershield **(see illustration)**.

4 The sensor if fitted to the left-hand side of the cylinder block, adjacent to the transmission bell housing, above the starter motor. Where fitted, undo the bolt and remove the sensor heatshield.

5 Disconnect the sensor wiring plug **(see illustration)**.

6 Undo the retaining bolt and withdraw the sensor.

7 Refitting is a reversal of removal, tightening the sensor retaining bolt to the specified torque.

Coolant temperature sensor

8 Removal of the sensor is described in Chapter 3 Section 7.

Accelerator pedal position sensor

9 The sensor is integral with the accelerator pedal assembly, see Section 5.

Mass airflow/Intake air temperature sensor

10 Remove the plastic cover from the top of the engine.

In-line engines

11 Remove the air cleaner housing as described in Section 2.

12 Undo the fasteners and detach the mass airflow/intake temperature sensor from the air cleaner housing **(see illustration)**.

13 Refitting is a reversal of removal.

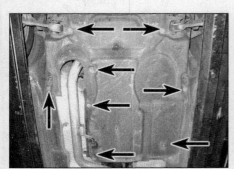

13.3 Engine/transmission undershield fasteners

13.5 Crankshaft position sensor wiring plug

13.12 Mass air flow sensor/intake air temperature sensor – in-line engines

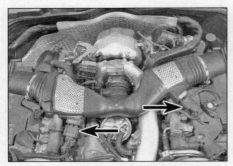

13.15 Disconnect the mass air flow sensors' wiring plugs

13.16 Breather hose heating element wiring plug

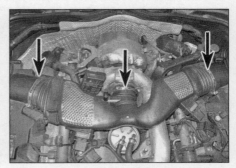

13.18 Air duct securing clamps

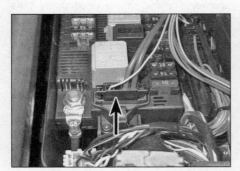

13.24 Disconnect the wiring plug at the front of the SAM unit and move the harness to one side

13.25 As the locking catches are slid out, the wiring plugs will disconnect

V6 engines

14 Remove the right-hand side air filter housing as described in Section 2.

15 Disconnect the wiring plugs from the left-, and right-hand side mass air flow sensors **(see illustration)**.

16 Disconnect the wiring plug from the breather hose heating element **(see illustration)**.

17 Disconnect the breather hose from the oil separator.

18 Slacken the clamp securing the air duct to the turbocharger **(see illustration)**.

19 Slacken the clamp securing outlet ducting to the left-hand air filter housing, then manoeuvre the ducting from place.

20 Note that the mass airflow sensors and the integral air intake temperature sensors can

only be replaced complete with the air outlet ducting.

21 Refitting is a reversal of removal.

Stop-light switch

22 The engine control module receives a signal from the stop-light switch which indicates when the brakes are being applied. Stop-light switch removal and refitting details can be found in Chapter 9 Section 18.

Engine electronic control module (ECM)

Caution: Electronic Control Units (ECMs) contain components that are sensitive to the levels of static electricity generated by a person during normal activity. Once the multiway harness connector has been unplugged, the exposed ECM connector

pins can freely conduct stray static electricity to these components, damaging or even destroying them – the damage will be invisible and may not manifest itself immediately. Expensive repairs can be avoided by observing the following basic handling rules:

a) *Handle a disconnected ECM by its case only; do not allow fingers or tools to come into contact with the pins.*

b) *When carrying an ECM, earth yourself from time to time, by touching a metal object such as an unpainted water pipe, this will discharge any potentially damaging static that may have built-up.*

c) *Do not leave the ECM unplugged from its connector for any longer than is absolutely necessary.*

Note: *If the ECM is to be renewed, prior to removal, Mercedes Benz diagnostic equipment (or equivalent) must be connected to the diagnostic plug and the stored data in the ECM retrieved. This information is essential for correctly programming the replacement ECM. Entrust this task to a Mercedes dealer or suitably equipped specialist.*

In-line engines

23 Remove the cover from the fusebox on the right-hand side of the engine compartment.

24 Disconnect the wiring plug from the front of the SAM **(see illustration)**.

25 Release the wiring harness cable ties, then unlock and disconnect the wiring plugs from the ECM **(see illustration)**.

26 Undo the retaining clips and remove the ECM **(see illustration)**.

27 Refitting is a reversal of removal. Note that if a new ECM has been fitted, it must be configured/programmed using Mercedes diagnostic equipment (or equivalent).

V6 engines

28 Remove the fuse/relay box cover in the engine compartment.

29 Unlock and disconnect the wiring plugs from the ECM **(see illustration)**.

30 Release the retaining clips and slide the ECM from place **(see illustration 13.26)**.

31 Refitting is a reversal of removal. Note that if a new ECM has been fitted, it must

13.26 Release the clip at each end, and slide the ECM upwards from place

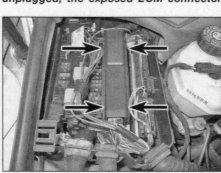

13.29 Slide out the catches to disconnect the wiring plugs

13.33 Fuel temperature sensor

13.36a MAP sensor – in-line engines...

13.36b...and V6 engines

be configured/programmed using Mercedes diagnostic equipment (or equivalent).

Fuel temperature sensor

32 Remove the plastic cover from the top of the engine.
33 The fuel temperature sensor is located on the injection pump. Disconnect the sensor wiring plug **(see illustration)**.
34 Ensure that the area around the sensor is scrupulously clean, then unscrew the sensor from the pump. Renew the sealing ring.
35 Refitting is a reversal of removal, tightening the sensor to the specified torque.

Manifold absolute pressure sensor

36 The MAP sensor is fitted to the air filter outlet ducting **(see illustrations)**.
37 Disconnect the sensor wiring plug, undo the fasteners and remove the sensor. Renew any sealing ring.
38 Refitting is a reversal of removal.

Boost pressure sensor

In-line engines

39 The boost pressure sensor is located under the fuel filter. Remove the filter as described in Chapter 1 Section 25. Note there is no need to disconnect the hoses from the filter.
40 Disconnect the sensor wiring plug, undo the retaining screws and remove the sensor. Renew any sealing ring.
41 Refitting is a reversal of removal.

V6 engines

42 Remove the plastic cover from the top of the engine.
43 The boost pressure sensor is fitted to the intake manifold, adjacent to the throttle body **(see illustration)**.
44 Disconnect the boost pressure sensor wiring plug.
45 Undo the retaining screws, and remove the boost pressure sensor. Renew the O-ring seal.
46 Refitting is a reversal of removal.

Camshaft position sensor

47 Remove the plastic cover from the top of the engine.
48 Disconnect the camshaft position sensor wiring plug **(see illustrations)**.
49 Undo the retaining bolt and withdrawn the sensor from place. Renew the sensor sealing ring.
50 Refitting is a reversal of removal, tightening the sensor retaining bolt to the specified torque.
51 Refit the engine top cover.

Knock sensor

In-line engines only

52 The knock sensor is located on the right-hand side of the cylinder block. Raise the front of the vehicle and support it securely on axle stands (see 'Vehicle jacking and support'). Undo the fasteners and remove the engine undershield.
53 Ensure the steering wheel and front

wheels are in the 'straight-ahead' position, then undo the pinch bolt/nut, pull the steering shaft from the steering rack pinion, and move it to one side. Renew the self-locking nut. Ensure that the steering wheel/road wheel remains unaltered until reassembled.
54 Disconnect the wiring plug, undo the retaining bolt and withdraw the knock sensor.
55 Refitting is a reversal of removal. It's essential that the sensor retaining bolt is tightened to the specified torque.

14 Throttle body – removal and refitting

Removal

In-line engines

1 Remove the plastic cover from the top of the engine.
2 Raise the front of the vehicle and support it securely on axle stands (see 'Vehicle jacking and support'). Release the fasteners and remove the engine undershield.
3 Undo the top bolt, slacken the lower bolt and move the top of the engine oil level dipstick guide tube to one side.
4 Undo the 3 retaining bolts, release the fuel pipes (no need to disconnect) and position the support brace to one side.
5 Release the clamps and disconnect the EGR pipe from the throttle body.
6 Remove the fuel filter as described in Chapter 1 Section 25.

13.43 Boost pressure sensor

13.48a On in-line engines, the sensor is at the rear of the cylinder head cover

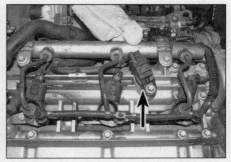

13.48b On V6 engines, the sensor is on the left-hand cylinder head cover

14.14 Prise out the air ducting clip

14.18 Remove the throttle body-to-cylinder head bracket

14.20a Remove the bracket above the mixing chamber

14.20b Unbolt the EGR pipe

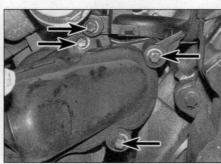

14.20c Mixing chamber retaining bolts

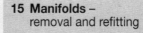

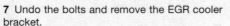

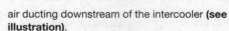

7 Undo the bolts and remove the EGR cooler bracket.

8 Disconnect the boost pressure sensor from beneath the fuel filter location.

9 Undo the 5 retaining bolts and manoeuvre the intake manifold upwards from place. Renew the seals.

10 Disconnect the throttle valve actuator wiring plug.

11 Undo the 4 retaining bolts and remove the throttle body. Renew the throttle body seals.

V6 engines

12 Remove the plastic cover on the top of the engine.

13 Undo the 3 retaining bolts and remove the noise damper from above the throttle body. Check the condition of the sealing ring and replace if necessary.

14 Prise out the clips and remove the charge

air ducting downstream of the intercooler (**see illustration**).

15 Remove the right-hand air filter housing as described in Section 2.

16 Remove the right-hand exhaust manifold shield.

17 Disconnect the throttle valve wiring plug.

18 Remove the bracket between the throttle body and the cylinder head (**see illustration**).

19 Undo the bolts and remove the throttle body. Renew the gasket.

20 To remove the mixing chamber, undo the bolts securing the EGR pipe, remove the bolt securing the bracket above the chamber to the cylinder head, then undo the retaining bolts and manoeuvre the chamber from position (**see illustrations**), Disconnect any wiring plugs as the assembly is withdrawn. Renew the gaskets/seals as necessary.

Refitting

21 Refitting is a reversal of removal, tightening the fasteners to their specified torque where given.

15 Manifolds –
removal and refitting

Intake manifold

1 Disconnect the battery negative lead as described in Chapter 5A Section 4.

2 Remove the plastic cover from the top of the engine.

3 Drain the cooling system as described in Chapter 1 Section 30.

In-line engines

4 Remove the common fuel rail as described in Section 12.

5 Remove the fuel filter as described in Chapter 1 Section 25, then undo the bolts and remove the filter bracket.

6 Undo the upper bolt, slacken the lower bolt and move the top of the engine oil level dipstick guide tube to one side.

7 Undo the bolts and move the EGR cooler support bracket to one side (**see illustration**).

8 Release the clamps and disconnect the coolant hoses from the EGR cooler (**see illustration**).

9 Undo the retaining bolts and remove the EGR cooler. Renew the gasket.

10 Release the clamps and remove the EGR pipe.

11 Remove the mixing chamber.

12 Undo the bolt and disconnect the EGR pipe from the cylinder head.

13 Working under the vehicle, disconnect the wiring plugs from the glow plug output stage (where applicable).

14 Undo the retaining bolts and remove the glow plug output stage.

15 Check to ensure all wiring/hoses that would impede the removal of the manifold have been released, then undo the retaining bolts and manoeuvre the intake manifold from place. Renew the manifold seals.

15.7 Remove the bracket between the intake manifold and the EGR cooler

15.8 Disconnect the coolant hose at each end of the EGR cooler

16 Refitting is a reversal of removal, tightening all fasteners to their specified torque.

V6 engines

17 Release the clamp and disconnect the coolant hose from the thermostat housing.
18 Remove the throttle body and mixing chamber as described in Section 14.
19 Disconnect the wiring plugs from the charge air temperature sensor and charge air pressure sensor.
20 Remove the turbocharger as described in Section 16.
21 Undo the retaining bolts and remove the turbocharger oil feed fitting (see illustration). Replace the gasket.
22 Remove the left-hand fuel common rail as described in Section 12.
23 Unscrew the union nuts securing the connecting pipe between the common rails. Plug the openings to prevent contamination.
24 Disconnect the fuel return pipe from the fuel pipes.
25 Remove the fuel filter as described in Chapter 1 Section 25.
26 Disconnect the fuel supply pipe from the high-pressure injection pump.
27 Undo the bolts and remove the fuel pipe from above the left-hand cylinder head cover.
28 Undo the bolts and remove the fuel filter cage.
29 Undo the bolts securing the fuel return hose distributor (see illustration).
30 Disconnect the engine wiring harness at the control unit (see illustration 13.29).
31 Disconnect the wiring plugs from:
a) Glow plugs.
b) Injectors.
c) Intake port shut-off motor.
d) Exhaust back pressure sensor (see illustration)
32 Disconnect the wiring plug from the EGR motor.
33 Undo the bolts securing the EGR motor to the charge air duct.
34 Disconnect the coolant hose, and remove the EGR valve motor.
35 Remove the lower bolt from the thermostat housing (see illustration).
36 Move the engine wiring harness to one side.
37 Make a final check to ensure all wiring/hoses that may impeded manifold removal have been disconnected.
38 Gradually, evenly, undo the retaining bolts and lift the intake manifold from place. Renew the manifold seal.
39 Refitting is a reversal of removal, noting the following points:
a) Tighten all fasteners to their specified torque, where given.
b) Tighten the intake manifold bolts in the sequence shown (see illustration).
c) Top up the cooling system as described in Chapter 1 Section 30 .
d) Check for leaks before refitting the engine cover/undershield.

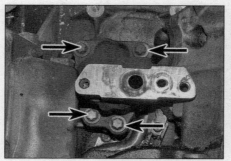
15.21 Undo the bolts and remove the turbocharger oil feed/return fitting

15.29 Unbolt the fuel return hose distributor

15.31 The exhaust back pressure sensor is located on the EGR valve housing

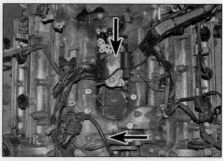
15.35 Undo the lower thermostat housing bolt, and move the wiring harness to one side

Exhaust manifold

In-line engines

40 Remove the turbocharger as described in Section 16.
41 Undo the retaining nuts and remove the exhaust manifold. Renew the self-locking nuts and the manifold gasket.
42 Ensure the manifold and cylinder head mating surfaces are clean, then check the condition/security of the mounting studs. Renew as necessary.

43 Refit the manifold and tighten the new retaining nuts to the specified torque.
44 Refit the turbocharger as described in Section 16.

V6 engines

45 Remove the air filter housings as described in Section 2.
46 Disconnect the wiring plug from the EGR valve motor.
47 Undo the bolt securing the EGR valve motor to the charge air manifold.
48 Apply a clamp to the hose, then

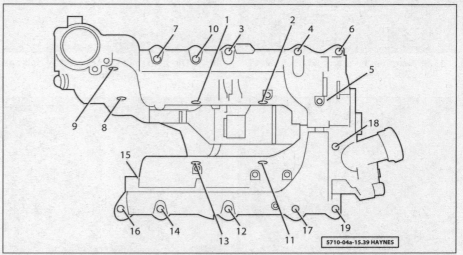
15.39 V6 engine intake manifold bolt tightening sequence

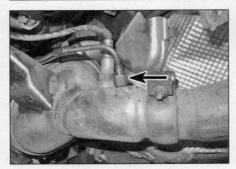

15.50 Trace the wiring back from the sensor and disconnect the wiring plug

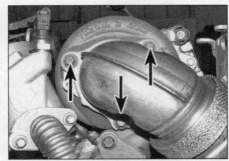

15.51 Remove the upper bolts and slacken the lower

15.52 Remove the EGR pipe

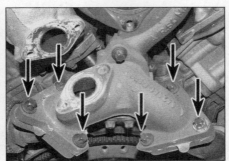

15.53 Exhaust collector bolts

15.55 Remove the manifold heat shield

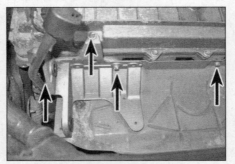

16.2a The heatshield is secured by bolts at the rear...

16.2b ...and at the front

16.4 Slacken the clamp bolt

16.7 Remove the turbocharger oil feed pipe

disconnect the coolant hose from the EGR valve. Be prepared for coolant spillage. Plug the openings to prevent contamination.
49 Remove the EGR valve motor.

50 On models with a particulate filter, disconnect the wiring plug and remove the exhaust back pressure sensor **(see illustration)**.

51 Remove the top bolts, and slacken the lower bolt securing the exhaust pipe to the turbocharger **(see illustration)**.
52 Undo the nuts and remove the EGR pipe **(see illustration)**. Renew the gaskets.
53 Remove the 6 retaining bolts from the exhaust collector **(see illustration)**.
54 Release the clamp and detach the primary catalytic converter from the manifold.
55 Undo the bolts and remove the heat shields above the manifolds **(see illustration)**.
56 Undo the retaining nuts and manoeuvre the exhaust manifolds from place. Renew the self-locking nuts and the manifold gaskets.
57 Ensure the manifold and cylinder head mating surfaces are clean, then check the condition/security of the mounting studs. Renew as necessary.
58 Refit the manifold and tighten the new retaining nuts to the specified torque.
59 The remainder of refitting is a reversal of removal. Top up the cooling system as described in 'Weekly checks'.

16 Turbocharger – removal and refitting

Removal

In-line engines

1 Remove the air filter housing as described in Section 2.
2 Remove the heatshield above the turbocharger **(see illustrations)**.
3 Raise the front of the vehicle and support it securely on axle stands (see 'Vehicle jacking and support'). Undo the fasteners and remove the engine undershield.
4 Release the clamp securing the catalytic converter/particulate filter to the turbocharger **(see illustration)**.
5 Undo the bolts securing the catalytic converter/particulate filter to the brackets on the transmission and cylinder block.
6 Undo the retaining bolt, unclip the wiring harness, and remove the charge air pipe upstream of the intercooler.
7 Undo the banjo bolts and remove the turbocharger oil feed pipe **(see illustration)**. Renew the sealing washers.

16.9 Disconnect the boost pressure control motor wiring plug

16.15 Undo the retaining plate bolt, and the air duct retaining bolts

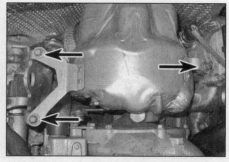

16.18 Turbocharger heatshield retaining bolts

8 Undo the retaining bolts and remove the support bracket beneath the turbocharger.

9 Disconnect the wiring plugs from the boost pressure control motor and exhaust gas temperature sensor upstream of the turbocharger **(see illustration)**.

10 Remove the bolts securing the turbocharger to the exhaust manifold. Note that if Torx bolts are fitted, they must be replaced by 12-point star bolts.

11 Manoeuvre the turbocharger upwards from position, complete with the oil drain tube. Be prepared for oil spillage. Renew the drain tube O-ring seal.

12 If required, undo the bolts and detach the oil drain tube from the underside of the turbocharger.

V6 engines

13 Remove the plastic cover from the top of the engine.

14 Remove the air intake duct downstream of the air filter.

15 Undo the bolt, and remove the charge air duct upstream of the intercooler retaining plate in a forwards direction **(see illustration)**.

16 Unclip the coolant hose, undo the 2 retaining bolts, and remove the charge air duct upstream of the intercooler **(see illustration 16.15)**.

17 Undo the retaining bolt and remove the charge air duct from the turbocharger. Check and renew the sealing rings if necessary.

18 Remove the heatshield above the turbocharger, and its support bracket **(see illustration)**.

19 Undo the top bolt, slacken the lower bolt and disconnect the exhaust pipe from the turbocharger. Renew the bolts and seal.

20 Undo the bolts and remove the EGR pipe from the exhaust collector **(see illustration 15.52)**. Renew the gaskets.

21 Undo the bolts securing the exhaust collector to the exhaust pipes **(see illustration 15.53)**. Renew the gaskets.

22 Undo the bolts securing the exhaust collector bracket to the cylinder block **(see illustration)**.

23 Remove the bolts securing the turbocharger oil supply fitting **(see illustration)**.

24 Undo the bolts securing the support bracket to the front of the turbocharger **(see illustration)**.

25 Disconnect the wiring plug from the boost pressure control motor.

26 Manoeuvre the turbocharger from place. Renew the gasket between the turbocharger and the oil feed fitting. Plug the openings to prevent contamination.

27 If required, detach the exhaust collector from the turbocharger. Renew the gasket and the retaining bolts.

Refitting

In-line engines

28 Ensure the turbocharger and exhaust manifold mating faces are clean.

29 If the turbocharger oil drain tube has been removed, renew the O-ring seal, attach the tube to the turbocharger, but only loosely fit the retaining bolts at this stage.

30 Manoeuvre the turbocharger assembly into position, ensuring the oil drain tube locates correctly in the cylinder block.

31 Fit the bolts securing the turbocharger to the manifold, and tighten the retaining bolts to the specified torque.

32 Tighten the oil drain tube retaining bolts to the specified torque.

V6 engines

33 Renew the oil supply fitting seal, and align it according to the hole pattern, ensuring the the oil supply channel is not obscured.

34 If the exhaust collector has been removed, loosely assembly it to the turbocharger and cylinder block, ensuring it's correctly aligned before tightening the new bolts.

All engines

35 The remainder of refitting is a reversal of removal, noting the following points:

a) *Tighten all fasteners to their specified torque where given.*

b) *We consider it prudent to change the engine oil and filter following turbocharger renewal.*

c) *Ensure the charge air ducts are clean and free from debris prior to refitting.*

d) *Check for correct operation and fluid leaks.*

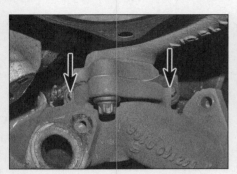

16.22 Exhaust collector bracket bolts

16.23 Undo the bolt each side securing the turbocharger

16.24 Support bracket bolts

18.3 Prise out the clips and disconnect the air hoses from each side of the intercooler

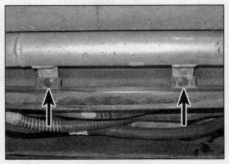

18.4 Prise up the centre pins, and lever out the expansion rivets

18.5 Unclip the lower mounting each side

17 Turbocharger – examination and overhaul

1 With the turbocharger removed, inspect the housing for cracks or other visible damage.
2 Spin the turbine or the compressor wheel to verify that the shaft is intact and to feel for excessive shake or roughness. Some play is normal since in use the shaft is 'floating' on a film of oil. Check that the wheel vanes are undamaged.
3 The wastegate and actuator are integral with the turbocharger, and cannot be checked or renewed separately. Consult a Mercedes Benz dealer or other specialist if it is thought that the wastegate may be faulty.
4 If the exhaust or induction passages are excessively oil-contaminated, the turbo shaft oil seals have probably failed (On the induction side, this will also have contaminated the intercooler, where applicable, which if necessary should be flushed with a suitable solvent). It's normal to find a little oil residue in the ducts/intercooler due to the crankcase ventilation system.
5 Check the condition of the air duct sealing rings and renew if necessary.
6 No DIY repair of the turbo is possible. A new unit may be available on an exchange basis.

18 Intercooler – removal and refitting

Removal

1 Raise the front of the vehicle and support it securely on axle stands (see *'Vehicle jacking and support'*). Undo the fasteners and remove the engine undershield.
2 Remove the front bumper as described in Chapter 11 Section 16.
3 Release the clamps and disconnect the intercooler intake and outlet hoses **(see illustration)**.

4 Release the plastic expansion rivets securing the air scoop **(see illustration)**.
5 Unclip the intercooler lower mountings **(see illustration)**.
6 Carefully, gently, push the lower edge of the intercooler rearwards a little, and out of the lower guides.
7 Manoeuvre the intercooler and air scoop downwards from place. Carefully pull the lower edge of the bumper forwards a little to prevent damage to the scoop as it's withdrawn.

Refitting

8 Ensure the intercooler and air ducts are free from oil and debris. If the induction passages are excessively oil-contaminated, the turbo shaft oil seals may have failed, although it's normal to find a little oil residue in the ducts/ intercooler due to the crankcase ventilation system.
9 Check the condition of the air duct sealing rings, and renew if necessary. Do not apply grease or lubricant to the new seals.
10 Refit the intercooler, reversing the removal procedure.

19 Exhaust system – general information and component renewal

General information

1 The exhaust system consists of 2, or 3 sections, and depending on model, may include 1, or 2 rear silencers, 1 or 2 catalytic converters and a diesel particulate filter. The secondary catalytic converter/particulate filter is secured to the transmission by means of a bracket and rubber mounting.
2 A primary catalytic converter is fitted close to the exhaust manifold, whilst the secondary catalytic converter/particulate filter is integral with the front exhaust pipe.
3 The rear silencers are integral with the tailpipes, and are secure to the front pipe by means of bolted flanges or clamping rings **(see illustration)**.

Removal

4 Each exhaust section can be removed individually or, alternatively, the complete system can be removed at a unit.
5 Before removing any part of the system, raise the vehicle and support it securely on axle stands (see *'Vehicle jacking and support'*). Where necessary, undo the fasteners and remove the engine/transmission undershield.

Rear silencer(s)

6 Slacken the clamp or undo the bolts/nuts at the flange connection (as applicable) securing the rear pipe/silencer to the front exhaust pipe/catalytic converter/particulate filter.
7 Where fitted, remove the support bracket between the silencers.
8 Unhook the rubber mountings, and with the help of an assistant, manoeuvre the rear silencer/pipe assembly from under the vehicle.

Secondary catalytic converter/ particulate filter

In-line engines

9 Remove the air filter housing as described in Section 2.
10 Trace the wiring back from the oxygen sensor and DPF pressure differential sensor (where applicable) and disconnect the wiring plugs.
11 Undo the bolts and remove the heatshield above the turbocharger.
12 Undo the bolt securing the clamp from the

19.3 Exhaust system bolted flanges

19.12 Catalytic converter-to-turbocharger clamp

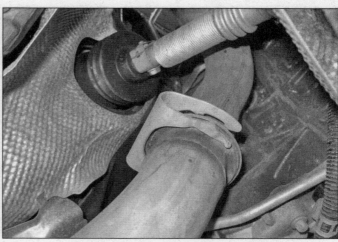

19.13 Prise off the clamp

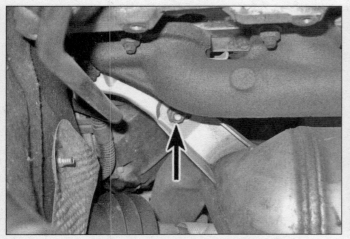

19.15 Catalytic converter rear mounting nut

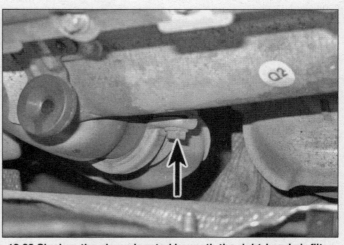

19.20 Slacken the clamp located beneath the right-hand air filter housing area

catalytic converter to the turbocharger **(see illustration)**.

13 Slide off the clamp securing the catalytic converter/particulate filter to the rear exhaust pipe assembly **(see illustration)**.

14 Using a split-type socket, unscrew the temperature sensor(s) from the catalytic converter.

15 Support the catalytic converter/particulate filter, then undo the mounting bolts/nuts and lower it from place **(see illustration)**.

16 Undo the pipe support bracket bolts, and undo the union nuts securing the pressure take-off pipes to the particulate filter.

17 Undo the bolts securing the catalytic converter to the particulate filter (where applicable). Discard the bolts – new ones must be fitted.

18 Note it's fitted position in relation to the particulate filter, then detach the catalytic converter. Renew the seal.

V6 engines

19 Remove the right-hand air filter housing as described in Section 2.

20 Slacken the clamp securing the primary catalytic converter to the secondary catalytic converter **(see illustration)**.

21 Trace the wiring for the upstream O2 sensor and temperature sensor back their connectors, then unplug them. Release the wiring harness from any retaining clips, noting their routing.

22 Undo the bolt securing the clamp between the secondary catalytic converter/particulate filter (as applicable) and the exhaust pipe **(see illustration)**.

23 Undo the mounting nut(s) and manoeuvre the catalytic converter from place.

Primary catalytic converter

In-line engines

24 Remove the air filter housing as described in Section 2.

25 Undo the bolts and remove the heatshield above the turbocharger.

26 Prise off the collar clamp between the turbocharger and the catalytic converter.

27 Prise off the collar clamp between the primary, and secondary catalytic converters.

28 Undo the mounting nut at the base of the primary catalytic converter and manoeuvre it upwards from place. Renew the nut, and the seals between the turbocharger, primary catalytic converter and secondary catalytic converter.

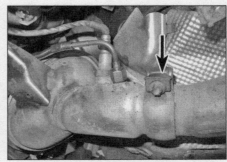

19.22 Slacken the clamp at the rear of the particulate filter/catalytic converter

19.29 Depress the catch each side, and fully open the bonnet

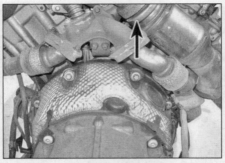

19.33 Primary catalytic converter clamp

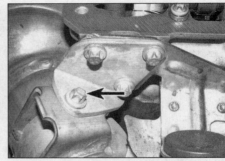

19.35 Catalytic converter retaining bolt

V6 engines

29 Open the bonnet, press the locking catch on the hinge each side, and raise the bonnet to its fully upright position **(see illustration)**.

30 Pull up the plastic panel on the top of the engine.

31 Undo the bolts and remove the heatshield above the turbocharger.

32 Undo the top bolt, and slacken the lower bolt securing the exhaust pipe to the turbocharger **(see illustration 15.51)**.

33 Remove the clamp securing the exhaust pipe to the primary catalytic converter, and remove the exhaust pipe **(see illustration)**.

34 Release the clamp between the primary, and secondary catalytic converter **(see illustration 19.20)**.

35 Undo the retaining bolt at the cylinder head and lift the catalytic converter from place **(see illustration)**.

Refitting

36 Each section is refitted by reversing the removal sequence, noting the following points:

a) Ensure that all traces of corrosion have been removed from the flanges and renew all gaskets.

b) Inspect the rubber mountings for signs of damage or deterioration, and renew as necessary.

c) Prior to tightening the exhaust system fasteners to the specified torque, ensure that all rubber mountings are correctly located, and that there is adequate clearance between the exhaust system and vehicle underbody.

Chapter 4 Part B
Emission control systems

Contents

Degrees of difficulty

Easy, suitable for novice with little experience	Fairly easy, suitable for beginner with some experience	Fairly difficult, suitable for competent DIY mechanic	Difficult, suitable for experienced DIY mechanic	Very difficult, suitable for expert DIY or professional

Specifications

Torque wrench settings	Nm	lbf ft
EGR cooler:		
M6	10	7
M8	10	15
EGR valve	10	7
Oil separator:		
In-line engines	12	8
V6 engines	N/A	

1 General information

1 All diesel engine models are also designed to meet strict emission requirements. All models are fitted with a crankcase emission control system, a catalytic converter(s), an exhaust gas recirculation (EGR) system, and on some models, a particulate filter, to keep exhaust emissions down to a minimum.

2 The emission control systems function as follows.

Crankcase emission control

3 To reduce the emission of unburned hydrocarbons from the crankcase into the atmosphere, the engine is sealed and the blow-by gases and oil vapour are drawn from inside the crankcase, through a wire mesh oil separator, into the intake tract to be burned by the engine during normal combustion.

Exhaust emission control

4 To minimise the level of exhaust pollutants released into the atmosphere, most models are fitted with 2 catalytic converters fitted into the exhaust system, and on some models, a diesel particulate filter.

5 The catalytic converter consists of a canister containing a fine mesh impregnated with a catalyst material, over which the hot exhaust gases pass. The catalyst speeds up the oxidation of harmful carbon monoxide, unburned hydrocarbons and soot, effectively reducing the quantity of harmful products released into the atmosphere via the exhaust gases.

Particulate filter

6 This device is designed to trap carbon particulates produced by the combustion process. The particle filter is fitted downstream of the catalytic converter. In order to prevent the filter blocking, pressure and temperature sensors are fitted to the filter. Under the normal, high-speed driving conditions, the soot particles are burnt off in the filter by the high temperature of the exhaust gases. However, where the driving conditions are such that the exhaust gases are not sufficiently high, the engine management system injects fuel into the cylinders after the point of combustion. These are called post-injections, and raise the temperature of the exhaust gases, causing the soot particles in the filter to be burnt off.

7 On some models, an additive known as Adblue is added to the fuel to help clean the particulate filter. For more information concerning Adblue, consult your vehicle handbook or Mercedes Dealer.

Exhaust gas recirculation (EGR) system

8 This system is designed to recirculate small quantities of exhaust gas into the intake tract, and therefore into the combustion process. This process reduces the level of unburnt hydrocarbons present in the exhaust gas before it reaches the catalytic converter. The system is controlled by the engine management system ECM, using the information from its various sensors, via the EGR valve which is fitted to the metal pipe connecting the intake and exhaust manifolds. On some models, the exhaust gasses are cooled prior to entering the intake manifold by passing through a cooler mounted on the side of the EGR valve. Engine coolant circulates through the cooler.

2 Engine emission control systems – testing and component renewal

Crankcase emission control

Testing

1 The components of this system require no attention other than to check that the hose(s) are clear and undamaged at regular intervals. If the system is thought to be faulty, renew the crankcase pressure limiting valve as follows.

Oil separator

In-line engines

2 Some models are fitted with an oil separator located at the front, right-hand corner of the cylinder head, whereas on other models the separator is located on the top of the cylinder head cover (see illustration).
3 Undo the fasteners and remove the plastic cover on the top of the engine.
4 On front mounted separators, disconnect the hose from the side of the oil separator (see illustration).
5 On front mounted separators, unclip the plastic cap (see illustration).
6 Undo the retaining bolt(s) and manoeuvre the oil separator from place. Renew the gasket.
7 Refitting is a reversal of removal, tightening the retaining bolt to the specified torque.

V6 engines

8 Pull the plastic cover upwards from the top of the engine.
9 The oil separator is located on the top of the right-hand cylinder head cover. Undo the retaining bolts, and pull the separator upwards

2.2 Oil separator fitted to the right-hand corner of the cylinder head

from the cover (see illustration). Renew the oil seal.
10 Refitting is a reversal of removal. Tighten the retaining bolts securely.

Exhaust emission control

Testing

11 The performance of the catalytic converter or diesel particulate filter can be checked only by using Mercedes Benz diagnostic equipment (or equivalent). Entrust this task to a dealer or suitable equipped specialist.
12 Before assuming that the catalytic converter/particulate filter is faulty, it is worth checking whether the problem is not due to a faulty injector(s). Refer to your Mercedes Benz dealer for further information.

Catalytic converter and particulate filter – renewal

13 Refer to Chapter 4A Section 19 for removal and refitting details.

Exhaust gas recirculation (EGR) system

Testing

14 Comprehensive testing of the system can only be carried out using specialist electronic equipment which is connected to the injection system diagnostic wiring connector (see Chapter 4A).

EGR cooler – renewal

15 Drain the coolant as described in Chapter 1 Section 30.

2.4 Disconnect the breather hose

4-cylinder in-line engines

16 Remove the upper bolt, and slacken the oil level dipstick guide tube lower bolt.
17 Slacken the lower bolt, and remove the upper bolts securing the EGR cooler support bracket. Move the support bracket to one side a little.
18 Release the clamps and disconnect the coolant hoses from the EGR cooler.
19 Undo the EGR cooler retaining bolts and remove the upper support bracket.
20 Manoeuvre the EGR cooler from place. Renew the gasket.
21 Refitting is a reversal of removal.

5-, and 6-cylinder in-line engines

22 Remove the EGR valve as described later in this Section.
23 Working underneath the vehicle, remove the EGR cooler lower mounting bolts.
24 Release the clamp and disconnect the coolant hose from the top of the EGR cooler (see illustration).
25 Remove the bolt securing the support brace to the top of the cooler.
26 Undo the remaining 2 retaining bolts, and remove the EGR cooler. Renew the gasket.
27 Refitting is a reversal of removal.

V6 engines

28 Remove the intake manifold as described in Chapter 4A Section 15.
29 Undo the bolts and remove the EGR cooler. Renew the gasket.

All engines

30 Refitting is a reversal of removal.

2.5 Unclip the plastic cap

2.9 Undo the separator retaining bolts

2.24 Disconnect the hose from the EGR cooler

2.32 EGR valve wiring plug – in-line engines

2.38 EGR valve retaining bolts – V6 engines

Exhaust gas recirculation (EGR) valve – renewal

In-line engines

31 Undo the fasteners and remove the plastic cover from the top of the engine.
32 Disconnect the EGR valve wiring plug **(see illustration)**.
33 Undo the retaining bolts and remove the EGR valve. Renew the O-ring seal.

V6 engines

34 Drain the coolant as described in Chapter 1 Section 30, or have a clamp ready to close-off the coolant pipe attached to the EGR valve.
35 Pull the plastic cover upwards from the top of the engine.
36 Disconnect the EGR valve wiring plug.

37 Release the clamp and disconnect the coolant hose from the EGR valve. Where applicable, apply a hose clamp to minimise coolant loss.
38 Undo the retaining bolts and remove the EGR valve **(see illustration)**. Renew the seal/gasket.

All engines

39 Refitting is a reversal of removal.

3 Catalytic converter – general information and precautions

1 The catalytic converter is a reliable and simple device which needs no maintenance in itself, but there are some facts of which an owner should be aware if the converter is to function properly for its full service life.

a) *DO NOT use fuel or engine oil additives – these may contain substances harmful to the catalytic converter.*
b) *DO NOT continue to use the car if the engine burns oil to the extent of leaving a visible trail of blue smoke.*
c) *Remember that the catalytic converter operates at very high temperatures. DO NOT, therefore, park the car in dry undergrowth, over long grass or piles of dead leaves after a long run.*
d) *Remember that the catalytic converter is FRAGILE - do not strike it with tools during servicing work.*

Chapter 5 Part A
Starting and charging systems

Contents

Degrees of difficulty

Easy, suitable for novice with little experience	**Fairly easy,** suitable for beginner with some experience	**Fairly difficult,** suitable for competent DIY mechanic	**Difficult,** suitable for experienced DIY mechanic	**Very difficult,** suitable for expert DIY or professional 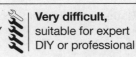

Specifications

System type	12-volt, negative earth
Alternator	160 to 200 A @ 25°C
Battery charge condition:	
Poor	12.5 volts
Normal	12.6 volts
Good	12.7 volts

Torque wrench settings	Nm	lbf ft
Alternator bolts	20	15
Starter motor bolts	40	30

1 General information and precautions

General information

1 The engine electrical system consists mainly of the charging and starting systems. Because of their engine-related functions, these components are covered separately from the body electrical devices such as the lights, instruments, etc (which are covered in Chapter 12). Refer to Chapter 5B for information on the pre-heating system.

2 The electrical system is of the 12-volt negative earth type.

3 The battery is of the low maintenance or "maintenance-free" (sealed for life) type and is charged by the alternator, which is belt-driven from the crankshaft pulley.

4 The starter motor is of the pre-engaged type incorporating an integral solenoid. On starting, the solenoid moves the drive pinion into engagement with the flywheel ring gear before the starter motor is energised. Once the engine has started, a one-way clutch prevents the motor armature being driven by the engine until the pinion disengages from the flywheel.

Precautions

5 Further details of the various systems are given in the relevant Sections of this Chapter. While some repair procedures are given, the usual course of action is to renew the component concerned. The owner whose interest extends beyond mere component renewal should obtain a copy of the "Automotive Electrical & Electronic Systems Manual", available from the publishers of this manual.

6 It is necessary to take extra care when working on the electrical system to avoid damage to semi-conductor devices (diodes and transistors), and to avoid the risk of personal injury. In addition to the precautions given in "Safety first!" at the beginning of this manual, observe the following when working on the system:

7 Always remove rings, watches, etc before working on the electrical system. Even with the battery disconnected, capacitive discharge could occur if a component's live terminal is earthed through a metal object. This could cause a shock or nasty burn.

8 Do not reverse the battery connections. Components such as the alternator, electronic control units, or any other components having semi-conductor circuitry could be irreparably damaged.

9 If the engine is being started using jump leads and a slave battery, connect the batteries positive-to-positive and negative-to-negative (see "Jump starting 0 Section 4 "). This also applies when connecting a battery charger.

10 Never disconnect the battery terminals,

the alternator, any electrical wiring or any test instruments when the engine is running.

11 Do not allow the engine to turn the alternator when the alternator is not connected.

12 Never "test" for alternator output by "flashing" the output lead to earth.

13 Never use an ohmmeter of the type incorporating a hand-cranked generator for circuit or continuity testing.

14 Always ensure that the battery negative lead is disconnected when working on the electrical system.

15 Before using electric-arc welding equipment on the car, disconnect the battery, alternator and components such as the fuel injection/ignition electronic control unit to protect them from the risk of damage.

2 Electrical fault finding – general information

1 Refer to Chapter 12 Section 2.

3 Battery – testing and charging
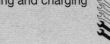

Standard and low maintenance battery – testing

1 If the vehicle covers a small annual mileage, it is worthwhile checking the specific gravity of the electrolyte every three months to determine the state of charge of the battery. Use a hydrometer to make the check and compare the results with the following table. Note that the specific gravity readings assume an electrolyte temperature of 15°C (60°F); for every 10°C (18°F) below 15°C (60°F) subtract 0.007. For every 10°C (18°F) above 15°C (60°F) add 0.007.

Ambient temperature	Above 25°C (77°F)	Below 25°C (77°F)
Fully charged	1.210 to 1.230	1.270 to 1.290
70% charged	1.17 to 1.190	1.230 to 1.250
Discharged	1.050 to 1.070	1.110 to 1.130

2 If the battery condition is suspect, first check the specific gravity of electrolyte in each cell. A variation of 0.040 or more between any cells indicates loss of electrolyte or deterioration of the internal plates.

3 If the specific gravity variation is 0.040 or more, the battery should be renewed. If the cell variation is satisfactory but the battery is discharged, it should be charged as described later in this Section.

Maintenance-free battery – testing

4 In cases where a "sealed for life" maintenance-free battery is fitted, topping-up

and testing of the electrolyte in each cell is not possible. The condition of the battery can therefore only be tested using a battery condition indicator or a voltmeter.

5 Models may be fitted with a "Delco" type maintenance-free battery, with a built-in charge condition indicator. The indicator is located in the top of the battery casing, and indicates the condition of the battery from its colour. If the indicator shows green, then the battery is in a good state of charge. If the indicator turns darker, eventually to black, then the battery requires charging, as described later in this Section. If the indicator shows clear/yellow, then the electrolyte level in the battery is too low to allow further use, and the battery should be renewed. Do not attempt to charge, load or jump start a battery when the indicator shows clear/yellow.

6 If testing the battery using a voltmeter, connect the voltmeter across the battery and compare the result with those given in the Specifications under "charge condition". The test is only accurate if the battery has not been subjected to any kind of charge for the previous six hours. If this is not the case, switch on the headlights for 30 seconds, then wait four to five minutes before testing the battery after switching off the headlights. All other electrical circuits must be switched off, so check that the doors and tailgate are fully shut when making the test.

7 If the voltage reading is less than 12.2 volts, then the battery is discharged, whilst a reading of 12.2 to 12.4 volts indicates a partially discharged condition.

8 If the battery is to be charged, remove it from the vehicle (Section 4) and charge it as described later in this Section.

Standard and low maintenance battery – charging

Note: *The following is intended as a guide only. Always refer to the manufacturer's recommendations (often printed on a label attached to the battery) before charging a battery.*

9 Charge the battery at a rate of 3.5 to 4 amps and continue to charge the battery at this rate until no further rise in specific gravity is noted over a four hour period.

10 Alternatively, a trickle charger charging at the rate of 1.5 amps can safely be used overnight.

11 Specially rapid "boost" charges which are claimed to restore the power of the battery in 1 to 2 hours are not recommended, as they can cause serious damage to the battery plates through overheating.

12 While charging the battery, note that the temperature of the electrolyte should never exceed 37.8°C (100°F).

Maintenance-free battery – charging

Note: *The following is intended as a guide only. Always refer to the manufacturer's recommendations (often printed on a label*

attached to the battery) before charging a battery.

13 This battery type takes considerably longer to fully recharge than the standard type, the time taken being dependent on the extent of discharge, but it can take anything up to three days.

14 A constant voltage type charger is required, to be set, when connected, to 13.9 to 14.9 volts with a charger current below 25 amps. Using this method, the battery should be usable within three hours, giving a voltage reading of 12.5 volts, but this is for a partially discharged battery and, as mentioned, full charging can take considerably longer.

15 If the battery is to be charged from a fully discharged state (condition reading less than 12.2 volts), have it recharged by your Mercedes Benz dealer or local automotive electrician, as the charge rate is higher and constant supervision during charging is necessary.

Caution: Do not charge AGM batteries above 14.8 volts, or the battery may be damaged.

16 The battery can only be charged by connecting the charger positive lead to the battery positive terminal, and the charger negative lead to the vehicle earth connection. Do not connect a battery charger negative lead directly to the battery terminal. These vehicles are fitted with an Battery Control unit (up to 31.05.06) or a Battery Sensor (01.06.06-on), which monitors the flow of current to and from the battery. If it calculates the state of the battery is getting low, it will ask the various car electrical systems to shut down certain electrical consumers. Eventually, the control unit/sensor may decide the battery state is so poor it decides the starting system must be disabled. Consequently, if a battery charger is connected directly to the terminals of the battery, even though the battery may be completely recharged, the system may still believe the battery state to be poor, as it has registered no current passing into the battery. Therefore, even though the battery is charged, the starter circuit may still be disabled.

4 Battery – disconnection, removal and refitting

Battery

Main battery

Disconnection

1 Ensure that all electrical consumers are switched off, all windows are closed, and the alarm is disarmed. Remove the remote control from the vehicle, and wait at least 2 minutes for the electrical systems to 'power down'.

2 On models equipped with 'Keyless GO', remove the transmitter key from the vehicle, and store it at least 2m away, out of transmitter range.

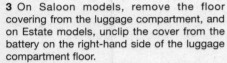

4.4 Slacken the nut and pull the negative terminal clamp from the battery post

4.5 Disconnect the positive terminal clamp in the same manner

4.8 Battery retaining clamp bolt

3 On Saloon models, remove the floor covering from the luggage compartment, and on Estate models, unclip the cover from the battery on the right-hand side of the luggage compartment floor.

4 Slacken the nut and disconnect the negative terminal clamp from the battery **(see illustration)**. Position the negative lead in such a way that it cannot accidentally touch the battery terminal.

5 If required, lift up the plastic cover, slacken the nut and disconnect the positive terminal clamp from the battery **(see illustration)**.

Removal

6 Disconnect the battery as described previously in this Section.

7 Where fitted, release the retaining strap around the battery.

8 Unscrew the bolt and remove the battery retaining clamp then lift the battery out of the engine compartment **(see illustration)**. Disconnect the vent pipe as the battery is withdrawn.

Refitting

9 Refitting is a reversal of removal, but smear petroleum jelly on the terminals when reconnecting the leads, and always reconnect the positive lead first, and the negative lead last.

10 After reconnection, the following procedures may need to be carried out:

Set time in instrument cluster

11 Refer to the owners handbook.

Reset the electric windows

12 Operate the window switch to fully close the window, then hold the switch in this position for approximately 1 second. Repeat this procedure for each window.

Steering angle sensor reset

13 On vehicles upto 2004 models year, after reconnection of the battery, the message 'El.-STAB.-PROGRAM – LOCATE WORKSHOP' may appear in the multifunction display. Reset the steering angle sensor as follows:
a) *Start the engine and allow it to idle.*
b) *Turn the steering wheel fully to the left, then to the right, then recentre it.*
c) *The message in the multifunction display should now disappear.*

Panoramic glass roof

14 Remove the panoramic glass roof fuse, then refit it.

15 Turn on the ignition, then move the the the glass roof fully to the front position, then fully rearwards and hold the switch in this position for approximately 1 second.

16 Again, move the glass roof fully to the front position, then fully rearwards and hold the switch in this position for approximately 1 second.

Tilt/sliding roof

17 Remove the tilt/sliding roof fuse, the refit it.

18 Turn on the ignition, then move the roof to the front and rear stops and hold the switch in this position for approximately 1 second.

Additional battery

19 On some models, an additional battery is fitted in the engine compartment. Remove the pollen filter housing as described in Chapter 1 Section 19.

20 Undo the bolt and disconnect the battery negative lead **(see illustration)**.

21 Undo the bolt and disconnect the battery positive lead.

22 Undo the retaining nut and lift open the battery clamp.

23 Manoeuvre the battery from place.

24 Refitting is a reversal of removal.

4.20 Additional battery terminals and battery clamp nut

| 5 | Charging system – testing | |

1 Refer to the warnings given in "Safety first!" and in Section 1 of this Chapter before starting work.

2 If the ignition warning light fails to illuminate when the ignition is switched on, first check the alternator wiring connections for security. If the light still fails to illuminate, check the continuity of the warning light feed wire from the alternator to the instrument. If all is satisfactory, the alternator maybe at fault and should be renewed or taken to an auto-electrician for testing and repair. Bear in mind that the E-Class is equipped with a sophisticated self-diagnosis system, and any

fault detected by the system will generate a fault code. Use Mercedes Benz diagnostic equipment (or equivalent) connected to the vehicles diagnostic plug (see Chapter 4A Section 6) to interrogate the ECM, read the code, and investigate the fault recorded.

3 If the ignition warning light illuminates when the engine is running, stop the engine and check that the drivebelt is correctly tensioned (see Chapter 1 Section 6) and that the alternator connections are secure. If all is so far satisfactory, have the alternator checked by an auto-electrician for testing and repair.

4 If the alternator output is suspect even though the warning light functions correctly, the regulated voltage may be checked as follows.

5 Connect a voltmeter across the battery terminals and start the engine.

6 Increase the engine speed until the voltmeter reading remains steady; the reading should be approximately 12 to 13 volts, and no more than 14 volts.

7 Switch on as many electrical accessories (eg, the headlights, heated rear window and heater blower) as possible, and check that the alternator maintains the regulated voltage at around 13 to 14 volts.

8 If the regulated voltage is not as stated, the fault may be due to worn brushes, weak brush springs, a faulty voltage regulator, a faulty diode, a severed phase winding or worn or damaged slip rings. The alternator should be renewed or taken to an auto-electrician for testing and repair.

6.9 Alternator upper mounting bolts

6.14 Prise off the plastic cap to access the alternator connection

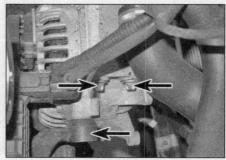

6.17a Undo the 3 upper retaining bolts...

6 Alternator – removal and refitting

Removal

1 Raise the front of the vehicle and support it securely on axle stands (see 'Vehicle jacking and support'). Undo the fasteners and remove the engine undershield.
2 Disconnect the battery negative lead as described in Section 4.

4 and 5 cylinder in-line engines

3 Undo the fasteners and remove the plastic cover from the top of the engine.
4 Remove the auxiliary drivebelt as described in Chapter 1 Section 6.
5 Remove the air filter housing as described in Chapter 4A Section 2.
6 Undo the bolts and remove the heatshield above the exhaust manifold.
7 Undo the mounting bracket bolts and remove the air intake pipe from turbocharger.
8 Disconnect the wiring from the alternator **(see illustration 6.14)**.
9 Undo the 4 mounting bolts, and manoeuvre the alternator downwards from place **(see illustration)**.

6 cylinder in-line engines

10 Undo the fasteners and remove the plastic cover from the top of the engine.

11 Remove the cooling fan shroud as described in Chapter 3 Section 6.
12 Remove the auxiliary drivebelt as described in Chapter 1 Section 6.
13 Remove the air duct between the intercooler and the turbocharger.
14 Prise off the plastic cap and disconnect the wiring from the alternator **(see illustration)**.
15 Undo the bolts securing the oil pipes bracket to the engine sump.
16 On automatic transmission models, disconnect the transmission fluid pipes beneath the alternator. Plug the openings to prevent contamination. Be prepared for fluid spillage.
17 Undo the 5 mounting bolts and lower the alternator from place **(see illustrations)**.

V6 engines

18 Remove the throttle body as described in Chapter 4A Section 14.
19 Remove the auxiliary drivebelt as described in Chapter 1 Section 6.
20 Disconnect the wiring from the alternator, and release the wiring harness cable ties **(see illustration)**.
21 Undo the 4 mounting bolts and lower the alternator from place **(see illustration)**.

Refitting

22 Refitting is the reverse of removal tightening all mounting bolts to their specified torque settings (where given). Ensure the

drivebelt is correctly refitted and tensioned as described in Chapter 1 Section 6.

7 Alternator – testing and overhaul

1 If the alternator is thought to be suspect, it should be removed from the vehicle and taken to an auto-electrician for testing. Most auto-electricians will be able to supply and fit brushes at a reasonable cost. However, check on the cost of repairs before proceeding as it may prove more economical to obtain a new or exchange alternator.

8 Starting system – testing

Note: Refer to the precautions given in Safety first! and in Section 1 of this Chapter before starting work.
1 If the starter motor fails to operate when the ignition key is turned to the appropriate position, the following possible causes may be responsible.
a) The battery is faulty.
b) The electrical connections between the switch, solenoid, battery and starter

6.17b...and the 2 lower bolts

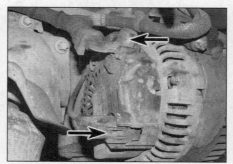

6.20 Prise off the cap, undo the nut, then depress the catch and disconnect the wiring plug

6.21 The alternator is secured by 2 bolts above, and 2 bolts below

motor are somewhere failing to pass the necessary current from the battery through the starter to earth.

c) *The solenoid is faulty.*

d) *The starter motor is mechanically or electrically defective.*

2 To check the battery, switch on the headlights. If they dim after a few seconds, this indicates that the battery is discharged – recharge (see Section 3) or renew the battery. If the headlights glow brightly, operate the ignition switch and observe the lights. If they dim, then this indicates that current is reaching the starter motor; therefore the fault must lie in the starter motor. If the lights continue to glow brightly (and no clicking sound can be heard from the starter motor solenoid), this indicates that there is a fault in the circuit or solenoid – see following paragraphs. If the starter motor turns slowly when operated, but the battery is in good condition, then this indicates that either the starter motor is faulty, or there is considerable resistance somewhere in the circuit.

3 If a fault in the circuit is suspected, disconnect the battery leads (including the earth connection to the body), the starter/solenoid wiring and the engine/transmission earth strap. Thoroughly clean the connections, and reconnect the leads and wiring, then use a voltmeter or test lamp to check that full battery voltage is available at the battery positive lead connection to the solenoid, and that the earth is sound. Smear petroleum jelly around the battery terminals to prevent corrosion – corroded connections are amongst the most frequent causes of electrical system faults

4 If the battery and all connections are in good condition, check the circuit by disconnecting the trigger wire from the solenoid terminal. Connect a voltmeter or test lamp between the wire end and a good earth (such as the battery negative terminal), and check that the wire is live when the ignition switch is turned to the 'start' position. If it is, then the circuit is sound – if not the circuit wiring can be checked as described in Chapter 12 Section 2.

5 The solenoid contacts can be checked by connecting a voltmeter or test lamp between the battery positive feed connection on the starter side of the solenoid and earth. When the ignition switch is turned to the 'start' position, there should be a reading or lighted bulb, as applicable. If there is no reading or lighted bulb, the solenoid is faulty and should be renewed.

6 If the circuit and solenoid are proved sound, the fault must lie in the starter motor. Begin checking the starter motor by removing it and having the brushes checked. If the fault does not lie in the brushes, the motor windings must be faulty. In this event, it may be possible to have the starter motor overhauled by a specialist, but check on the availability and cost of spares before proceeding, as it may prove more economical to obtain a new or exchange motor.

9 Starter motor – removal and refitting

Removal

In-line engines

1 The starter motor is bolted to the transmission bellhousing, at the rear of the engine on the left-hand side. Access is best achieved from under the front of the car.

2 Disconnect the battery negative lead as described in Section 4.

3 Raise the front of the vehicle and support it securely on axle stands (see *'Vehicle jacking and support'*). Undo the fasteners and remove the engine undershield.

4 Disconnect the wiring from the starter. Where necessary unbolt the wiring harness bracket **(see illustration)**.

5 Undo the mounting bolts, and lower the starter motor from place. In order to access the upper mounting bolt, use Torx socket and long extensions accross the top of the gearbox.

V6 engines

6 The starter is fitted to the left-hand side of the cylinder block.

7 Disconnect the battery negative lead as described in Section 4.

8 Raise the front of the vehicle and support it securely on axle stands as described in *'Vehicle jacking and support'*. Undo the fasteners and remove the engine/transmission undershield.

9 Disconnect the wiring from the starter motor **(see illustration)**.

10 Undo the mounting bolts and lower the starter motor from place **(see illustration)**.

Refitting

11 Refitting is a reversal of removal tightening the mounting bolts to the specified torque. Ensure all wiring is correctly routed and its retaining nuts are securely tightened.

10 Starter motor – testing and overhaul

1 If the starter motor is thought to be suspect, it should be removed from the vehicle and taken to an auto-electrician for testing. Most auto-electricians will be able to supply and fit brushes at a reasonable cost. However, check on the cost of repairs before proceeding as it may prove more economical to obtain a new or exchange motor.

11 Start control unit – removal and refitting

Removal

1 Disconnect the battery negative lead as described in Section 4.

Electronic start switch control unit

Note: *If a new control unit is to be fitted, the stored data must be transferred to Mercedes Benz diagnostic equipment (or equivalent) prior to removal. This data is then used to program/configure the new unit.*

2 Using a pair of circlip pliers (or similar)

9.4 Disconnect the wiring from the front of the starter motor, and unbolt the harness bracket

9.9 Starter motor wiring connections. Prise off the plastic cap to access the upper connection

9.10 Starter motor mounting bolts

11.2 Unscrew the start control unit collar

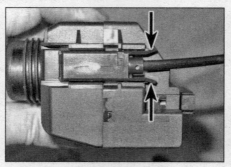

11.6 Squeeze together the clips and disconnect the release cable

12.3 Battery earth lead connection, and BCM wiring plug

unscrew the collar around the control unit **(see illustration)**.

3 Remove the drivers side lower facia panel as described in Chapter 11 Section 34.

4 On models where the footwell air duct is separate from the drivers side lower facia panel, remove it from below the facia.

5 Lower the start switch control unit, and disconnect the wiring plugs.

6 Where applicable, unclip the selector lever release cable from the control unit **(see illustration)**.

Keyless Go control units

Luggage compartment control unit

7 Remove the left-hand side luggage compartment side panel trim as described in Chapter 11 Section 34.

8 Undo the retaining bolt and swivel the control unit holder forwards.

9 Unclip the control unit from the top of the holder and disconnect the wiring plugs.

Interior compartment control unit

10 On automatic transmission models, move the selector lever to position 'D'.

11 Open the front ashtray and pull up the front edge of the gear/selector lever surround trim panel.

12 Pull out the ashtray a little, and disconnect the wiring plugs as they become accessible.

13 Unclip the Keyless Go module from the ashtray.

Rear door control unit

14 Remove the rear door inner trim panel and weather shield as described in Chapter 11 Section 34.

15 Disconnect the wiring plugs, and unhook the control unit.

Refitting

16 Refitting is a reversal of removal. Note that if a new control unit has been fitted, the data stored (see Paragraph 1) must be loaded into the new unit using the Mercedes Benz diagnostic equipment (or equivalent).

12 Battery control module (BCM) – removal and refitting

Removal

1 The battery control module (BCM) is fitted to the tailgate/boot sill panel. Remove the spare wheel and lift out the floor from the luggage compartment.

2 In order to preserve the vehicle setting, attach a bridging wire from the battery earth lead to a suitable vehicle earth point.

3 Undo the nut and disconnect the battery earth lead from the BCM, then disconnect the wiring plug **(see illustration)**.

4 Undo the mounting bolts and remove the BCM.

Refitting

5 Refitting is a reversal of removal.

Chapter 5 Part B
Pre-heating system

Contents

Degrees of difficulty

Easy, suitable for novice with little experience	**Fairly easy,** suitable for beginner with some experience	**Fairly difficult,** suitable for competent DIY mechanic	**Difficult,** suitable for experienced DIY mechanic	**Very difficult,** suitable for expert DIY or professional

Specifications

Torque wrench settings	Nm	lbf ft
Glow plugs:		
M8	10	7
M10	18	13

1 General information

1 To assist cold starting, diesel-engined models are fitted with a preheating system, which comprises glow plugs (one per cylinder), a glow plug output stage, a facia-mounted warning lamp, a coolant temperature sensor and the associated electrical wiring.

2 The glow plugs are miniature electric heating elements, encapsulated in a metal case with a probe at one end and electrical connection at the other. Each combustion chamber has one glow plug threaded into it. When the glow plug is energised, it heats up rapidly causing the temperature of the air charge drawn into each of the combustion chambers to rise. The glow plug probe is positioned directly in line with the incoming spray of fuel from the injectors. Hence the fuel passing over the glow plug probe is also heated, allowing its optimum combustion temperature to be achieved more readily. In addition, small particles of the fuel passing over the glow plugs are ignited and this helps to trigger the combustion process.

3 A warning light informs the driver that pre-heating is taking place. The lamp extinguishes when sufficient pre-heating has taken place to allow the engine to be started, but power will still be supplied to the glow plugs for a further period until the engine is started. If no attempt is made to start the engine, the power supply to the glow plugs is switched off to prevent battery drain and glow plug burn-out.

4 The system employs post-glowing (after-heating), which operates as follows. After the engine has been started, the glow plugs continue to operate for a further period of time. This helps to improve fuel combustion whilst the engine is warming-up, resulting in quieter, smoother running and reduced exhaust emissions. The duration of the after-heating period is dependent on the coolant temperature.

3.3 Glow plug locations

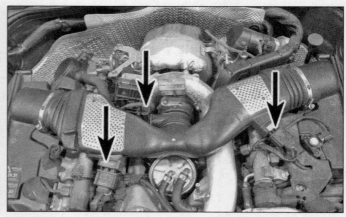

3.8 Disconnect the mass airflow sensors and breather pipe heater element wiring plugs

2 Pre-heating system – testing

1 Full testing of the system can only be carried out using specialist diagnostic equipment which is connected to the engine management system diagnostic wiring connector (see Chapter 4A Section 6). If the pre-heating system is thought to be faulty, some preliminary checks of the glow plug operation may be made as described in the following paragraphs.

2 Connect a voltmeter or 12-volt test lamp between the glow plug supply cable, and a good earth point on the engine.

Caution: Make sure that the live connection is kept well clear of the engine and bodywork

3 Have an assistant activate the pre-heating system by turning the ignition key to the second position, and check that battery voltage is applied to the glow plug electrical connection.

Note: *The supply voltage will be less than battery voltage initially, but will rise and settle as the glow plug heats up. It will then drop to zero when the pre-heating period ends and the safety cut-out operates.*

4 If no supply voltage can be detected at the glow plug, then the glow plug output stage or the supply cable may be faulty.

5 To locate a faulty glow plug, first operate the pre-heating system to allow the glow plugs to reach working temperature, then disconnect the battery negative lead as described in Chapter 5A Section 4.

6 Refer to Section 3, and remove the supply cable from No 2 glow plug terminal. Measure the electrical resistance between the glow plug terminal and the engine earth. A reading of anything more than a few Ohms indicates that the glow plug is defective.

7 As a final check, remove the glow plugs and inspect them visually, as described in Section 3.

8 If no problems are found, take the vehicle to a Mercedes Benz dealer or suitably equipped specialist for testing using the appropriate diagnostic equipment.

3 Glow plugs – removal, inspection and refitting

Removal

1 Disconnect the battery negative lead as described in Chapter 5A Section 4.

In-line engines

2 Undo the fasteners and remove the plastic cover on the top of the engine.

3 Disconnect the glow plug wiring connectors **(see illustration)**.

4 Clean the area around the glow plugs to prevent contamination, then using a deep socket, unscrew and remove them.

5 If the torque required to remove a glow plug exceeds 25 Nm, Mercedes recommend to bring the engine upto operating temperature and trying again. Bear in mind that if the hexagonal section of the plug breaks off, the plug will then need to be drilled out, which may involve cylinder head removal.

V6 engines

6 Pull the plastic cover on the top of the engine upwards from the rubber mountings.

7 Remove the right-hand air filter housing as described in Chapter 4A Section 2.

8 Disconnect the wiring plugs from the left-hand mass airflow sensor, right-hand mass airflow sensor, and breather pipe heater element **(see illustration)**.

9 Disconnect the breather hose from the oil separator.

10 Release the clamps and remove the air ducts between the air filter housing and the turbocharger **(see illustration)**.

11 Disconnect the glow plug wiring connectors **(see illustration)**.

12 Clean the area around the glow plugs to prevent contamination, then using a deep socket, unscrew and remove them **(see illustration)**.

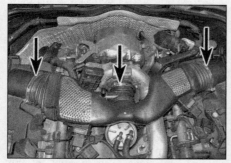

3.10 Release the clamps and remove the air duct

3.11 Pull the glow plug connectors upwards

3.12 Unscrew the glow plug from the cylinder head

4.5 The glow plug output stage is under the coolant expansion tank

4.7 Remove the bracket above the output stage

4.8 Disconnect the output stage wiring plugs

13 If the torque required to remove a glow plug exceeds 25 Nm, Mercedes recommend to bring the engine upto operating temperature and trying again. Bear in mind that if the hexagonal section of the plug breaks off, the plug will then need to be drilled out, which may involve cylinder head removal.

Inspection

14 Inspect the glow plugs for signs of damage. Burnt or eroded glow plug tips can be caused by a bad injector spray pattern. Have the injectors checked if this sort of damage is found.

15 If the glow plugs are in good condition, check them electrically, as described in Section 2.

16 The glow plugs can be energised by applying 12 volts to them to verify that they heat up evenly and in the required time. Observe the following precautions:

a) *Support the glow plug by clamping it carefully in a vice or self-locking pliers. Remember it will be red hot.*

b) *Make sure that the power supply or test lead incorporates a fuse or overload trip to protect against damage from a short-circuit.*

c) *After testing, allow the glow plug to cool for several minutes before attempting to handle it.*

17 A glow plug in good condition will start to glow red at the tip after drawing current for 5 seconds or so. Any plug which takes much longer to start glowing, or which starts glowing in the middle instead of at the tip, is probably defective.

Refitting

18 Thoroughly clean the glow plugs, and the glow plug seating areas in the cylinder head.

19 Apply a smear of anti-seize compound to the glow plug threads, then refit the glow plug and tighten it to the specified torque.

20 Reconnect the wiring to the glow plug. The connectors are a push-fit.

21 The remainder of refitting is a reversal of removal.

4 Glow plug output stage – removal and refitting

Removal

1 Disconnect the battery negative lead as described in Chapter 5A Section 4.

In-line engines

646.8xx engines

2 Raise the front of the vehicle and support it

securely on axle stands (see *'Vehicle jacking and support'*). Undo the fasteners and remove the engine undershield.

3 The glow plug output stage is located on the left-hand side of the engine/transmission. Undo the retaining bolts, lower the output stage, and disconnect the wiring plugs.

646.9xx, 647.9xx and 648.9xx engines

4 On models with these engines, the glow plug output stage is located on the left-hand side of the engine compartment, beneath the coolant expansion tank.

5 Disconnect the wiring from the output stage, then undo the 2 retaining nuts and manoeuvre the output stage from place **(see illustration)**.

V6 engines

6 The glow plug output stage is located at the front of the engine. Pull the plastic cover on the top of the engine upwards from its rubber mountings.

7 Undo the retaining nuts/bolts and lift the bracket above the output stage upwards **(see illustration)**.

8 Disconnect the wiring plugs and manoeuvre the output stage from place **(see illustration)**.

Refitting

9 Refitting is a reversal of removal.

Notes

Chapter 6
Clutch

Contents

Section number

Degrees of difficulty

Easy, suitable for novice with little experience | **Fairly easy,** suitable for beginner with some experience | **Fairly difficult,** suitable for competent DIY mechanic | **Difficult,** suitable for experienced DIY mechanic | **Very difficult,** suitable for expert DIY or professional

Specifications

Type	Self-adjusting, single dry plate with diaphragm spring, hydraulically-operated

Friction plate
  Diameter . . . . 240 mm
  Lining thickness:
    New (approximate) . . . . 3.6 to 4.0 mm
    Service limit . . . . 2.6 to 3.0 mm

Torque wrench settings	Nm	lbf ft
Master cylinder retaining nuts*	13	9
Pressure plate retaining bolts:		
Stage 1	16	12
Stage 2	25	18
Slave cylinder mounting bolt	11	8
Steering column pinch bolt*	25	18

*Do not re-use

1 General information and precautions

1 All models are fitted with a single dry plate clutch system. The main components consist of a friction disc, pressure plate (or cover), hydraulic master cylinder and release bearing/slave cylinder.

2 The clutch pressure plate is bolted to the rear face of the flywheel, and the friction disc is located between the pressure plate and the flywheel friction surface. The friction disc is splined to the transmission input shaft and is free to slide along the splines. Friction lining material is riveted to each side of the disc, and the disc hub incorporates cushioning springs to absorb transmission shocks and ensure a smooth take-up of drive. The pressure plate incorporates an internal diaphragm spring mounted on a fulcrum ring. When the inner fingers of the spring are depressed, the outer perimeter draws the pressure plate away from the friction disc.

3 The release bearing is part of the slave cylinder and is operated by the clutch pedal, using hydraulic pressure. The pedal acts on the hydraulic master cylinder pushrod, and hydraulic pressure operates the slave cylinder, which incorporates the release bearing.

4 When the clutch pedal is depressed, the release bearing is pushed forwards, to bear against the centre of the diaphragm spring, thus pushing the centre of the diaphragm spring inwards.

5 When the clutch pedal is released, the diaphragm spring forces the pressure plate into contact with the friction linings on the friction disc, and simultaneously pushes the friction disc forwards on its splines, forcing it against the flywheel. The friction disc is now firmly sandwiched between the pressure plate and the flywheel, and drive is taken up.

6 The clutch is self-adjusting. As wear takes place on the friction disc over a period of time, the pressure plate automatically moves closer to the friction plate to compensate.

⚠ **Warning: Dust created by clutch wear and deposited on the clutch components may contain asbestos, which is a health hazard. DO NOT blow it out with compressed air, or inhale any of it. DO NOT use petrol (or petroleum-based solvents) to clean off the dust. Brake system cleaner or methylated spirit should be used to flush the dust into a suitable receptacle. After the clutch components are wiped clean with rags, dispose of the contaminated rags and cleaner in a sealed, marked container.**

⚠ **Warning: Hydraulic fluid is poisonous; wash off immediately and thoroughly in the case of skin contact, and seek immediate medical advice if any fluid is swallowed or gets into the eyes. Certain types of hydraulic fluid are inflammable, and may ignite when allowed into contact with hot components; when servicing any hydraulic system, it is safest to assume that the fluid is inflammable, and to take precautions against the risk of fire as though it is petrol that is being handled. Hydraulic fluid is also an effective paint stripper, and will attack plastics; if any is spilt, it should be washed off immediately, using copious quantities of fresh water. Finally, it is hygroscopic (it absorbs moisture from the air) – old fluid may be contaminated and unfit for further use. When topping-up or renewing the fluid, always use the recommended type, and ensure that it comes from a freshly opened, sealed container.**

2 Clutch master cylinder – removal and refitting

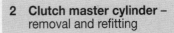

Note: *Refer to the precautions given in Section 1 regarding the use of hydraulic fluid.*

Removal

1 To reduce fluid loss, draw off as much fluid as possible from the appropriate chamber of the brake fluid reservoir, using a clean syringe, until the fluid level is below the level of the clutch master cylinder supply pipe. Alternatively, fit a hose clamp to the supply pipe.

2 Remove the brake light switch as described in Chapter 9 Section 18.

3 Depress the clip, rotate the clutch pedal switch 90° clockwise and detach it from the pedal bracket **(see illustration)**.

4 Unclip the plastic cover from the pedal bracket.

5 Carefully prise out the clevis pin securing the master cylinder pushrod to the pedal.

6 Undo the master cylinder retaining nuts. Note that new nuts must be fitted.

7 Prise out the wire clip a little, and disconnect the fluid pressure pipe from the master cylinder **(see illustration)**. Replace the pressure pipe O-ring seal. Be prepared for fluid spillage. Plug the openings to prevent contamination.

8 Similarly, prise out the wire clip and disconnect the fluid supply pipe from the master cylinder. Be prepared for fluid spillage. Plug the openings to prevent contamination.

9 Manoeuvre the master cylinder out from under the facia.

Refitting

10 Refitting is a reversal of removal. Bleed the clutch hydraulic system as described in Section 4.

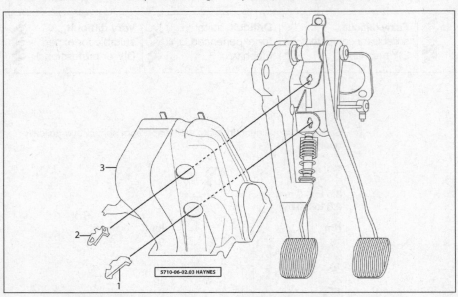

2.3 Stop light switch (1), clutch pedal switch (2) and plastic cover (3)

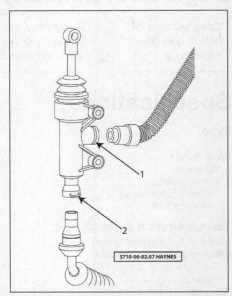

2.7 Clutch pressure pipe clip (2) and fluid supply pipe clip (1)

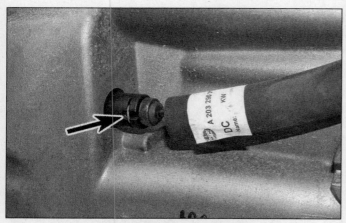

3.2 Clutch fluid pipe retaining clip

3.3 Release bearing/slave cylinder retaining bolts

3 Clutch slave cylinder – removal, inspection and refitting

Removal

1 Remove the transmission as described in Chapter 7A Section 7.

2 If not already disconnected, release the retaining clip from the clutch fluid hose on the transmission bellhousing, and remove the hose (see illustration).

3 Undo the retaining bolts and withdraw the release bearing/slave cylinder from the transmission housing, complete with bleed screw connection (see illustration).

Inspection

4 Spin the release bearing, and check it for excessive roughness. If any excessive movement or roughness is evident, renew the bearing. If a new clutch has been fitted, it is wise to renew the release bearing as a matter of course.

Refitting

5 Refitting is a reversal of removal. Tighten the retaining bolts to the specified torque, and bleed the clutch hydraulic system as described in Section 4.

4 Clutch hydraulic system – bleeding

Note: Refer to the precautions given in Section 1 regarding the use of hydraulic fluid.

1 The correct operation of the hydraulic system is only possible after removing all air from the circuit, and this is achieved by bleeding the system.

2 During the bleeding procedure, add only clean, unused hydraulic fluid of the recommended type. Never re-use fluid that has already been bled from the system. Ensure that sufficient fluid is available before starting work.

3 If there is any possibility of incorrect fluid being already in the system, both the clutch and brake circuits must be flushed completely with uncontaminated, correct fluid, and new seals should be fitted to the various components.

4 If hydraulic fluid has been lost from the system, or air has entered because of a leak, ensure that the fault is cured before proceeding further.

5 Apply the parking brake, then jack up the front of the vehicle and support it on axle stands (see 'Vehicle jacking and support'). Undo the fasteners and remove the transmission undershield.

6 Remove the dust cap from the slave cylinder bleed screw, and clean away any dirt.

7 Note that the brake fluid reservoir feeds both the brake and clutch hydraulic systems.

8 Mercedes-Benz recommended that pressure-bleeding equipment be used to bleed the system. Some pressure-bleeding kits are operated by the reservoir of pressurised air contained in a spare tyre; however, note that it will probably be necessary to reduce the pressure to a lower level than normal. Refer to the instructions supplied with the kit. If a pressure-bleeding kit is not available,

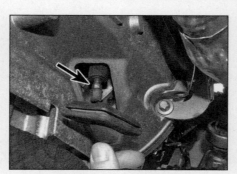

4.11 Clutch slave cylinder bleed screw

use the normal bleeding method described for the brake hydraulic circuit in Chapter 9 Section 2.

9 By connecting a pressurised, fluid-filled container to the brake fluid reservoir, bleeding can be carried out simply by opening the bleed screw on the clutch slave cylinder, and allowing the fluid to flow out until no more air bubbles can be seen in the expelled fluid. This method has the advantage that the large reservoir of fluid provides an additional safeguard against air being drawn into the system during bleeding.

10 Collect a clean glass jar, a suitable length of plastic or rubber tubing which is a tight fit over the bleed screw, and a ring spanner to fit the screw.

11 Fit the spanner and tube to the slave cylinder bleed screw (see illustration), place the other end of the tube in the jar, and pour in sufficient fluid to cover the end of the tube.

12 Connect the pressure-bleeding equipment to the brake/clutch fluid reservoir in accordance with its manufacturer's instructions.

13 Loosen the bleed screw half a turn using the spanner, and allow fluid to drain into the jar until no more air bubbles emerge.

14 When bleeding is complete, tighten the bleed screw, and disconnect the hose and the pressure bleeding equipment.

15 Wash off any spilt fluid, check once more that the bleed screw is tightened securely, and refit the dust cap.

16 Check the hydraulic fluid level in the reservoir, and top-up if necessary (see "Weekly checks").

17 Discard any hydraulic fluid that has been bled from the system, as it will not be fit for re-use.

18 Check the feel of the clutch pedal. If it feels at all spongy, air must still be present in the system, and further bleeding is required. Failure to bleed satisfactorily after a reasonable repetition of the bleeding procedure may be due to worn master or slave cylinder seals.

19 On completion, refit the undershield and lower the vehicle to the ground.

5.3 Pressure plate retaining bolts

5.4 Note the fitted position of the clutch plate/friction disc

5 Clutch assembly – removal, inspection and refitting

⚠ **Warning: Dust created by clutch wear and deposited on the clutch components may contain asbestos, which is a health hazard. DO NOT blow it out with compressed air, or inhale any of it. DO NOT use petrol or petroleum-based solvents to clean off the dust. Brake system cleaner or methylated spirit should be used to flush the dust into a suitable receptacle. After the clutch components are wiped clean with rags, dispose of the contaminated rags and cleaner in a sealed, marked container.**

Removal

1 Remove the transmission as described in Chapter 7A Section 7.

2 If the original clutch is to be refitted, make alignment marks between the clutch pressure plate assembly and the flywheel, so that the clutch can be refitted in its original position.

3 Progressively unscrew the bolts securing the clutch pressure plate assembly to the flywheel, and recover the washers (where fitted) **(see illustration)**.

4 Withdraw the clutch pressure plate assembly (cover) and disc from the flywheel **(see illustration)**. Be prepared to catch the friction disc, and note which way round the friction disc is fitted – the two sides of the disc may be marked Engine side and Transmission side, or the side with the part number on faces the flywheel. The greater projecting side of the hub faces away from the flywheel.

Inspection

Note: *Due to the amount of work involved in removing the clutch assembly, it is considered*

to be normal practice to replace the assembly regardless of condition.

5 Clean the cover, disc, and flywheel. Do not inhale the dust, as it may contain asbestos, which is dangerous to health.

6 Examine the fingers of the diaphragm spring for wear or scoring. If the depth of any scoring is excessive, a new cover assembly must be fitted.

7 Examine the pressure plate for scoring, cracking and discoloration. Light scoring is acceptable, but if excessive, a new assembly must be fitted.

8 Examine the friction disc linings for wear cracking, and for contamination with oil or grease. Using vernier calipers, check the thickness of the linings and compare with the details given in the Specifications. Check the disc hub and splines for wear by temporarily fitting it on the transmission input shaft. Renew the friction disc as necessary.

9 Examine the flywheel friction surface for scoring, cracking and discoloration (caused by overheating). If excessive, it may be possible to have the flywheel machined by an engineering works, otherwise it should be renewed.

10 Ensure that all parts are clean, and free of oil or grease, before reassembling. Do not apply any lubricant to the splines of the friction disc hub. Note that a new pressure plate may be coated with protective grease. It is only permissible to clean the grease away from the friction disc lining contact area. Removal of the grease from other areas will shorten the service life of the clutch.

11 Check the spigot bearing in the end of the crankshaft or in the centre of the flywheel. Make sure that it turns smoothly and quietly. If the transmission input shaft contact face on the bearing is worn or damaged, fit a new bearing.

Refitting

12 If you are re-using the pressure plate, the adjustment ring will need to be reset. Position the pressure plate in a hydraulic press (Mercedes technicians use a special tool) **(see illustrations)**, with a block of wood placed under the central portion of the pressure plate, directly below the diaphragm spring fingers (not on the friction face). Apply pressure to the diaphragm spring fingers until the adjusting ring is loose. While still applying pressure,

5.12a Special tool to adjust the pressure plate...

5.12b ...which presses down on the diaphragm spring fingers

5.12c Turn the adjusting ring anti-clockwise...

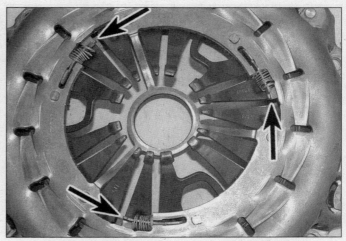
5.12d...and release the pressure on the diaphragm

5.16a Centralise the clutch plate...

5.16b...and fit the assembly onto the flywheel

use a screwdriver to rotate the adjusting ring anti-clockwise (see illustrations). Hold the adjustment ring in place, and then release the pressure on the diaphragm spring fingers.

13 It is important to ensure that no oil or grease gets onto the friction disc linings, or the pressure plate and flywheel faces. It is advisable to refit the clutch assembly with clean hands, and to wipe down the pressure plate and flywheel faces with a clean rag before assembly begins.

14 Offer the disc to the flywheel, with the greater projecting side of the hub facing away from the flywheel (most friction discs will have an Engine side marking which should face the flywheel). Hold the friction disc against the flywheel while the pressure plate assembly is offered into position, or alternatively use the centralising tool described later to hold the disc on the flywheel.

15 Fit the clutch pressure plate assembly, where applicable aligning the marks with those on the flywheel. Ensure that the pressure plate assembly locates over the dowels on the flywheel. Insert the securing bolts and washers, and tighten them finger-tight, so that the friction disc is gripped, but can still be moved.

16 The friction disc must now be centralised, to ensure correct alignment of the transmission input shaft with the spigot bearing in the crankshaft/flywheel (see illustrations). To do this, a proprietary tool may be used, or alternatively, use a wooden mandrel made to fit inside the friction disc hub and spigot bearing. Insert the tool through the friction disc into the spigot bearing, and make sure that it is central.

17 Tighten the clutch pressure plate bolts progressively and in diagonal sequence, until the specified torque setting is achieved, and then remove the centralising tool.

18 Check the release bearing in the front of the transmission for smooth operation, and if necessary renew it with reference to Section 3.

19 Refit the transmission as described in Chapter 7A Section 7.

Chapter 7 Part A
Manual gearbox

Contents

Degrees of difficulty

Easy, suitable for novice with little experience	Fairly easy, suitable for beginner with some experience	Fairly difficult, suitable for competent DIY mechanic	Difficult, suitable for experienced DIY mechanic	Very difficult, suitable for expert DIY or professional

Specifications

General
Type . . . . 6-speed with optional sequential automated operation
Code . . . . 716.60, 716.62, 716.63, 716.64, 716.65 or 716.66

Lubrication
Recommended oil . . . . See 'Lubricants and fluids'
Capacity:
   Upto transmission code 716.634 . . . . 1.2 litres
   From transmission code 716.646 . . . . 1.5 litres

Torque wrench settings

	Nm	lbf ft
Drain plug	30	22
Filler plug	35	25
Gearbox-to-engine bolts	40	30
Gearbox mounting bracket bolts:		
M8	24	18
M12	80	59
Output flange retaining nut*	110	78
Release bearing sleeve bolt	12	9

*Do not re-use

1 General information

1 A 6-speed manual transmission is bolted to the rear of the engine. Drive is transmitted from the crankshaft via the clutch to the input shaft, which has a splined extension to accept the clutch friction disc. The transmission output shaft transmits the drive via the propeller shaft to the rear differential. The input shaft runs in line with the output shaft. The input shaft and output shaft gears are in constant mesh with the layshaft gear cluster. Selection of gears is by sliding synchromesh hubs, which lock the appropriate output shaft gears to the output shaft.

2 Gear selection is via a floor-mounted lever and selector mechanism incorporating a gearchange rod or cable. The selector mechanism causes the appropriate selector fork to move its respective synchro-sleeve along the shaft, to lock the gear pinion to the synchro-hub. Since the synchro-hubs are splined to the output shaft, this locks the pinion to the shaft, so that drive can be transmitted. To ensure that gear-changing can be made quickly and quietly, a synchromesh system is fitted to all forward gears, consisting of baulk rings and spring-loaded fingers, as well as the gear pinions and synchro-hubs. The synchromesh cones are formed on the mating faces of the baulk rings and gear pinions.

3 Some models have an optional Sequentronic six-speed manual transmission that has an electro/hydraulic-operated clutch and shifting system. The result is a transmission that is conventional in its gears and internal components; but which is operated instead in response to commands from the gear lever through the ECU, so when changing gear it operates more like an automatic transmission. Mercedes call it an 'automated manual transmission'.

2 Gearbox oil – draining and refilling

Note: *Models with sequentronic transmissions, will need to be taken to a Mercedes Dealer to check the transmission oil level, as special tools are required.*

1 Raise the vehicle and support it securely on axle stands (see *'Vehicle jacking and support'*). Undo the fasteners and remove the transmission undershield.

2 Place a suitable container beneath the transmission drain plug, at the bottom of the casing, then unscrew the plug. Unscrew the level/filler plug, located on the right-hand side of the transmission, to assist draining. A hexagonal key should be used to unscrew the plugs, but a tool can be improvised using a long nut, or a length of hexagonal bar, and a spanner **(see illustrations)**.

3 Once all the fluid has drained, refit and tighten the drain plug.

4 Fill the transmission until the fluid level is 10 mm below the filler opening. Note that the vehicle must be in a level position.

5 When the level is correct, refit the plug, and tighten to the specified torque.

3 Gearchange lever asembly – removal and refitting

Removal

Rod/cable gearshift

1 Position the gear lever in the neutral position.

2 Remove the centre console as described in Chapter 11 Section 35.

3 To remove the gear knob from the gear lever, lift the gaiter from around the lever and turn the gaiter inside out, pulling it upwards over the gear knob. Turn the locking ring, below the gear knob anti-clockwise, and then pull the gear knob upwards to remove it from the gear lever.

4 Unclip the rubber boot from around the gearchange lever.

5 On models with a gearchange cable, disconnect the cable from the lever assembly as described in Section 4.

6 Undo the bolts at the rear of the gearchange lever.

7 With reference to Chapter 2A Section 16, or Chapter 2B Section 15, remove the rear engine/transmission mounting.

8 Remove the reinforcing brace beneath the propeller shaft.

9 Remove the bracket for the transmission undershield.

10 Detach the front of the propeller shaft from the transmission as described in Chapter 8 Section 7.

11 Pull out the pin securing the support bracket to the rear of the transmission **(see illustrations)**.

12 Pull out the pin securing the linkage rod to the selector shaft **(see illustrations)**.

13 Where fitted, disconnect the selector cable from the lower left-hand corner of the

2.2a Transmission fluid drain plug location

2.2b Transmission fluid filler/level plug location

3.11a Lift the securing clip...

3.11b...and slide it out of the transmission casing

3.12a Pull the locking clip out of the selector rod...

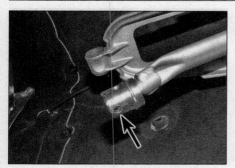

3.12b...and the gear linkage rod

transmission housing. Turn the locking ring anti-clockwise to disconnect the cable.
14 Lower the gearchange lever assembly from place.

Sequentronic transmission

15 Remove the key from the ignition lock.
16 Remove the centre console as described in Chapter 11 Section 35.
17 Disconnect the wiring plug from the rear of the gearchange lever assembly.
18 Undo the 3 retaining bolts, and manoeuvre the gearchange lever assembly from place.

Refitting

19 Refitting is the reverse of the removal procedure, applying a smear of the specified grease to all linkage pivot points (see *"Lubricants and fluids"*). Ensure all nuts and bolts are securely tightened'.

4 Gearchange cable – removal, refitting and adjustment

Removal

1 Raise the front of the vehicle and support it securely on axle stands (see *'Vehicle jacking and support'*).
2 Remove the centre console as described in Chapter 11 Section 35.
3 Unclip the outer rubber gaiter from the gearchange lever and fold it upwards.
4 Carefully prise the cable end fitting from the balljoint on the gearchange lever.
5 Working underneath the vehicle, prise out the retaining clip and pull the cable downwards from the base of the gear lever housing.
6 Unclip the cover from the cable housing at the rear of the gearbox housing.
7 Carefully prise the cable end fitting from the gearbox lever balljoint, and detach the outer cable from the housing bracket.

Refitting

8 Apply a little multi-purpose grease to the cable end fittings.
9 Refit the cable to the gearbox lever and gearchange lever, then adjust the cable as described later in this Section.

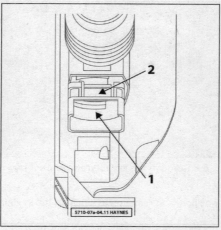

4.11 Press-up the lock button (1) until it's held by the catch (2)

10 After adjustment, the remainder of refitting is a reversal of removal.

Adjustment

11 Working underneath the vehicle, press-up the cable lock button until it is held in place by the catch **(see illustration)**.
12 With the gear lever in the neutral position, move the lever to the right-hand side, lift it slightly, then insert Mercedes tool No. 716 589 00 23 00 under the lever collar. Ensure the tool is inserted with the cut-out upwards **(see illustrations)**.
13 Slide the tool forwards until it touches the contact surface of the reverse gear lock **(see illustration)**.
14 Move the lever slightly to the left, and hold it against the tool.
15 Working under the vehicle, have an assistant press the catch and release the cable lock button.

5 Output flange oil seal – renewal

1 With reference to Chapter 8 Section 7, detach the front of the propeller shaft from the rear of the transmission.
2 Ensure that the transmission is in neutral.

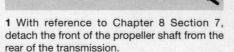
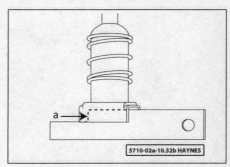

4.13 The tool must touch the contact surface of the reverse gear lock (a)

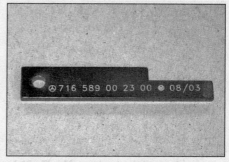

4.12a The Mercedes tool dimensions are: Length 1 = 75 mm, Length 2 – 50 mm, Width 1 = 14 mm, Width 2 = 8 mm

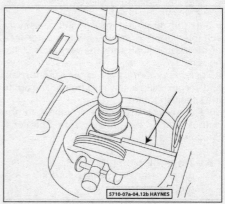

4.12b Ensure the tool is inserted with the cut-out upwards

3 Bolt a suitable holding tool to the transmission output flange. A suitable tool can be made up using two pieces of flat bar and bolts – engage the tool with two of the bolts holes in the output flange, and use it to counterhold the flange. Note that it must be possible to gain access to the output flange nut with the tool in place.
4 Counterhold the output flange, then unscrew the flange securing nut. Discard the nut, a new one must be used on refitting **(see illustration)**.
5 Pull the output flange from the shaft, using a suitable puller if necessary.
6 Prise the oil seal from the housing using a screwdriver.

5.4 The flange securing nut will be tight

6.1 Reversing light switch location

6.6 Remove the polystyrene impact pad

6.7 Step plate retaining nuts

7 Thoroughly clean the oil seal seating in the rear transmission cover.

8 Tap the new seal into position, using a suitable socket or tube, until the outer face of the seal is flush with the end face of the housing.

9 Refit the output flange to the output shaft, and secure using a new nut. Tighten the nut to the specified torque.

10 Reconnect the propeller shaft to the output flange, with reference to Chapter 8 Section 7.

6 Transmission electronic components – removal and refitting

Removal

Reversing light switch

Note: *Some models do not have a reversing light switch fitted to the transmission, on these models the ECU controls the operation of the reversing lights.*

1 Where fitted, the reversing light circuit is controlled by a switch located at the rear of the transmission **(see illustration)**. If a fault develops in the circuit, first ensure that the circuit fuse has not blown.

2 For access to the switch, it will be necessary to apply the parking brake, and then jack up the front of the vehicle and support it on axle stands (see *'Vehicle jacking and support'*). Undo the fasteners and remove the transmission undershield.

3 To test the switch, disconnect the wiring connector, and use a multimeter (set to the resistance function) or a battery-and-bulb test circuit to check that there is continuity between the switch terminals only when reverse gear is selected. If this is not the case, and there are no obvious breaks or other damage to the wires, the switch is faulty, and must be renewed.

4 To remove the switch, disconnect the wiring plug, undo the retaining bolt and withdrawn the switch from the transmission.

Electronic control unit (Sequentronic transmissions)

5 Move the passengers seat to the rearmost

position, and remove the key from the ignition lock.

6 Fold back the carpet from the floor, and remove the impact absorber material **(see illustration)**.

7 Undo the 3 retaining nuts and remove the step plate **(see illustration)**.

8 Disconnect the wiring plugs and remove the ECU.

Refitting

9 Refitting is a reversal of removal.

7 Gearbox – removal and refitting

Note: *This is a difficult operation, due to the limited access to the engine-to-transmission bolts. It is suggested that the procedure is read through thoroughly before starting the operation. Suitable ratchet extensions will be required to reach some of the engine-to-transmission bolts.*

Removal

1 Disconnect the battery negative lead as described in Chapter 5A Section 4.

2 Ensure the transmission is in position 'N', then raise the vehicle and support it securely on axle stands (see *'Vehicle jacking and support'*). Undo the fasteners and remove the engine/transmission undershield.

3 Remove the undershield rear support bracket.

4 Remove the catalytic converter and

particulate filter (where applicable) as described in Chapter 4A Section 19.

5 Remove the bracket each side securing the catalytic converter to the transmission.

6 Detach the earth lead from the rear of the transmission.

7 Undo the retaining bolts, remove the cover from the right-hand side of the transmission, then disconnect the wiring plugs.

8 Detach the fluid pipe from the engine sump.

9 Support the transmission using a transmission jack, then remove the rear transmission mounting complete with support bracket.

10 Detach the front of the propeller shaft from the transmission coupling as described in Chapter 8 Section 7.

11 Release the securing clip and disconnect the clutch fluid pipe from the transmission **(see illustration)**, with reference to Chapter 6. Place a suitable container beneath the pipe to catch the fluid which will be released, and plug or cover the open ends of the pipe and hose.
Note: The hydraulic fluid pipe from the clutch master cylinder loops over the transmission bellhousing, and an alternative method is to disconnect the union on the side of the transmission **(see illustration)**, and leave the pipe in position while the transmission is being removed. If this course of action is taken, fit a hose clamp to the fluid supply hose leading from the brake fluid reservoir to the clutch master cylinder. Place a suitable container beneath the union to catch the fluid which will be released, and plug or cover the open ends of the pipe and hose.

12 Prise off the securing clips, and

7.11a Release the securing clip...

7.11b ...or undo the fluid pipe connection

7.14a On models with soundproofing...

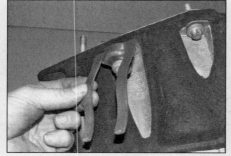

7.14b...remove the bolts with brackets first...

7.14c...and then pull out the soundproofing

disconnect the gear selector rods from the rear of the transmission.

13 Support the engine, as otherwise it will tilt rearwards and damage the brake pipes at the engine compartment bulkhead.

14 Unscrew all the engine-to-transmission bolts, leaving one bolt on either side of the transmission. Access to the upper bolts is very difficult, even with the assembly tilted, and several long socket extensions will be required. Remove the two upper, outer bolts first, removing the retaining brackets and soundproofing from the top of the transmission **(see illustrations)**.

15 Unscrew the two remaining engine-to-transmission bolts, and then, with the help of an assistant, pull the transmission rearwards and release the transmission input shaft from the clutch. Take care not to allow the weight of the transmission to hang on the clutch and input shaft, and where applicable take care not to damage the clutch fluid pipe during this procedure. If necessary, rotate the transmission to enable the top of the bellhousing to clear the vehicle body.

16 Once the input shaft is clear of the clutch, lower the transmission to the ground and withdraw from under the vehicle.

Refitting

17 The gearbox is refitted by a reversal of the removal procedure, bearing in mind the following points:
a) *Do not apply any lubricant to the transmission input shaft splines.*
b) *Ensure the locating dowels are correctly*
c) *positioned prior to installation.*
d) *Tighten all nuts and bolts to the specified torque (where given).*
e) *On completion, refill the gearbox with the specified type and quantity of lubricant (see "Lubricants and fluids") then check the oil level as described in Section 2.*
f)

8 Gearbox overhaul – general information

1 Overhauling a manual gearbox unit is a difficult and involved job for the DIY home mechanic. In addition to dismantling and reassembling many small parts, clearances must be precisely measured and, if necessary, changed by selecting shims and spacers. Internal gearbox components are also often difficult to obtain, and in many instances,

extremely expensive. Because of this, if the gearbox develops a fault or becomes noisy, the best course of action is to have the unit overhauled by a specialist repairer, or to obtain an exchange reconditioned unit.

2 Nevertheless, it is not impossible for the more experienced mechanic to overhaul the gearbox, provided the special tools are available, and the job is done in a deliberate step-by-step manner, so that nothing is overlooked.

3 The tools necessary for an overhaul include internal and external circlip pliers, bearing pullers, a slide hammer, a set of pin punches, a dial test indicator, and possibly a hydraulic press. In addition, a large, sturdy workbench and a vice will be required.

4 During dismantling of the gearbox, make careful notes of how each component is fitted, to make reassembly easier and more accurate.

5 Before dismantling the gearbox, it will help if you have some idea what area is malfunctioning. Certain problems can be closely related to specific areas in the gearbox, which can make component examination and replacement easier. Refer to the '*Fault finding*' Section of this manual for more information.

Chapter 7 Part B
Automatic gearbox

Contents

Degrees of difficulty

Easy, suitable for novice with little experience	**Fairly easy,** suitable for beginner with some experience	**Fairly difficult,** suitable for competent DIY mechanic	**Difficult,** suitable for experienced DIY mechanic	**Very difficult,** suitable for expert DIY or professional

Specifications

Type . . . . Five forwards speeds and reverse.

Model	Transmission code
200 CDI.	722.699
220 CDI.	722.699
270 CDI.	722.640
280 CDI.	722.626
320 CDI.	722.626

Type . . . . Seven forwards speeds, and two reverse speeds.

Model	Transmission code
280 CDI (V6)	722.9
320 CDI (V6)	722.9

Transmission fluid capacity (initial fill)
5-speed transmission. . . . . 7.5 L
7-speed transmission. . . . . 9.0 L

Installed height of torque converter:
  5-speed transmission. . . . . 7.0 mm
  7-speed transmission:
    Helical screwed connection . . . . 9.5 mm
    Axial screwed connection. . . . . 19.5 mm

Torque wrench settings

	Nm	lbf ft
Gearbox housing-to-engine bolts	38	28
Oil drain plug	20	15
Rear mounting-to-transmission	50	37
Rear support bracket-to-body	50	37
Torque converter bolts:		
Straight-threaded connection bolts (M8)	42	32
Angle-threaded connection bolts:		
Stage 1	4	2
Stage 2	30	22
Stage 3	Angle-tighten a further 90°	
Torque converter drain plug:		
M8	10	7
M10	15	11

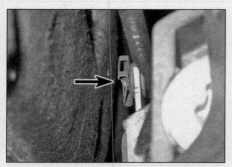

2.3 Prise off the selector rod retaining clip

2.5 Lever up the catch and rotate the collar 90°

2.7 Selector lever assembly rear retaining bolts

1 General information

1 The vehicles covered in this manual are equipped with a five-speed (model 722.6) or seven-speed (model 722.9) automatic transmission. All transmissions have a torque converter clutch system that improves fuel economy. The TCC engages in drive and overdrive modes. The TCC system consists of a solenoid, controlled by the ECU, which locks the torque converter when the vehicle is cruising on level ground and the engine is fully warmed-up. A transmission oil cooler is also fitted.

2 The transmission comprises a torque converter, an epicyclic geartrain, and hydraulically-operated brakes and clutches.

3 The torque converter provides a fluid coupling between the engine and transmission, and acts as a clutch, also providing a degree of torque multiplication when accelerating.

4 The epicyclic geartrain provides the forward and reverse gear ratios, according to which of its component parts are held stationary or allowed to turn. The components of the geartrain are held or released by brakes and clutches, which are activated by a hydraulic control unit. A fluid pump within the transmission provides the necessary hydraulic pressure to operate the brakes and clutches.

5 Driver control of the transmission is by a selector lever or optional steering wheel controls, and a two-position switch. This alters the hydraulic control pressure in the transmission, according to throttle position. The 'drive' position (D) provides automatic changing throughout the range of all forward gear ratios, and is the position selected for normal driving. An automatic kickdown facility shifts the transmission down a gear if the accelerator pedal is fully depressed. The 'hold' facility is similar to the 'drive' position, but limits the number of gear ratios available – ie, when the selector lever is in the 3 position, only the first three ratios can be used; in the 2 position, only the first two can be used, and so on. The lower ratio 'hold' is useful when travelling down steep gradients, or for preventing unwanted selection of high gears on twisty roads.

6 Due to the complexity of the automatic transmission, any repair or overhaul work must be left to a Mercedes-Benz dealer or automatic transmission specialist with the necessary special equipment for fault diagnosis and repair. The contents of the following Sections are therefore confined to supplying general information, and any service information and instructions that can be used by the owner.

2 Selector lever assembly – removal and refitting

Removal

1 Ensure the selector lever is in position 'P', then disconnect the battery negative lead as described in Chapter 5A Section 4.

2 Apply the parking brake, then jack up the front of the vehicle, and support securely on axle stands (see 'Vehicle jacking and support'). Undo the fasteners and remove the rear section of the engine/transmission undershield.

3 Working under the vehicle, prise off the metal retaining clip, and disconnect the selector rod from the bottom of the selector lever (see illustration).

4 Working inside the vehicle, remove the centre console as described in Chapter 11 Section 35.

5 At the front of the gear lever housing, disconnect the ignition switch control cable from the housing by levering up the catch, rotating the collar 90° and pulling it from place (see illustration).

6 Disconnect the wiring plugs from the selector lever assembly.

7 The selector lever assembly is retained by 1 bolt at the front, and 2 at the rear (see illustration). Undo the bolts and manoeuvre the lever assembly from place.

Refitting

8 Refitting is a reversal of removal.

3 Selector rod – removal, refitting and adjustment

Removal

1 Apply the parking brake, then jack up the front of the vehicle and support it on axle stands (see 'Vehicle jacking and support'). Undo the fasteners and remove the rear section of the engine/transmission undershield.

2 Prise the securing clips from the ends of the selector rod, at the the selector lever and at the lever on the transmission, and then withdraw the rod from under the vehicle (see illustration).

Refitting

3 Refitting is a reversal of removal, but check and adjust the selector rod as follows.

Adjustment

4 An assistant will be required to hold the selector lever in position D. This needs to be held in this position, throughout the complete procedure.

5 Working under the vehicle, slacken the grub

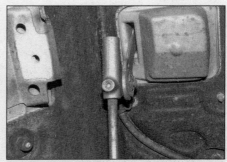

3.2 Slide off the clip and detach the rod from the lever

3.5 Slacken the grub screw at the base of the selector lever

4.9 Use a pair of pliers to unscrew the trim ring

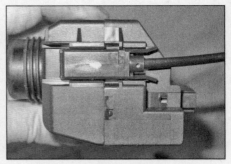

4.11 Squeeze together the lugs and disconnect the cable

screw at the bottom of the selector lever **(see illustration)**.

6 Ensure the selector lever on the transmission is in the 'D' position (fully forwards), then tighten the grub screw securely.

4 Ignition lock control cable
– removal, refitting and adjustment

Removal

1 On models without the 'Keyless Go' system, turn the ignition key to position 'O'.
2 On models with the 'Keyless Go' system, press the start-stop button repeatedly until the ignition is switched off.
3 Remove the centre console as described in Chapter 11 Section 35.
4 Remove the facia mounted audio system as described in Chapter 12 Section 16.
5 At the front of the gear lever housing, disconnect the ignition switch control cable from the housing **(see illustration 2.5)**. Raise the retaining lug, and pressing against the spring pressure, rotate the collar through 90° and detach the cable.
6 Lift up the air duct to expose the control cable.
7 Remove the drivers side lower facia panel as described in Chapter 11 Section 34.
8 Pull the air duct in the drivers footwell from the heater housing, and move it to one side.

9 Carefully unscrew the trim ring from the ignition control switch **(see illustration)**.
10 Remove the electronic ignition switch from the facia, without disconnecting the wiring plugs.
11 Squeeze together the retaining lugs and disconnect the control cable from the ignition switch **(see illustration)**.
12 Note its routing, then release any retaining clips and manoeuvre the control cable from the facia.

Refitting

13 Refitting is a reversal of removal.

5 Automatic transmission oil renewal

5-speed transmission

Note: *Note that the top of the fluid level dipstick tube is fitted with a tamperproof cap incorporating a plastic clip. The clip is broken when the cap is removed, and a new clip must be fitted when the cap is refitted. The dipstick is not fitted inside the tube, but must be obtained as a separate tool (number 140 589 15 21 00) from a Mercedes-Benz dealer. The alternative is to take the vehicle to a dealer for the fluid level check.*

1 With the parking brake fully applied, shift the selector lever to position 'N' and turn off the ignition.

2 Raise the vehicle and support it securely on axle stands (see *'Vehicle jacking and support'*). Release the fasteners and remove the transmission undershield. Note that the vehicle should be level to ensure accurate fluid level.
3 Position a container under the transmission, undo the drain plug and allow the fluid to flow in to the container **(see illustration)**. Renew the drain plug sealing ring.
4 When the fluid has stopped draining, refit the drain plug with a new washer, and tighten it to the specified torque.
5 Prise out the cover from the lower part of the bell housing, then using a socket on the crankshaft pulley, rotate the engine clockwise until the torque converter drain plug is accessible through the bell housing aperture **(see illustration)**.
6 Move the container under the bell housing, remove the torque converter drain plug and allow the fluid to flow out. Renew the drain plug sealing washer.
7 When the fluid has stopped draining, refit the plug with a new sealing washer and tighten it to the specified torque.
8 Break the plate of the locking pin, and remove the cap from the top of the filler tube. Note that a new cap will be required.
9 With the transmission cold (approximately 25°C) add 5 litres of new fluid through the filler tube.
10 Move the selector lever to position 'P', start the engine and allow it to idle.
11 Move the selector lever through the various positions several times, ending in position 'P'.
12 Insert the dipstick into the filler tube, remove it and examine the oil level on the dipstick. The 'MAX' and 'MIN' marks at the lower end of the dipstick are for fluid at 25°C.
13 If necessary, add fluid through the filler tube to bring the level upto the cold 'MAX' mark on the dipstick.
14 Mercedes recommend that if shifting problems occur, the fluid level should be checked with the transmission fluid temperature at 80°C. At this temperature, the upper marks on the dipstick should be used.
15 When the fluid level is correct, stop the engine, fit the new cap to the filler tube, and press it down until it latches.

5.3 5-speed automatic transmission fluid drain plug

5.5 Prise the cover from the bell housing

16 Refit the transmission undershield and lower the vehicle to the ground.

7-speed transmission

17 Renewal of the fluid in the 7-speed transmission requires access to Mercedes STAR diagnostic equipment (or equivalent), and several special tools. In order to obtain the correct fluid level, the fluid must be accessed accurately at several different temperatures, depending on vehicle specification. Consequently, we recommend this task is entrusted to a Mercedes dealer or suitably equipped repairer.

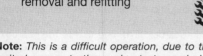

6 Automatic transmission – removal and refitting

Note: *This is a difficult operation, due to the limited access to the engine-to-transmission bolts, and to the weight of the transmission assembly. It is suggested that the procedure is read through thoroughly before starting the operation. Suitable ratchet extensions will be required to reach some of the engine-to-transmission bolts.*

Removal

1 Move the transmission selector lever to position 'N', then disconnect the battery negative lead as described in Chapter 5A Section 4.
2 Raise the bonnet to its fully open position **(see illustration)**. Take care to protect any brake pipes or wiring at the rear of the engine compartment.
3 Apply the parking brake, then jack up the front of the vehicle and support it on axle stands (see *'Vehicle jacking and support'*). The vehicle must be raised sufficiently high to enable the transmission to be lowered and removed from under the vehicle. Remove the engine undershield.
4 On 7-speed transmissions, remove the right-hand air filter housing and catalytic converter/particulate filter as described in Chapter 4A.
5 Remove the plastic cover from the top of the engine.

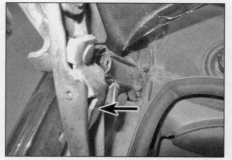

6.2 Depress the catch each side, and fully open the bonnet

6 On 5-speed transmissions, undo the bolt securing the upper end of the transmission oil filler pipe.
7 Drain the transmission fluid as described in Section 5.
8 Remove the undershield rear support bracket.
9 Remove the exhaust support bracket from the rear of the transmission.
10 Release the retaining clip and detach the selector rod from the transmission.
11 Disconnect the earth lead from the transmission **(see illustration)**.
12 Remove the heatshield from the right-hand side of the transmission, and disconnect any wiring plugs from the transmission **(see illustration)**.
13 Remove the cover in the lower section of the sump casing to access the torque converter bolts **(see illustration)**.
14 Unscrew and remove the torque converter retaining bolts. It will be necessary to turn the engine, using the crankshaft pulley bolt, so that each of the bolts can be unscrewed through the aperture **(see illustration)**.
Caution: Ensure the engine is turned only in the correct direction of rotation (clockwise).
15 Disconnect and remove the transmission fluid cooler pipes. Be prepared for fluid spillage. Plug the openings to prevent contamination. Renew the cooler O-ring seals.
16 The engine and transmission must now be supported. Mercedes technicians use a support bar which locates in the tops of the

6.11 Disconnect the transmission earth lead

inner wing panels – proprietary engine support bars are available from tool outlets.
17 If a support bar is not available, an engine hoist should be used. With an engine hoist the engine/transmission can be manoeuvred more easily and safely, balancing the engine on a jack is not recommended.
18 Undo the bolts and remove the rear crossmember, complete with rear transmission mounting.
19 Disconnect the propeller shaft flexible coupling from the transmission output shaft as described in Chapter 8, and pull the shaft rearwards a little. Support the shaft to prevent damage.
20 Lower the engine/transmission slightly and support it on a transmission jack.
21 Undo the bolts securing the transmission to the engine, pull it rearwards a little, and move the starter to one side with the wiring still attached. The help of an assistant will be required.
22 On 5-speed transmissions, slacken the retaining bolt and pull the oil filler pipe from the transmission. Renew the O-ring seal.
23 With the help of an assistant, withdraw the transmission squarely from the engine, making sure that the torque converter comes away with the transmission, and does not stay in contact with the driveplate. If this precaution is not taken, there is a risk of the torque converter falling out and being damaged. converter remains on the transmission input shaft.
24 Lower the transmission to the ground.

6.12 Remove the heatshield to access the wiring plug

6.13 Prise out the cover...

6.14...to access the torque converter bolts

9.3 Remove the polystyrene impact absorber

9.4 The floor plate is secured by 3 nuts

9.5 Remove the electronic transmission control module

Refitting

25 Where removed, refit the torque converter as follows:

a) Lightly grease the torque converter drive flange. Molykote grease is recommended.

b) Using 2 bolts, manipulate the converter into position. Move the converter back-and forth-as it is fitted to ensure that it is fully engaged with the input shaft and primary pump. The converter is fully engaged when the distance between the bellhousing face and torque converter driveplate face is as specified at the start of this Chapter.

c) Turn the torque converter until two of the converter-to-driveplate bolt holes are positioned at the access hole of the transmission bellhousing.

26 With the help of an assistant, raise the transmission, and locate it on the rear of the driveplate. Ensure the transmission is correctly aligned with the locating dowels, before pushing it fully into engagement with the engine. **Note:** The torque converter must remain in full engagement with the fluid pump at the correct installation depth throughout the fitting procedure.

27 Working your way around the transmission casing, refit the transmission-to-engine bolts. Do not fully tighten the retaining bolts until all the bolts are in place, then tighten to the specified torque setting.

28 Tighten the torque converter retaining bolts to the specified torque. Turn the engine as required to bring each of the bolts into view. **Note:** Insert all of the bolts before fully tightening them to the specified torque.

29 The remainder of the refitting procedure is a reversal of the removal procedure, noting the following special points:

a) Tighten all retaining bolts to their specified torque wrench setting (where given).

b) Reconnect and adjust the selector rod, as described in Section 3.

c) Renew the transmission fluid as described in Section 5.

d) If a new unit has been fitted, depending on the transmission type, it may be necessary to have the transmission ETC 'matched' to the engine management ECM electronically, to ensure correct operation – seek the advice of your Mercedes dealer or automatic transmission specialist.

e) Road test the car to check the transmission for correct operation.

7 Automatic transmission overhaul – general information

1 In the event of a fault occurring on the transmission, it is first necessary to determine whether it is of an electrical, mechanical or hydraulic nature, and to achieve this, special test equipment is required. It is therefore essential to have the work carried out by a Mercedes dealer, or a suitably-equipped specialist if a transmission fault is suspected.

2 Do not remove the transmission from the vehicle for possible repair before professional fault diagnosis has been carried out, since most tests require the transmission to be in the vehicle.

8 Torque converter oil seal – renewal

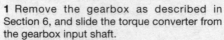

1 Remove the gearbox as described in Section 6, and slide the torque converter from the gearbox input shaft.

2 Using a flat-bladed screwdriver, prise the oil seal from the input shaft housing. Note the fitted depth of the seal.

3 Ensure that the oil seal recess in the gearbox, and the torque converter spigot are clean and dry. Lubricate the new oil seal with clean gearbox fluid, and fit it to the gearbox. Use a tubular drift that bears only on the hard outer edge of the seal. Fit the seal squarely into the housing, with the inner lip facing the gearbox.

4 Position the torque converter over the input shaft, and check that it is fully located.

9 Electronic transmission control module (ETC) – removal and refitting

Removal

Note: This procedure only applies to vehicles fitted with the 5-speed transmission. On 7-speed transmissions, the electronic control unit is integrated into the transmission casing.

1 Remove the ignition key.

2 Move the passengers seat to the rearmost position, and fold the footwell carpet back. The ETC is located under the passengers floor.

3 Remove the impact absorber **(see illustration)**.

4 Undo the fasteners and remove the floor plate **(see illustration)**.

5 Undo the retaining nuts, move the ETC rearwards and disconnect the wiring plugs **(see illustration)**.

Refitting

6 Refitting is a reversal of removal. Note that if a new ETC module has been fitted, it may need to be configured using Mercedes Benz diagnostic equipment. Entrust this task to a Mercedes dealer or suitably equipped specialist.

Chapter 8
Driveshafts, propeller shaft and final drive

Contents

Degrees of difficulty

| Easy, suitable for novice with little experience | | Fairly easy, suitable for beginner with some experience | Fairly difficult, suitable for competent DIY mechanic | Difficult, suitable for experienced DIY mechanic | Very difficult, suitable for expert DIY or professional | |

Specifications

Final drive
Type . . . . Rubber bush-mounted to rear suspension crossmember

Driveshaft
Type . . . . Steel shafts with ball-and-cage type constant velocity joints at each end

Propeller shaft
Type . . . . Two-piece tubular shaft with centre bearing and universal joint. Rubber coupling at front and rear joints

Constant velocity joint grease capacity:
82 mm diameter joint housing 80g
95 mm diameter joint housing 100g
102 mm diameter joint housing 120g
106 mm diameter joint housing 130g
112 mm diameter joint housing 140g
116 mm diameter joint housing 150g

Torque wrench settings

	Nm	lbft
Driveshaft nut: *		
Self-locking nut	350	258
Not self-locking nut:		
Stage 1	170	125
Stage 2	Angle-tighten a further 45°	
Final drive:		
Filler plug	50	37
Drain plug	50	37
Front mount bracket to crossmember: *		
Stage 1	50	37
Stage 2	Angle-tighten a further 90°	
Front mounting bolts (M10)*	65	48
Rear mounting bolt (M14): *		
Stage 1	80	60
Stage 2	Angle-tighten a further 60°	
Pinion nut: *		
Vehicles with 198 mm diameter differential	See text	
All other vehicles	160	118
Propeller shaft:		
Front or rear flexible coupling: *		
M10	40	30
M12	60	44
Centre bearing-to-crossbrace	25	18
Crossbrace-to-floor	23	17
Roadwheel bolts	130	96

Do not re-use

1 General information

1 Power is transmitted from the transmission to the rear axle by a two-piece propeller shaft, joined in front of the centre bearing by a 'slip joint': a sliding, splined coupling. The slip joint allows slight fore-and-aft movement of the propeller shaft. The propeller shaft is attached to the flanges of the transmission and final drive unit by flexible rubber couplings, a vibration damper being fitted between the front coupling and the shaft. The middle of the propeller shaft is supported by the centre bearing, which is bolted to the vehicle body. A universal joint is located at the rear of the centre bearing, to compensate for movement of the transmission and differential on their mountings, and for any flexing of the chassis.

2 The final drive assembly includes the drive pinion, the ring gear, the differential and the output flanges. The drive pinion, which drives the ring gear, is also known as the differential input shaft, and is connected to the propeller shaft via an input flange. The differential is bolted to the ring gear and drives the rear wheels through a pair of output flanges bolted to driveshafts. The differential allows the wheels to turn at different speeds when cornering, although only to a limited amount on models fitted with ASD (limited-slip differential).

3 The driveshafts deliver power from the final drive unit output flanges to the rear wheels. The driveshafts are equipped with constant velocity (CV) joints at each end. The inner CV joints are bolted to the differential flanges; the outer CV joints engage the splines of the wheel hubs, and are secured by a large nut.

4 Major repair work on the differential assembly components (drive pinion, ring-and-pinion and differential) requires many special tools and a high degree of expertise, and therefore should not be attempted by the home mechanic. If major repairs become necessary, we recommend that they be performed by a Mercedes-Benz service department or other suitably-equipped automotive engineer.

2 Final drive unit – draining and refilling

1 This operation is much quicker and more efficient if the car is first taken on a journey of sufficient length to warm the final drive unit up to normal operating temperature.

2 Park the car on level ground, switch off the ignition and apply the parking brake firmly. For improved access, jack up the rear of the car and support it securely on axle stands (see 'Vehicle jacking and support'). Note that the car must be level, to ensure accuracy, when refilling and checking the oil level.

3 Wipe clean the area around the filler/level plug, which is situated on the left-hand side of the final drive unit, next to the driveshaft flange, and unscrew it **(see illustration)**.

4 Position a suitable container under the drain plug, and unscrew the plug from the right-hand side of the housing **(see illustration)**.

5 Allow the oil to drain completely into the container. If the oil is hot, take precautions against scalding. Clean both the filler/level and the drain plugs, being especially careful to wipe any metallic particles off the magnetic inserts.

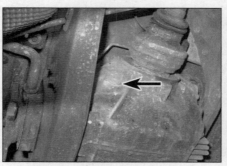

2.3 Final drive filler/level plug

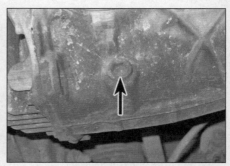

2.4 Final drive drain plug

3.10 Final drive rear mounting bolt

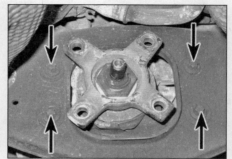

3.12 Final drive-to-bracket bolts

4.11 Release the staked area of the nut on the shaft

6 When the oil has finished draining, clean the drain plug threads and those of the final drive casing. Apply a little thread-locking compound to the plug, then tighten it to the specified torque. If the car was raised for the draining operation, now lower it to the ground.

7 Refilling the final drive unit is an extremely awkward operation. Above all, allow plenty of time for the oil level to settle properly before checking it. Note that the car must be parked on flat level ground when checking the oil level.

8 Refill the final drive unit with the exact amount of the specified type of oil (see "Lubricants and fluids"), until it begins to drip from the filler hole. Apply a little thread-locking compound to the plug, then tighten it to the specified torque. If the correct amount was poured into the final drive unit and a large amount flows out on checking the level, refit the filler/level plug and take the car on a short journey so that the new oil is distributed fully around the final drive components, then check the level again on your return.

3 Final drive unit – removal and refitting

Removal

1 On models with Sensotronic Brake Control (SBC) (upto 2007 pre-facelift models), have the system deactivated using Mercedes (or equivalent) diagnostic equipment. If access to this equipment is not available, deactivate the system as described in Chapter 9 Section 4.

2 Raise the rear of the vehicle and support it securely on axle stands (see 'Vehicle jacking and support'). Remove both rear roadwheels.

3 Remove the rear section of the exhaust system as described in Chapter 4A Section 19.

4 With reference to Chapter 9 Section 16, unhook the parking brake cable from the centre adjuster mechanism.

5 Undo the two bolts securing the propeller shaft centre support bearing to the crossbrace **(see illustration 7.5)**.

6 Make alignment marks between the coupling and flange, then undo the three nuts and remove the bolts securing the propeller

shaft rear flexible coupling to the differential pinion flange.

7 Push the propeller shaft forwards as far as it will go to disengage the pinion flange centring sleeves. Lower the disconnected propeller shaft, and fasten it to one side or support it securely to prevent any damage. Do not let it hang from the rear of the transmission.

8 Remove the rear driveshafts as described in Section 5.

9 Place a jack beneath the final drive housing and just take the weight of the unit.

10 Remove the rear bolt securing the final drive unit to the suspension crossmember/subframe **(see illustration)**.

11 Undo the bolt/nut each side securing the final drive front mounting bracket to the suspension crossmember/subframe. Note the positions of the shims – the triangular bulges must point upwards.

12 With the help of an assistant, carefully lower the final drive assembly from place. If required, undo the bolts and detach the front mounting bracket from the final drive unit **(see illustration)**.

Refitting

13 Refitting is a reversal of removal, noting the following points:
a) Only tighten the propeller shaft centre bearing bolts once the rear coupling has been refitted, and the bolts tightened.
b) Align the rear coupling previously made marks.
c) Tighten all fasteners to their specified torque where given.
d) Replenish the final drive fluid as described in Section 2.

4 Final drive unit seals – renewal

Driveshaft oil seals

1 Chock the front wheels and loosen the rear wheel bolts. Jack up the rear of the car and support it on axle stands (see 'Vehicle jacking and support'). Remove the rear wheels.

2 Remove the relevant driveshaft as described in Section 5.

3 Note the seal's fitted position in the

housing, and then using a lever, carefully prise the seal out of the final drive housing.

4 Clean out the recess in the housing for the seal, and then check the new seal against the old seal to make sure it is the correct one.

5 Using a seal drift/installer or a large deep socket, install the new oil seal into the housing, making sure it is fitted in the same location as noted on removal.

6 Lubricate the lip of the seal with clean gear oil, and then refit the driveshaft with reference to Section 5.

7 Check the oil level in the final drive unit as described in Section 2. Lower the vehicle to the ground and tighten the wheel bolts to the specified torque setting.

Pinion oil seal

8 Chock the front wheels and jack up the rear of the car and support it on axle stands (see 'Vehicle jacking and support').

9 Drain the final drive unit oil as described in Section 2.

10 Undo the three nuts and remove the bolts securing the propeller shaft rear flexible coupling to the differential pinion flange. Disconnect the propeller shaft from the flange on the differential and fasten it to the underside of the vehicle to prevent it getting damaged.

11 Before attempting to remove the large nut securing the flange to the pinion shaft **(see illustration)**, use a small drift to release the staked area of the nut in the depressions on the shaft.

12 On vehicles with a 198 mm diameter differential, use a beam-type (deflection) torque wrench to measure the torque required to rotate the pinion shaft. Is essential that when tightening the pinion nut, the same torque is achieved.

13 Using a tool/bar to prevent the flange from turning, undo the flange retaining nut.

14 Note the seal's fitted position in the housing, and then using a lever, carefully prose the seal out of the final drive housing.

15 Clean out the recess in the housing for the seal, and then check the new seal against the old seal to make sure it is the correct one.

16 Using a seal drift/installer or a large deep socket, install the new oil seal into the housing, making sure it is fitted in the same location as noted on removal.

17 Lubricate the lip of the seal with clean gear oil, and then refit the flange to the pinion shaft.

18 On vehicles with a 198 mm diameter differential, fit a new pinion nut, and tighten it gradually, checking with the beam-type (deflection) torque wrench until the torque measured during removal, is achieved. Stake the nut to the shaft using a chisel.

19 On all other vehicles, fit a new pinion nut and tighten it to the specified torque.

20 The remainder of refitting is a reversal of removal.

5 Driveshaft – removal and refitting

Removal

1 On models with Sensotronic Brake Control (SBC) (upto 2007 pre-facelift models), have the system deactivated using Mercedes (or equivalent) diagnostic equipment. If access to this equipment is not available, deactivate the system as described in Chapter 9 Section 4.

2 Slacken the 12-point driveshaft retaining nut with the car resting on its wheels. Note that this nut is extremely tight – ensure that the tools used to loosen it are of good quality, and a good fit. Do not remove the nut at this stage.

3 Chock the front wheels and slacken the rear wheel bolts. Jack up the rear of the car and support it on axle stands (see 'Vehicle jacking and support'). Remove the relevant rear roadwheel.

4 Undo the mounting bracket retaining bolts and slide the brake caliper from the disc. Suspend the caliper from the vehicle body to prevent strain on the flexible brake hose.

5 Remove the ABS wheel speed sensor as described in Chapter 9 Section 20.

6 Detach the anti-roll bar link from the hub carrier as described in Chapter 10 Section 19.

7 Detach all the suspension control arms from the hub carrier, with the exception of the lower spring control arm, as described in Chapter 10 Section 17.

8 Lower the jack under the spring control arm, fold the hub carrier outwards and slide the outer driveshaft housing from the hub.

9 The driveshaft can now be removed from the final drive unit. Carefully lever the driveshaft out from the final drive unit, taking care not to damage the seal in the final drive unit housing. Note the circlip on the driveshaft splined section to locate it in the final drive. Discard this circlip – a new one must be fitted.

Refitting

10 Refitting is the reverse of removal, noting the following points.

a) Slide the driveshaft back into the final drive, making sure that the new circlip locates inside the differential securely.

b) Clean the threads of the driveshaft outer coupling, and fit a new driveshaft nut.

c) Tighten all fasteners to their specified torque where given.

d) Once the vehicle is resting on its wheels, tighten the driveshaft retaining nut to the specified torque. Where non-self-locking nut is fitted, stake it firmly into the driveshaft groove using a hammer and punch.

6 Driveshaft gaiters – renewal

Note: *This is a difficult procedure for the DIY'er to successfully carry out without access to a hydraulic press and suitable crimping tools. It may be prudent to simply obtain a complete replacement driveshaft.*

1 Remove the driveshaft as described in Section 5.

2 Secure the driveshaft in a vice equipped with soft jaws, and release the two outer joint gaiter retaining clips. If necessary, the retaining clips can be cut to release them.

3 Cut off the rubber gaiter and discard it, scoop out all the old dirty grease.

4 Using a hacksaw, carefully cut the sealing cup from the joint housing **(see illustrations)**.

5 Clamp the outer constant velocity joint in a vice, and make alignment marks between the inner ring, ball retainer, and outer joint housing **(see illustration)**.

6 Align the shaft so the narrow bar of the inner ring points upwards.

7 Using a suitable thin-bladed screwdriver, prise out the upper balls from the retainer **(see illustration)**.

8 Slightly rotate the shaft and remove it, complete with the retainer and remaining balls, from the outer joint housing. Hold onto the balls to prevent them falling out.

9 Remove the remaining balls from the

6.4a Cut through the sealing cup lip...

6.4b...then use a chisel...

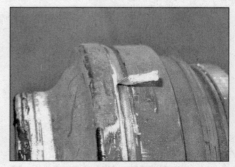

6.4c...to prise out the lip...

6.4d...and drive the sealing cup from the housing

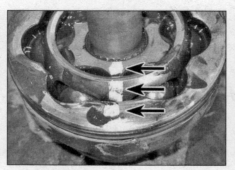

6.5 Make alignment marks between the inner ring, ball retainer and joint housing

6.7 Prise the balls from the retainer

retainer.

10 Note its orientation, then use a hydraulic press or puller to remove the inner ring from the shaft **(see illustration)**.

11 Release the two inner joint gaiter retaining clips, and slide the gaiter from place. Do not attempt to dismantle the inner joint.

12 Using a hacksaw, carefully cut the sealing cup from the joint housing **(see illustrations 6.4a, 6.4b, 6.4c and 6.4d)**.

13 Thoroughly clean the joints, balls, etc, and examine them for wear and damage. If the either joint is worn or damaged, the complete driveshaft must be replaced.

14 Fill the inner joint with the correct quantity of grease as given in the Specifications, then renew the O-ring seal, slide the new sealing cup into place, and secure it using a hammer and a 4 mm rod to push the cup rim into the groove.

15 Slide the inner joint gaiter into place, and secure it with the new retaining clips.

16 Slide the new outer joint gaiter onto the shaft – small diameter first.

17 Slide the new sealing cup onto the shaft – small diameter first.

18 Press the outer joint inner ring onto the shaft (observing the orientation previously noted), so that the shaft protrudes 4.2 mm through the ring **(see illustration)**.

19 'Stake' the ring to the shaft at 3 points 120° apart. The stakings must be applied between the original stakings, and as close as possible to the splined profile of the shaft.

20 Fill the outer joint with the correct quantity of grease as given in the Specifications, then renew the O-ring seal, slide the new sealing cup into place, and secure it using a hammer and a 4 mm rod to push the cup ring into the groove.

21 Slide the outer joint gaiter into place, and secure it with the new retaining clips.

22 The remainder of refitting is a reversal of removal, noting the following points:

a) *Align the previously made marks between the outer joint housing, retainer and inner ring.*

b) *Fill the outer joint with the correct quantity of grease as given in Specifications.*

c) *Crimp the new retaining clips in place, with the 'open end' of the clips facing opposite to the normal direction of rotation.*

7 Propeller shaft – removal and refitting

Removal

1 Chock the front wheels. Jack up the rear of the car and support it on axle stands (see *'Vehicle jacking and support'*).

2 Remove the rear section of the exhaust system as described in Chapter 4A Section 19.

3 Remove the heatshields from above the exhaust system.

4 Remove the crossbrace under the front of the propeller shaft.

5 Have an assistant support the propeller shaft, then undo the bolts securing the centre bearing crossbrace to the vehicle floor **(see illustration)**.

6 Make alignment marks between the flexible coupling and the transmission output flange **(see illustration)**. Repeat this process at the rear of the propeller shaft.

7 Slacken and remove the retaining nuts and bolts securing the flexible coupling to the transmission flange **(see illustrations)**. Discard the nuts; new ones should be used on refitting.

8 Unscrew the nuts and bolts securing the coupling to the final drive unit flange and discard them; new ones must be used on refitting **(see illustration)**.

9 Slide the rear of the shaft forwards and disengage the shaft from the final drive unit. Free the front of the shaft from the transmission, and remove the shaft assembly from underneath the vehicle.

Note: *Do not separate the two halves of the shaft without first making alignment marks. If the shafts are incorrectly joined, the propeller shaft assembly may become imbalanced, leading to noise and vibration during operation. On some models, there are alignment marks already on the shaft; the raised mark on the front section must be positioned in between the two marks on the rear section universal joint.*

10 Inspect the rubber couplings, the support bearing and shaft universal joint as described later in this Chapter.

Refitting

11 Lubricate the shaft bushes with multi-purpose grease, and the shaft splines with molybdenum disulphide grease.

12 Manoeuvre the shaft into position, aligning the marks made prior to removal, and engage the shaft with the transmission and final drive

6.10 Remove the inner ring from the shaft

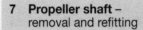

6.18 The shaft must protrude 4.2 mm

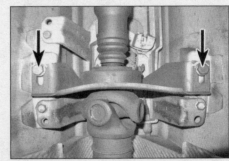

7.5 Centre bearing crossbrace retaining bolts

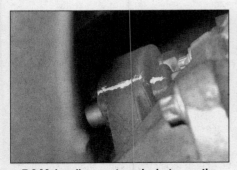

7.6 Make alignment marks between the coupling and the transmission output flange

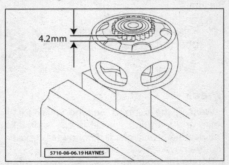

7.7 Remove the bolts/nuts securing the flexible coupling to the transmission flange

7.8 Undo the 3 bolts/nuts securing the coupling to the final drive flange

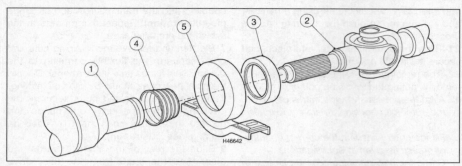

9.5 Propeller shaft centre bearing components – typical

1 Propeller shaft, 2 Propeller shaft, 3 Bearing, 4 Rubber gaiter, 5 Centre bearing

unit flanges. With the marks correctly aligned, refit the centre bearing retaining bolts, tightening them lightly only at this stage.

13 Making sure the marks are correctly aligned, insert the retaining bolts securing the rear coupling to the final drive unit and fit the new retaining nuts. Tighten the retaining nuts to the specified torque setting.

14 Make sure the front coupling is correctly aligned with the transmission flange and refit the coupling bolts. Fit the new retaining nuts and tighten them to the specified torque.

15 With both the front and rear couplings correctly tightened, tighten the centre bearing retaining bolts to the specified torque setting.

16 The remainder of refitting is a reversal of removal.

8 Propeller shaft rubber coupling – check and renewal

Check

1 Raise the vehicle and support it securely on axle stands (see *'Vehicle jacking and support'*).
2 To improve access to the coupling, unscrew the heat shield retaining nuts and manoeuvre the heat shield out from around the exhaust system.
3 Closely examine the rubber couplings which link the propeller shaft to the transmission and final drive, looking for signs of damage such as cracking or splitting or for signs of general deterioration. If necessary, renew the coupling as follows.

Renewal

4 Remove the propeller shaft as described in Section 7.

Front coupling

5 Make alignment marks between the coupling and propeller shaft.
6 Unscrew the retaining nuts and washers, then withdraw the bolts and remove the coupling from the propeller shaft. Note carefully any additional markings or wording (which may be in German) for use when refitting. Inspect the vibration damper for signs of wear or damage, and renew if necessary.
7 Check the centring sleeve fitted to the

centre of the coupling for signs of wear or damage. If necessary, the centring sleeve can be pressed out of position for renewal, having first noted its fitted depth.
8 Fit the new rubber coupling to the shaft, ensuring that (where applicable) any additional markings or wording are orientated as noted on removal. Insert the retaining bolts then fit the new retaining nuts and washers, and tighten them to the specified torque.
9 Refit the propeller shaft as described in Section 7.

Rear coupling

10 Unscrew the retaining nuts then withdraw the bolts and remove the coupling from the propeller shaft.
11 Fit the new coupling, then fit the retaining bolts and new nuts, tightening them to the specified torque.
12 Refit the propeller shaft as described in Section 7.

9 Propeller shaft centre bearing – check and renewal

Check

1 Wear in the support bearing will lead to noise and vibration when the car is driven. The bearing is best checked with the propeller shaft removed (see Section 7).
2 Rotate the bearing and check that it turns smoothly with no sign of free play; if it's difficult to turn, or if it has a gritty feeling, renew it. Also inspect the rubber portion. If it's cracked or deteriorated, renew it.

Renewal

Note: *Bearing renewal requires the use of a puller and hydraulic press, as well as suitable spacers. If access to suitable equipment cannot be gained, entrust the task to your Mercedes-Benz dealer or suitably equipped repairer.*

3 Remove the propeller shaft as described in Section 7.
4 Make alignment marks between the front and rear sections of the propeller shaft, noting that on some models there are alignment

marks already on the shaft; the raised mark on the front section must be positioned in between the two marks on the rear section universal joint.
5 Separate the two halves of the propeller shaft **(see illustration)**.
6 Remove the rubber gaiter from the front section of the shaft.
7 Using a suitable puller, draw the centre mounting assembly off the end of the shaft, noting which way around the bracket is fitted.
8 Support the mounting bracket assembly, and carefully press the bearing out of position using a tubular drift.
9 Inspect all components for signs of wear or damage and renew as necessary.
10 Support the mounting bracket securely and press the new bearing fully into position using a tubular drift which bears only on the bearing outer race.
11 Remove all traces of dirt from the propeller shaft, ensure that the mounting bracket is positioned the correct way around, and then press the assembly fully onto the shaft using a tubular drift which bears only on the bearing inner race.
12 Lubricate the propeller shaft splines with molybdenum disulphide grease. Carefully slide the two halves of the propeller shaft together, making sure the alignment marks are correctly positioned.
13 Refit the propeller shaft as described in Section 7.

10 Propeller shaft universal joint – check and renewal

Check

1 Wear in the universal joint is characterised by vibration in the transmission, noise during acceleration, and metallic squeaking and grating sounds as the bearings disintegrate. The joint can be checked with the propeller shaft still fitted.
2 Hold the front half of the propeller shaft, and try to turn the rear half of the shaft. Free play between the propeller shaft halves indicates excessive wear. If the axial movement is excessive, renew the propeller shaft.

Renewal

3 At the time of writing, no spare parts were available to enable renewal of the universal joints to be carried out. Therefore, if any joint shows signs of damage or wear the propeller shaft assembly must be renewed. Consult your Mercedes-Benz dealer or parts supplier for latest information on parts availability.
4 If renewal of the propeller shaft is necessary, it may be worthwhile seeking the advice of an automotive engineering specialist. They may be able to repair the original shaft assembly, or supply a reconditioned shaft on an exchange basis.

Chapter 9
Braking system

Contents

Degrees of difficulty

Easy, suitable for novice with little experience	**Fairly easy,** suitable for beginner with some experience	**Fairly difficult,** suitable for competent DIY mechanic	**Difficult,** suitable for experienced DIY mechanic	**Very difficult,** suitable for expert DIY or professional

Specifications

Front brakes
Caliper type . . . . Single piston sliding caliper or twin-piston fixed caliper
Disc:
   Type Ventilated
   Thickness:
      New . . . . 28 or 32 mm
         28 mm discs . . . . 25.4 mm
         32 mm discs . . . . 29.4 mm
Pad friction material minimum thickness . . . . 2.0 mm

Rear brakes
Caliper type . . . . Single piston sliding caliper
Disc:
   Type . . . . Ventilated
   Thickness:
     New
        28 mm discs . . . . 25.4 mm
        32 mm discs . . . . 30.0 mm
   Maximum runout . . . . 0.08 mm
Pad friction material minimum thickness . . . . 2.0 mm
Parking brake shoe friction material minimum thickness. . . . . N/A

Parking brake
Type . . . . Cable operated brake shoes with drum machined into rear disc hub
Number of notches on gear segment. . . . . See text

Torque wrench settings

	Nm	lbf ft
Bleed screw	7	5
Brake operating unit (BOU)-to-bulkhead	20	15
Front brake caliper-to-hub carrier: *		
M12	115	85
M14:		
Stage 1	80	60
Stage 2	Angle-tighten a further 45°	
Front caliper guide pin bolts: *		
T45 Internal Torx	27	20
13 mm Hexagon head	40	30
7 mm Allen key	27	20
9 mm Allen key	55	41
Disc retaining screw	10	7
Master cylinder nuts	25	18
Rear caliper bracket-to-hub carrier bolts*	115	85
Rear caliper guide pin bolts*	28	21
Roadwheel bolts	130	96
Servo/BOU pushrod-to-pedal pivot pin	20	15
Servo retaining nuts	20	15
Vacuum pump bolts:		
In-line engines	14	10
V6 engines	9	7
Wheel speed sensors: *		
Front wheel sensor	25	17
Rear wheel sensor	8	6

*Do not re-use

1 General information

1 The braking system is of the servo-assisted, dual-circuit hydraulic type. The layout is such that under normal circumstances, both circuits operate in unison. Should a hydraulic failure occur in one of the circuits, full braking force will still be available in the other circuit (operating on two diagonally-opposite roadwheels), albeit with increased pedal travel.

2 All models have disc brakes at the front and rear wheels as standard. An Anti-lock Braking System (ABS) is fitted as standard to all models (refer to the appropriate section for further information on the operation of the ABS). **Note:** On models equipped with electronic traction control (ASR), this function is also carried out by the ABS.

3 Models are equipped with the Mercedes-Benz Brake Assist System (BAS), which ensures that, in an emergency braking situation, full braking effort is applied immediately, reducing stopping distances. Models are also equipped with the Electronic Stability Program (ESP), which uses the braking system to help steer the car in extreme circumstances. Information on these systems was limited at time of writing and, in any case, any problems would have to be referred to a Mercedes-Benz dealer.

4 The front and rear disc brakes are actuated by sliding single-piston or fixed opposed-piston type calipers. This design of caliper

ensures that equal pressure is applied to each disc pad.

5 The parking brake provides an independent, mechanical means of applying the rear brakes. A drum and shoe arrangement is fitted in the centre of each rear brake disc. The parking brake is applied by a foot pedal, and is released by a hand lever on the facia panel; both controls actuate the brake shoes via cables.

Caution: When servicing any part of the system, work carefully and methodically; also observe scrupulous cleanliness when overhauling any part of the hydraulic system. Always renew components (in axle sets, where applicable) if in doubt about their condition, and use only genuine Mercedes-Benz parts, or at least those of known good quality. Note the warnings given in Safety first! and at relevant points in this Chapter concerning the dangers of asbestos dust and hydraulic fluid.

6 Vehicles upto 2007 model year, are equipped with Sensotronic Brake Control (SBC). The SBC braking system uses a microcomputer to monitor the car and driver actions. In the event it's needed, such as emergency braking, the system monitors brake pressure, and applies the appropriate stopping power necessary, even if the driver doesn't exert enough power. SBC features a host of other features as well, including distributing brake force to different wheels during cornering, to ensure greater stability in the vehicle as well as maximum stopping power; the SBC system even dries the brake discs if a film of water forms on them.

⚠ *Warning: On models with SBC, it's absolutely essential that the system is deactivated prior to commencing any repair procedure. Failure to do so could result in serious personal injury. See Section 4.*

2 Hydraulic system – bleeding

⚠ *Warning: Hydraulic fluid is poisonous; wash off immediately and thoroughly in the case of skin contact, and seek immediate medical advice if any fluid is swallowed or gets into the eyes. Certain types of hydraulic fluid are flammable, and may ignite when allowed into contact with hot components; when servicing any hydraulic system, it is safest to assume that the fluid is flammable, and to take precautions against the risk of fire as though it is petrol that is being handled. Hydraulic fluid is also an effective paint stripper, and will attack plastics; if any is spilt, it should be washed off immediately, using copious quantities of fresh water. Finally, it is hygroscopic (it absorbs moisture from the air) – old fluid may be contaminated and unfit for further use. When topping-up or renewing the fluid, always use the recommended type, and ensure that it comes from a freshly-opened sealed container.*

General

1 The correct operation of any hydraulic

system is only possible after removing all air from the components and circuit; this is achieved by bleeding the system.

2 During the bleeding procedure, add only clean, unused hydraulic fluid of the recommended type; never re-use fluid that has already been bled from the system. Ensure that sufficient fluid is available before starting work.

3 If there is any possibility of incorrect fluid being already in the system, the brake components and circuit must be flushed completely with uncontaminated, correct fluid, and new seals should be fitted to the various components.

4 If hydraulic fluid has been lost from the system, or air has entered because of a leak, ensure that the fault is cured before continuing further.

5 Park the car on level ground, switch off the engine and select first or reverse gear, then chock the wheels and release the parking brake.

6 Check that all pipes and hoses are secure, unions tight and bleed screws closed. Clean any dirt from around the bleed screws.

7 Unscrew the master cylinder reservoir cap, and top the master cylinder reservoir up to the MAX level line; refit the cap loosely, and remember to maintain the fluid level at least above the MIN level line throughout the procedure, or there is a risk of further air entering the system.

⚠️ *Warning: On vehicles equipped with Sensotronic Brake Control (SBC) only the pressure-bleeding method should be employed. If the brake pedal is used, the system will automatically enter self-test mode and apply the brakes. This could cause foreseen problems with air trapped in the system.*

8 There are a number of one-man, do-it-yourself brake bleeding kits currently available from motor accessory shops. It is recommended that one of these kits is used whenever possible, as they greatly simplify the bleeding operation, and reduce the risk of expelled air and fluid being drawn back into the system. If such a kit is not available, the basic (two-man) method must be used, which is described in detail below.

9 If a kit is to be used, prepare the car as described previously, and follow the kit manufacturer's instructions, as the procedure may vary slightly according to the type being used; generally, they are as outlined below in the relevant sub-section.

10 Whichever method is used, the same sequence must be followed (paragraphs 11 and 12) to ensure that all air is removed from the system. On completion, test the operation of the braking system exhaustively, before bringing the car back into service on the road.

Bleeding sequence

11 If the system has been only partially disconnected, and suitable precautions were taken to minimise fluid loss, it should

be necessary only to bleed that part of the system.

12 If the complete system is to be bled, then it should be done working in the following sequence:
a) *Right-hand rear brake*
b) *Left-hand rear brake*
c) *Right-hand front brake*
d) *Left-hand front brake*

Basic (two-man) method

13 Collect a clean glass jar, a suitable length of plastic or rubber tubing which is a tight fit over the bleed screw, and a ring spanner to fit the screw. The help of an assistant will also be required.

14 Remove the dust cap from the first screw in the sequence. Fit the spanner and tube to the screw, place the other end of the tube in the jar, and pour in sufficient fluid to cover the end of the tube.

15 Ensure that the master cylinder reservoir fluid level is maintained at least above the MIN level line throughout the procedure.

16 Have the assistant fully depress the brake pedal several times to build-up pressure, and then maintain it on the final downstroke.

17 While pedal pressure is maintained, unscrew the bleed screw (approximately one turn) and allow the compressed fluid and air to flow into the jar. The assistant should maintain pedal pressure, following it down to the floor if necessary, and should not release it until instructed to do so. When the flow stops, tighten the bleed screw again, have the assistant release the pedal slowly, and recheck the reservoir fluid level.

18 Repeat the steps given in paragraphs 16 and 17 until the fluid emerging from the bleed screw is free from air bubbles. If the master cylinder has been drained and refilled, and air is being bled from the first screw in the sequence, allow approximately five seconds between cycles for the master cylinder passages to refill.

19 When no more air bubbles appear, tighten the bleed screw to the specified torque, remove the tube and spanner, and refit the dust cap. Do not overtighten the bleed screw.

20 Repeat the procedure on the remaining screws in the sequence, until all air is removed from the system and the brake pedal feels firm again.

Using a one-way valve kit

21 As their name implies, these kits consist of a length of tubing with a one-way valve fitted, to prevent expelled air and fluid being drawn back into the system; some kits include a translucent container, which can be positioned so that the air bubbles can be more easily seen flowing from the end of the tube.

22 The kit is connected to the bleed screw, which is then opened. The user returns to the driver's seat, depresses the brake pedal with a smooth, steady stroke, and slowly releases it; this is repeated until the expelled fluid is clear of air bubbles.

23 Note that these kits simplify work so much that it is easy to forget the master cylinder reservoir fluid level; ensure that this is maintained at least above the MIN level line at all times.

Using a pressure-bleeding kit

24 These kits are usually operated by the reservoir of pressurised air contained in a spare tyre. However, note that it will probably be necessary to reduce the pressure to a lower level than normal; refer to the instructions supplied with the kit.
Note: *Mercedes-Benz specify that a pressure of 2 bar (29 psi) should not be exceeded.*

25 By connecting a pressurised, fluid-filled container to the master cylinder reservoir, bleeding can be carried out simply by opening each brake caliper bleed screw in turn (in the specified sequence – see paragraph 12), and allowing the fluid to flow out until no more air bubbles can be seen in the expelled fluid.

26 This method has the advantage that the large reservoir of fluid provides an additional safeguard against air being drawn into the system during bleeding.

27 Pressure-bleeding is particularly effective when bleeding 'difficult' systems, or when bleeding the complete system at the time of routine fluid renewal.

All methods

28 When bleeding is complete, and firm pedal feel is restored, wash off any spilt fluid, tighten the bleed screws to the specified torque, and refit their dust caps.

29 Check the hydraulic fluid level in the master cylinder reservoir, and top-up if necessary (see '*Weekly checks*').

30 Discard any hydraulic fluid that has been bled from the system; it will not be fit for re-use.

31 Check the feel of the brake pedal. If it feels at all spongy, air must still be present in the system, and further bleeding is required. Failure to bleed satisfactorily after a reasonable repetition of the bleeding procedure may be due to worn master cylinder seals.

---

3 Hydraulic pipes and hoses – renewal

Note: *Before starting work, refer to the warnings in Section 1 and Section 2.*

1 Before disturbing any part of the brake hydraulic system, on models with Sensotronic Brake Control (SBC), it's essential that the system is deactivated prior to commencing work, as described in Section 4.

2 If any pipe or hose is to be renewed, minimise fluid loss by first removing the master cylinder reservoir cap, then tightening it down onto a piece of polythene to obtain an airtight seal. Alternatively, flexible hoses can be sealed, if required, using a proprietary

3.3 Undo the union nut and remove the clip

4.1 Models with Sensotronic Brake Control have 'SBC' cast into the modulator housing

brake hose clamp; metal brake pipe unions can be plugged (if care is taken not to allow dirt into the system) or capped immediately they are disconnected. Place a wad of rag under any union that is to be disconnected, to catch any spilt fluid.

3 If a flexible hose is to be disconnected, unscrew the brake pipe union nut and remove the clip, which secures the hose to its mounting bracket **(see illustration)**.

4 To unscrew the union nuts, it is preferable to obtain a brake pipe spanner of the correct size; these are available from most large motor accessory shops. Failing this, a close-fitting open-ended spanner will be required, though if the nuts are tight or corroded, their flats may be rounded-off if the spanner slips. In such a case, a self-locking wrench is often the only way to unscrew a stubborn union, but it follows that the pipe and the damaged nuts must be renewed on reassembly. Always clean a union and surrounding area before disconnecting it; this helps to prevent the entry of dirt into the hydraulic system. If disconnecting a component with more than one union, make a careful note of the connections before disturbing any of them.

5 If a brake pipe is to be renewed, it can be obtained, cut to length and with the union nuts and end flares in place, from Mercedes-Benz dealers. All that is then necessary is to bend it to shape, following the line of the original, before fitting it to the car. Alternatively, most motor accessory shops can make up brake pipes from kits, but this requires very careful measurement of the original, to ensure that the new one is of the correct length. The safest answer is usually to take the original to the shop as a pattern.

6 On refitting, do not overtighten the union nuts. It is not necessary to exercise brute force to obtain a sound joint!

7 Ensure that the pipes and hoses are correctly routed, with no kinks, and that they are secured in the clips or brackets provided. After fitting, remove the polythene from the reservoir, and bleed the hydraulic system as described in Section 2. Wash off any spilt fluid, and check carefully for fluid leaks.

8 Finally, test the operation of the braking system exhaustively, before bringing the car back into service on the road.

4 Sensotronic Brake Control (SBC) system – de-activation and re-activation

1 Vehicles upto 2007 model year may be equipped with Sensotronic Brake Control – see Section 1. In order to positively identify the presence of SBC, open the bonnet and examine the brake master cylinder. Models with SBC have no conventional brake servo unit, and 'SBC' cast into the modulator housing **(see illustration)**.

De-activation

2 It's absolutely essential that the system is de-activated prior to working on the brake, as otherwise, the hydraulic system may be pressurised (upto 140 psi), and the caliper pistons moved, without warning. This could result in spilled brake fluid, piston ejection, and personal injury.

3 Mercedes Benz technicians use dedicated diagnostic equipment (STAR tester) to deactivate the system. However, alternative electronic tools are readily available from specialist automotive suppliers. In the absence of an suitable electronic tool, the SBC system may be de-activated using the following procedure. Alternatively, disconnect the battery as described in Chapter 5A Section 4, then wait 10 minutes for any residual energy to dissipate.

Caution: The following procedures must be strictly adhered to. Any deviation may result in the SBC entering self-test mode, and applying the brakes.

 Warning: Brake pad replacement and brake bleeding must not be carried out at the same time.

 Warning: The brake pedal must not be depressed under any circumstances.

Warning: The doors or boot lid/ tailgate must not be unlocked or opened.

Note: *Before starting work, it's essential to read and comprehend the complete work description. Operations have to be completed in rapid succession.*

4 Open the drivers window.

5 Switch off all electrical consumers, and

remove the key from the ignition switch. On models with 'Keyless Go', press Start/Stop repeatedly until the ignition is switched off.

6 Remove the 'Keyless Go' or key from the vehicle, and store it outside of the transmitter range.

7 Close and lock all doors for a minimum of 30 seconds.

8 Unlock the vehicle for a minimum of 15 seconds (the SBC may self-test in this time).

9 Lock the vehicle, and wait at least 10 minutes before commencing work.

Re-activation

10 Raise the vehicle so the wheels are free to rotate.

11 Working through the open window, turn the ignition on.

Caution: On models with 'Keyless go', do not activate any of the 'Keyless Go' functions.

Caution: Do not start the engine.

12 Turn the ignition off, wait for 1 to 5 seconds then turn it on again.

13 Rotate the rear left-hand wheel in the normal direction of rotation for a minimum of 3 seconds (1 – 2 rotations), then slow and stop the wheel by hand.

14 Within 60 seconds of the previous step, rotate the front left-hand wheel a minimum of 2 revolutions. Automatically, the wheel brake will be applied, and the brake lights will flash 3 times. This signals successful re-activation, and the SBC brake pad application routine will automatically commence – the front and rear pads will be applied several times, over a 50 second period.

15 Lower the vehicle and turn the ignition off.

16 Start the engine, and depress the brake pedal 5 – 10 times. If a fault message appears, repeat the re-activation procedure. If after 2 or 3 attempts the fault message is still displayed, have the system re-activated, and the fault code(s) erased using Mercedes STAR diagnosis equipment or aftermarket equivalent.

5 Front brake pads – renewal

 Warning: Renew both sets of front brake pads at the same time – never renew the pads on only one wheel, as uneven braking may result. Note that the dust created by wear of the pads may contain asbestos, which is a health hazard. Never blow it out with compressed air, and don't inhale any of it. An approved filtering mask should be worn when working on the brakes. DO NOT use petrol or petroleum-based solvents to clean brake parts; use brake cleaner or methylated spirit only.

1 Apply the handbrake, then slacken the front roadwheel bolts. Jack up the front of the vehicle and support it on axle stands (see

'*Vehicle jacking and support*'). Remove both front roadwheels.

2 If new pads are to be fitted, reduce the fluid level in the master cylinder reservoir to the minimum level using a syringe (or similar).

3 On models with Sensotronic Brake Control (SBC), de-activate the system as described in Section 4.

Single-piston floating calipers

4 Follow the relevant accompanying photos **(illustrations 5.4a to 5.4s)** for the actual pad replacement procedure. Be sure to stay in order and read the caption under each illustration, and note the following points:

a) New pads may have an adhesive foil on the backplates. Remove this foil prior to installation.

b) Apply a thin smear of anti-seize grease only to the areas shown.

c) When pushing the caliper piston back to accommodate new pads, keep a close eye on the fluid level in the reservoir.

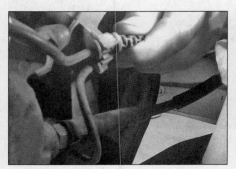
5.4a Unclip the pad wear sensor wiring harness

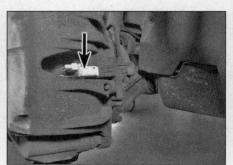
5.4b Unplug the wear sensor wiring plug

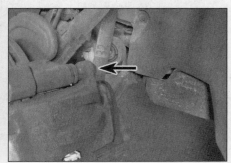
5.4c Remove the caliper upper guide pin bolt...

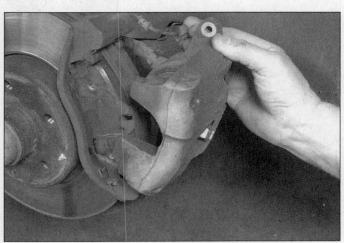
5.4d ...and pivot the caliper away

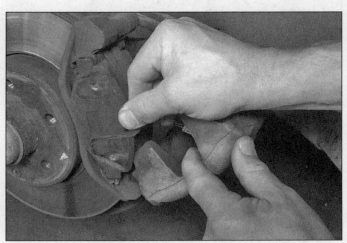
5.4e Remove the outer pad...

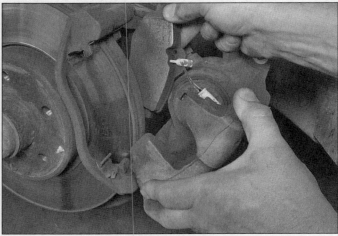
5.4f ...and the inner pad

5.4g Remove the shim from the caliper piston

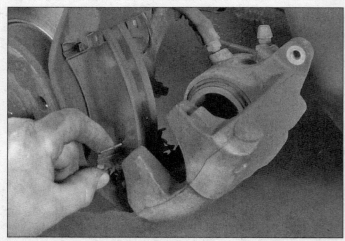

5.4h Remove the upper and lower shims from the caliper mounting bracket

5.4i Clean the caliper and bracket with aerosol cleaner and a soft brush

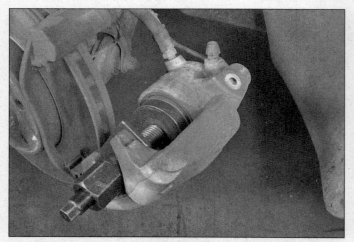

5.4j If new pads are to be fitted, push the piston fully into the caliper body using a piston retraction tool. Keep an eye on the reservoir fluid level as the piston is pushed back.

5.4k Fit the new shim to the caliper piston...

5.4l ...then to the upper, and lower caliper mounting bracket locations

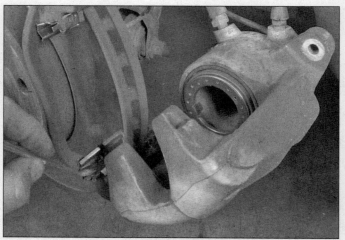

5.4m Apply a smear of anti-seize grease to the mounting bracket shims where the pads make contact

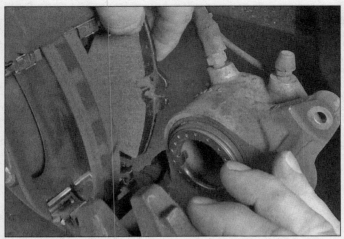

5.4n Fit the inner brake pad – ensure the friction material is against the disc face!

5.4o Fit the outer brake pad

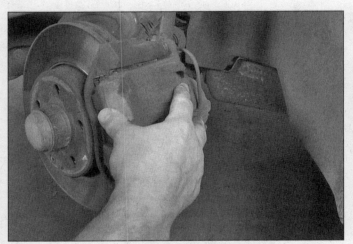

5.4p Pivot the caliper back into place

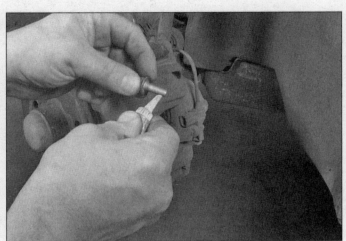

5.4q Apply a little thread-locking compound...

5.4r...then refit the upper guide pin bolt and tighten it to the specified torque

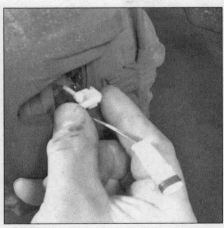

5.4s Press the wear sensor into the hole in the brake pad friction material, reconnect the wiring plug, and secure the harness

5 Repeat the above procedure on the remaining caliper.

6 Re-activate the SBC system (where fitted) as described in Section 4.

7 Depress the brake pedal repeatedly, until the pads are pressed into firm contact with the brake disc, and normal (non-assisted) pedal pressure is restored.

8 Apply a little anti-seize grease to the hub surface, then refit the roadwheels, lower the vehicle to the ground and tighten the roadwheel bolts to the specified torque.

9 Check the hydraulic fluid level as described in 'Weekly checks'.

Caution: New pads will not give full braking efficiency until they have bedded-in. Be prepared for this, and avoid hard braking as far as possible for the first hundred miles or so after pad renewal.

Twin piston fixed calipers

10 Follow the relevant accompanying photos **(illustrations 5.10a to 5.10s)** for the actual pad replacement procedure. Be sure to stay in order and read the caption under each illustration, and note the following points:

a) *New pads may have an adhesive foil on the backplates. Remove this foil prior to installation.*

b) *The pad guide pins are likely to be seized in place. Gently apply heat and penetrating fluid to the pins/caliper body prior to driving the pins from place. It may be prudent to obtain replacement pins prior to commencing work – they're likely to be damaged during the procedure.*

c) *When pushing the caliper pistons back to accommodate new pads, keep a close eye on the fluid level in the reservoir.*

11 Repeat the above procedure on the remaining caliper.

12 Re-activate the SBC system (where fitted) as described in Section 4.

13 Depress the brake pedal repeatedly, until the pads are pressed into firm contact with the brake disc, and normal (non-assisted) pedal pressure is restored.

14 Apply a little anti-seize grease to the hub surface, then refit the roadwheels, lower the vehicle to the ground and tighten the roadwheel bolts to the specified torque.

15 Check the hydraulic fluid level as described in 'Weekly checks'.

Caution: New pads will not give full braking efficiency until they have bedded-in. Be prepared for this, and avoid hard braking as far as possible for the first hundred miles or so after pad renewal.

5.10a Pull the wear sensor from the pad backing plate, and disconnect the wiring plug

5.10b Use a thin metal punch...

5.10c...to drive out the upper...

5.10d...and lower pad retaining pins

5.10e Recover the pad retaining spring

5.10f If there's a wear lip on the disc, use a screwdriver to push the pads away from the disc a little

5.10g Remove the outer pad/shim...

5.10h...then the inner pad and shim

5.10i Undo the bolt securing the wear sensor wiring

5.10j Clean the caliper using aerosol brake cleaner and a soft brush

5.10k If new pads are to be fitted, push both pistons fully into the caliper body using a piston retraction tool. Keep an eye on the fluid level in the reservoir as the pistons are retracted

5.10l Fit the new shims to the pad backplates, ensuring the arrow points in the normal direction of rotation

5.10m Slide in the inner pad/shim. Ensure the pad friction material is against the disc face

5.10n Slide in the outer pad/shim

5.10o Position the pad retaining spring...

5.10p Apply a little anti-seize grease to the pad retaining pins, and slide them into place

5.10q Use a metal punch to drive the pins fully into place

5.10r Insert the wear sensor into the hole in the pad friction material/backplate...

5.10s...and reconnect the wiring plug

6 Rear brake pads – renewal

Warning: Renew both sets of rear brake pads at the same time – never renew the pads on only one wheel, as uneven braking may result. Note that the dust created by wear of the pads may contain asbestos, which is a health hazard. Never blow it out with compressed air, and don't inhale any of it. An approved filtering mask should be worn when working on the brakes. DO NOT use petrol or petroleum-based solvents to clean brake parts; use brake cleaner or methylated spirit only.

1 Apply the handbrake, then slacken the rear roadwheel bolts. Jack up the rear of the vehicle and support it on axle stands (see 'Vehicle jacking and support'). Remove both rear roadwheels.

2 If new pads are to be fitted, reduce the fluid level in the master cylinder reservoir to the minimum level using a syringe (or similar).

3 On models with Sensotronic Brake Control (SBC), de-activate the system as described in Section 4.

4 Follow the relevant accompanying photos **(illustrations 6.4a to 6.4q)** for the actual pad replacement procedure. Be sure to stay in order and read the caption under each illustration, and note the following points:

a) *New pads may have an adhesive foil on the backplates. Remove this foil prior to installation.*

b) *Apply a thin smear of anti-seize grease only to the areas shown.*

c) *When pushing the caliper piston back to accommodate new pads, keep a close eye on the fluid level in the reservoir.*

5 Depress the brake pedal repeatedly, until the pads are pressed into firm contact with the brake disc, and normal (non-assisted) pedal pressure is restored.

6 Repeat the above procedure on the remaining rear brake caliper.

7 Re-activate the SBC system (where fitted) as described in Section 4.

8 Apply a little anti-seize grease to the hub surface, then refit the roadwheels,

6.4a Pull the wear sensor from the brake pad/backplate

lower the vehicle to the ground and tighten the roadwheel bolts to the specified torque.

9 Check the hydraulic fluid level as described in 'Weekly checks'.

Caution: New pads will not give full braking efficiency until they have bedded-in. Be prepared for this, and avoid hard braking as far as possible for the first hundred miles or so after pad renewal.

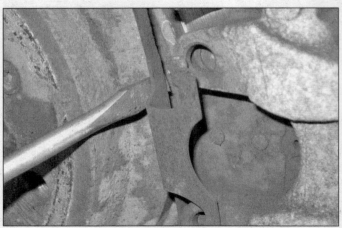

6.4b Use a screwdrive to prise the caliper spring from place

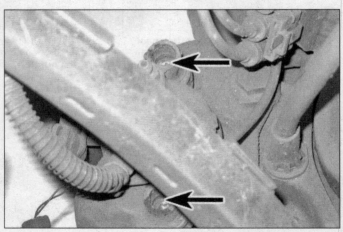

6.4c Prise out the caps (where fitted), then use a Torx key to unscrew the upper and lower guide pin bolts

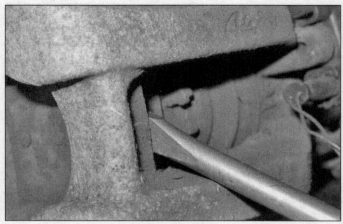

6.4d If there's a wear lip on the disc, use a screwdriver to lever the caliper to the outside, forcing the piston into the caliper body a little

6.4e Slide the caliper from place...

6.4f...and unclip the inner pad from the piston

6.4g Suspend the caliper from the anti-roll bar to prevent straining the brake hose

6.4h Remove the outer pad from the mounting bracket

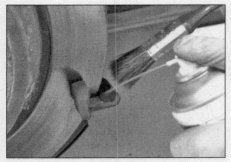

6.4i Clean the caliper and mounting bracket using aerosol brake cleaner and a soft brush

6.4j If new pads are to be fitted, push the piston fully into the caliper body using a piston retraction tool. Keep an eye on the fluid level in the reservoir as the piston is pushed back.

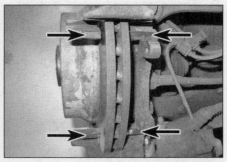

6.4k Apply a smear of anti-seize grease to the pad mounting surfaces on the bracket

6.4l Clip the new inner pad into the caliper piston

6.4m Fit the outer pad to the bracket. Ensure the pad friction material is against the disc face

6.4n Slide the caliper back into place...

6.4o Refit the upper and lower guide pin bolts, and tighten them to the specified torque

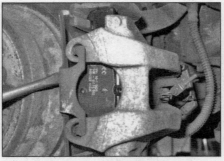

6.4p Refit the caliper retaining spring

6.4q Press the wear sensor into the hole in the pad friction material and backplate

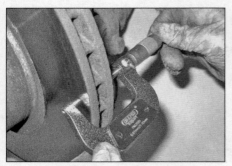

7.3 Use a micrometer to check the thickness of the disc

7 Front brake disc – inspection, removal and refitting

Note: *Before starting work, refer to the note at the beginning of Section 5 concerning the dangers of asbestos dust.*

Inspection

Note: *If either disc requires renewal, BOTH should be renewed at the same time, to ensure even and consistent braking. New brake pads should also be fitted.*

1 Apply the handbrake, then jack up the front of the car and support it on axle stands (see *'Vehicle jacking and support'*. Remove the appropriate front roadwheel.

2 Slowly rotate the brake disc so that the full area of both sides can be checked; remove the brake pads if better access is required to the inboard surface. Light scoring is normal in the area swept by the brake pads, but if heavy scoring or cracks are found, the disc must be renewed.

3 It is normal to find a lip of rust and brake dust around the disc's perimeter; this can be scraped off if required. If, however, a lip has formed due to excessive wear of the brake pad swept area, then the disc's thickness must be measured using a micrometer **(see illustration)**. Take measurements at several places around the disc, at the inside and outside of the pad swept area; if the disc has worn at any point to the specified minimum thickness or less, the disc must be renewed.

4 If the disc is thought to be warped, it can be

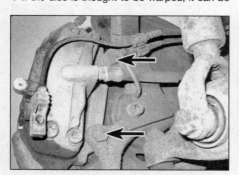

7.10 Undo the caliper retaining bolts

checked for run-out. Either use a dial gauge mounted on any convenient fixed point, while the disc is slowly rotated, or use feeler blades to measure (at several points all around the disc) the clearance between the disc and a fixed point, such as the caliper mounting bracket. If the measurements obtained are at the specified maximum or beyond, the disc is excessively warped, and must be renewed; however, it is worth checking first that the hub bearing is in good condition (Chapters 1 and/or 10). If the run-out is excessive, the disc must be renewed.

5 Check the disc for cracks, especially around the wheel stud holes, and any other wear or damage, and renew if necessary.

Removal

6 Remove the front brake pads as described in Section 5.

Single-piston floating calipers

7 Using a piece of wire or string, tie the caliper to the front suspension coil spring, to avoid placing any strain on the hydraulic brake hose.

8 Unscrew the two bolts securing the brake caliper mounting bracket to the hub carrier, then slide the bracket assembly off the disc. Discard the bolts – new ones must be fitted.

Twin-piston fixed calipers

9 Unbolt the sensor connector from the caliper **(see illustration)**.

10 Undo the retaining bolts and slide the caliper from place **(see illustration)**. Suspend the caliper from the suspension coil spring to avoid placing any strain on the hydraulic hose.

7.9 Unbolt the wear sensor connector

7.11 Undo the Torx screw and remove the disc

All calipers

11 Use chalk or paint to mark the relationship of the disc to the hub, then remove the screw securing the brake disc to the hub, and remove the disc **(see illustration)**. If it is tight, lightly tap its rear face with a hide or plastic mallet.

Refitting

12 Refitting is the reverse of the removal procedure, noting the following points:
a) Ensure that the mating surfaces of the disc and hub are clean and flat.
b) Align (if applicable) the marks made on removal, and tighten the disc retaining screw to the specified torque.
c) If a new disc has been fitted, use a suitable solvent to wipe any preservative coating from the disc, before refitting the caliper.
d) Tighten the new caliper mounting bolts to the specified torque setting.
e) Fit the brake pads as described in Section 5.
f) Refit the roadwheel, then lower the vehicle to the ground and tighten the roadwheel nuts to the specified torque. On completion, repeatedly depress the brake pedal until normal (non-assisted) pedal pressure returns.

8 Rear brake disc – inspection, removal and refitting

Note: *Before starting work, refer to the note at the beginning of Section 6 concerning the dangers of asbestos dust.*

Inspection

Note: *If either disc requires renewal, BOTH should be renewed at the same time, to ensure even and consistent braking. New brake pads should also be fitted.*

1 Firmly chock the front wheels, then jack up the rear of the car and support it on axle stands (see *'Vehicle jacking and support'*). Remove the appropriate rear roadwheel. Release the handbrake.

2 Inspect the disc as described in Section 7.

Removal

3 Undo the 2 caliper mounting bracket bolts, and slide the bracket, complete with caliper and brake pads, from place **(see illustration)**. Discard the bolts – new ones must be fitted.

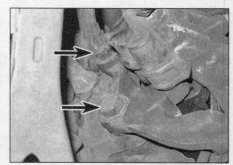

8.3 Caliper mounting bracket bolts

8.6 Rear brake disc retaining screw

4 Suspend the caliper assembly from the vehicle suspension/body to prevent straining the brake hose.
5 Insert a screwdriver through a wheel bolt hole in the brake disc, and rotate the adjuster knurled wheel on the pivot to retract the shoes **(see illustrations 14.6a and 14.6b)**.
6 Slacken and remove the brake disc retaining screw **(see illustration)**.
7 If the disc is to be refitted, make alignment marks between the disc and hub.
8 It should now be possible to withdraw the brake disc from the rear hub by hand. If it is tight, lightly tap its rear face with a hide or plastic mallet.

Refitting

9 If a new disc is been fitted, use a suitable solvent to wipe any preservative coating from the disc. Ensure the disc mounting surface on the hub is free from dirt and corrosion.
10 Align (if applicable) the marks made on removal, then fit the disc and tighten the retaining screw to the specified torque.
11 Refit the caliper mounting bracket, and tighten the new bolts to the specified torque.
12 Adjust the parking brake shoes and cable as described in Section 14.
13 Fit the brake pads as described in Section 6.

9 Front brake caliper – removal, overhaul and refitting

Note: *Before starting work, refer to the note at the beginning of Section 2 concerning the dangers of hydraulic fluid, and to the warning at the beginning of Section 5 concerning the dangers of asbestos dust.*

Removal

1 Apply the handbrake, then jack up the front of the vehicle and support it on axle stands (see 'Vehicle jacking and support'). Remove the appropriate roadwheel.
2 On vehicles with Sensotronic Brake Control (SBC), de-activate the system as described in Section 4.
3 Make a note of the wiring harness routing, then disconnect the wiring plugs from the caliper.

4 Minimise fluid loss by using a brake hose clamp, a G-clamp or a similar tool to clamp the flexible hose.
5 Clean the area around the union, then slacken the brake hose union nut.
6 Remove the brake pads as described in Section 5.

Single-piston floating caliper

7 Unscrew the caliper from the end of the brake hose and remove it from the vehicle.

Twin-piston fixed caliper

8 Undo the caliper mounting bolts, slide the caliper from place, and unscrew the caliper from the brake hose.

Overhaul

9 At the time of writing, no replacement parts appear to be available for the front calipers. If they are defective, replacement calipers must be fitted.

Refitting

10 Screw the caliper fully onto the flexible hose union.
11 On models with twin-piston fixed calipers, slide the caliper into position, fit the new retaining bolts and tighten them to the specified torque.
12 Refit the brake pads as described in Section 5.
13 Securely tighten the brake pipe union nut.
14 Remove the brake hose clamp, and bleed the hydraulic system as described in Section 2. Note that, providing the precautions described were taken to minimise brake fluid loss, it should only be necessary to bleed the relevant front brake.
15 On models with SBC, re-activate the system as described in Section 4.
16 Refit the roadwheel, then lower the vehicle to the ground and tighten the roadwheel nuts to the specified torque. On completion, check the hydraulic fluid level as described in 'Weekly checks'.

10 Rear brake caliper – removal, overhaul and refitting

Note: *Before starting work, refer to the note at the beginning of Section 2 concerning the dangers of hydraulic fluid, and to the warning at the beginning of Section 6 concerning the dangers of asbestos dust.*

Removal

1 Chock the front wheels, then jack up the rear of the vehicle and support on axle stands (see 'Vehicle jacking and support'). Remove the relevant rear wheel.
2 On vehicles with Sensotronic Brake Control (SBC), de-activate the system as described in Section 4.
3 Minimise fluid loss by using a brake hose clamp, a G-clamp or a similar tool to clamp the flexible hose.

4 Clean the area around the union, then loosen the brake hose union nut.
5 Remove the brake pads as described in Section 6.
6 Unscrew the caliper from the end of the flexible hose, and remove it from the vehicle.

Overhaul

7 At the time of writing, it would appear that no replacement parts are available for the rear caliper. If defective, the complete caliper must be replaced.

Refitting

8 Screw the caliper fully onto the flexible hose union.
9 Refit the brake pads as described in Section 6.
10 Securely tighten the brake pipe union nut.
11 Remove the brake hose clamp, and bleed the hydraulic system as described in Section 2. Note that, providing the precautions described were taken to minimise brake fluid loss, it should only be necessary to bleed the relevant rear brake.
12 On models with SBC, re-activate the system as described in Section 4.
13 Refit the roadwheel, then lower the vehicle to the ground and tighten the roadwheel nuts to the specified torque. On completion, check the hydraulic fluid level as described in 'Weekly checks'.

11 Master cylinder – removal, overhaul and refitting

Note: *Before starting work, refer to the warning at the beginning of Section 2 concerning the dangers of hydraulic fluid.*

Vehicles without Sensotronic Brake Control (SBC)

Removal

1 Disconnect the battery negative terminal (Chapter 5A Section 4) and then depress the brake pedal several times to remove the vacuum from the brake servo unit.
2 Remove the right-hand cover from the engine compartment **(see illustration)**.

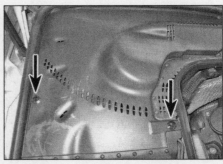

11.2 Release the fasteners and remove the cover

11.15 Unclip the plastic cover

11.16 Disconnect the wiring plug from the level switch

3 Unscrew the reservoir cap, lift out the filter, and remove as much brake fluid as possible using a syringe (or similar).

 Warning: Do not syphon the fluid by mouth, as it is poisonous; use a syringe or an old antifreeze tester.

4 Disconnect the wiring plug from the reservoir.

5 Place absorbent rags around the reservoir/master cylinder, then undo the retaining bolt and pull the reservoir upwards from the master cylinder. Renew the reservoir-to-master cylinder seals.

6 Make a note of the correct fitted positions of the unions, then unscrew the union nuts and carefully withdraw the pipes. Plug or tape over the pipe ends and master cylinder orifices, to minimise the loss of brake fluid, and to prevent the entry of dirt into the system. Wash off any spilt fluid immediately with cold water.

7 Release any wiring from the master cylinder, then undo the mounting nuts and pull the master cylinder from the servo unit. Renew the master cylinder-to-servo O-ring seal.

Overhaul

8 At the time of writing, it would appear that no replacement parts are available for the master cylinder. If defective, the complete master cylinder must be replaced.

Refitting

9 Remove all traces of dirt from the master cylinder and servo unit mating surfaces, and renew the seal.

10 Fit the master cylinder to the servo unit, ensuring that the servo unit pushrod enters

the master cylinder bore centrally. Fit the master cylinder retaining nuts, and tighten them to the specified torque.

11 Wipe clean the brake pipe unions, then refit them to the master cylinder/hydraulic unit ports and tighten them securely.

12 Press the new reservoir seals firmly into the master cylinder ports, then ease the reservoir into position. Refit the reservoir locking pin securely. Reconnect the fluid hose(s) to the reservoir, and reconnect the wiring connector(s).

13 The remainder of refitting is a reversal of removal, noting the following points:
a) *Tighten all fasteners to their specified torque where given.*
b) *Refill the master cylinder reservoir with new fluid, and bleed the complete hydraulic system as described in Section 2.*

Models with Sensotronic Brake Control (SBC)

Removal

Note: *Refitting of the BOU requires the brake hydraulic system to be bleed upon completion. This can only be done using Mercedes STAR diagnostic equipment (or after-market equivalent) – see Section 2.*

14 De-activate the SBC system as described in Section 4, or disconnect the battery negative lead as described in Chapter 5A Section 4.

15 On these models, Mercedes refer to the master cylinder as the Brake Operating Unit (BOU). Begin removal, by lifting away

the black plastic cover over the BOU fluid reservoir **(see illustration)**.

16 Disconnect the level warning switch wiring plug from the reservoir **(see illustration)**.

17 Unscrew the reservoir cap, lift out the filter, and remove as much brake fluid as possible using a syringe (or similar).

18 Thoroughly clean the area around the reservoir and pipe. Absolute cleanliness is essential.

19 Disconnect the return and feed pipes from the fluid reservoir. Mop up any spilled fluid, and plug the openings to prevent contamination.

20 Place absorbent rags around the BOU, then remove the retaining bolt and pull the fluid reservoir upwards from the BOU. Renew the O-ring seals.

21 Disconnect the wiring plug from the pedal value sensor located on the top of the BOU.

22 Note their fitted positions then disconnect the brake pipes from the BOU. Plug the openings to prevent contamination.

23 Remove the stop light switch as described in Section 18.

24 On models with manual transmission, depress the locking clip, rotate the clutch pedal switch 90° clockwise and remove it from the bracket.

25 Unclip the plastic cover from the brake/clutch pedal. Unclip the wiring harness from the cover as it's withdrawn.

26 Undo and remove the bolt securing the BOU pushrod to the brake pedal **(see illustration)**.

27 Undo the nuts securing the BOU to the bulkhead, and manoeuvre the complete assembly from place **(see illustration)**.

28 No further dismantling of the BOU is recommended.

Refitting

29 Refitting is a reversal of removal, noting the following points:
a) *Tighten all fasteners to their specified torque where given.*
b) *If a new BOU has been fitted, it must be configured using Mercedes STAR diagnosis equipment, or equivalent.*
c) *Bleed the hydraulic system as described in Section 2.*

12 Vacuum servo unit – testing, removal and refitting

Note: *Note that a vacuum servo unit is only fitted to models without Sensotronic Brake Control (SBC)*

Testing

1 To test the operation of the servo unit, depress the footbrake several times with the engine off, to exhaust the vacuum from the servo. Now start the engine whilst keeping the pedal firmly depressed. There should be a noticeable 'give' in the brake pedal as the engine starts and the vacuum builds-up.

2 Allow the engine to run for at least two

11.26 Remove the pushrod bolt

11.27 BOU retaining nuts

13.1 Pull the vacuum hose connection from the servo

minutes, then switch it off. If the brake pedal is now depressed it should feel normal, but further applications should result in the pedal feeling progressively firmer, with the pedal stroke decreasing on each application.

3 If the servo does not operate as described, first inspect the servo unit check valve as described in Section 13.

4 If the servo uni still fails to operate correctly, the fault lies within the unit itself. Repairs to the unit are not possible – if faulty, the servo unit must be replaced.

Removal

5 Remove the master cylinder as described in Section 11.

6 Disconnect the vacuum pipe from the servo unit.

7 Unclip the 'U frame' from the engine compartment bulkhead.

8 Unscrew the centre screws, and prise out the plastic expansion rivets securing the water collector above the servo.

9 Remove the brake light switch as described in Section 18.

10 Unclip the plastic cover from the brake pedal.

11 Unscrew the servo pushrod pivot pin **(see illustration 11.26)**.

12 Undo the 2 nuts securing the servo unit to the bulkhead.

13 Working in the engine compartment, lift the water collector a little, and manoeuvre the servo unit from place.

Refitting

14 Refitting is a reversal of removal, noting the following points:

14.4 Rotate the eccentric bolt to the left, and push it backwards in the slot

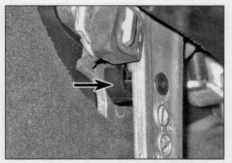

14.2 The colour of the plastic 'pawl' determines the handbrake adjustment details

a) *Renew the gasket between the servo unit and the engine compartment bulkhead.*
b) *Tighten all fasteners to their specified torque where given.*
c) *Check for correct braking system operation before venturing out onto the road.*

13 Vacuum servo unit check valve – removal, testing and refitting

Removal

1 Pull the vacuum hose connection from the servo unit **(see illustration)**.

2 Trace the hose back and disconnect it from the vacuum pump.

3 The valve is integral with the hose. If the valve is faulty, the complete hose assembly must be renewed.

Testing

4 Examine the vacuum hose, check the valve for signs of damage, and renew if necessary.

5 The valve may be tested by blowing through the hose in both directions; air should glow through the valve in one direction only – when blown through the from the servo unit end of the hose. Renew the hose assembly is this not the case.

Refitting

6 Ensuring the hose is correctly routed, securely reconnect it to the pump and the servo unit.

7 On completion, start the engine and check

14.6a Insert a screwdriver through one of the wheel bolt holes...

the valve to servo unit connection for signs of air leaks. Test the operation of the braking system before venturing out onto the road.

14 Parking brake – adjustment

Note: *If the parking brake shoe clearance requires significant amount of adjustment, it is advisable to inspect the brake shoe lining thickness.*

1 The parking brake cable is self-adjusting on all models, The following procedure is intended merely to compensate for wear of the shoe friction material, which should occur at a very slow and even rate and make routine adjustment unnecessary.

2 Two different types of parking brake ratchet mechanisms may be fitted – the type of mechanism determines the number of notches the lever should travel before the brake is fully applied. Examine the parking brake lever – to the left-hand side of the lever is the ratchet pawl. Early models with a 'pushed' pawl will be coloured black, and the brake should be fully applied after 5 notches. Later models with a 'pulled' pawl will be coloured grey, and the brake should be fully applied after 1 notch **(see illustration)**.

3 Chock the front wheels, slacken the rear wheel bolts, raise the rear of the vehicle and support it securely on axle stands (see *'Vehicle jacking and support'*). Remove the rear wheels, and fully release the parking brake.

4 Working underneath the vehicle, pre-tension the automatic cable slack adjuster as follows: Using an Allen key, rotate the detent eccentric bolt to the left approximately half a turn, and at the same time push it backwards in the slot until the spring loaded detent eccentric engages with the raised section in the hold-down clip **(see illustration)**.

5 Turn one of the rear brake discs so that access can be gained to the parking brake shoe adjuster, situated between the parking brake shoes, at the rear.

6 Using a long slim screwdriver engaged in the teeth of the adjuster, turn the adjuster until the parking brake shoes make contact with the drum and the disc can no longer be turned **(see illustrations)**. Repeat the procedure on

14.6b...and engage it with the teeth of the adjuster

the other rear brake. To apply the brake shoes, the adjuster on the left-hand brake is turned from the rear forwards, whist the adjuster on the right-hand brake is turned from the front forwards.

7 Now back both adjusters off exactly 10 teeth. It must now be possible to freely rotate both discs by hand.

8 Working underneath the vehicle, release the hold down clip, and allow the cable slack adjuster to automatically reset itself.

9 Upon completion, refit the rear wheels, lower the vehicle to the ground and tighten the wheel bolts to the specified torque.

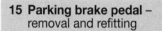

15 Parking brake pedal – removal and refitting

Removal

1 Chock the front wheels, slacken the rear wheel bolts, raise the vehicle and support is securely on axle stands (see 'Vehicle jacking and support'). Fully release the parking brake and remove the rear wheels.

2 Undo the bolts and remove the crossbrace beneath the exhaust system.

3 Undo the fasteners and slide the heatshields away to access the hand brake cable in the transmission tunnel.

4 Working underneath the vehicle, pre-tension the automatic cable slack adjuster as follows: Using an Allen key, rotate the detent eccentric bolt to the left approximately half a turn, and at the same time push it backwards in the slot until the spring loaded detent eccentric engages with the raised section in the hold-down clip (see illustration 14.4).

5 Detach the front parking brake cable at the automatic slack adjuster (see illustration).

6 Undo the fasteners and remove the drivers side lower facia panel as described in Chapter 11 Section 36. Disconnect any wiring plugs as the panel is withdrawn.

7 Release the fasteners and remove the parking brake pedal cover (see illustration).

8 Disconnect the parking brake warning switch wiring plug.

9 Remove the circlip securing the pedal to the bracket (see illustration).

15.9 Remove the circlip

15.5 Disconnect the front cable from the adjuster arm

10 Unclip the cable from the pedal (see illustration).

11 Unclip the unlocking cable from the pedal as it's withdrawn.

Refitting

12 Refitting is a reversal of removal. Adjust the parking brake as described in Section 14.

16 Parking brake cables – removal and refitting

Rear cables

Removal

1 Chock the front wheels, slacken the rear wheel bolts, raise the vehicle and support is securely on axle stands (see 'Vehicle jacking and support'). Fully release the parking brake and remove the rear wheels.

2 On models with Sensotronic Brake Control (SBC), de-activate the system as described in Section 4.

3 Undo the bolts and remove the crossbrace beneath the exhaust system.

4 Undo the fasteners and slide the heatshields away to access the parking brake cable in the transmission tunnel.

5 Unhook the cable adjuster return spring from the bracket.

6 Working underneath the vehicle, pre-tension the automatic cable slack adjuster as follows: Using an Allen key, rotate the detent eccentric bolt to the left approximately half a turn, and

15.10 Unclip the cable from the pedal and bracket

15.7 Unclip the pedal cover

at the same time push it backwards in the slot until the spring loaded detent eccentric engages with the raised section in the hold-down clip (see illustration 14.4).

7 Unhook the relevant cable from the adjuster.

8 Unclip the outer cable from the bracket rearwards of the adjuster.

9 Remove the parking brake shoes as described in Section 17.

10 Work along the cable length, and release it from any grommets/retaining brackets/clips. Release it from the hub carrier bracket by squeezing the retaining collar.

Refitting

11 Refitting is a reversal of removal. Adjust the parking brake as described in Section 14.

Front cable

Removal

12 Chock the front wheels, slacken the rear wheel bolts, raise the rear of the vehicle and support it securely on axle stands (see 'Vehicle jacking and support'). Fully release the parking brake, and remove the rear wheels.

13 Undo the fasteners and remove the rear section of the engine/transmission undershield.

14 Undo the bolts and remove the crossbrace above the exhaust system.

15 Undo the fasteners and slide the heatshields rearwards a little beneath the parking brake slack adjuster.

16 Working underneath the vehicle, pre-tension the automatic cable slack adjuster as follows: Using an Allen key, rotate the detent eccentric bolt to the left approximately half a turn, and at the same time push it backwards in the slot until the spring loaded detent eccentric engages with the raised section in the hold-down clip (see illustration 14.4).

17 Detach the rear of the cable from the slack adjuster arm (see illustration 15.5).

18 Work along the length of the cable, and release any retaining clips/grommets.

19 Undo the fasteners and remove the drivers side lower facia panel. Disconnect the wiring plugs as the panel is withdrawn.

20 Release the clips and remove the plastic cover from the side of the pedal/bracket assembly.

21 Unclip the cable from the pedal and support bracket, then gently pull the cable into the passenger compartment, and manoeuvre it from the vehicle (see illustration 15.10).

Refitting

22 Refitting is a reversal of removal. Adjust the parking brake cable as described in Section 14.

17 Parking brake shoes –
removal and refitting

17.2a Note the positions of the components at the front...

17.2b...and rear of the parking brake assembly

Removal

1 Remove the rear brake discs as described in Section 8.

2 Make a note of the correct fitted location of all components, then clean the parking brake shoe assembly using brake cleaner (see illustrations). Place rags below the brake assembly to catch any spillage. DO NOT use compressed air to blow out the brake dust.

3 Carefully unhook and remove the parking brake shoe front return spring, noting which way round the spring is fitted – it is not symmetrical (see illustration).

4 Using a pair of thin-nosed pliers, compress the upper shoe retaining spring then rotate it through 90° and remove it from the backplate. Access to the spring can be gained through the hub flange holes (see illustration).

5 Lift the upper shoe, remove the adjuster mechanism, and disengage the rear return spring (see illustrations).

6 Using a pair of thin-nosed pliers, compress the lower shoe retaining spring then rotate it through 90° and remove it from the backplate. Access to the spring can be gained through the hub flange holes

7 Fold open the expansion lock, press out the pin, and detach the parking brake cable (see illustration).

8 With the shoes removed, clean and inspect the condition of the shoe adjuster and expander mechanisms, and renew them if they show signs of wear or damage. If all is well, apply a fresh coat of brake grease (Mercedes-Benz recommend Molykote Paste

17.3 Unhook the front return spring

17.4 Compress the retaining spring then rotate it 90° and remove it

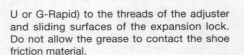

U or G-Rapid) to the threads of the adjuster and sliding surfaces of the expansion lock. Do not allow the grease to contact the shoe friction material.

Refitting

9 Prior to installation, clean the backplate, and apply a thin smear of high-temperature brake grease (see paragraph 9) or anti-seize compound to all those surfaces of the backplate which bear on the shoes. Do not allow the lubricant to foul the friction material.

10 Fully retract the adjuster mechanism.

11 Reconnect the parking brake cable to the expansion lock.

12 Manoeuvre the shoes into position, engaging them with the adjuster and expansion lock, then refit the front and rear return springs.

13 Refit the shoe retaining springs.

14 Refit the discs as described in Section 8.

18 Braking system switches –
removal and refitting

Parking brake warning light switch

Removal

1 Undo the fasteners and remove the drivers side lower facia panel as described in Chapter 11 Section 36. Disconnect any wiring plugs as the panel is withdrawn.

2 Release the fasteners and remove the parking brake pedal cover (see illustration 15.7).

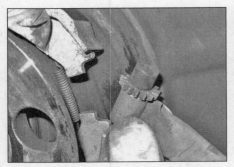

17.5a Remove the adjuster mechanism...

17.5b...and unhook the rear return spring

17.7 Press out the pin securing the cable to the expansion lock

18.4 Parking brake warning light switch

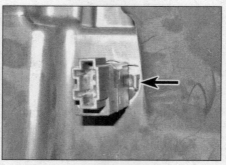

18.8 Depress the clip and rotate the stop light switch clockwise

18.9 Fully extend the switch plunger

3 Disconnect the switch wiring plug.
4 Squeeze the switch retaining lugs and detach it from the bracket **(see illustration)**.

Refitting

5 Refitting is a reversal of removal.

Stop light switch

Removal

6 Undo the fasteners and remove the drivers side lower facia panel as described in Chapter 11 Section 36. Disconnect any wiring plugs as the panel is withdrawn.
7 Disconnect the switch wiring plug.
8 Depress the locking clip, rotate the switch clockwise and remove it from the bracket **(see illustration)**.

Refitting

9 Fully extend the stop-light switch plunger from the switch body to reset the switch **(see illustration)**.
10 Fully depress the brake pedal and hold it in position, then manoeuvre the switch into position. Rotate the switch until the locking lug clips into position. Slowly release the brake pedal and allow it to return to its stop. This will automatically adjust the stop-light switch.
11 Reconnect the wiring connector, and check the operation of the stop-lights. The stop-lights should illuminate after the brake pedal has travelled approximately 5 mm. If the switch is not functioning correctly, it is faulty and must be renewed; no other adjustment is possible.
12 Refit the drivers side lower facia panel.

19 Sensotronic Brake Control (SBC) unit – general information

General information

1 Due to the complexity of the SBC system and the need for specialist equipment (Mercedes STAR), replacement is considered to be outside the scope of this manual. Consequently, we recommend this task be entrusted to a Mercedes Benz dealer or suitably equipped specialist.
2 Note that it may be possible to obtain a

reconditioned replacement unit rather than a new unit – consult your Mercedes parts specialist.

20 Anti-lock braking system (ABS) – general information, sensor and ECU replacement

General information

1 Depending on model, specification and market, the E-Class W211 range may be equipped with Anti-lock braking system (ABS), Anti-clip regulation (ASR), Emergency Brake Assist (BAS), Active brake assist (ABA), Adaptive brake (ABR) and Electronic stability program (ESP).
2 Essentially, all of these systems use sensors to monitor the speed of each roadwheel, combined with sensors to monitor the position/rate of change of the brake pedal, and vehicle yaw (lateral acceleration) rate, then control the fluid pressure to each wheel brake caliper to prevent wheel lock, and assist in vehicle directional control during emergency situations. The systems are capable on interpreting the drivers braking patterns, anticipating emergency braking, and applying the brakes accordingly.
3 The fluid pressure to each wheel is modulated by a electro/hydraulic control unit, incorporating solenoid valves and pump(s). The system is equipped with a sophisticated self-diagnosis system, and communicates with vehicles other electronic control modules via a data network. If a fault should develop, and warning light on the instrument cluster will illuminate, and one or more fault codes will be generated and stored in the control module. The system can then be interrogated using diagnostic equipment via the 16-pin connector on the lower, right-hand side of the facia.
4 The electro/hydraulic control units are extremely complex, and specialist tools are required to remove, refit and configure them. Consequently, the replacement procedures detailed in this manual are restricted to sensor removal and replacement. Any other tasks should be entrusted to a Mercedes dealer or suitably equipped specialist.

Sensor replacement

Front wheel speed sensor

5 Slacken the front roadwheel bolts, raise the front of the vehicle and support it securely on axle stands (see 'Vehicle jacking and support'). Remove the front roadwheels.
6 Undo the fasteners and remove the front section of the engine undershield.
7 Trace the sensor wiring back to the connector. Prise the connector from the retaining clip, and disconnect it.
8 Unclip the sensor wiring from any retaining clips, noting the loom routing.
9 Undo the retaining bolt and remove the chafe protection **(see illustration)**. Discard the bolt – a new one must be fitted.
10 Pull the sensor from the hub carrier.
11 Refitting is a reversal of removal. Tighten the chafe protection/sensor new retaining bolt to the specified torque.

Rear wheel speed sensor

12 Slacken the rear roadwheel bolts, chock the front wheels, raise the rear of the vehicle and support it securely on axle stands (see 'Vehicle jacking and support'). Remove the rear wheels.
13 Release the fasteners and remove the rear wheel arch liner(s).
14 Trace the sensor wiring back to the connector, then using a screwdriver, release the spring retaining clip and disconnect the wiring plug.
15 Release the sensor wiring loom from any retaining clips, noting the loom routing.

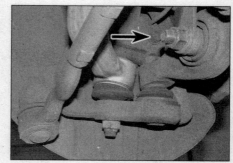

20.9 Front wheel speed sensor retaining bolt

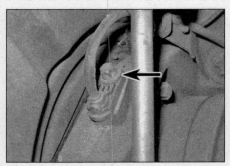

20.16 Rear wheel speed sensor retaining bolt

20.25 The wiring plug will disconnect as the catch is slid out

20.26 Unclip and remove the ECU

16 Undo the retaining bolt, and pull the sensor from the hub carrier **(see illustration)**. Discard the bolt – a new one must be fitted.

17 Refitting is a reversal of removal. Tighten the new sensor retaining bolt to the specified torque.

Yaw rate/lateral acceleration sensor

18 Remove the drivers seat as described in Chapter 11 Section 29.

19 Unclip and remove the floor vent grille.

20 Fold back the carpet under the seat, and disconnect the sensor wiring plug.

21 Undo the retaining nuts and remove the sensor.

Caution: Handle the sensor with extreme care. Rough handling/knocks may cause damage to the sensor.

22 Refitting is a reversal of removal. If a new sensor has been fitted, it may need to be initialized using Mercedes STAR diagnostic equipment (or after-market equivalent).

ECU replacement

23 Disconnect the battery negative lead as described in Chapter 5A Section 4.

24 Remove the cover from the fuse box in the right-hand corner of the engine compartment.

25 Slide out the catches and disconnect the wiring plugs from the top of the ECU **(see illustration)**.

26 Release the clip at each end, and slide the ECU upwards from place **(see illustration)**.

27 Refitting is a reversal of removal.

---

21 Vacuum pump – testing, removal and refitting

Testing

1 The operation of the braking system vacuum pump can be checked using a vacuum gauge.

2 Disconnect the vacuum pipe from the pump, and connect the gauge to the pump union using a suitable length of hose.

3 Start the engine and allow it to idle, and then measure the vacuum created by the pump. As a guide, a minimum of approximately 500 mm Hg should be recorded. If the vacuum registered is significantly less than this, it is likely that the pump is faulty. However, seek the advice of a Mercedes-Benz dealer or specialist before condemning the pump.

Removal

In-line engines

4 Undo the fasteners and remove the engine top cover.

5 Squeeze together the sides, and disconnect the pipe from the vacuum pump **(see illustration)**.

6 Detach the breather hose above the vacuum pump.

7 Undo the retaining bolts and remove the engine cover mounting bracket.

8 Pull the vacuum pump from place. Renew the pump seals.

V6 engines

9 Pull the plastic cover on the top of the engine upwards from its mountings. The pump is located at the front of the right-hand cylinder head.

10 Depress the clips and disconnect the pipe from the vacuum pump **(see illustration)**.

11 Undo the retaining bolts and remove the noise baffle from in front of the pump.

12 Undo the 4 retaining bolts and remove the vacuum pump **(see illustration)**. Renew the pump seals.

Refitting

13 Refitting is a reversal of removal.

21.5 Disconnect the vacuum pipe

21.10 Depress the clips and disconnect the pipe

21.12 Renew the vacuum pump seals

Notes

Chapter 10
Suspension and steering

Contents

Degrees of difficulty

Easy, suitable for novice with little experience	**Fairly easy,** suitable for beginner with some experience	**Fairly difficult,** suitable for competent DIY mechanic	**Difficult,** suitable for experienced DIY mechanic	**Very difficult,** suitable for expert DIY or professional

Specifications

Front suspension
Type . . . .   Independent, multi-link suspension, with MacPherson struts incorporating coil springs, telescopic shock absorbers and anti-roll bar connected to lower arms by connecting drop links. Anti-roll bar fitted to all models. Self-leveling air suspension available as an option.

Rear suspension
Type . . . .   Independent, multi-link with coil springs and telescopic shock absorbers. Anti-roll bar fitted to all models. Self-leveling air suspension available as an option.

Steering system
Type . . . .   Hydraulic power assisted, with rack and pinion.

Front wheel alignment and steering angles
Camber. . . . .   Permissible difference between sides 20'
Castor. . . . .   Permissible difference between sides 30'
Toe-in . . . .   0°10' ± 10'

Rear wheel alignment angles
Toe-in . . . .   0°20' ± 7'

Front hub bearing
Endfloat . . . .   0.01 to 0.02 mm

Front hub grease capacity
Grease cap. 15g
Hub and bearing. 70g

Tyre pressures . . . .   see end of 'Weekly checks'

Torque wrench settings

	Nm	lbf ft
Front suspension:		
Anti-roll bar clamp bolts	50	37
Anti-roll bar link rod nut*	130	96
Front subframe/axle carrier bolts:		
Front bolts	50	37
Rear bolts	100	74
Hub nut clamp bolt	11	8
Spring control arm:		
To axle carrier: *		
Stage 1	80	60
Stage 2	Angle-tighten a further 120°	
To hub carrier: *		
Stage 1	50	37
Stage 2	Angle-tighten a further 60°	
Suspension strut:		
Upper mounting nuts	30	22
Lower mounting bolt/nut	165	122
Piston rod nut*	23	17
Torque strut:		
To axle carrier: *		
Stage 1	80	60
Stage 2	Angle-tighten a further 120°	
To hub carrier: *		
Stage 1	50	37
Stage 2	Angle-tighten a further 60°	
Upper control arm:		
Pivot bolt nut*	50	37
Balljoint nut*		
Stage 1	20	15
Stage 2	Angle-tighten a further 90°	
Outer balljoint-to-control arm: *		
Stage 1	20	15
Stage 2	Angle-tighten a further 45°	
Rear suspension		
Air suspension spring-to-control arm	150	110
Anti-roll bar:		
Clamp bolts	70	52
Link rod bolt/nut*	50	37
Axle/subframe bolts: *		
Stage 1	90	66
Stage 2	Angle-tighten a further 60°	
Camber strut: *		
M12:		
Stage 1	50	37
Stage 2	Angle-tighten a further 90°	
M14:		
Stage 1	80	59
Stage 2	Angle-tighten a further 90°	
Driveshaft retaining nut: *		
Self-locking nut	350	258
Non-self-locking nut: *		
Stage 1	170	125
Stage 2	Angle-tighten a further 45°	
Shock absorber upper mounting nut	20	15
Shock absorber lower mounting nut: *		
Steel coil suspension	55	41
Air suspension:		
Stage 1	50	37
Stage 2	Angle-tighten a further 90°	
Spring control arm: *		
To-rear subframe/axle carrier:		
Stage 1	50	37
Stage 2	Angle-tighten a further 90°	
To-hub carrier:		
Aluminium	150	110
Steel:		
Stage 1	80	59
Stage 2	Angle-tighten a further 90°	

Torque wrench settings (continued)

	Nm	lbf ft
Rear suspension (continued)		
Thrust arm: *		
M12:		
Stage 1	50	37
Stage 2	Angle-tighten a further 90°	
M14:		
Stage 1	80	59
Stage 2	Angle-tighten a further 90°	
Tie-rod: *		
M12:		
Stage 1	50	37
Stage 2	Angle-tighten a further 90°	
M14:		
Stage 1	80	59
Stage 2	Angle-tighten a further 90°	
Torque strut: *		
M12:		
Stage 1	50	37
Stage 2	Angle-tighten a further 90°	
M14:		
Stage 1	80	59
Stage 2	Angle-tighten a further 90°	
Wheel bearing assembly bolts	80	59
Steering		
Column:		
Column mounting bolts	20	15
Lower pinch bolt nut*	24	18
Upper UJ pinch bolt	30	22
Power steering pump mounting bolts:		
Normal threads	20	15
Self-tapping threads	35	26
Power steering pump pulley bolts	25	18
Steering rack-to-subframe:		
Stage 1	70	52
Stage 2	Angle-tighten a further 90°	
Steering wheel bolt	80	59
Track rod end nut: *		
Stage 1	50	37
Stage 2	Angle-tighten a further 90°	

*Do not re-use

1 General information

1 The independent front suspension is of the MacPherson strut type, incorporating coil springs and integral telescopic shock absorbers. The lower end of the strut is attached to the spring control arm. The hub carrier, which carry the wheel bearings, brake calipers and the hub/disc assemblies, is located by the torque strut at the front, the spring control arm at the rear, and the upper control arm. These struts/arms are attached to the hub carrier by means of balljoints, and to the front axle/sub frame/vehicle body by bolts through metal/rubber bushes **(see illustration)**. A front anti-roll bar is fitted to all models. The anti-roll bar is rubber-mounted, and is connected to both hub carriers by short drop links.

2 The independent rear suspension also incorporates coil springs and telescopic shock absorbers. The shock absorbers are

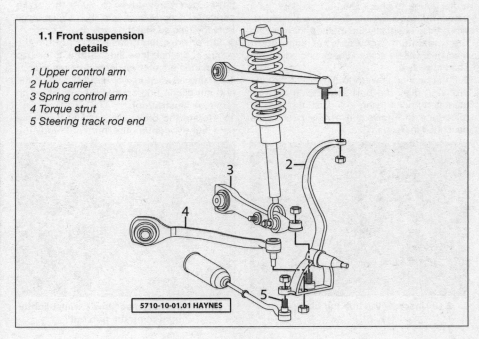

1.1 Front suspension details

1 Upper control arm
2 Hub carrier
3 Spring control arm
4 Torque strut
5 Steering track rod end

5710-10-01.01 HAYNES

located by transverse lower suspension arms, which use rubber mounting bushes. The hub assemblies are fastened to the lower arms, and are joined to the rear subframe by four control arms; two upper arms and two lower ones. Coil springs are fitted between the lower arms and vehicle body. A rear anti-roll bar is fitted to all models. The anti-roll bar is rubber-mounted and is connected to the hub carrier by connecting links.

3 Air suspension was an option for these vehicles, where the conventional spring coil spring was replaced by pressurised air bellows. The system is self-leveling, and dependent on specification, has adaptive damping. The main components of the system are the air bellows, compressor, reservoir, control module, and the necessary sensors/valves/pipework.

4 The steering gear is mounted onto the front subframe, and is connected by two track rods, with balljoints at their inner and outer ends, to the steering arms projecting forwards from the wheel hub carriers. The track rod ends are threaded to the track rods in order to allow adjustment of the front wheel toe setting.

5 Power-assisted steering is standard on all models. The hydraulic steering system is powered by a belt-driven pump which is driven off the crankshaft pulley.

Note: *Many of the suspension and steering components are secured in position with self-locking nuts and bolts. Whenever a self-locking nut or bolt is disturbed, it must be discarded and a new nut/bolt fitted.*

2 Front hub bearing – checking and adjustment

1 Mercedes-Benz recommend the use of a dial gauge to check the hub endfloat, as a means of checking the bearing adjustment. While this is certainly the method for assuring the maximum accuracy, a competent mechanic will be able to check and adjust the bearing by feel.

2 If the bearing is worn to the extent that the droning noise can be heard inside the car, there is no point trying to 'adjust' the bearing to reduce the noise. Fit a new bearing as described in Section 3.

2.4 Shake the wheel to assess play in the bearing

Without a dial gauge

3 Chock the rear wheels and firmly apply the parking brake. Jack up the front of the car and support it on axle stands (see *'Vehicle jacking and support'*).

4 Grasp the wheel at the top and bottom, and shake it to assess free play **(see illustration)**. Repeat the check with the wheel held on the left and right sides. A very small amount of play may be noticed, but if the play is excessive, the bearings should be adjusted as described below.

5 If adjustment is required, the wheel must be removed. This will probably entail lowering the car temporarily to loosen the wheel bolts, then raising the car once more.

6 Refit one of the wheel bolts, in the hole opposite the brake disc retaining screw. This is simply to prevent the disc from moving in relation to the hub.

7 On vehicles with Sensotronic Brake Control (SBC), de-activate the system as described in Chapter 9 Section 4.

8 Taking care not to damage the pad friction material or the disc surface, use a large flat-bladed screwdriver to push the brake pads and pistons back into the caliper, away from the disc so that the pads do not drag.

9 Tap or prise the grease cap out from the centre of the hub **(see illustration)**. If the cap is damaged on removal, it must be renewed.

10 Using an Allen key or socket, slacken the hub nut clamp bolt so that the nut is free to turn **(see illustration)**.

11 Rotate the brake disc and at the same time lightly tighten the hub nut until the

2.9 Tap the grease cap out from the centre of the hub (brake disc removed)

disc starts to become difficult to turn **(see illustration)**. From this point, slacken the hub nut by approximately one-third of a turn, and then tap the end of the hub spindle with a soft-faced mallet to relieve the tension on the bearing.

12 Slacken the hub nut fully, then very lightly tighten it by hand only until resistance is felt. A few attempts may be required, but there should be a clear point at which, without effort, all free play is eliminated without loading the bearing. Do not tighten the hub nut using tools, or any tighter than described, as this will quickly destroy it.

13 Tighten the hub nut clamp bolt to the specified torque.

14 Pack the grease cap with fresh grease, and tap it fully back into place **(see illustration)**.

15 Refit the wheel, then lower the car to the ground and tighten the wheel bolts to the specified torque.

16 Where applicable, re-activate the Sensotronic Brake Control (SBC) system as described in Chapter 9 Section 4.

17 On models without Sensotronic Brake Control (SBC), depress the brake pedal repeatedly until normal pressure returns.

18 If a new bearing has been fitted, recheck the adjustment within approximately 500 miles.

With a dial gauge

19 Chock the rear wheels and firmly apply the parking brake. Loosen the front wheel bolts, and then jack up the front of the car and support it on axle stands (see *'Vehicle jacking*

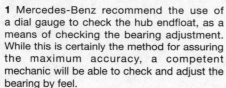

2.10 Unscrew the hub nut clamp bolt

2.11 Turn the hub/disc slowly whilst lightly tightening the hub nut

2.14 Tap the cap into place

and support'). Remove the relevant front roadwheel.

20 On vehicles with Sensotronic Brake Control (SBC), de-activate the system as described in Chapter 9 Section 4.

21 Using spacers if necessary, refit two of the wheel bolts (to locate the brake disc), positioning them on opposite sides, and tightening them securely.

22 Taking care not to damage the pad friction material or the disc surface, use a large flat-bladed screwdriver to push the brake pads and pistons back into the caliper, away from the disc so that the pads do not drag.

23 Tap the grease cap out from the centre of the hub. If the cap is damaged on removal, it must be renewed.

24 Mount a dial gauge onto the front face of the hub/disc, and position the gauge probe so that it is in contact with the end of the axle shaft. Zero the gauge scale, then grasp the disc at two opposite points and pull it in and out. Note the reading obtained on the gauge, and check that the hub bearing endfloat is within the limits given in the Specifications at the start of this Chapter.

25 If all is well, remove the dial gauge. Pack the grease cap with grease, and tap the cap into position. Remove the wheel bolts and refit the roadwheel, then lower the car to the ground and tighten the wheel bolts to the specified torque. Where applicable, re-activate the SBC system as described in Chapter 9 Section 4.

26 If adjustment is required, use an Allen key to slacken the hub retaining nut clamp bolt until the retaining nut is free to turn.

27 Rotate the brake disc while lightly tightening the hub nut, until the disc starts to become difficult to turn. From this point, slacken the hub nut by approximately one-third of a turn, and then tap the end of the hub spindle with a soft-faced mallet to relieve the tension on the bearing.

28 Check the hub bearing endfloat as previously described. If necessary adjust the endfloat by rotating the hub nut as required.

29 Recheck the bearing endfloat, then refit all disturbed components as described.

30 Where applicable, re-activate the SBC system as described in Chapter 9 Section 4.

31 If a new bearing has been fitted, recheck the adjustment within approximately 500 miles.

---

3 Front hub and bearing – removal, overhaul and refitting

Note: *The hub assembly should not be removed unless the bearings are to be renewed; the hub bearing inner race is a press-fit on the hub carrier, and removal of the hub will almost certainly damage the bearings. A press will be required to dismantle and rebuild the assembly; if such a tool is not available, a large bench vice and spacers (such as large sockets) will serve as an adequate substitute. The bearing's*

3.3 Slacken and remove the hub nut

inner races are an interference fit on the hub; if the inner race remains on the hub when it is pressed out of the hub carrier, a knife-edged bearing puller will be required to remove it.

Removal

1 Remove the front brake disc, disc shield and ABS sensor as described in Chapter 9.

2 Tap the grease cap out from the centre of the hub. If the cap is damaged on removal, it must be renewed.

3 Slacken the hub nut clamp bolt, then slacken and remove the hub nut from the axle **(see illustration)**.

4 Take off the hub outer bearing, and place it to one side where it can be kept clean **(see illustration)**.

5 The front hub assembly can now be withdrawn from the hub carrier. If the hub assembly is a tight fit on the axle, a puller will be required to draw it off.

6 If the inner bearing race remains on the hub carrier, a knife-edge type puller will be required to remove it. With the race removed, slide off the hub oil seal.

7 Inspect the hub carrier axle shaft for signs of damage, and renew if necessary.

Overhaul

8 No overhaul of the hub or bearings is possible. If wear or damage is evident, the hub and bearing assembly must be replaced.

Refitting

9 Apply a smear of grease to the hub rear oil seal lip, and locate the hub assembly onto the hub carrier shaft.

10 Pack the outer bearing with grease, working it well into the bearing tracks. Fit the outer bearing into position over the hub carrier shaft, and slide it fully into the hub location.

11 Screw on the hub nut. Rotate the hub assembly whilst using the hub nut to press the hub assembly onto the hub carrier shaft. Once the hub assembly is correctly seated, adjust the hub bearing endfloat as described in Section 2.

12 Pack the grease cap with grease, then tap it squarely into position.

13 Refit the brake disc shield, ABS wheel speed sensor and brake disc as described in Chapter 9.

3.4 Remove the hub outer bearing

---

4 Front hub carrier – removal and refitting

Removal

1 Chock the rear wheels and firmly apply the parking brake. Loosen the front wheel bolts, and then jack up the front of the car and support it on axle stands (see *'Vehicle jacking and support'*). Remove the relevant front roadwheel.

2 Remove the front hub assembly as described in Section 3.

3 Undo the fasteners and remove the brake disc shield.

4 Slacken and remove the nut securing the track rod balljoint to the hub carrier, and release the balljoint tapered shank using a universal balljoint separator **(see illustration 28.3)**.

5 Similarly, release the balljoints securing the hub carrier to the two suspension lower arms, and upper arm, with reference to Section 7. Manoeuvre the hub carrier from place.

6 Inspect the carrier for signs of wear or damage, and renew as necessary.

Refitting

7 Refitting is a reversal of removal, noting the following points:

a) Clean any threads by running a tap of the correct thread size and pitch down them.

b) Thoroughly clean the balljoint tapers and their locating holes, also clean the balljoint threads if necessary, using a wire brush.

c) Check all the balljoint rubbers for signs of damage or perishing. If the rubber has split, this will lead to loss of lubricant and dirt entry, which will destroy the joint. If any balljoints are suspect, take the opportunity to fit new components.

d) Fit a new locking nuts, where fitted.

e) Tighten bolts and nuts to the specified torque setting where applicable.

f) Refit the hub and bearing assembly as described in Section 3.

g) Where new parts have been fitted, it is advisable to the front wheel tow setting ('tracking') checked on completion.

5.2 Front suspension strut upper mounting bolts

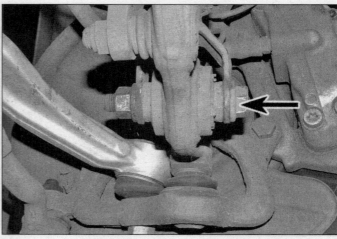

5.3 Strut lower mounting bolt/nut

5 Front suspension strut – removal and refitting

Note: *Refer to the note at the end of Section 1 before proceeding. Shock absorbers should always be renewed in pairs on the same axle, to preserve safe handling.*

Conventional steel coil spring (non-air suspension)

Removal

1 Chock the rear wheels, and firmly apply the parking brake. Loosen the front wheel bolts, and then jack up the front of the car and support it on axle stands (see *'Vehicle jacking and support'*). Remove the relevant front roadwheel.
2 Working in the engine compartment, undo the suspension strut upper mounting nuts **(see illustration)**.
3 Undo the nut and remove the bolt securing the lower end of the strut to the spring control arm **(see illustration)**. Note which way around the bolt is fitted – from the front.
4 With the help of an assistant, press the strut control arm downwards, and manoeuvre the suspension strut from place.

Refitting

5 Check the strut body for leaking fluid, dents, cracks and other obvious signs of damage. Also check the coil spring for any cracks and inspect the spring seat for any general deterioration. Renew any faulty components.
6 Refitting is a reversal of removal, noting the following points:
a) *Renew all self-locking nuts.*
b) *Tighten all fasteners to their specified torque, where given.*
c) *Only tighten the suspension strut lower*

bolt/nut once the weight of the vehicle is back on its' wheels.

Air suspension strut (Airmatic)

Removal

Caution: On models with front air suspension struts, replacement of the units is only possible once the system has been depressurised. This can only safely be done using Mercedes STAR diagnostic equipment (or after-market equivalent). Using any other method of depressurisation will probably result in expensive damage.
7 Raise the front, and rear of the vehicle, then support it securely on axle stands (see *'Vehicle jacking and support'*). Remove the front roadwheels.
8 Using Mercedes STAR diagnostic equipment, de-pressurise the air suspension system.
9 Working in the engine compartment, disconnect the wiring plug from the top of the suspension strut.
10 Undo the union and disconnect the air pressure pipe from the top of the strut. Plug or seal the openings to prevent contamination.
11 Remove the strut upper retaining nuts.
12 Release the fasteners and remove the wheel arch liner.
13 Trace the wiring back to the damping valve unit, and disconnect the wiring plug. Release the wiring from any retaining clips.
14 Undo the nut, and use a balljoint splitter to detach the upper control arm from the hub carrier. Support the hub carrier to prevent damage.
15 Undo the nut and withdraw the bolt securing the lower end of the strut to the spring control arm. Note that the bolt is fitted from the rear.
16 With the help of an assistant, press down the strut control arm, and manoeuvre the strut assembly from place.

17 Examine the strut for signs of excessive wear, damage or leaks. If defective, the complete strut assembly must be replaced. No overhaul is recommended.

Refitting

18 Refitting is a reversal of removal, noting the following points:
a) *Only tighten the strut lower mounting bolt/ nut once the weight of the vehicle is back on its' wheels.*
b) *Tighten all fasteners to their specified torque, where given.*
c) *Re-pressurise the air system using Mercedes STAR diagnostic equipment (or equivalent).*

6 Front suspension coil spring – removal and refitting

Note: *Refer to the note at the end of Section 1 before proceeding. Springs should always be renewed in pairs on the same axle, to preserve safe handling.*

⚠ *Warning: Before attempting to dismantle the suspension strut, a suitable tool to hold the coil spring in compression must be obtained. Adjustable coil spring compressors are readily available, and are recommended for this operation. Any attempt to dismantle the strut without such a tool is likely to result in damage or personal injury.*

Removal

1 With the strut removed from the car as described in Section 5, clean away all external dirt. If necessary, mount it upright in a vice during the dismantling procedure
2 Fit the spring compressor, and compress

6.2 Compress the spring until the seats are not under tension

6.3 Remove the piston nut and washer...

6.4a Remove the spring retainer/seat...

6.4b...gaiter...

6.4c...and bump stop

6.6 Spring cup, contact washer and support washer

the coil spring until all tension is relieved from the upper spring seat **(see illustration)**.

3 Remove the cap (where fitted), then unscrew and remove the piston rod retaining nut, whilst retaining the strut piston with a suitable spanner **(see illustration)**.

4 Remove the upper spring retainer and seat, complete with gaiter and bump stop. If required, separate the bump stop and gaiter from the seat **(see illustrations)**.

5 Make alignment marks between the spring and lower seat, then slide the shock absorber from the spring.

6 Inspect the lower spring cup, contact washer and support washer **(see illustration)**.

7 With the strut assembly now completely dismantled, examine all the components for

wear, damage or deformation, and check the bearing for smoothness of operation. Renew any of the components as necessary.

8 Examine the strut for signs of fluid leakage. Check the strut piston for signs of pitting along its entire length, and check the strut body for signs of damage.

9 If any doubt exists about the condition of the coil spring, carefully remove the spring compressors, and check the spring for distortion and signs of cracking. Renew the spring if it is damaged or distorted, or if there is any doubt as to its condition.

10 Inspect all other components for signs of damage or deterioration, and renew as necessary.

Refitting

11 Ensure the support washer, contract washer and lower spring cup are in place.

12 Fit the coil spring (together with the compressor tool) onto the strut, making sure its lower end is correctly located against the spring seat stop, as noted on removal.

13 Refit the upper spring retainer and seat, complete with bump stop and gaiter. Ensure the end of the coil spring engages correctly with the step in the spring seat **(see illustration)**.

14 Fit a new piston rod nut and tighten it to the specified torque, whilst counterholding the piston rod **(see illustration)**.

15 Refit the strut as described in Section 5.

6.13 The end of the coil spring must rest against the stop in the spring seat

6.14 Counterhold the piston rod whist tightening the nut

7.2 Detach the upper arm from the hub carrier

7.4a The engine compartment fusebox is secured by 2 bolts at the upper rear edge...

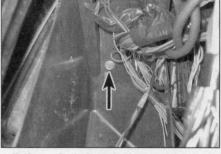

7.4b...and a bolt at the lower rear edge

7 Front suspension arms – removal and refitting

Removal

Upper control arm

1 Remove the suspension strut as described in Section 5.

2 Undo the nut and detach the upper arm outer balljoint from the hub carrier using a universal balljoint separator **(see illustration)**. Secure the hub carrier to prevent any strain on the brake hose or wiring harnesses.

3 If removing the left-hand upper control arm, remove the pollen filter housing (Chapter 1 Section 19) and additional battery (Chapter 5A Section 4).

4 If removing the right-hand upper control arm, remove the engine management control unit (Chapter 4A Section 13), ESP control unit and SAM unit, then move the engine compartment fusebox to one side **(see illustrations)**. Access is extremely limited.

5 Undo the retaining nuts, remove the bolts and manoeuvre the upper control arm from the vehicle **(see illustrations)**.

6 Examine the inner mounting bushes and outer balljoint for wear, damage and deterioration. From 02/2003, the upper control arm was modified. From this date the arm is manufactured from sheet aluminium with a bolted-on outer balljoint. On this type of arm, the balljoint can be replaced as described in Section 8. On the earlier cast-aluminium arms, the balljoint is integral with the arm, and if defective, the complete assembly must be replaced.

Torque strut

7 Slacken the relevant front roadwheel bolts, raise the front of the vehicle and support it securely on axle stands (see 'Vehicle jacking and support'). Remove the roadwheel, then undo the fasteners and remove the engine undershield.

8 Undo the retaining nut, then using a universal balljoint separator, detach the outer end of the torque strut from the hub carrier **(see illustration)**.

9 At the inner end of the torque strut, undo the retaining nut and remove the pivot bolt **(see illustration)**. Note that the bolt must not be allowed to rotate at all as the nut is slackened, otherwise the locating lugs for the caster adjustment on the bush will be sheared off. Note the fitted position of the bolt in relation to the bush in the strut.

10 Manoeuvre the torque strut from position.

11 Examine the strut and bush. If required, the bush can be renewed separately from the strut, but a press will be required. Note orientation and fitted depth of the bush before removing it. Press the new bush into the same position. Note that there are several variations of bush design. Ensure the replacement bush matches the one removed.

Spring control arm

Caution: On models with front air suspension struts, replacement of the control arm is only possible once the system has been depressurised. This can only safely be done using Mercedes STAR diagnostic equipment (or after-market equivalent). Using any other method of depressurisation will probably result in expensive damage.

12 Raise the front, and rear of the vehicle, then support it securely on axle stands (see 'Vehicle jacking and support'). Remove the front roadwheels.

13 On models with front air suspension, using Mercedes STAR diagnostic equipment, de-pressurise the air suspension system.

14 Undo the fasteners and remove the rear section of the engine undershield.

15 Undo the retaining bolt and remove the front wheel speed sensor and scuff plate from the hub carrier. There's no need to disconnect the wiring.

7.5a Undo the nuts...

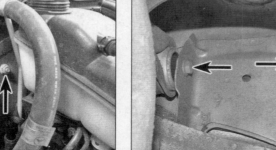

7.5b...and remove the bolts

7.8 Torque strut balljoint retaining nut

7.9 Torque strut inner pivot bolt

7.18 Spring control arm inner pivot bolt and nut

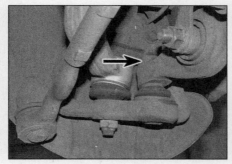

7.19 Spring control arm balljoint retaining nut

8.4 The balljoint is secured by 3 bolts/nuts

16 Undo the nut/bolt securing the lower end of the suspension strut to the control arm (**see illustration 5.3**).

17 Undo the nut and detach the lower end of the anti-roll bar link rod from the spring control arm.

18 Undo the nut and pull the inner pivot bolt from the arm (**see illustration**). Note that the bolt must not be allowed to rotate at all as the nut is slackened, otherwise the locating lugs for the camber adjustment in the mounting will be sheared off. Note the fitted position of the bolt in relation to the bush in the arm.

19 Undo the retaining nut, then using a universal balljoint separator, detach the outer end of the spring control arm from the hub carrier (**see illustration**).

20 Manoeuvre the control arm from place.

21 Examine the arm and bushes. If required, the bushes can be renewed separately from the arm, but a press will be required. Note orientation and fitted depth of the bush(es) before removing it. Press the new bush(es) into the same position. Note that there are several variations of bush design. Ensure the replacement bush matches the one(s) removed. If the balljoint is damaged or worn, the complete arm assembly must be replaced.

Refitting

22 Refitting is a reversal of removal, noting the following points:
a) Renew all self-locking nuts.
b) The arms' inner pivot bolt nuts must only be tightened once the weight of the vehicle is back on its' wheels.
c) Tighten all fasteners to their specified torque where given.
d) Have the front wheel alignment checked at the earliest opportunity.

8 Front suspension upper arm outer balljoint – renewal

1 From 02/2003, the upper control arm was modified. From this date the arm is manufactured from sheet aluminium with a bolted-on outer balljoint. On this type of arm, the balljoint can be replaced as described in this Section. On the earlier cast-aluminium

arms, the balljoint is integral with the arm, and if defective, the complete assembly must be replaced as described in Section 7.

2 Slacken the relevant roadwheel bolts, raise the front of the vehicle and support it securely on axle stands (see *'Vehicle jacking and support'*). Remove the roadwheel.

3 Undo the retaining nut, and use a universal balljoint separator tool to detach the control arm balljoint from the top of the hub carrier.

4 Undo the 3 retaining bolts/nuts and detach the balljoint from the upper control arm (**see illustration**). Note that new nuts and bolts are supplied in the genuine Mercedes balljoint replacement kit.

5 Slide the new balljoint fully into the control arm, fit the new nuts/bolts, and tighten them to the specified torque.

6 The remainder of refitting is a reversal of removal.

9 Front anti-roll bar – removal and refitting

Removal

1 On models with front air suspension struts, replacement of the anti-roll bar is only possible once the system has been depressurised. This can only safely be done using Mercedes STAR diagnostic equipment (or after-market equivalent). Using any other method of depressurisation will probably result in expensive damage.

2 Remove the plastic cover from the top of the engine, then remove the air cleaner housing as described in Chapter 4A Section 2.

3 Slacken the front roadwheel bolts, raise the front of the vehicle and support it securely on axle stands (see *'Vehicle jacking and support'*). Remove the roadwheels.

4 On models with front air suspension, using Mercedes STAR diagnostic equipment, de-pressurise the air suspension system.

5 Undo the fasteners and remove the engine undershield.

6 Attach a lifting hoist to the engine. The engine must be raised a little, and the subframe must be lowered a little to facilitate the anti-roll bar removal.

7 Remove the bolt each side securing the engine mountings to the subframe. Raise the engine a little, taking care not to stretch any hoses or wiring harnesses.

8 Undo the nuts and detach the upper ends of the link rods from the anti-roll bar (**see illustration**).

9 Position a workshop jack(s) under the front subframe, then undo the retaining bolts and lower the subframe a little, ensuring the steering column coupling is not stretched.

10 Undo the bolts and remove the anti-roll bar clamps. Mercedes insist that once removed, the clamps must be renewed.

11 Manoeuvre the anti-roll bar from under the vehicle.

12 If required, note their fitted positions, then prise the anti-roll bar bushes from place.

Refitting

13 Refitting is a reversal of removal, tightening all fasteners to their specified torque where given.

10 Front anti-roll bar link rods – removal and refitting

Removal

1 Slacken the front roadwheel bolts, raise the front of the vehicle and support it securely on axle stands (see *'Vehicle jacking and support'*). Remove the roadwheels.

2 Using an Allen key to counterhold the balljoint, undo the retaining nut at the upper,

9.8 Counterhold the anti-roll bar link nut with an Allen key in the bolt

and lower end of the anti-roll bar link rod **(see illustration 9.8)**. Discard the retaining nuts – new ones must be fitted.

3 Manoeuvre the link rod from place.

Refitting

4 Refitting is a reversal of removal. Tighten the fasteners to their specified torque where given.

11 Front subframe – removal and refitting

Removal

Caution: On models with front air suspension struts, removal of the subframe is only possible once the system has been depressurised. This can only safely be done using Mercedes STAR diagnostic equipment (or after-market equivalent). Using any other method of depressurisation will probably result in expensive damage.

1 Ensure the front wheels are in the 'straight-ahead' position. During this procedure, the steering wheel must not be rotated.

2 Remove the plastic covers from the top of the engine.

3 Remove the air cleaner housing as described in Chapter 4A Section 2.

4 Use syringe or poultry baster to remove as much fluid as possible from the power steering fluid reservoir.

5 Slacken the front roadwheel bolts, raise the front of the vehicle and support it securely on axle stands (see 'Vehicle jacking and support'). Remove the roadwheels.

6 Undo the fasteners and remove the engine undershield.

7 Where applicable, depressurise the front air suspension system with the Mercedes STAR diagnostic equipment.

8 Detach the trackrod end balljoints from the hub carriers, as described in Section 28.

9 Detach the anti-roll bar link rods from the spring control arms as described in Section 10.

10 Detach the spring control arms and torque struts from the subframe/axle carrier as described in Section 7.

11 Move the steering wheel to its fully extended position.

12 Working in the engine compartment, undo the pinch bolt/nut and slide the steering column lower shaft upwards from the steering rack pinion. Discard the bolt – a new one must be fitted.

13 In order to support the engine whilst the subframe is removed, attach a suitable lifting hoist to the engine.

14 Remove the bolts securing the left-, and right-hand engine mountings to the subframe.

15 Note its fitted position, then disconnect any wiring plugs/harness from the steering rack.

16 Thoroughly clean the area around the steering rack pinion housing/pipes, then undo the bolts, remove the retaining plate, and pull the fluid pipes from the pinion housing **(see illustration)**. Plug the openings to prevent contamination. Renew the O-ring seals.

17 Support the front subframe using workshop jack(s) and suitable pieces of wood.

18 Remove the retaining bolts each side, the lower the subframe/axle carrier from place.

Refitting

19 Refitting is a reversal of removal, noting the following points:

a) *Replace all self-locking nuts.*
b) *Tighten all fasteners to their specified torque where given.*
c) *Bleed the power steering system as described in Section 27.*
d) *Where applicable, re-pressurise the front air suspension system using Mercedes STAR diagnostic equipment (or equivalent).*
e) *Have the wheel alignment checked at the earliest opportunity.*

12 Rear hub carrier – removal and refitting

Note: *Before proceeding, refer to the note in Section 1.*

Removal

Caution: On models with rear air suspension, removal of the hub carrier is only possible once the system has been depressurised. This can only safely be done using Mercedes STAR diagnostic equipment (or after-market equivalent). Using any other method of depressurisation will probably result in expensive damage.

1 Where applicable, de-pressurise the rear air suspension system using Mercedes STAR diagnostic equipment (or after-market equivalent).

2 On models with Sensotronic Brake Control (SBC), de-activate the system as described in Chapter 9 Section 4.

3 Prise out the cap from the centre of the rear wheel, then using a hammer and pointed-nose chisel, carefully relieve the driveshaft retaining nut staking (where applicable) **(see illustration)**.

4 Slacken the driveshaft retaining nut with the car resting on its wheels. Note that this nut is extremely tight – ensure that the tools used to loosen it are of good quality, and a good fit. Discard the nut – a new one must be fitted.

5 Chock the front wheels, slacken the rear roadwheel bolts, raise the rear of the vehicle and support it securely on axle stands (see 'Vehicle jacking and support'). Remove the rear roadwheels.

6 Remove the parking brake shoes as described in Chapter 9 Section 17, then pull the parking brake cable from the hub carrier.

7 Undo the retaining bolt and pull the wheel speed sensor from the hub carrier – see Chapter 9 Section 20.

8 Undo the nut and detach the lower end of the anti-roll bar link rod from the hub carrier.

9 Position a workshop jack under the hub carrier, then raise it until the driveshaft is approximately horizontal.

10 With reference to Section 17, detach the torque strut, camber strut, tie rod and thrust arm from the hub carrier.

11 Lower the jack supporting the hub carrier, then remove the bolt securing the spring control arm to the hub carrier.

12 Withdraw the hub assembly from the end of the driveshaft joint. If necessary, tap the joint out of the hub using a soft-faced mallet. If this fails to free it from the hub, the joint will have to be pressed out using a suitable tool which is bolted to the hub.

Note: *Support the driveshaft by hanging it from the vehicle underbody using a piece of wire. Do not allow the driveshaft to hang under its own weight, as the CV joint may be damaged.*

Refitting

13 Refitting is a reversal of removal, noting the following points:

a) *Loosely attach the torque strut, camber strut, tie-rod, thrust arm and spring control arm. Tighten the bolts fully only when the weight of the vehicle is back on its wheels.*
b) *Tighten all fasteners to their specified torque, where given.*
c) *Re-pressurise the air suspension system (where applicable) using Mercedes STAR diagnostic equipment (or equivalent).*

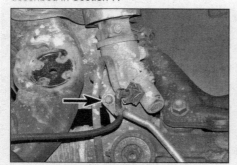

11.16 Power steering fluid pipes plate retaining bolt

12.3 Relieve the nut staking

d) Re-activate the SBC system (where applicable) as described in Chapter 9 Section 4.

e) Where a non-self-locking driveshaft nut is fitted, once fully tightened, 'stake' the nut to the shaft using a chisel or punch.

f) Have the rear wheel alignment checked at the earliest opportunity.

13 Rear hub bearing – renewal

Note: *In order to fit the driveshaft flange/hub, Mercedes technicians use tool nos. 210 589 03 43 00 and 211 589 00 33 00. These tools attach to the end of the driveshaft, and pull the flange into place. If these tools are not available, it will be necessary to remove the hub carrier in order to renew the bearing.*

With the Mercedes special tools

1 On models with Sensotronic Brake Control (SBC), de-activate the system as described in Section 9 Section 4.

2 Prise out the cap from the centre of the rear wheel, then using a hammer and pointed-nose chisel, carefully relieve the driveshaft retaining nut staking (where applicable) **(see illustration 12.3)**.

3 Slacken the driveshaft retaining nut with the car resting on its wheels. Note that this nut is extremely tight – ensure that the tools used to loosen it are of good quality, and a good fit. Discard the nut – a new one must be fitted.

4 Chock the front wheels, slacken the rear roadwheel bolts, raise the rear of the vehicle and support it securely on axle stands (see 'Vehicle jacking and support'). Remove the rear roadwheels.

5 Remove the parking brake shoes as described in Chapter 9 Section 17.

6 Using a slide hammer and suitable attachments, pull the driveshaft flange from the bearing assembly.

7 The wheel bearing assembly is bolted to the hub carrier. Undo the bolts and remove the bearing assembly. Press the driveshaft slightly to one side to access the bolts.

Caution: Take care not to damage any of the aluminium surfaces of the rear axle/suspension. Any scratches, cracks or notches may shorten the service life of the components.

8 The inner race of the bearing remains on the hub flange. If the flange is to be re-used, remove the bearing race with a knife-edged bearing puller.

9 Before commencing refitting, clean the water drain channel in the hub carrier.

10 Position the new bearing assembly on the hub carrier, refit the bolts and tighten them to the specified torque.

11 Use Mercedes tools Nos. 210 589 03 43 00 and 211 589 00 33 00 to draw the driveshaft flange/hub into place.

12 The remainder of refitting is a reversal of removal, noting the following points:

a) Tighten all fasteners to their specified torque where given.

b) Re-activate the SBC system (where applicable) as described in Chapter 9 Section 4.

c) Where a non-self-locking driveshaft nut is fitted, once fully tightened, 'stake' the nut to the shaft using a chisel or punch.

Without the Mercedes special tools

13 Remove the hub carrier as described in Section 12.

14 Undo the retaining bolts and detach the hub bearing/driveshaft flange from the hub carrier.

15 If the driveshaft flange/hub is to be re-used, press it from the bearing assembly, then use a knife-edge puller to remove the bearing inner race which will have remained on the flange.

16 Before commencing reassembly, clean the water channel in the hub carrier.

17 Press the new bearing assembly onto the driveshaft flange. Take care to only press on the inner race of the bearing assembly.

18 Position the flange/bearing assembly on the hub carrier and tighten the retaining bolts to the specified torque.

19 Refit the hub carrier as described in Section 12.

14 Rear suspension shock absorber – removal, testing and refitting

Note: *Refer to the note at the end of Section 1 before proceeding. Shock absorbers should always be renewed in pairs on the same axle, to preserve safe handling.*

Caution: On models with rear air suspension, removal of the shock absorber is only possible once the system has been depressurised. This can only safely be done using Mercedes STAR diagnostic equipment (or after-market equivalent). Using any other method of depressurisation will probably result in expensive damage.

Removal

1 Chock the front wheels, and loosen the rear wheel bolts. Jack up the rear of the car and support it on axle stands (see 'Vehicle jacking and support'). To improve access, remove the rear roadwheel.

2 Prise up the centre pins, lever out the plastic rivets, and unclip the protective cover from the base of the suspension lower arm **(see illustration)**.

Vehicles with air suspension

3 De-pressurise the rear air suspension system using Mercedes STAR diagnostic equipment (or after-market equivalent), then immediately raise the lower arm approximately 30 mm using a workshop jack under the hub carrier.

All vehicles

4 Remove the luggage compartment side trim panel as described in Chapter 11 Section 34.

5 Slacken and unscrew the upper mounting nut, taking care to ensure that the shock absorber body/piston rod does not rotate, and lift off the large washer and rubber bush **(see illustration)**.

6 From underneath the car, slacken and remove the shock absorber lower mounting nut, then withdraw the bolt and washers.

7 Lift the lower half of the shock absorber to collapse it slightly, and then manoeuvre it out from underneath the wheel arch.

Testing

8 Examine the shock absorber for signs of fluid leakage. Check the piston for signs of pitting along its entire length, and check the body for signs of damage.

9 While holding it in an upright position, test the operation of the shock absorber by moving the piston through a full stroke, and then through short strokes of 50 to 100 mm. In both cases, the resistance felt should be smooth and continuous. If the resistance is jerky, or uneven, or if there is any visible sign of wear or damage, renewal is necessary.

10 Inspect all other components for signs of damage or deterioration, and renew any that are suspect.

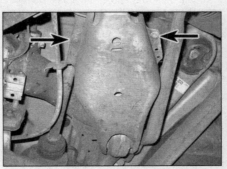

14.2 Remove the plastic rivets and unclip the lower cover

14.5 Rear shock absorber upper mounting nut

Refitting

11 If a new shock absorber is being fitted, gently compress and release the unit a few times, to prime it before fitting.

12 Slide the bump stop onto the shock absorber piston, then refit the dust cover and spacer.

13 Manoeuvre the unit into position so that the threaded top section passes through the hole at the top of the wheel arch. Raise the lower arm slightly if necessary, and engage the lower mounting loosely with the mounting point on the lower arm; fully insert the lower mounting bolt with its washer.

14 Working from above, fit the rubber bush and large washer, then screw on the upper mounting nut, and tighten by hand only.

15 Fit the new nut and washer (where fitted) to the lower mounting bolt, and tighten it by hand only.

Vehicles with steel coil springs

16 Refit the roadwheel, then lower the car to the ground and tighten the wheel bolts to the specified torque.

17 With the car resting on its wheels, push down on the wing, and then release it. Repeat this a few times, to settle the components.

18 Tighten the shock absorber upper mounting nut to the specified torque, making sure the piston rod does not turn. Where fitted, fit a new locknut, and tighten it to its specified torque while counter-holding the first nut.

19 Refit the luggage compartment side trim panel as described in Chapter 11 Section 34.

20 Tighten the lower mounting nut to the specified torque, counterholding the bolt against rotation if necessary.

21 Refit the lower protective cover to the lower arm, secure it with the plastic expansion rivets.

Vehicles with air suspension

22 Repressurise the air suspension system using Mercedes STAR diagnostic equipment (or after-market equivalent).

23 Refit the roadwheel, tighten the bolts to the specified torque, and lower the vehicle to the ground.

24 Tighten the shock absorber upper mounting nut to the specified torque, and refit the luggage compartment side trim panel as described in Chapter 11 Section 34.

25 Tighten the lower mounting nut, counterholding the bolt to prevent rotation.

26 Refit the lower arm protective cover, and tighten the retaining screws securely.

15 Rear suspension coil spring
– removal and refitting

⚠️ *Warning: A suitable tool to hold the coil spring in compression must be obtained. Adjustable coil spring compressors are readily available, and are recommended for this operation. Any attempt to remove the spring without such a tool is likely to result in damage or personal injury.*
Note: *Refer to the note at the end of Section 1 before proceeding.*

Removal

1 Chock the front wheels, and loosen the rear wheel bolts. Jack up the rear of the car and support it on axle stands (see *'Vehicle jacking and support'*). Remove the relevant rear roadwheel.

2 Prise out the centre pins, lever out the plastic expansion rivets, and remove the protective cover from the base of the lower suspension arm.

3 Fit the spring compressor, and compress the coil spring until all tension is relieved from the spring seats.
Note: *There's only room for the type of compressor that inserts into the spring centre from underneath.*

4 Position a jack beneath inner end of the lower arm, and raise the jack head until the arm is securely supported.

5 Slacken and remove the nut and bolt securing the shock absorber mounting to the lower arm.

6 Carefully lower the lower suspension arm until it is possible to remove the coil spring and upper spring seat **(see illustration)**.

7 Inspect the coil spring for signs of wear or damage, and renew if necessary. The upper spring seat should also be renewed if it is damaged or shows signs of deterioration.

Refitting

8 Ensure that the lower arm spring seat is clean, then fit the upper spring seat to the coil spring and manoeuvre the spring into position.

9 Locate the lower end of the spring correctly against the stop on the lower arm seat. Align the upper spring seat with the body mounting, and carefully raise the lower arm whilst also aligning it with the subframe.

10 Check that the spring is correctly located, and then insert the lower arm pivot bolt. Fit a new nut to the pivot bolt, tightening it lightly only at this stage. Refit the shock absorber mounting bolt, and tighten the new retaining nut to the specified torque.

11 Remove the jack from beneath the lower arm, and then carefully release the spring compressor whilst making sure both its upper and lower ends are correctly located.

12 Refit the roadwheel, then lower the car to the ground and tighten the wheel bolts to the specified torque.

13 With the car resting on its wheels, rock it to settle the spring and lower arm in position.

14 Tighten the lower arm pivot bolt nut to the specified torque setting.

15 Refit the protective cover to the lower arm, and securely tighten its retaining screws.

16 Rear suspension air spring
– removal and refitting

Removal

1 Chock the front wheel, slacken the rear wheel bolts, raise the rear of the vehicle and support it securely on axle stands (see *'Vehicle jacking and support'*). Remove the rear wheels.

2 De-pressurise the air suspension system using Mercedes STAR diagnostic equipment (or equivalent).Using any other method of depressurisation will probably result in expensive damage.

3 Release the cable tie, then disconnect the air pressure pipe from the top of the air spring **(see illustration)**. Use a deep, split-type 10 mm socket to undo the pipe union.

4 Disconnect the wiring plug from the top of the air spring.

5 Where necessary, release the fasteners and remove the protective cover from the base of the spring control arm.

6 Undo the nut and withdraw the bolt securing the air spring to the spring control arm **(see illustration)**.

7 Undo the bolt securing the tie-rod to the hub carrier.

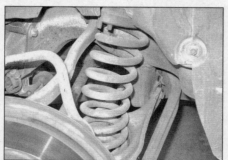

15.6 Manoeuvre the coil spring from place

16.3 Disconnect the air pipe from the spring

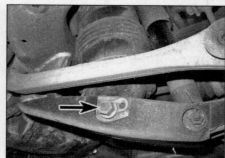

16.6 Rear air spring lower retaining bolt/nut

8 Prise the air spring from the retaining clip on the vehicle floor. Note that this causes irreparable damage to the retaining clip, which must be renewed.

9 Press the base of the air spring upwards from the control arm, press the tie-rod downwards a little, and manoeuvre the air spring to the rear, and out from under the wheelarch.

Caution: Do not twist the air spring as its removed. Twisting will produce creases in the bellows, which will cause premature failure.

10 Remove the fragments of the air spring retaining clip from the vehicle floor, and the top of the spring.

Refitting

11 Check the condition of the air spring bellows, noting the following points:
a) *The folds in the bellows must be correctly formed, with no twisting/creases.*
b) *There must be no damage to the bellows (cracks, etc).*
c) *The air spring must be straight – not buckled or twisted.*
d) *The overall length of the air spring (from lower mounting eye to upper contact surface) must not exceed 300 mm. If the air spring is unrolled or too long it must be renewed.*

12 If in any doubt about the condition of the air spring, renew it, or at least have it examined by a Mercedes dealer or specialist.

13 Press the new air spring retaining clip fully over the locating stud on the vehicle body.

14 Manoeuvre the air spring into position, align it with the retaining clip and push it fully upwards into place. Do not twist the spring as it's being fitted.

15 The remainder of refitting is a reversal of removal, noting the following points:
a) *Tighten all fasteners to their specified torque where given.*
b) *Refit the air spring lower bolt/nut, and tie-rod outer bolt loosely. They must be fully tightened once the weight of the vehicle is back on its wheels.*
c) *Re-pressurise the system using Mercedes STAR diagnostic equipment (or after-market equivalent).*
d) *Check for correct operation/leaks before venturing out onto the road.*

---

17 Rear suspension control arms – removal and refitting

Note: *Refer to the note at the end of Section 1 before proceeding.*

Removal

1 Chock the front wheels, slacken the rear wheel bolts, raise the rear of the vehicle and support it securely on axle stands (see 'Vehicle jacking and support'). Remove the rear wheels.

17.3a Remove the bolt/nut securing the camber strut to the axle/subframe...

Camber strut

2 Position a workshop jack under the hub carrier, and raise the jack until the rear driveshaft is approximately horizontal.

3 Undo the nuts, and withdraw the bolts at the inner, and outer ends of the camber strut **(see illustrations)**. Note the locations of any washers/shims.

4 Manoeuvre the camber strut from position.

Torque strut

Note: *This is an involved procedure requiring the rear axle/subframe assembly to be lowered. Ensure you have enough working space/lifting equipment before starting.*

Caution: On models with rear air suspension, removal of the strut is only possible once the system has been depressurised. This can only safely be done using Mercedes STAR diagnostic equipment (or after-market equivalent). Using any other method of depressurisation will probably result in expensive damage.

Note: *Lowering the rear axle/subframe requires the fuel filler pipe to be disconnected from the tank. Consequently, this procedure is best done when the tank is almost empty.*

5 On models with Sensotronic Brake Control (SBC) de-activate the system as described in Chapter 9 Section 4.

6 Where applicable, de-pressurise the air suspension system using Mercedes STAR diagnostic equipment (or after-market equivalent).

7 Remove the complete exhaust system as described in Chapter 4A Section 19.

8 Undo the fasteners and remove the rear underfloor panelling.

17.16 Torque strut-to-hub carrier bolt/nut

17.3b...and to the hub carrier

9 Unhook the parking brake cables from the automatic slack adjuster as described in Chapter 9 Section 16.

10 With reference to Chapter 8 Section 7, detach the propeller shaft rear flexible coupling from the final drive flange.

11 Remove the rear brake pads as described in Chapter 9 Section 6.

12 Working along their lengths, unclip the left- and right-hand wheel speed sensor/brake pad contact sensor wiring harnesses from their retaining clips.

13 On models with air suspension, prise the top of the air spring downwards from the vehicle floor. This will destroy the retaining clips, which must be renewed as described in Section 16.

14 Undo the nuts, and withdraw the bolts securing the base of both shock absorbers to the control arms.

15 Position a workshop jack under each hub carrier, then raise the jack until the driveshafts are approximately horizontal.

16 Remove the bolt securing the outer end of the torque strut to the hub carrier **(see illustration)**.

17 Release the clamp and disconnect the fuel filler hose from the tank.

18 Position workshop jacks under the rear axle/subframe, undo the bolts and lower the assembly a little. The help of an assistant will make the task easier. Ensure no strain is placed on any wiring or hoses as the assembly is lowered. Note that new bolts must be fitted.

19 Use a marker pen to make alignment marks between the inner end of the torque strut and the axle/subframe. If a new strut is to be fitted, the marks can be transferred to

17.20 Torque strut-to-axle/subframe bolt

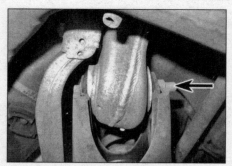

17.27 Spring control arm-to-axle carrier/subframe bolt

17.28 Spring control arm-to-hub carrier bolt

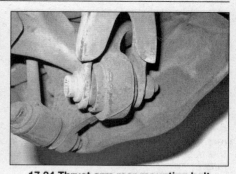

17.34 Thrust arm rear mounting bolt

the new strut.

20 Remove the bolt securing the inner end of the torque strut to the axle/subframe, and manoeuvre it from place **(see illustration)**.

Spring control arm

Caution: On models with rear air suspension, removal of the arm is only possible once the system has been depressurised. This can only safely be done using Mercedes STAR diagnostic equipment (or after-market equivalent). Using any other method of depressurisation will probably result in expensive damage.

Vehicles with steel coil spring

21 Remove the steel coil spring as described in Section 15.

Vehicles with air suspension

22 Detach the lower end of the air spring from the control arm as described in Section 16. This procedure includes de-pressurising the system using Mercedes STAR diagnostic equipment (or after-market equivalent).

All vehicles

23 Detach the shock absorber from the control arm as described in Section 14.
24 Position a workshop jack under the hub carrier, and raise the jack until the driveshaft is approximately horizontal.
25 Detach the tie-rod from the hub carrier **(see illustration 17.37a)**.
26 Prise out the cap and remove the brake caliper lower guide bolt – see Chapter 9 Section 10.
27 Remove the bolt securing the control

arm to the rear axle carrier/subframe **(see illustration)**.
28 Remove the bolt securing the control arm to the hub carrier **(see illustration)**.
29 Manoeuvre the spring control arm from place.
30 Check the arm for signs of wear or damage. If necessary, the rubber bush can be replaced using a suitable press. Note the fitted orientation of the bush prior to removal.

Thrust arm

31 Undo the fasteners and remove the rear section of the underbody panelling.
32 Undo the axle carrier/subframe front mounting bolt and remove the washer.
33 Place a workshop jack under the hub carrier, then raise the jack until the driveshaft is approximately horizontal.
34 Undo the nuts, and withdraw the bolts securing the inner and outer ends of the thrust arm **(see illustration)**. Manoeuvre the arm from place.
35 Examine the rubber bush. If it is damaged/worn, the complete thrust arm must be replaced.

Tie-rod

36 Place a workshop jack under the hub carrier, then raise the jack until the driveshaft is approximately horizontal.
37 Undo the nut(s), and withdraw the bolts securing the inner and outer ends of the rod to the hub carrier and axle carrier/subframe **(see illustrations)**.
38 Examine the rubber bushes for wear or damage. If the bushes are defective, the

complete tie-rod must be replaced.

Refitting

39 Refitting is a reversal of removal, noting the following points:
a) *Install the arms/rod/strut mounting bolts, but only tighten them once the weight of the vehicle is back on its' wheels.*
b) *Tighten all fasteners to their specified torque where given.*
c) *Where applicable, re-pressurise the air suspension system using Mercedes STAR diagnostic equipment (or after-market equivalent).*
d) *Have the rear wheel alignment checked at the earliest opportunity.*

18 Rear anti-roll bar – removal and refitting

Note: *Refer to the note at the end of Section 1.*

Removal

1 As described in Section 17 (Torque strut removal), lower the rear axle carrier/subframe a little to gain access to the anti-roll bar mounting clamps.
2 Undo the nuts and detach the outer ends of the anti-roll bar from the link rods **(see illustration 19.3)**.
3 Undo the bolts securing the anti-roll bar clamps to the rear axle carrier/subframe **(see illustration)**. Manoeuvre the anti-roll bar from place.

17.37a Detach the tie-rod from the hub carrier...

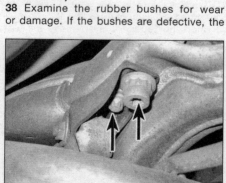

17.37b ...then undo the bolts and detach the tie-rod bracket from the subframe

18.3 Undo the bolt securing the anti-roll bar clamp to the subframe

Refitting

4 Refitting is a reversal of removal. Tighten all fasteners to their specified torque.

19 Rear anti-roll bar link rods – removal and refitting

1 Refer to the note at the end of Section 1.

Removal

2 Chock the front wheels, and then jack up the rear of the car and support it on axle stands (see 'Vehicle jacking and support'). If required, to make access easier remove the relevant rear roadwheel.
3 Slacken and remove the nut securing the connecting link to the anti-roll bar **(see illustration)**.
4 Unscrew the bolt securing the lower part of the connecting link to the hub carrier and remove it from the car **(see illustration)**.
5 Inspect the connecting link mounting bush for signs of damage or deterioration. Also check that the balljoint is free to move easily, and that its gaiter is undamaged. Renew the connecting link if necessary.

Refitting

6 Manoeuvre the link rod into position, and fit lower retaining bolt to the hub carrier. Tighten the bolt to the specified torque.
7 Engage the upper end of the link rod with the anti-roll bar, and tighten the nut to the specified torque.
8 Where applicable, refit the roadwheel, and lower the vehicle to the ground.

20 Air suspension system – general information and component renewal

General information

1 E-Class (211) models may be fitted with air suspension. Depending on specification, only the rear suspension, or front and rear

19.3 Detach the upper end of the link from the anti-roll bar

suspension may have the traditional steel springs replaced by air springs. This self leveling system consists of a compressor, electronic control unit (ECU), central reservoir, and the interconnecting pipework. With the exception of the ECU, before any procedure is attempted, the system must be de-pressurised using Mercedes STAR diagnostic equipment (or after-market equivalent). Upon completion, the system must be re-pressurised, again using the diagnostic equipment.
2 If access to the appropriate diagnostic equipment is not available, any work on the suspension system must be entrusted to a Mercedes dealer or suitably equipped repairer. Any attempt to de-pressurise the system, or drive the vehicle with the system de-pressurised, will probably result in expensive damage.

Component renewal

Air springs

3 Replacement of the front air spring is described in Section 5, and the rear spring in Section 16.

Central reservoir

4 De-pressurise the system using Mercedes STAR diagnostic equipment (or after-market equivalent).
5 Remove the right-hand side luggage compartment side panel as described in Chapter 11 Section 34.
6 Where applicable, remove the bass speaker module.

19.4 Detach the lower end of the link from the hub carrier

7 Disconnect the pressure pipe connection from the central reservoir. Plug the openings to prevent contamination.
8 Undo the 3 retaining bolts and remove the central reservoir.
9 Refitting is a reversal of removal. Re-pressurise the system using Mercedes STAR diagnostic equipment (or equivalent).

Air suspension control unit (ECU)

10 Disconnect the battery negative lead as described in Chapter 5A Section 4.
11 Fold the passengers side carpet back, and remove the plastic impact absorber.
12 Undo the 3 plastic nuts and fold the control unit rack rearwards **(see illustration)**.
13 Undo the 2 mounting bolts, and detach the control unit from the carrier **(see illustration)**.
14 Slide out the locking catches, and disconnect the wiring plugs from the control unit.
15 Refitting is a reversal of removal. Note that if a new control unit is fitted, it must be configured using Mercedes STAR diagnostic equipment or equivalent.

Compressor

16 De-pressurise the suspension system using Mercedes STAR diagnostic equipment (or equivalent).
17 Remove the front bumper as described in Chapter 11 Section 16.
18 Disconnect the pressure pipe from the compressor **(see illustration)**. Plug the openings to prevent contamination.

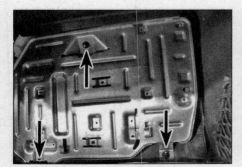

20.12 Control rack retaining nuts

20.13 Air suspension control unit

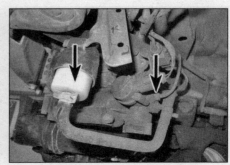

20.18 Compressor pressure pipe and intake filter

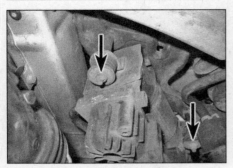

20.20 Compressor mounting nuts (one hidden)

21.4 Undo the bolt from the centre of the steering wheel

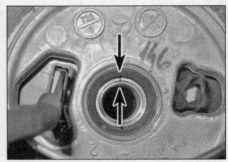

21.5 If necessary, make alignment marks between the column shaft and the steering wheel

19 Disconnect the hose from the compressor air intake filter.

20 Undo the 3 retaining nuts and remove the compressor **(see illustration)**. Disconnect the wiring plug(s) as the compressor is withdrawn.

21 When replacing the compressor, Mercedes insist that the compressor relay is renewed at the same time.

22 Refitting is a reversal of removal. Re-pressurise the system using Mercedes STAR diagnostic equipment (or equivalent).

21 Steering wheel – removal and refitting

Removal

1 Set the front wheels in the straight-ahead position, and remove the ignition key. Pull the steering wheel out to its fully-extended position.

2 Remove the drivers airbag as described in Chapter 12 Section 20.

3 Disconnect any wiring plugs from the steering wheel.

4 Slacken and remove the steering wheel retaining bolt **(see illustration)**. Hold the steering wheel firmly to prevent rotation.

5 If marks do not already exist, mark the steering wheel and steering column shaft in relation to each other, then lift the steering

wheel off the column splines. If it is tight, tap it up near the centre, using the palm of your hand, or twist it from side-to-side, whilst pulling upwards to release it from the shaft splines **(see illustration)**.

Caution: Do not turn the column shaft or airbag contact unit whilst the steering wheel is removed.

Refitting

6 Refitting is a reversal of removal, noting the following points:

a) *Ensure that the steering wheel locates correctly with the contact unit as the steering wheel is refitted.*

b) *Engage the wheel with the column splines, aligning the marks made on removal, and tighten the steering wheel retaining bolt to the specified torque setting.*

c) *Reconnect the wiring plug(s)*

d) *Refit the airbag as described in Chapter 12 Section 20.*

22 Steering column – removal, inspection and refitting

Note: Refer to the note at the end of Section before proceeding.

Removal

1 Fully extend the steering column, and

ensure the front wheels are in the 'straight-ahead' position.

2 Raise the front of the vehicle and support it securely on axle stands (see *'Vehicle jacking and support'*). Release the fasteners and remove the engine undershield.

3 Working from underneath, remove the bolt securing the steering column upper universal joint **(see illustration)**.

4 Pull the steering column upper universal joint from the lower shaft.

5 Pull the locking plate from the lower shaft. Upon reassembly, replace the self-locking nut.

6 Remove the steering wheel as described in Section 21.

7 With reference to Chapter 12 Section 5, remove the steering column switch assembly.

8 Remove the instrument cluster as described in Chapter 12 Section 10.

9 Remove the drivers side lower facia panel as described in Chapter 11 Section 36.

10 Note their fitted positions, then disconnect the wiring plugs from the steering column.

11 Undo the 4 retaining screws, and remove the plastic trim surround from the end of the steering column **(see illustration)**.

12 Undo the bolts and remove the side brace **(see illustration)**.

13 Remove the mounting bolts, and manoeuvre the steering column from place.

22.3 Universal joint pinch bolt and locking plate

22.11 Steering column surround trim retaining screws

22.12 Side brace bolts

22.13a Undo the 2 bolts above the column...

22.13b...and the horizontal bolt beneath

23.3 Align the attachment pin with the recess

Ensure the bulkhead grommet remains in place (see illustrations).

Inspection

14 The steering column incorporates a telescopic safety feature. In the event of a front-end crash, the lower section of the shaft collapses and prevents the steering wheel injuring the driver. Before refitting the steering column, examine the column and mountings for signs of damage and deformation, and renew as necessary.

15 Check the steering shaft for signs of free play in the column bushes. If any damage or wear is found on the steering column bushes, the column should be overhauled. Overhaul of the column is a complex task requiring several special tools, and should be entrusted to a Mercedes-Benz dealer.

Refitting

16 Refitting is a reversal of removal.

23 Steering lock control unit – removal and refitting

Removal

1 Set the ignition control to position 'I'. The control unit can only be removed if the steering column is unlocked.

2 Remove the drivers side lower facia panel as described in Chapter 11 Sections 34 and 36.

3 Rotate the attachment pin, aligning it with the recess and pull it from place (see illustration).

4 Manoeuvre the steering lock control unit from the column and disconnect the wiring plug.

Refitting

5 Refitting is a reversal of removal.

24 Steering rack – removal, overhaul and refitting

Removal

1 Ensure the front wheels are in the 'straight-ahead' position, then fully extend the steering column. It's essential that the steering wheel is not rotated during the following procedures.

2 Slacken the front wheel bolts, raise the front of the vehicle and support it securely on axle stands (see 'Vehicle jacking and support'). Remove the front roadwheels.

3 Release the fasteners and remove the engine undershield.

4 Remove the plastic cover from the top of the engine.

5 Using a syringe or poultry baster, remove as much fluid as possible from the power steering fluid reservoir.

6 Detach the track rods ends from the hub carriers as described in Section 28.

7 Undo the fasteners and remove the heat shield (where fitted) from the subframe.

8 Undo the bolt, slide the upper steering column shaft from the lower shaft, and recover the locking plate/nut (see illustration 22.3). Renew the nut.

9 Disconnect any wiring plugs from the steering rack, and release any wiring harness clips.

10 Undo the bolts, and pull the fluid pipes from the steering rack pinion housing (see illustration). Plug the openings to prevent contamination. Be prepared for fluid spillage. Renew the pipe O-ring seals.

11 Place a workshop jack under the steering rack, undo the mounting bolts and lower the assembly from place (see illustration). The help of an assistant during this procedure will be helpful – the assembly is heavy!

Overhaul

12 Examine the steering rack assembly for signs of wear, leakage or damage. If overhaul of the steering rack assembly is necessary, the task must be entrusted to a Mercedes-Benz dealer or specialist.

Refitting

13 Manoeuvre the steering rack into position. Ensure the marks made on removal are correctly aligned.

14 Fit the steering rack mounting bolts and tighten them to the specified torque.

15 The remainder of refitting is a reversal of removal, noting the following points:
a) Renew the fluid pipes' O-ring seals.
b) Tighten all fasteners to their specified torque where given.
c) Bleed the power steering system as described in Section 27.
d) Have the front wheel alignment checked at the earliest opportunity.

25 Steering rack gaiter – renewal

1 Remove the track rod end as described in Section 28.

2 Release the inner and outer clamp, then slide the gaiter from the steering rack (see

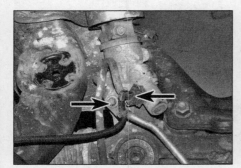
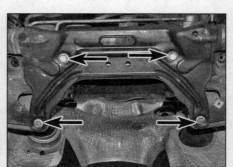

24.10 Undo the bolt securing the fluid pipes, and disconnect the wiring plug

24.11 Undo the bolts and remove the bracket along with the steering rack

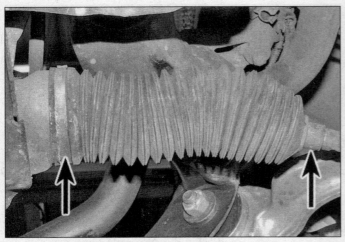

25.2 Steering rack gaiter inner, and outer clamps

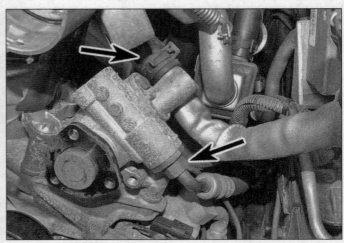

26.7 Disconnect the fluid hose and pressure pipe

illustration). Renew the O-ring seal on the steering rack.

3 With the new O-ring in place, slide the gaiter over the track rod, and into position on the steering rack. Note that some gaiters incorporate a diaphragm valve. This valve must point rearwards.

4 Position the new inner, and outer clamp, then tighten them.

5 Refit the track rod end with reference to Section 28.

26 Power steering pump –
removal and refitting

Removal

In-line engines

1 Undo the fasteners and remove the plastic cover from the top of the engine.

2 Using a syringe or poultry baster, remove as much fluid as possible from the power steering fluid reservoir.

3 Remove the throttle body as described in Chapter 4A Section 14.

4 Remove the cooling fan and shroud as described in Chapter 3 Section 6.

5 Slacken the power steering pump pulley bolts, then remove the auxiliary drivebelt as described in Chapter 1 Section 6.

6 Remove the bolts followed by the power steering pump pulley.

7 Release the clamp and disconnect the fluid supply hose from the pump **(see illustration)**. Be prepared for fluid spillage.

8 Undo the union and pull the fluid pressure pipe from the pump. Renew the union O-ring seal. Be prepared for fluid spillage.

9 Undo the 3 retaining bolts and manoeuvre the power steering plump from place. Plug the openings to prevent contamination.

V6 engines

10 Release the clip and place the coolant expansion reservoir to one side **(see illustration)**.

11 Using a syringe or poultry baster, remove as much fluid as possible from the power steering fluid reservoir.

12 Release the clamp and disconnect the fluid return hose from the fluid reservoir. Be prepared for fluid spillage. Plug the openings to prevent contamination.

13 Unclip the wiring harness from the fluid reservoir, and disconnect any wiring plugs as necessary.

14 Undo the 3 retaining bolts and lift the fluid reservoir from place **(see illustration)**.

15 Release the clamp, and disconnect the fluid supply hose from the base of the reservoir. Be prepared for fluid spillage. Plug the openings to prevent contamination.

16 Remove the auxiliary drivebelt as described in Chapter 1 Section 6.

17 Disconnect the fluid pressure pipe from the pump. Renew the O-ring seal. Plug the openings to prevent contamination.

26.10 Coolant expansion tank clip

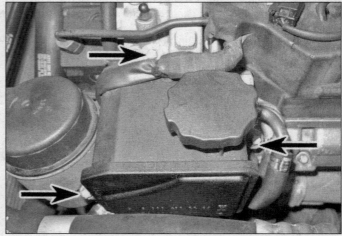

26.14 Power steering fluid reservoir retaining bolts

26.19 Power steering pump-to-timing cover bolts

26.20 Undo the bolt securing the bracket to the block

18 Disconnect the wiring plug from the regulator valve on the pump.

19 Undo the 2 bolts securing the pump to the timing cover **(see illustration)**.

20 Release the cable strap, then undo the retaining bracket bolt at the rear of the pump, and manoeuvre the pump from place **(see illustration)**.

Refitting

21 If the power steering pump is faulty, seek the advice of your Mercedes-Benz dealer as to the availability of spare parts. If spares are available, it may be possible to have the pump overhauled by a suitable specialist or alternately obtain an exchange unit. If not, the pump must be renewed.

22 Refitting is a reversal of removal, noting the following points:

a) *Tighten all fasteners to their specified torque where given.*

b) *Bleed the power steering system as described in Section 27.*

27 Power steering system – bleeding

1 Raise the front of the vehicle and support it securely on axle stands (see *'Vehicle jacking and support'*).

2 Release the fasteners and remove the plastic cover from the top of the engine.

3 With the engine stopped, fill the fluid reservoir to within 10 mm of the top of the reservoir. Use only the specified type of fluid (see *"Lubricants and fluids"*).

4 With the engine stopped, slowly move the steering from lock-to-lock several times to purge out the trapped air, then top-up the level in the fluid reservoir. Repeat this procedure

until the fluid level in the reservoir does not drop any further.

5 Have an assistant start the engine, whilst you keep watch on the fluid level. Be prepared to add more fluid as the engine starts, as the fluid level is likely to drop quickly. The fluid level must not be allowed to drop too far, or more air will be drawn into the system. Don't turn the steering wheel during this process.

6 With the engine running at idle speed, turn the steering wheel slowly two or three times approximately 45° to the left and right of the centre, then turn the wheel twice from lock-to-lock. Do not hold the wheel on either lock, as this imposes strain on the hydraulic system. Repeat this procedure until bubbles cease to appear in fluid reservoir.

7 If, when turning the steering, an abnormal noise is heard from the fluid lines, it indicates that there is still air in the system. Check this by turning the wheels to the straight-ahead position and switching off the engine. If the fluid level in the reservoir rises, then air is present in the system and further bleeding is necessary.

8 Once all traces of air have been removed from the power steering hydraulic system,

turn the engine off and allow the system to cool. Once cool, check that fluid level is up to the maximum mark, topping-up if necessary.

28 Track rod end – removal and refitting

Note: *Refer to the note at the end of Section 1 before proceeding.*

Removal

1 Chock the rear wheels, and loosen the front wheel bolts. Jack up the front of the car and support it on axle stands (see *'Vehicle jacking and support'*). Remove the relevant front roadwheel.

2 Clean the end of the track rod and slacken the locknut **(see illustrations)**. Make a mark on the track rod arm threads to aid refitting. It will be needed to ensure that the wheel alignment remains correctly set when the balljoint is installed.

3 Slacken and remove the balljoint nut, and free the balljoint from the hub carrier. If necessary, free the balljoint tapered shank

28.2a Slacken the locknut...

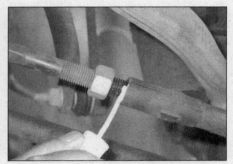

28.2b...and mark the position on the threads

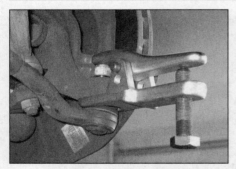

28.3 Use a balljoint separator

using a universal balljoint separator **(see illustration)**.

4 Counting the exact number of turns necessary to do so, unscrew the balljoint from the track rod.

5 Carefully clean the balljoint and the threads – the balljoint taper must not have any lubricant on it, otherwise it will not lock into position. Renew the balljoint if its movement is sloppy or too stiff, is excessively worn, or is damaged in any way; carefully check the stud taper and threads.

Refitting

6 Screw the balljoint back onto the track rod by the number of turns noted on removal, and tighten the locknut. This should position the balljoint at the relevant marks made on removal.

7 Refit the balljoint shank to the hub carrier, then fit a new retaining nut and tighten it to the specified torque.

8 Refit the roadwheel, then lower the car to the ground and tighten the roadwheel bolts to the specified torque.

9 Have the front wheel alignment checked at the earliest opportunity.

29 Wheel alignment and steering angles – general information

Definitions

1 A car's steering and suspension geometry is defined in four basic settings – all angles are expressed in degrees; the steering axis is defined as an imaginary line drawn through the axis of the suspension strut, extended where necessary to contact the ground **(see illustration)**.

2 Camber is the angle between each roadwheel and a vertical line drawn through its centre and tyre contact patch, when viewed from the front or rear of the car. Positive camber is when the roadwheels are tilted outwards from the vertical at the top; negative camber is when they are tilted inwards.

3 The front camber angle is adjusted by removing the nut, withdrawing the spring control arm inner bolt, and reinserting it into one of two positions. The angle should be measured using a camber angle gauge. The rear wheel camber is not adjustable.

4 Castor is the angle between the steering axis and a vertical line drawn through each roadwheel's centre and tyre contact patch, when viewed from the side of the car. Positive castor is when the steering axis is tilted so that it contacts the ground ahead of the vertical; negative castor is when it contacts the ground behind the vertical.

5 The front castor angle is adjusted by removing the nut, withdrawing the torque strut inner bolt, and re-inserting in one of two positions. The setting must measured using a castor angle gauge. The rear wheel castor is not adjustable.

6 Toe is the difference, viewed from above, between lines drawn through the roadwheel centres and the car's centre-line. 'Toe-in' is when the roadwheels point inwards, towards each other at the front, while 'toe-out' is when they splay outwards from each other at the front.

7 The front wheel toe setting is adjusted by screwing the track rod in or out of its balljoints, to alter the effective length of the track rod assembly.

8 Rear wheel toe setting is also adjustable. The toe setting is adjusted by slackening the tie-rod inner mounting bracket bolts, rotating the adjusting nut to achieve the desired setting, then tightening the bolts again.

Checking and adjustment

9 Due to the special measuring equipment necessary to check the wheel alignment and steering angles, and the skill required to use it properly, the checking and adjustment of these settings is best left to a Mercedes-Benz dealer or similar expert. Note that most tyre-fitting shops now possess sophisticated checking equipment.

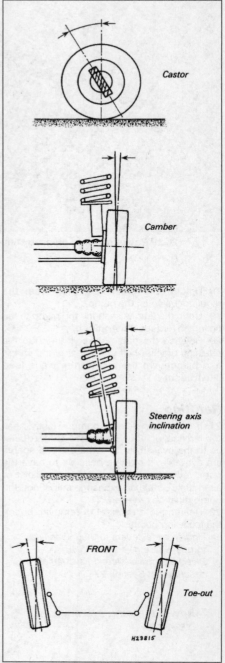

29.1 Wheel alignment details

Chapter 11
Bodywork and fittings

Contents

Degrees of difficulty

Easy, suitable for novice with little experience		**Fairly easy,** suitable for beginner with some experience		**Fairly difficult,** suitable for competent DIY mechanic		**Difficult,** suitable for experienced DIY mechanic		**Very difficult,** suitable for expert DIY or professional	

Specifications

Torque wrench settings	Nm	lbf ft
Seat belt anchorage	32	24
Seat belt inertia reel	32	24
Seat belt rear inertia reel bracket-to-pillar	8	6
Seat bolts*	45	33

*Do not re-use

1 General information

1 The body is of unitary all-steel construction, and incorporates computer-calculated impact crumple zones at the front and rear, with a central safety cell passenger compartment. During manufacture the body is dip-primed, fully sealed and undercoated, then painted with multi-layered base and top-coats.

2 The bodyshell on all models covered by this manual is of four-door Saloon or five-door Estate configuration.

3 A number of structural components and body panels are made of galvanised steel to provide a high level of protection against corrosion. Extensive use is also made of plastic materials, mainly in the interior, but also in exterior components. The front and rear bumpers are moulded from a synthetic material that is very strong and yet light. Plastic components such as wheel arch liners are fitted to the underside of the vehicle to further improve corrosion resistance.

2 Maintenance – bodywork and underframe

1 The general condition of a vehicle's bodywork is the one thing that significantly affects its value. Maintenance is easy but needs to be regular. Neglect, particularly after minor damage, can lead quickly to further deterioration and costly repair bills. It is important also to keep watch on those parts of the vehicle not immediately visible, for instance the underside, inside all the wheel arches and the lower pan of the engine compartment.

2 The basic maintenance routine for the bodywork is washing – preferably with a lot of water, from a hose. This will remove all the loose solids, which may have stuck to the vehicle. It is important to flush these off in such a way as to prevent grit from scratching the finish. The wheel arches and underframe need washing in the same way to remove any accumulated mud, which will retain moisture and tend to encourage rust. Paradoxically, the best time to clean the underframe and wheel arches is in wet weather when the mud is thoroughly wet and soft. In very wet weather the underframe is usually cleaned of large accumulations automatically and this is a good time for inspection.

3 Periodically, except on vehicles with a wax-based underbody protective coating, it is a good idea to have the whole of the underframe of the vehicle steam cleaned, engine compartment included, so that a thorough inspection can be carried out to see what minor repairs and renovations are necessary. Steam cleaning is available at many

garages and is necessary for removal of the accumulation of oily grime, which sometimes is allowed to become thick in certain areas. If steam-cleaning facilities are not available, there are some excellent grease solvents available which can be brush applied. The dirt can then be simply hosed off. Note that these methods should not be used on vehicles with wax-based underbody protective coating or the coating will be removed. Such vehicles should be inspected annually, preferably just prior to winter, when the underbody should be washed down and any damage to the wax coating repaired. Ideally, a completely fresh coat should be applied. It would also be worth considering the use of such wax-based protection for injection into door panels, sills, box sections, etc, as an additional safeguard against rust damage where such protection is not provided by the vehicle manufacturer.

4 After washing paintwork, wipe off with a chamois leather to give an unspotted clear finish. A coat of clear protective wax polish will give added protection against chemical pollutants in the air. If the paintwork sheen has dulled or oxidised, use a cleaner/polisher combination to restore the brilliance of the shine. This requires a little effort, but such dulling is usually caused because regular washing has been neglected. Care needs to be taken with metallic paintwork, as special non-abrasive cleaner/polisher is required to avoid damage to the finish. Always check that the door and ventilator opening drain holes and pipes are completely clear so that water can be drained out. Bright work should be treated in the same way as paintwork. Windscreens and windows can be kept clear of the smeary film that often appears by the use of a proprietary glass cleaner. Never use any form of wax or other body or chromium polish on glass.

3 Maintenance – upholstery and carpets

1 Mats and carpets should be brushed or vacuum cleaned regularly to keep them free of grit. If they are badly stained remove them from the vehicle for scrubbing or sponging and make quite sure they are dry before refitting. Seats and interior trim panels can be kept clean by wiping with a damp cloth. If they do become stained (which can be more apparent on light coloured upholstery) use a little liquid detergent and a soft nail brush to scour the grime out of the grain of the material. Do not forget to keep the headlining clean in the same way as the upholstery. When using liquid cleaners inside the vehicle do not over-wet the surfaces being cleaned. Excessive damp could get into the seams and padded interior causing stains, offensive odours or even rot. If the inside of the vehicle gets wet accidentally it is worthwhile taking

some trouble to dry it out properly, particularly where carpets are involved. Do not leave oil or electric heaters inside the vehicle for this purpose.

4 Minor body damage – repair

Minor scratches

1 If the scratch is very superficial, and does not penetrate to the metal of the bodywork, repair is very simple. Lightly rub the area of the scratch with a paintwork renovator, or a very fine cutting paste, to remove loose paint from the scratch and to clear the surrounding bodywork of wax polish. Rinse the area with clean water.

2 In the case of metallic paint, the most commonly found scratches are not in the paint, but in the lacquer top coat, and appear white. If care is taken, these can sometimes be rendered less obvious by very careful use of paintwork renovator (which would otherwise not be used on metallic paintwork); otherwise, repair of these scratches can be achieved by applying lacquer with a fine brush.

3 Apply touch-up paint to the scratch using a fine paintbrush; continue to apply fine layers of paint until the surface of the paint in the scratch is level with the surrounding paintwork. Allow the new paint at least two weeks to harden, and then blend it into the surrounding paintwork by rubbing the scratch area with a paintwork renovator or a very fine cutting paste. Finally, apply wax polish.

4 Where the scratch has penetrated right through to the metal of the bodywork, causing the metal to rust, a different repair technique is required. Remove any loose rust from the bottom of the scratch with a penknife, and then apply rust-inhibiting paint to prevent the formation of rust in the future. Using a rubber or nylon applicator, fill the scratch with bodystopper paste. If required, this paste can be mixed with cellulose thinners to provide a very thin paste, which is ideal for filling narrow scratches. Before the stopper-paste in the scratch hardens, wrap a piece of smooth cotton rag around the top of a finger. Dip the finger in cellulose thinners, and then quickly sweep it across the surface of the stopper-paste in the scratch; this will ensure that the surface of the stopper-paste is slightly hollowed. The scratch can now be painted over as described earlier in this Section.

Dents

5 When deep denting of the vehicle's bodywork has taken place, the first task is to pull the dent out, until the affected bodywork almost attains its original shape. There is little point in trying to restore the original shape completely, as the metal in the damaged area will have stretched on impact and cannot be reshaped fully to its original contour. It is better to bring the level of the dent up to a point which is about 3 mm below the level of the surrounding bodywork. In cases where the dent is very shallow anyway, it is not worth trying to pull it out at all. If the underside of the dent is accessible, it can be hammered out gently from behind, using a mallet with a wooden or plastic head. Whilst doing this, hold a suitable block of wood firmly against the outside of the panel to absorb the impact from the hammer blows and thus prevent a large area of the bodywork from being 'belled-out'.

6 Should the dent be in a section of the bodywork, which has a double skin or some other factor making it inaccessible from behind, a different technique is called for. Drill several small holes through the metal inside the area – particularly in the deeper section. Then screw long self-tapping screws into the holes just sufficiently for them to gain a good purchase in the metal. Now the dent can be pulled out by pulling on the protruding heads of the screws with a pair of pliers.

7 The next stage of the repair is the removal of the paint from the damaged area, and from an inch or so of the surrounding 'sound' bodywork. This is accomplished most easily by using a wire brush or abrasive pad on a power drill, although it can be done just as effectively by hand using sheets of abrasive paper. To complete the preparation for filling, score the surface of the bare metal with a screwdriver or the tang of a file, or alternatively, drill small holes in the affected area. This will provide a really good 'key' for the filler paste.

8 To complete the repair see the Section on filling and re-spraying.

Rust holes or gashes

9 Remove all paint from the affected area and from an inch or so of the surrounding 'sound' bodywork, using an abrasive pad or a wire brush on a power drill. If these are not available a few sheets of abrasive paper will do the job just as effectively. With the paint removed you will be able to gauge the severity of the corrosion and therefore decide whether to renew the whole panel (if this is possible) or to repair the affected area. New body panels are not as expensive as most people think and it is often quicker and more satisfactory to fit a new panel than to attempt to repair large areas of corrosion.

10 Remove all fittings from the affected area except those, which will act as a guide to the original shape of the damaged bodywork. Then, using tin snips or a hacksaw blade, remove all loose metal and any other metal badly affected by corrosion. Hammer the edges of the hole inwards in order to create a slight depression for the filler paste.

11 Wire-brush the affected area to remove the powdery rust from the surface of the remaining metal. Paint the affected area with rust-inhibiting paint – if the back of the rusted area is accessible, treat this also.

12 Before filling can take place it will be necessary to block the hole in some way. This can be achieved by the use of aluminium or plastic mesh, or aluminium tape.

13 Aluminium or plastic mesh is probably the best material to use for a large hole. Cut a piece to the approximate size and shape of the hole to be filled, then position it in the hole so that its edges are below the level of the surrounding bodywork. It can be retained in position by several blobs of filler paste around its periphery.

14 Aluminium tape should be used for small or very narrow holes. Pull a piece off the roll and trim it to the approximate size and shape required, then pull off the backing paper (if used) and stick the tape over the hole; it can be overlapped if the thickness of one piece is insufficient. Burnish down the edges of the tape with the handle of a screwdriver or similar, to ensure that the tape is securely attached to the metal underneath.

Filling and re-spraying

15 Before using this Section, see the Sections on dent, deep scratch, rust holes and gash repairs.

16 Many types of bodyfiller are available, but generally speaking those proprietary kits which contain a tin of filler paste and a tube of resin hardener are best for this type of repair. A wide, flexible plastic or nylon applicator will be found invaluable for imparting a smooth and well-contoured finish to the surface of the filler.

17 Mix up a little filler on a clean piece of card or board – measure the hardener carefully (follow the maker's instructions on the pack) otherwise the filler will set too rapidly or too slowly. Using the applicator, apply the filler paste to the prepared area; draw the applicator across the surface of the filler to achieve the correct contour and to level the filler surface. As soon as a contour that approximates to the correct one is achieved, stop working the paste – if you carry on too long, the paste will become sticky and begin to 'pick up' on the applicator. Continue to add thin layers of filler paste at twenty-minute intervals until the level of the filler is just proud of the surrounding bodywork.

18 Once the filler has hardened, excess can be removed using a metal plane or file. From then on, progressively finer grades of abrasive paper should be used, starting with a 40-grade production paper and finishing with 400-grade (or higher) wet-and-dry paper. Always wrap the abrasive paper around a flat rubber, cork, or wooden block – otherwise the surface of the filler will not be completely flat. During the smoothing of the filler surface, the wet-and-dry paper should be periodically rinsed in water. This will ensure that a very smooth finish is imparted to the filler at the final stage.

19 At this stage the 'dent' should be surrounded by a ring of bare metal, which in turn should be encircled by the finely 'feathered' edge of the good paintwork. Rinse the repair area with clean water, until all of the dust produced by the rubbing-down operation has gone.

20 Spray the whole repair area with a light coat of primer – this will show up any imperfections in the surface of the filler. Repair these imperfections with fresh filler paste or bodystopper, and once more smooth the surface with abrasive paper. If bodystopper is used, it can be mixed with cellulose thinners to form a really thin paste, which is ideal for filling small holes. Repeat this spray-and-repair procedure until you are satisfied that the surface of the filler, and the feathered edge of the paintwork are perfect. Clean the repair area with clean water, and allow to dry fully.

21 The repair area is now ready for final spraying. Paint spraying must be carried out in a warm, dry, windless and dust-free atmosphere. This condition can be created artificially if you have access to a large indoor working area, but if you are forced to work in the open, you will have to pick your day very carefully. If you are working indoors, dousing the floor in the work area with water will help to settle the dust that would otherwise be in the atmosphere. If the repair area is confined to one body panel, mask off the surrounding panels; this will help to minimise the effects of a slight mis-match in paint colours. Bodywork fittings (e.g. rubbing strips, door handles, etc) will also need to be masked off. Use genuine masking tape and several thicknesses of newspaper for the masking operations.

22 Before commencing to spray, agitate the aerosol can thoroughly, and then spray a test area (an old tin, or similar) until the technique is mastered. Cover the repair area with a thick coat of primer; the thickness should be built up using several thin layers of paint rather than one thick one. Using 400-grade (or higher) wet-and-dry paper, rub down the surface of the primer until it is really smooth. While doing this, the work area should be thoroughly doused with water, and the wet-and-dry paper periodically rinsed in water. Allow to dry before spraying on more paint.

23 Spray on the top coat, again building up the thickness by using several thin layers of paint. Start spraying at the top of the repair area and then, using a side-to-side motion, work downwards until the whole repair area and about 2 inches of the surrounding original paintwork is covered. Remove all masking material 10 to 15 minutes after spraying on the final coat of paint.

24 Allow the new paint at least two weeks to harden, then, using a paintwork renovator or a very fine cutting paste, blend the edges of the paint into the existing paintwork. Finally, apply wax polish.

Plastic components

25 With the use of more and more plastic body components by the vehicle manufacturers (e.g. bumpers, spoilers, and in some cases major body panels), rectification of more serious damage to such items has become a matter of either entrusting repair work to a specialist in this field, or renewing complete components. Repair of such damage by the DIY owner is not really feasible, owing to the cost of the equipment and materials required for effecting such repairs. The basic technique involves making a groove along the line of the crack in the plastic using a rotary burr in a power drill. The damaged part is then welded back together by using a hot-air gun to heat up and fuse a plastic filler rod into the groove. Any excess plastic is then removed and the area rubbed down to a smooth finish. It is important that a filler rod of the correct plastic is used, as body components can be made of a variety of different types (e.g. polycarbonate, ABS, polypropylene).

26 Damage of a less serious nature (abrasions, minor cracks etc) can be repaired by the DIY owner using a two-part epoxy filler repair material. Once mixed in equal proportions, this is used in similar fashion to the bodywork filler used on metal panels. The filler is usually cured in twenty to thirty minutes, ready for sanding and painting.

27 If the owner is renewing a complete component himself, or if he has repaired it with epoxy filler, he will be left with the problem of finding a suitable paint for finishing which is compatible with the type of plastic used. At one time the use of a universal paint was not possible, owing to the complex range of plastics encountered in body component applications. Standard paints, generally speaking, will not bond to plastic or rubber satisfactorily. However, it is now possible to obtain a plastic body parts finishing kit, which consists of a pre-primer treatment, a primer and coloured top coat. Full instructions are normally supplied with a kit, but basically the method of use is to first apply the pre-primer to the component concerned and allow it to dry for up to 30 minutes. Then the primer is applied and left to dry for about an hour

before finally applying the special coloured top coat. The result is a correctly coloured component where the paint will flex with the plastic or rubber, a property that standard paint does not normally possess.

5 Major body damage – repair

1 Where serious damage has occurred, or large areas need renewal due to neglect, it means that complete new panels will need welding in, and this is best left to professionals. If the damage is due to impact, it will also be necessary to completely check the alignment of the bodyshell, and this can only be carried out accurately by a Mercedes-Benz dealer using special jigs. If the body is left misaligned, it is primarily dangerous as the car will not handle properly, and secondly, uneven stresses will be imposed on the steering, suspension and possibly transmission, causing abnormal wear, or complete failure, particularly to such items as the tyres.

6 Bonnet – removal, refitting and adjustment

Removal

1 Raise the bonnet to the vertical position.
2 Release the fasteners and remove the cover from the lower section of the bonnet (see illustration).
3 Disconnect the washer jet hose. Unclip the hose from any retainers on the bonnet.
4 Disconnect the washer jet wiring plugs (where applicable).
5 With the aid of an assistant to support the bonnet, extract the strut upper retaining clip, then unhook and remove the strut from the bonnet on both sides (see illustration).
6 Mark the position of the hinge bolts on both sides, so that the bonnet can be refitted in its original position.

7 With the help of an assistant, loosen and withdraw the hinge bolts, and carefully lift off the bonnet. Store the bonnet in a safe place to prevent any damage.

Refitting and adjustment

8 With the bonnet closed, check the gap between the bonnet and front wings on both sides (transverse adjustment), the alignment of the front edge of the bonnet with the front edge of the wing when looking down (longitudinal adjustment), and the height of the bonnet front edge and top edge in relation to the wing (height adjustment). The help of an assistant would be useful when adjusting the bonnet.
9 Open the bonnet and slacken the two bolts securing the lock striker plate to the bonnet. There are two striker plates fitted to the bonnet, one on the left and one on the right.
10 By trial and error, move the striker plate until an equal gap exists between the bonnet and the front wings on each side.
11 From within the engine compartment, slacken the locknut and screw down the bonnet rubber buffer.
12 Slacken the hinge retaining bolts.
13 By trial and error, move the bonnet as necessary, tightening the hinge bolts each time until the bonnet upper edge and front wing edge are aligned.
14 Now raise the rubber buffer a few turns at a time until the front edge of the bonnet and the edge of the wing, when viewed from the front, are aligned. Tighten the buffer locknut when adjustment is correct.

7 Bonnet support strut – removal and refitting

Removal

1 Raise the bonnet to the vertical position and have an assistant support the bonnet.
2 Extract the strut retaining clip, then unhook and remove the strut from the bonnet (see illustration 6.5).
3 Working at the lower end of the strut, extract the retaining clip, then unhook and remove the strut from the inner wing panel.

Refitting

4 Refitting is a reversal of removal.

8 Bonnet release cables – removal and refitting

Removal

1 Open the bonnet. If the bonnet release cable has broken, it is probably best to seek the advice of a Mercedes dealer or specialist, as to the best course of action.

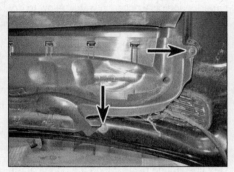
6.2 Bonnet lower cover left-hand fasteners

6.5 Prise out the strut clip a little

2 Remove the bonnet release lever, and disconnect the cable **(see illustrations)**.
3 Tie string to the release cable so that, as the cable is pulled through the bulkhead, it will pull the string with it.
4 Remove the cover from the engine compartment fuse/relay box, and release the cable.
5 Remove the cable junction box, prise it open with a screwdriver, and disconnect the rear cable.
6 Pull the rear cable from the bulkhead, leaving the string in place to aid refitting.
7 If required, undo the bolts and remove the right-, and left hand bonnet catches, then disconnect the cables **(see illustration)**. Release the cables from any retaining clips.

Refitting

8 Refitting is the reverse sequence to removal – use the string to draw the new cable through the bulkhead into the car. With the help of an assistant, make sure that the lock is working satisfactorily before closing the bonnet.

9 Radiator grille – removal and refitting

Removal

1 Open the bonnet, and from the inside at the front, undo the grille retaining bolts **(see illustration)**.
2 Remove the grille surround and grille from the bonnet, taking care not to damage the paintwork.

Refitting

3 Refitting is a reversal of removal.

8.2a Undo the screw...

8.2b...remove the lever and disconnect the cable

10 Bonnet emblem – removal and refitting

Removal

1 From the underside of the bonnet, turn the emblem retaining clip 90° anti-clockwise – the clip has raised sides to make it easier to grip with pliers **(see illustration)**.
2 Pull the emblem upwards out of the bonnet to remove.

Refitting

3 Refitting is a reversal of removal.

11 Boot lid (Saloon) – removal and refitting

Removal

1 Remove the high-level stop light as described in Chapter 12 Section 8.
2 Disconnect the wiring plugs from the boot lid lock and number plate lights, then release the wiring harness from the retaining clips.
3 Mark the outline of the hinges on the boot lid using a pencil.

8.7 Bonnet catch retaining bolts

4 Place some rags beneath the lower corners of the boot lid and, with the help of an assistant, undo the hinge retaining bolts. Remove the boot lid upwards out of the restraining hooks, and out from the car.

Refitting

5 Refitting is the reverse sequence to removal, but align the hinges with the outline marks made prior to removal before tightening the bolts. Adjust the lock striker plate as necessary to achieve satisfactory opening and closing of the boot lid.

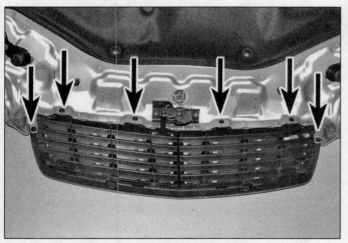
9.1 Radiator grille retaining bolts

10.1 Rotate the emblem retaining clip anti-clockwise

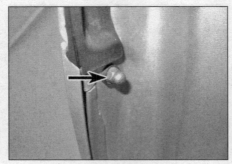

12.4a Undo the nut in the centre...

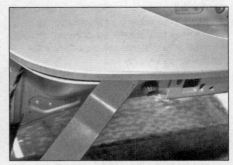

12.4b...and the nut each side...

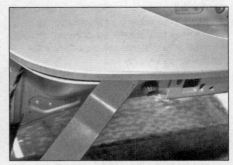

12.4c...then prise the outer panel from the boot lid

12 Boot lid lock (Saloon) – removal and refitting

Removal

1 Open the boot lid, then disconnect the battery negative lead as described in Chapter 5A Section 4.
2 Remove the number plate from the boot lid.
3 Remove the boot lid inner trim panel as described in Section 34.
4 Undo the 3 retaining nuts and carefully prise the outer panel from the boot lid (see illustrations).
5 Undo the bolt each side of the boot lid release handle, manoeuvre the lock/handle from position, then disconnect the wiring plugs and detach the cable (see illustrations).
6 If required, undo the retaining bolts, manoeuvre the boot lid catch(es) from place and disconnect the wiring plug (see illustration). On models with 2 catches, detach the connecting rod as the catch is withdrawn.
7 If required, remove the boot lid sill trim panel (Section 34), undo the bolts and remove the lock striker(s) from the vehicle body (see illustration).

12.5a Boot lid release handle screws

12.5b Pull the outer cable from the bracket, and disengage the inner cable fitting

Refitting

8 Refitting is a reversal of removal. Adjust the lock striker plate as necessary to achieve satisfactory opening and closing of the boot lid.

13 Tailgate and support struts (Estate) – removal and refitting

Removal

1 Open the tailgate, then disconnect the battery as described in Chapter 5A Section 4.
2 Remove the tailgate trim panels as described in Section 34.

3 Disconnect the wiring connectors and washer hose from their connections in the tailgate.
4 Remove the hinge cover from each side, release the harness guide tubes, and pull the harnesses/hoses from each side.
5 Mark the fitted positions of the hinges on the tailgate, so that the tailgate can be accurately aligned when refitting.
6 Have an assistant support the tailgate, then undo the bolts and remove the tailgate.
7 Removal of the support struts, requires the removal of the headlining. Entrust this tank to a Mercedes specialist or upholstery specialist.

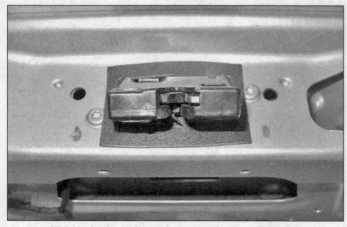

12.6 Undo the bolts and remove the boot lid catch

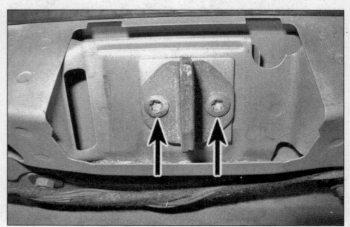

12.7 Lock striker retaining bolts

14.2a Undo the bolts on the outside...

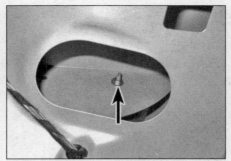

14.2b...the nut each side on the inside, and remove the handle trim strip

14.3 Remove the bolt each side of the handle

14 Tailgate lock (Estate) – removal and refitting

Removal

1 Remove the tailgate trim panel as described in Section 34.
2 Undo the retaining nuts/bolts and remove the tailgate release handle trim strip **(see illustrations)**.
3 Undo the retaining bolt each side of the release handle **(see illustration)**.
4 Disconnect the wiring plug, and control cables, then undo the bolt and remove the tailgate release handle **(see illustration)**.
5 Undo the 3 retaining bolts, manoeuvre the tailgate lock from position, and disconnect the wiring plug **(see illustration)**.

Refitting

6 Refitting is a reversal of removal. If necessary, adjust the position of the striker to achieve satisfactory opening and closing.

15 Tailgate automatic opening/ closing – component renewal

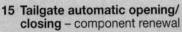

Hydraulic unit

1 Access to the hydraulic unit requires the

headlining to be removed. Consequently, we recommend that this task is entrusted to a Mercedes dealer or suitably experienced repairer.

Control module

2 Open the tailgate, then disconnect the battery negative lead as described in Chapter 5A Section 4.
3 Remove the left-hand side luggage compartment side trim panel as described in Section 34.
4 Depress the retaining clip, manoeuvre the control module from place and disconnect the wiring plugs.
5 Refitting is a reversal of removal. If a new control module has been fitted, it must be 'normalised' using the following procedure:

Models upto 06/06:
a) *Close the tailgate manually.*
b) *Open the tailgate using the release handle on the outside of the tailgate.*
c) *Operate the tailgate open/close switch in the drivers door, until the tailgate is completely open and switches off automatically. This should take approximately 5 seconds, and is complete when the tailgate 'relaxes' from the completely open position.*
d) *Using the information in the Owners Handbook reprogram the 'garage position' of the tailgate.*

Models from 06/06:
a) *Open the tailgate using the release handle on the outside of the tailgate. This will take approximately 5 seconds, and is complete when the tailgate 'relaxes'.*
b) *Using the switch at the base of the tailgate, close the tailgate, and allow it to lock. The normalisation is now complete.*
c) *Reprogram the 'garage position' of the tailgate using the information in the Owners Handbook.*

16 Bumpers – removal and refitting

Front bumper

1 Chock the rear wheels and firmly apply the parking brake, then jack up the front of the car and support it on axle stands (see *'Vehicle jacking and support'*).
2 Undo the fasteners and remove the front section of the wheel arch liner each side, for access to the bumper side mounting bolts. Where applicable, unclip the height sensor wiring harness.
3 Undo the bolt each side securing the bumper to the wing bracket and remove the strip **(see illustration)**.
4 Undo the 2 screws along the rear edge of

14.4 Tailgate release handle bolt

14.5 Tailgate lock retaining bolts

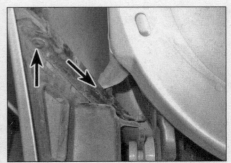

16.3 Undo the bolt, slide the strip forwards and remove it

16.4 Remove the screw each side at the rear edge of the bumper

16.6 Undo the bolts each side adjacent to the headlights

16.7 Push the bumper rearwards, then downwards to disengage the clip each side

the bumper accessible from underneath **(see illustration)**.

5 Disconnect the wiring plugs for the parking control sensors, fog lights and ambient temperature sensor (where applicable).

6 Undo the 2 bolts each side at the front of the bumper **(see illustration)**.

7 With the help of an assistant, push the bumper rearwards/downwards slightly to disengage the wing clip each side, then

carefully manoeuvre the bumper forwards and away from the vehicle **(see illustration)**.

8 Refitting is a reversal of removal.

Rear bumper

9 Open the boot lid/tailgate, then disconnect the battery negative lead as described in Chapter 5A Section 4.

Saloon models

10 Prise the luggage compartment lights from place, and disconnect the wiring plugs.

11 Remove the 3 plastic expansion rivets each side, and manoeuvre the boot lid sill trim panel from place **(see illustration)**.

12 Remove the luggage compartment rear side panels as described in Section 34.

13 Disconnect any bumper wiring plugs.

14 Undo the bumper retaining nuts on the inside of the boot sill **(see illustrations)**.

Estate models

15 Remove the luggage compartment side trim panels as described in Section 34.

16 Disconnect the bumper wiring plugs and undo the retaining nut each side in the luggage compartment **(see illustration)**.

All models

17 Undo the 2 bolts each side in the luggage compartment **(see illustration)**.

18 Release the fasteners, prise forwards the rear section of the wheelarch liner each side, then undo the bolt exposed **(see illustrations)**.

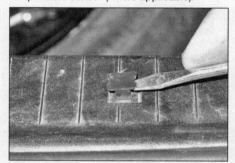

16.11 Prise out the plastic expansion rivets each side and remove the boot sill trim panel

16.14a Undo the nut each side at the outer edge...

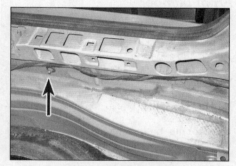

16.14b...and centre of the rear bumper

16.16 Undo the bumper retaining nut each side – Estate models

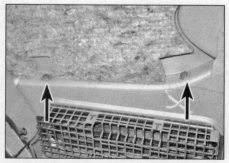

16.17 Remove the bolts each side in the luggage compartment

16.18a Remove the various fasteners, pull the wheelarch liner forwards...

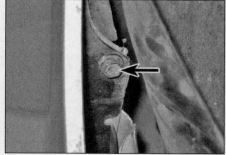

16.18b...and undo the bolt each side

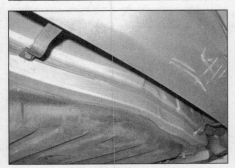

16.19 Undo the bolts on the bumper underside

17.3 Prise the triangular trim panel from the door

17.4 Use a flat, blunt tool to unclip the panel at the front of the door

19 Undo the 2 bolts on the underside of the bumper **(see illustration)**.
20 With the help of an assistant, manoeuvre the bumper rearwards from place.
21 Refitting is a reversal of removal.

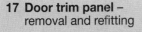

17 Door trim panel –
   removal and refitting

Removal

Front door

1 Lower the window glass approximately 175 mm (measured at the rear edge).
2 Disconnect the battery negative lead as described in Chapter 5A Section 4.
3 Unclip the mirror triangular trim panel **(see illustration)**. Disconnect any wiring plug as the panel is withdrawn.
4 Unclip the panel at the front of the door trim **(see illustration)**.
5 Undo the screw and disconnect the wiring plug **(see illustration)**.
6 Lift out the panel, and remove the 2 screws beneath **(see illustrations)**.
7 Undo the screw, and prise away the door lock cover **(see illustration)**.
8 Using a wide-bladed or wedge tool, carefully prise away the door trim panel, working progressively around the edge of the panel until all the clips have been released

(see illustration). Do not use excessive force; otherwise the clips will be broken.
9 Where applicable, unscrew and remove the lock control rod button.
10 Lift the panel away, and disconnect the

operating handle cable, and the door trim panel wiring plugs **(see illustration)**.
11 If the door weathershield is to be removed, disconnect the wiring plugs, and unclip the door control unit **(see illustration)**.

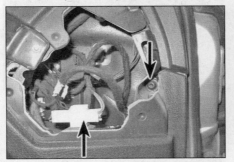

17.5 Disconnect/unclip the wiring plug, and remove the screw

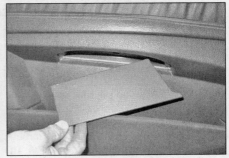

17.6a Remove the trim panel...

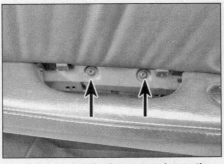

17.6b...and undo the screws beneath

17.7 Lock cover retaining screw

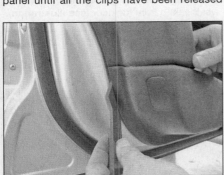

17.8 Working around the front, rear and lower edges, prise the panel from the door

17.10 Unclip the outer cable, and disengage the inner cable fitting from the handle lever

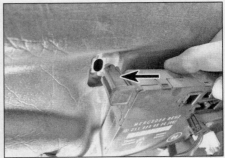

17.11 Depress the clip above, and below each side, then pull the control unit from the door

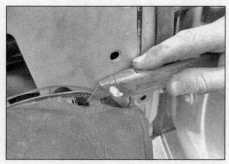

17.12 Use a sharp knife to cut through the sealant

17.14a Release the latch each side...

17.14b...then release the upper clips and remove the ashtray

17.17a Prise up the trim panel...

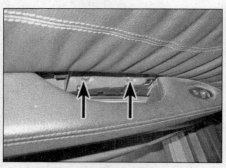
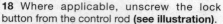

17.17b...and undo the 2 screws

17.18 Unscrew the lock button

12 Using a sharp 'craft' knife, cut through the sealant, and carefully remove the weathershield (see illustration).

Rear door

13 Disconnect the battery negative lead as described in Chapter 5A Section 4.

14 On models with a door astray, remove the insert, release the latch each side, fully open the ashtray, then release the 2 clips at the top edge and remove the ashtray (see illustrations).

15 On models without a door ashtray, prise the trim away from the front edge of the door trim panel with a blunt, flat-bladed tool.

16 On all models, remove the bolt exposed by the ashtray/trim removal.

17 Prise up the trim from the armrest aperture, and remove the 2 bolts beneath (see illustrations).

18 Where applicable, unscrew the lock button from the control rod (see illustration).

19 Prise out the plastic SRS emblem cover, and undo the screw exposed (see illustration).

20 Undo the screw and remove the lock cover (see illustration 17.7).

21 Using a wide-bladed or wedge tool, carefully prise off the door trim panel, working progressively around the edge of the panel until all the clips have been released (see illustration 17.8). Do not use excessive force; otherwise the clips will be broken.

22 Lift the panel away, disconnect the operating handle cable, and the door trim panel wiring plugs (see illustration 17.10).

23 If the door weathershield is to be removed, disconnect the wiring plugs, and unclip the door control unit (see illustration).

24 Using a sharp 'craft' knife, cut through

the sealant, and carefully remove the weathershield.

Refitting

25 Refitting is a reversal of removal. Renew any broken clips.

18 Front door window glass and regulator – removal and refitting

Removal

1 Remove the door inner trim panel and weathershield as described in Section 17.

2 Starting at the rear, unclip the window inner weatherstrip from the door (see illustration).

17.19 Prise out the cover and remove the screw

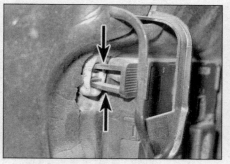

17.23 Compress the clips each side, and remove the door control unit

18.2 Pull up the inner weatherstrip

18.4a Slacken the window clamp bolts...

18.4b...lift the rear of the window and manoeuvre it from the door

18.6 Electric window motor retaining bolts

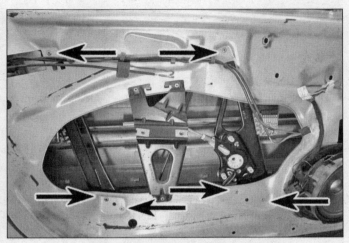

18.7 Drill out the window regulator rivets

3 Disconnect the wiring plug, undo the bolt and remove the window switch panel from the door.

4 Slacken the window glass clamp bolts, lift up the rear of the glass and manoeuvre it from the door **(see illustrations)**.

5 Release the cable ties, and disconnect the wiring plug from the electric window motor.

6 Undo the 3 retaining bolts and remove the electric window motor **(see illustration)**.

7 The regulator is secured by 6 rivets. Drill out the rivets, unhook the regulator and manoeuvre it from position **(see illustration)**. New rivets will be required.

Refitting

8 Refitting is the reverse sequence to removal.

Lubricate the regulator sliding channels when reassembling.

19 Rear door window glass and regulator

Removal

1 Lower the window glass approximately 50 mm.

2 Remove the door inner trim panel and weathershield as described in Section 17.

3 Where applicable, unclip the 'Keyless Go' control module from the door, and lay it to one side.

4 Slacken the window clamp bolt **(see illustration)**.

5 Reconnect the battery negative lead and fully lower the window glass.

6 Remove the bolt at the rear, upper section of the door **(see illustration)**.

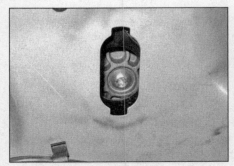

19.4 Slacken the window clamp bolt

19.6 Undo the bolt to the rear of the airbag

19.7 Remove the inner weatherstrip

19.8a Carefully remove the trim strip...

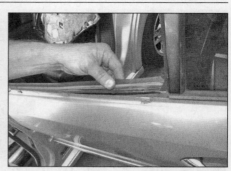

19.8b...then pull up the weather strip

19.9a Pull away the rubber channel, undo the bolt at the top...

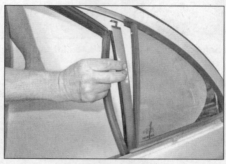

19.9b...and lower the bar into the door

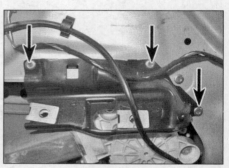

19.11 Drill out the rivets and remove the bracket

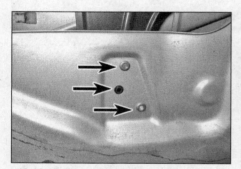

19.13a Drill out the 3 rivets at the base of the regulator...

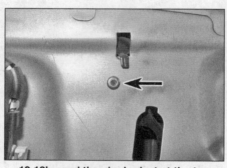

19.13b...and the single rivet at the top

window bar, then undo the bolt and carefully manoeuvre the bar downwards from place **(see illustrations)**.

10 Manoeuvre the window glass from the door.

11 Drill out the rivets securing the bracket above the electric window motor **(see illustration)**. Renew the rivets.

12 Undo the 3 retaining bolts and pull the electric window motor from place. Disconnect the wiring plug as the motor is withdrawn.

13 The window regulator is secured by 4 rivets. Drill out the rivets and manoeuvre the regulator from the door **(see illustrations)**. Renew the rivets.

Refitting

14 Refitting is the reverse sequence to removal. Lubricate the regulator sliding channels when reassembling.

7 Prise the inner door weather strip from place **(see illustration)**.
8 Carefully prise the trim strip away, then

unclip the outer weather strip from the door skin **(see illustrations)**.
9 Prise the rubber channel from the quarter

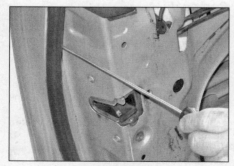

20.3a Undo the retaining bolt...

20.3b...and pull the lock cylinder/cover from the door

20 Front door exterior handle
– removal and refitting

Removal

1 Open the door, then disconnect the battery negative lead as described in Chapter 5A Section 4.
2 Unclip the sealing rubber at the rear of the door.
3 Undo the retaining bolt and pull the lock cylinder from place **(see illustrations)**.

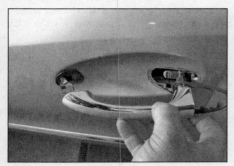

20.4 Pull the exterior handle rearwards from the door

21.2 Drill out the regulator rivets

21.5 Front door lock retaining bolts

Disconnect the wiring plug from the cylinder as it becomes accessible.

4 Pull the exterior handle rearwards, and manoeuvre it from the door **(see illustration)**. Disconnect any wiring plugs as the handle is withdrawn.

Refitting

5 Refitting is the reverse sequence to removal. Check the lock operation before closing the door.

---

21 Front door lock assembly – removal and refitting

Removal

1 Remove the front window as described in Section 18.

2 Drill out the 3 rivets securing the rear section of the window regulator, and position it forwards in the door **(see illustration)**. Renew the rivets.

3 Release the wiring harness clips, then trace the lock wiring loom forwards, and disconnect the wiring plugs at the front of the door.

4 Remove the front door lock cylinder as described in Section 20.

5 Undo the 3 bolts securing the lock to the rear of the door **(see illustration)**. Note that

when refitting, tighten the rear-facing bolts first.

6 Manoeuvre the lock from the door.

Refitting

7 Refitting is a reversal of removal. Upon completion, adjust the lock as follows:

a) *Prise out the grommet from the end of the door and slacken the release lever bolt* **(see illustration)**. *Note: Left-hand door – right-hand thread, right-hand door – left-hand thread!*

b) *Pull the exterior handle out to its full extent, then release it sharply.*

c) *Using moderate force press the exterior handle against the door.*

d) *Tighten the release lever bolt and refit the grommet.*

---

22 Rear door exterior handle – removal and refitting

Removal

1 Pull away the rubber sealing strip at the rear of the door.

2 Slacken the retaining bolt just enough until the door handle cover is loose **(see illustration)**.

3 Pull the exterior handle, and remove the door handle cover **(see illustration)**.

4 Pull the exterior handle rearwards and

21.7 Prise out the grommet from the end of the door

away from the door **(see illustration)**. Disconnect any wiring plugs as they become accessible.

Refitting

5 Refitting is a reversal of removal, ensuring the handle gaskets/seals are in place.

---

23 Rear door lock assembly – removal and refitting

Removal

1 Fully close the window glass, then remove the door inner trim panel and weathershield as described in Section 17.

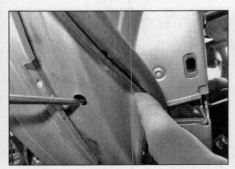

22.2 Use a screwdriver to slacken the retaining bolt

22.3 Operate the handle and pull out the cover

22.4 Slide/pull the handle from the door

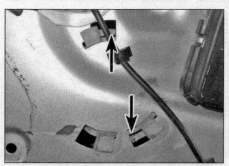

23.2 Depress the clips, and rotate the impact absorber clockwise

23.7 Unclip the plastic duct from the door

23.6 Exterior handle bearing bracket retaining bolts

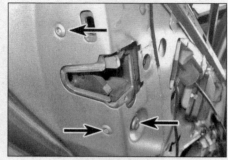

23.8 Rear door lock retaining bolts

2 Depress the clips, reach inside the door, rotate the impact absorber clockwise, and manoeuvre it from the door **(see illustration)**.

3 Unclip the inner release handle cable from the retaining clips on the door.

4 Detach the lock button/rod from the lock **(see illustration 17.18)**.

5 Remove the exterior door handle as described in Section 22.

6 Pull away the rubber gasket, slacken the 2 bolts on the outside of the door, and remove the exterior handle bearing bracket **(see illustration)**. Disconnect any wiring plugs as the bearing bracket is withdrawn.

7 Trace any wiring harness from the door lock forwards, release any retaining clips, disconnect any wiring plugs and manoeuvre the plastic duct from place **(see illustration)**.

8 Undo the 3 retaining bolts at the rear of the door, and manoeuvre the door lock from place **(see illustration)**.

Refitting

9 Refitting is a reversal of removal.

24 Central locking system components – removal and refitting

Lock switches and actuators

1 The switches and actuators are all part of the door lock assemblies. On most models, only the front door locks have switches which activate the complete system when either front door is locked/unlocked. Remove the lock assemblies as described in the relevant

Section. See your local Mercedes dealer for availability of components for the lock assembly.

Fuel filler flap

2 Remove the right-hand side luggage compartment side trim panel as described in Section 34.

3 Slacken the retaining bolts, and manoeuvre the locking motor until the wiring plugs can be disconnected **(see illustration)**.

4 If required, undo the screws and detach the locking motor from the mounting.

5 When refitting, feed the guide into the duct.

Infra-red receivers

6 The receivers are only fitted to those locks which are equipped with lock switches, ie, the front doors.

7 The receivers for the front doors are incorporated into the lock cylinders. Removal of the lock cylinder is described in Section 20.

Control module

8 There are control modules located behind the door trim/tailgate panels **(see illustrations)**.

9 Remove the door inner trim panel as described in Section 17, or the tailgate trim panel as described in Section 34.

10 Disconnect the module wiring plugs.

11 Release the retaining lugs (they either squeeze together, or are pressed apart)/undo the screws, and remove the module from the car.

12 Refitting is a reversal of removal.

'Keyless Go' control modules

Interior compartment module

13 On automatic transmission models, fully apply the parking brake, and place the selector lever in position 'D'.

14 Open the front ashtray, then pull up the front edge of the selector/gear change lever surround trim to unclip it – see Section 35.

15 Pull the ashtray from the centre console, and disconnect the wiring plugs as they become accessible.

16 Unclip the 'Keyless Go' control module from the ashtray.

17 Refitting is a reversal of removal.

24.3 Fuel filler flap locking motor bolts

24.8a Front door control module

24.8b Tailgate control module

25.5 Prise the cover from the check strap bolts

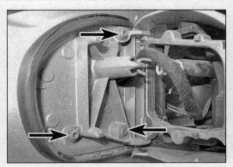
27.5 Door mirror retaining bolts

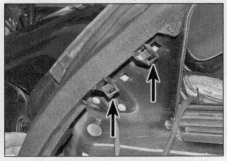
27.9a Release the catches...

27.9b...and unclip the window frame trim at the front

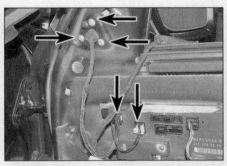
27.11 Mirror mounting bolts and wiring plugs

27.13 Prise up the clip and pull the mirror from place

Rear door control module

18 Remove the door inner trim panel and weathershield as described in Section 17.
19 Disconnect the wiring plugs, and unclip the 'Keyless Go' control module from the door.
20 Refitting is a reversal of removal.

25 Door – removal and refitting

Removal

1 Fully lower the door window, then prise the cover from the front edge of the door inner trim panel **(see illustration 17.4)**. On rear doors an ashtray may be fitted in place of the cover.
2 Disconnect the battery negative lead as described in Chapter 5A Section 4.
3 Disconnect the wiring plugs and push the harness into the door.
4 Unclip the harness gaiter from the door, and pull the harness from the door.
5 Remove the cover and undo the 2 bolts securing the check strap to the pillar **(see illustration)**.
6 Prise off the caps and remove both hinge bolts.
7 With the help of an assistant, lift the door from the hinge, and manoeuvre it from the vehicle.

Refitting

8 Refitting is a reversal of removal.

26 Windscreen and fixed window glass – general information

1 Due to the methods of attachment, and the special equipment required to complete the task successfully, removal and refitting of the windscreen, rear/tailgate window (and rear side windows on Estate models) should be entrusted to a dealer or an automotive glass specialist.

27 Door mirror – removal and refitting

Complete mirror assembly

Models upto 06/06

1 Unclip the mirror inner cover from the inside of the door **(see illustration 17.3)**.
2 Prise the cover from the front of the door **(see illustration 17.4)**.
3 Disconnect the mirror wiring plugs from the door control unit.
4 Remove the mirror outer cover as described in this Section.

5 Undo the retaining bolts at the outside of the door, and remove the mirror **(see illustration)**.
6 Manoeuvre the mirror along with wiring, from the door.
7 Refitting is a reversal of removal.

Models from 06/06

8 Remove the door inner trim panel as described in Section 17.
9 Unclip the door window frame trim until the mirror mounting bolt is accessible **(see illustrations)**.
10 Disconnect the wiring plugs from the door control unit.
11 Undo the mounting bolts and remove the complete mirror assembly **(see illustration)**. Disconnect any wiring plugs as the unit is withdrawn.
12 Refitting is a reversal of removal.

Mirror glass

Models upto 06/06

13 Tilt the top of the glass rearwards, then use a small screwdriver to prise up the retaining clip and remove the glass **(see illustration)**. Disconnect any wiring plugs as the glass is withdrawn.
14 Clip the glass back into place from the bottom upwards.

Models from 06/06

15 Pull the top edge of the mirror glass rearwards, then using a plastic wedge (or similar) lever the mirror rearwards to

27.15 Gentle lever the top edge of the mirror glass rearwards

27.19 Depress the clip and slide the mirror cover rearwards

27.22 Unclip the cover from the mirror interior

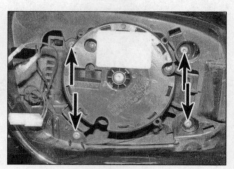

27.23 Mirror frame retaining bolts

27.24 Mirror adjustment motor retaining screws

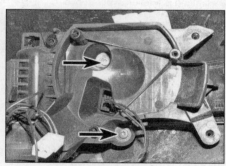

27.25a Undo the screws...

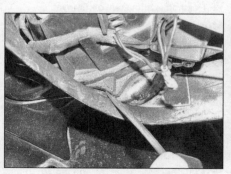

27.25b and release the catch

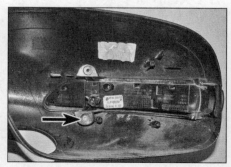

27.26 If required, undo the remaining screw and remove the side repeater

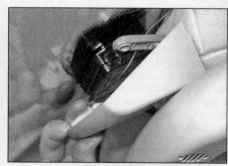

28.2 Prise the cover downwards

release the retaining clips **(see illustration)**. Disconnect any wiring plugs as the mirror is withdrawn.

16 Clip the glass back into place from the bottom upwards.

Mirror cover

Models upto 06/06

17 Remove the mirror glass as described earlier in this Section.
18 Fold the mirror rearwards.
19 Depress the retaining clip and remove the mirror cover **(see illustration)**.
20 Refitting is a reversal of removal.

Models from 06/06

21 Remove the mirror glass as described earlier in this Section.
22 Remove the cover from the mirror interior **(see illustration)**. Note that the cover may be damaged during the removal procedure – if necessary, renew it.
23 Undo the 4 retaining bolts and remove the mirror frame **(see illustration)**.
24 Undo the 3 screws and remove the mirror adjustment motor **(see illustration)**. Disconnect the wiring plugs as the motor is withdrawn.
25 Undo the 2 screws, release the catch and remove the mirror cover **(see illustrations)**.
26 Remove the side repeater light from the cover **(see illustration)**.
27 Refitting is a reversal of removal.

---

28 Interior mirror – removal and refitting

Removal

1 Switch off the ignition and remove the key from the EIS. On models with 'Keyless Go' place the transmitter key out of range of the vehicle.
2 Using a blunt, flat-bladed tool, carefully prise the rain/light sensor cover downwards and remove it **(see illustration)**.

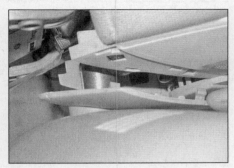

28.3 Unclip the mirror base cover

28.4 Pivot the mirror to one side, and pull it downwards

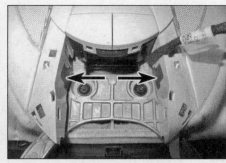

28.6 Depress the overhead console release buttons

3 Unclip the mirror base cover from the overhead console **(see illustration)**.
4 Remove the mirror by pivoting it to one side, and pulling downwards at the same time **(see illustration)**.
5 Disconnect the rain/light sensor wiring plug.
6 Depress the release buttons, prise down the rear edge, and release the overhead console **(see illustration)**.
7 Disconnect the wiring plugs and remove the rear view mirror.

Refitting

8 Refitting is a reversal of removal.

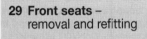

29 Front seats –
removal and refitting

Removal

1 Move the front seat fully upright, fully forward, and as high as possible.
2 Prise up the plastic covers, and undo the 2 bolts at the rear of the seat rails **(see illustration)**. Discard the bolts – new ones must be fitted.
3 Unclip the cover, undo the bolt and detach the seat belt from the seat **(see illustration)**.
4 Move the seat fully rearwards, prise up the plastic covers, then undo the bolts at the front of the seat rails. Discard the bolts – new ones must be fitted.

29.2 Slide out the plastic covers to expose the seat retaining bolts

5 Disconnect the battery negative lead as described in Chapter 5A Section 4.
6 Wait at least 10 minutes for any residual electric energy to dissipate.
7 Lift up the front of the seat, note their fitted positions, and disconnect the various wiring plugs **(see illustration)**.
8 Where applicable, disconnect the air pipe from the seat underside.
9 With the help of an assistant, carefully manoeuvre the seat from the passenger cabin.
Caution: The seats are extremely heavy!

Refitting

10 Refitting is a reversal of removal, noting the following points:

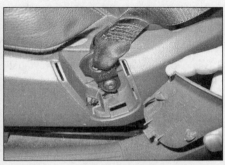

29.3 Prise out the cover to access the seat belt bolt

a) Renew the seat mounting bolts.
b) Tighten all fasteners to their specified torque where given.
c) Reconnect the battery negative lead as described in Chapter 5A Section 4.
d) If a new seat has been fitted, it must be 'Normalised' using Mercedes STAR diagnostic equipment or equivalent.

30 Rear seats –
removal and refitting

Seat cushion

Non through-loading – Saloon

1 Press-in the locking catches each side at the front edge, lift the cushion and manoeuvre it from place **(see illustration)**.

Through-loading – Saloon

2 Move the front seats fully forwards, then pull the release lever and move the rear seat cushion to the upright position.
3 Pull on the release mechanism handle and manoeuvre the seat cushion from place.

Estate

4 Pull the release handle at the side, and move the seat cushion to the fully vertical position.

29.7 Disconnect the wiring plugs from the underside of the front seat

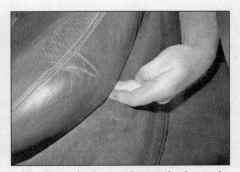

30.1 Press-in the catches at the front of the seat cushion

30.5 Pull the release lever and remove the seat cushion

30.7 Undo the nut each side...

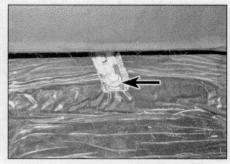

30.8...and the central screw

5 Pull the release lever, and manoeuvre the seat cushion from place (see illustration).

Seat backrest

Non-through loading – Saloon

6 Remove the seat cushion as previously described in this Section.
7 Undo the retaining nut each side at the front edge (see illustration).
8 Undo the central retaining screw (see illustration).
9 Lift the backrest a little, pull out the seat belts, and manoeuvre the backrest from place.

Through-loading – Saloon

10 Fold the seat cushion forwards, then operate the backrest release lever in the luggage compartment.
11 Undo the bolt securing the centre seat belt lower anchorage.
12 Undo the retaining nuts at the front, lower, outer edges.
13 Fold the backrest forwards, and slide the side upholstery upwards from place.
14 Undo the bolts securing the backrest pivot bearing each side.
15 Prise the cover from the centre hinge, and remove the bolt beneath.
16 Fold up the centre hinge clip, make alignment marks between the centre hinge journals and bracket, then manoeuvre the backrest(s) from place. Disconnect any wiring plugs as the backrest(s) are withdrawn.

Estate

17 Remove the rear seat cushions as described earlier in this Section.
18 Undo the centre seat belt lower anchorage bolt.
19 Working the luggage compartment, release the backrests, fold them forwards, then remove the luggage compartment cover.
20 Using a blunt, flat-bladed tool, unclip the side panel each side of the backrest (see illustration).
21 Undo the bolts securing the backrest pivot bearing bracket each side, then press the bearing inwards towards the backrest (see illustration).
22 Disconnect any wiring plugs/air pipe connections at the sides of the backrest.
23 Carefully prise up and remove the centre hinge cover (see illustration).
24 Undo the centre hinge bolt.
25 Fold up the centre hinge clip, make alignment marks between the outer hinge journals and bracket, then manoeuvre the backrest(s) from place. Disconnect any wiring plugs as the backrest(s) are withdrawn.

31 Seat belts –
removal and refitting

> **Warning: All models are equipped with spring-loaded automatic tensioning devices fitted to the front seat belt inertia reel**

assemblies. The belt tensioners are triggered by the airbag system in the event of an accident. For safety reasons, no attempt should be made to dismantle the front seat belt inertia reels, and no electrical testing should be performed on any of the wiring associated with the airbag or belt tensioner system – work of this nature must be entrusted to a Mercedes-Benz dealer.
Caution: Although no specific precautions are given by the manufacturer, it seems prudent to treat the seat belt tensioner with as much care as an airbag unit (see Chapter 12). Therefore, do not drop or strike the tensioner, nor subject it to extremes of heat. If there is any doubt about the condition of the seat belt or tensioner, refer to a Mercedes-Benz dealer – DO NOT attempt to dismantle the belt reel or tensioner, as this could be highly dangerous. If any noise has been noted from the seat belt mechanism, do not attempt to cure this by applying lubricants of any kind. A noise from the tensioner may indicate an internal fault, or it may be that the unit has 'fired', and is therefore no longer operative.

Front belts

Inertia reel

1 Disconnect the battery negative lead as described in Chapter 5A Section 4.
2 Remove the B-pillar trim panel as described in Section 34.

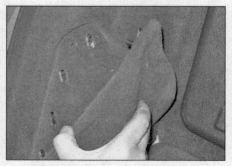

30.20 Unclip the panel each side

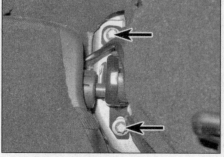

30.21 Undo the bearing bracket bolts each side

30.23 Prise up the centre hinge cover

31.3 Seat belt upper anchorage bolt

31.4 Front seat belt inertia reel retaining bolt and wiring plugs

31.13 Undo the seat belt lower anchorage bolt

3 Undo the nut and remove the seat belt upper anchorage **(see illustration)**.
4 Disconnect the wiring plugs from the seat belt inertia reel, then undo the retaining bolt and remove the reel **(see illustration)**.
5 Refitting is a reversal of removal, tightening the retaining bolts to their specified torque where given.

Buckle

6 Remove the relevant front seat as described in Section 29.

Upto 07/04

7 Undo the seat belt buckle retaining bolt.
8 Undo the screw, remove the seat base side panel to access the buckle wiring harness. Release the wiring/harness from the clips etc. and remove the buckle.

From 07/04

9 Undo the two screws and remove the trim panel from the side of the seat base.
10 Undo the nut securing the buckle to the seat base, then unclip the wiring.

Rear belts

Inertia reel – side belts

11 Disconnect the battery negative lead as described in Chapter 5A Section 4.

Saloon

12 Remove the parcel shelf as described in Section 34.
13 Undo the seat belt lower anchorage bolt **(see illustration)**.

14 If removing the left-hand seat belt, undo the nuts and move the antenna amplifier to one side.
15 Undo the seat belt upper anchorage bolt **(see illustration)**.
16 Undo the retaining bolt and slide the seat belt from the guide.
17 Move the insulation material to one side, undo the retaining bolt and manoeuvre the seat belt inertia reel from place **(see illustration)**. Disconnect the wiring plugs as the inertia reel is withdrawn.
18 Refitting is a reversal of removal, tightening the retaining bolts to their specified torque where given.

Estate

19 Both the rear seat and 3rd row side seat belts are accessed once the luggage compartment side panels have been removed.
20 Remove the luggage compartment side trim panel and C-pillar trim panel as described in Section 34.
21 On models with a 3rd row of seats, unclip the seat belt guide, and feed the belt through the side panel.
22 Undo the seat belt upper anchorage bolt **(see illustration)**.
23 Disconnect the wiring plugs from the inertia reel, then undo the 4 bolts and remove the reel along with the bracket **(see illustration)**.
24 If required, undo the bolt and detach the inertia reel from the bracket.
25 Refitting is a reversal of removal,

31.15 Undo the seat belt upper anchorage bolt

tightening the retaining bolts to their specified torque where given.

Inertia reel – centre belt

Estate, and Saloon models with through-loading

26 Where fitted, the centre seat belt is incorporated into the seat itself, and can only be removed by dismantling the seat, which includes removing the seat covering. This job is considered beyond the scope of this manual, and is best entrusted to a Mercedes-Benz dealer.

Saloon – without through-loading

27 Remove the rear parcel shelf as described in Section 34.
28 Fold back the insulation material, and undo the seat belt lower anchorage bolt.

31.17 Rear side seat belt inertia reel retaining bolt

31.22 Rear seat belt upper anchorage bolt

31.23 2nd and 3rd row rear seat belt inertia reels

29 Undo the retaining bolt and manoeuvre the seat belt inertia reel from place **(see illustration)**.
30 Refitting is a reversal of removal. Tighten the fasteners to their specified torque where given.

Buckle

31 Remove the rear seat cushion as described in Section 30.
32 Undo the bolt and remove the relevant seat belt stalk.
33 Refitting is a reversal of removal, tightening the retaining bolts to their specified torque where given.

32 Sunroof – general information

1 A sliding sunroof, either mechanically- or electrically-operated, is available as a factory-fitted option. Adjustment or repair of the sunroof or its component parts should be left to the dealer or specialist, as the complexity of the unit and the need for special tools and equipment renders these operations beyond the scope of this manual.

33 Body exterior fittings – removal and refitting

Wheelarch liners and body under-panels

1 The various plastic covers fitted to the underside of the vehicle are secured in position by a mixture of screws, nuts and retaining clips, and removal will be fairly obvious on inspection. Work methodically around, removing its retaining screws and releasing its retaining clips until the panel is free and can be removed from the underside of the vehicle. Most clips used on the vehicle are simply prised out of position. Other clips can be released by unscrewing/prising out the centre pins and then removing the clip.
2 On refitting, renew any retaining clips that

31.29 Rear centre belt inertia reel retaining bolt

may have been broken on removal, and ensure that the panel is securely retained by all the relevant clips and screws.

Body trim strips and badges

3 The various body trim strips and badges are held in position with a special adhesive tape. Removal requires the trim/badge to be heated, to soften the adhesive, and then cut away from the surface. Due to the high risk of damage to the vehicle's paintwork during this operation, it is recommended that this task should be entrusted to a Mercedes dealer or suitably-equipped specialist.

34 Interior trim – removal and refitting

Interior trim panels – general

1 The interior trim panels are secured using either screws or various types of trim fasteners, usually studs or clips.
2 Check that there are no other panels overlapping the one to be removed; usually there is a sequence that has to be followed that will become obvious on close inspection.
3 Remove all obvious fasteners, such as screws. If the panel will not come free, it is held by hidden clips or fasteners. These are usually situated around the edge of the panel and can be prised up to release them; note, however that they can break quite easily so new ones

should be available. The best way of releasing such clips, without the correct type of tool, is to use a large flat-bladed screwdriver. Note that some panels are secured by plastic expanding rivets, where the centre pin must be prised up before the rivet can be removed. Note in many cases that the adjacent sealing strip must be prised back to release a panel.
4 When removing a panel, never use excessive force or the panel may be damaged; always check carefully that all fasteners have been removed or released before attempting to withdraw a panel.
5 Refitting is the reverse of the removal procedure; secure the fasteners by pressing them firmly into place and ensure that all disturbed components are correctly secured to prevent rattles.

A-pillar trim panel

6 Due to the proximity of the headlining airbag, disconnect the battery negative lead as described in Chapter 5A Section 4, then wait at least 10 minutes for any residual electrical energy to dissipate.
7 Pull the rubber weatherstrip away adjacent to the A-pillar.
8 Using a blunt-, flat-bladed tool, carefully prise the A-pillar trim panel from place. Note how the lugs at the base of the trim panel engage **(see illustrations)**.
9 Refitting is a reversal of removal; secure the fasteners by pressing them firmly into place and ensure that all disturbed components are correctly secured to prevent rattles.

B-pillar trim panel

10 Move the front seat fully forwards and upwards, the prise the cover from the seat base, and remove the seat belt anchorage bolt **(see illustration 29.3)**.
11 Where applicable, prise the air grille from the B-pillar panel.
12 Where applicable, prise the air grille from the B-pillar trim panel.
13 Pull the rubber weatherstrip from each side of the B-pillar.
14 Starting at the rear edges, pull up and remove the front, and rear door sill trim panels **(see illustration)**.
15 Using a blunt, flat-bladed tool, carefully prise the upper and lower B-pillar panel

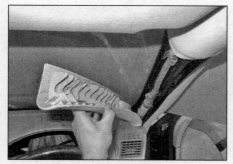

34.8a Prise the A-pillar trim panel from place

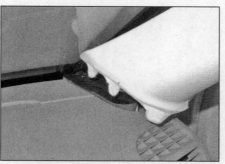

34.8b Note the lugs at the base of the panel

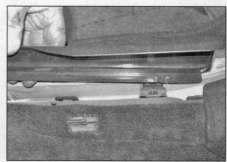

34.14 Pull up the front and rear door sill trim panels

34.15 Prise the pillar panel clip from the pillar

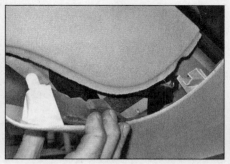

34.20a Pull the top of the C-pillar trim panel inwards...

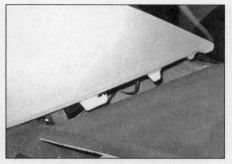

34.20b...then rotate it forwards to disengage it from the parcel shelf

retaining clips from the metal pillar. Feed the seat belt through the upper trim panel as it's withdrawn **(see illustration)**.

16 Refitting is a reversal of removal; secure the fasteners by pressing them firmly into place and ensure that all disturbed components are correctly secured to prevent rattles.

C-pillar trim panel

Saloon

17 Remove the rear seat cushion as described in Section 30. On models with through-loading system, it's sufficient to position cushion upright rather than completely remove it.
18 Pull away the rubber weatherstrip adjacent to the C-pillar.
19 Undo the rear side seatbelt lower anchorage bolt(s).
20 Pull the pillar trim panel inwards at the top edges to release the retaining clip, then rotate the panel forwards and manoeuvre it from place **(see illustrations)**. Note how the panel engages with the parcel shelf.
21 Refitting is a reversal of removal; fit the rear upper retaining clip to the panel prior to refitting.

Estate

22 Lift the rear seat cushion, then remove the rear side seat belt lower anchorage bolt.
23 Fold the seat backrest fully forwards.

24 Pull away the rubber weatherstrip adjacent to the C-pillar.
25 Pull the C-pillar trim panel inwards to release the retaining clips **(see illustration)**. Feed the seat belt through the panel as it's withdrawn.
26 Refitting is a reversal of removal.

D-pillar trim panel

27 Due to the proximity of the headlining airbag, disconnect the battery negative lead as described in Chapter 5A Section 4, then wait at least 10 minutes for any residual electrical energy to dissipate.
28 Remove the C-pillar trim panel as described earlier in this Section. Note that

34.25 Release the C-pillar trim panel retaining clips

there is no need to detach the seat belt lower anchorage.
29 Remove the rear section of the luggage compartment side panel. The left-hand side panel is removed by pressing the release button at the top, and lifting the panel from place, whilst the right-hand panel must be pulled inwards to release the retaining clips **(see illustrations)**.
30 Pull away the rubber weatherstrip, undo the screws and remove the trim panel at the base of the D-pillar.
31 Undo the retaining screws, then pull the D-pillar trim panel inwards at the rear edge to release the retaining clip **(see illustrations)**.
32 Push the panel forwards, out of the cover guide rail, then inwards until the wiring plug is

34.29a Press the release button and pull the panel inwards

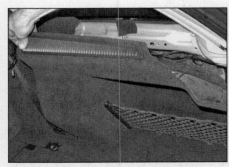

34.29b Pull the right-hand panel inwards to release the clips

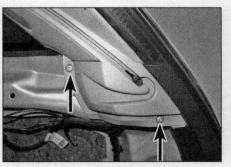

34.31a Undo the screws...

34.31b...and pull the rear edge inwards

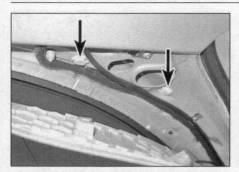

34.32 Push the panel forwards to release it from the clips

34.36 Prise the rear window surround trim from place

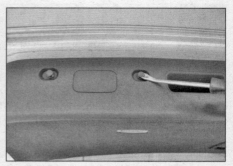

34.37 Prise up the centre pins, and remove the 12 expansion rivets

accessible **(see illustration)**. Disconnect the wiring plug and manoeuvre the panel from place.

33 Refitting is a reversal of removal.

Door trim panels

34 See Section 17.

Tailgate trim panels

35 Open the tailgate, then disconnect the battery negative lead as described in Chapter 5A Section 4.

36 Using a blunt, flat-bladed tool, carefully unclip the rear window trim surround **(see illustration)**.

37 Remove the 12 plastic expansion rivets

from the lower edge, and sides of the tailgate trim panel **(see illustration)**.

38 On models with an inner release handle, undo the retaining screw, and slide the inner release handle trim towards the front of the vehicle, and remove it **(see illustrations)**.

39 Undo the 2 screws securing the pull-down strap (where fitted), pull down the front edge of the trim panel and manoeuvre it from place **(see illustration)**. Disconnect any wiring plugs as the panel is withdrawn.

Boot lid trim panel

40 Remove the warning triangle and bracket (where fitted), then prise up the centre pins, and lever out the 6 plastic expansion rivets

securing the trim panel to the boot lid **(see illustration)**.

41 Undo the 6 retaining screws and remove the trim from the boot lid outer edge **(see illustration)**.

42 Prise out the boot lid lamp and disconnect the wiring plug **(see illustration)**.

43 Manoeuvre the boot lid trim panel from place.

44 Refitting is a reversal of removal.

Parcel shelf

Without through-loading

45 Remove the rear seat backrests as described in Section 30.

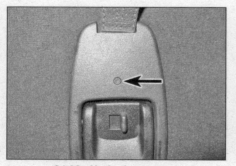

34.38a Undo the screw...

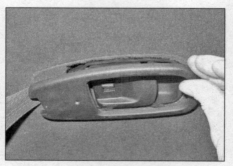

34.38b ...and slide the release handle trim forwards

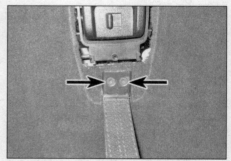

34.39 Remove the pull-down strap retaining screws

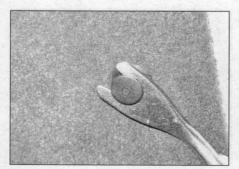

34.40 Prise up the centre pin, and lever out the plastic expansion rivets

34.41 Undo the 3 screws each side and remove the boot lid outer trim

34.42 Prise out the boot lid lamp

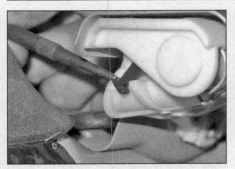

34.46 Insert a rod from the rear, press-down the catch and pull out the head restraint – parcel shelf removed for clarity

34.48 Prise out the seat belt guide trim

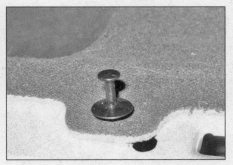

34.49 Prise up the centre pins, and lever out the plastic expansion rivets

46 Pull up the head restraints, unclip the rear head restraint mounting grommets from the parcel shelf, then use an 8 mm rod to release the catches and remove the head restraints **(see illustration)**.

47 Remove the C-pillar trim panels as described earlier in this Section. Note there is no need to detach the lower seat belt anchorages.

48 Unclip the centre seat belt guide trim from the parcel shelf **(see illustration)**.

49 Prise up the centre pins, lever out the plastic expansion rivets at the front edge of the parcel shelf, then lift the front edge, and slide the parcel shelf forwards **(see illustration)**. Guide the seat belt through the recess as the parcel shelf is withdrawn.

50 Refitting is a reversal of removal.

With through-loading

51 Remove both C-pillar trim panels as described earlier in this Section.

52 Prise up the centre pins, and lever out the plastic expansion rivet each side at the front edge of the parcel shelf.

53 Working in the luggage compartment, undo the 4 nuts/bolts securing the parcel shelf to the vehicle body.

54 Lift the parcel shelf a little, and unclip the speaker cover.

55 Disconnect the speaker wiring plugs, then rotate the speaker housing anti-clockwise until it unlocks.

56 Pull the parcel shelf forwards, and remove it along with the speaker housing.

57 Refitting is a reversal of removal.

Headlining

58 The rigid headlining is clipped to the roof, and can only be withdrawn once all fittings such as the grab handles, sunvisors, interior light, and related trim panels have been removed, and the door, tailgate and sunroof aperture sealing strips have been prised clear.

59 As with carpet removal, taking out the headlining is not especially difficult, just time-consuming.

Footwell kick panels

60 Pull away the rubber weatherstrip adjacent to the A-pillar.

61 Pull the door sill trim panel upwards at the front edge.

62 Using a blunt, flat-bladed tool, carefully prise the footwell kick panel from the side of the vehicle body. Disconnect any wiring plugs as the panel is withdrawn.

63 Refitting is a reversal of removal.

Luggage compartment side trim panel

Saloon

64 Where applicable, fold the rear seat backrests forwards.

65 Undo the bolts and remove the stowage anchors from the lower edge of the trim panel **(see illustration)**.

66 Remove the 2 plastic expansion rivets at the upper edge of the trim panel **(see illustration)**.

67 On models with through-loading, undo the screws and lift out the carrier plate cover from behind the rear seats.

68 Prise out the boot lid hinge surround trim, then manoeuvre the side trim panel from the vehicle **(see illustration)**.

69 Refitting is a reversal of removal.

Estate

Rear panel

70 If removing the left-hand side trim panel, operate the release button, lift the inner panel from place, then undo the 3 screws and remove the outer insulation panel **(see illustration)**.

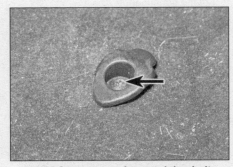

34.65 Stowage anchor retaining bolt

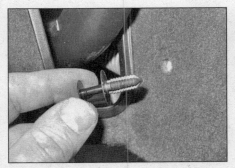

34.66 Prise up the centre pins, and lever out the plastic expansion rivets

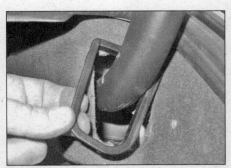

34.68 Remove the boot lid hinge surround trim

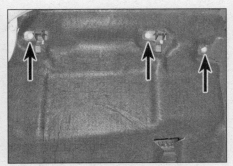

34.70 Insulation panel retaining screws

34.77 Remove the cover, then undo the 2 bolts exposed

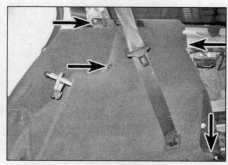

34.78a Undo the screws/nuts, unclip and side panel...

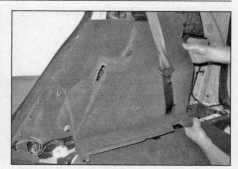

34.78b...and manoeuvre it from place

71 If removing the right-hand side trim panel, use a blunt, flat-bladed tool to carefully prise the panel from the vehicle **(see illustration 34.29b)**.

Front panel

72 Remove the rear seats as described in Section 30.

73 Remove the C-pillar trim panel as described earlier in this Section.

74 Prise up the rear edge of the door sill trim panel.

75 Remove the plastic expansion rivet and fold back the carpet under the rear seat location.

76 Pull away the rubber weatherstrip at the rear of the door aperture.

77 Remove the rubber cover then note their fitted positions, undo the 2 bolts and remove the backrest bracket **(see illustration)**.

78 The side trim panel is now secured by 3 screws, 1 nut, and 3 clips in the C-pillar area **(see illustrations)**. Undo the screws/nut, release the clips and remove the side trim panel. Disconnect any wiring plugs as the panel is withdrawn. On 7-seater models, if required, undo the seat belt lower anchorage bolt, unclip the seat belt guide, and feed the belt through the panel as it's withdrawn.

79 Refitting is a reversal of removal.

34.83 Remove the bolt each side of the air bag

Glovebox

Complete glovebox

80 Move the steering wheel to the fully lowered, rearmost position.

81 Move the front passengers seat fully rearwards, then disconnect the battery negative lead as described in Chapter 5A Section 4.

82 Remove the upper section of the facia as described in Section 36.

83 Undo the bolt each side of the passengers air bag **(see illustration)**.

84 Remove the centre console as described in Section 35.

85 Undo the 2 screws securing the passengers

34.86a The globebox is secured by a bolts at the outer edge...

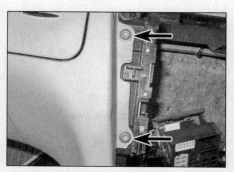

34.86b...2 bolts at the upper, inner edge...

34.86c...and a bolt at the lower, inner edge

34.85 Passengers side lower facia panel retaining screws

side lower facia panel, and manoeuvre it from place **(see illustration)**. Disconnect any wiring plugs as the panel is withdrawn.

86 The glovebox is now secured by 4 bolts **(see illustrations)**. Undo the bolts and manoeuvre the glovebox from the vehicle. Disconnect any wiring plugs as the glovebox is withdrawn.

87 Refitting is a reversal of removal.

Glovebox lid

88 Undo the fasteners securing the passengers side lower facia panel, and manoeuvre it from place **(see illustration 34.85)**. Disconnect any wiring plugs as the panel is withdrawn.

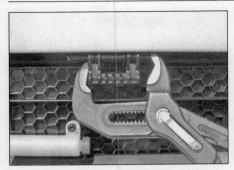

34.89 Press out the hinge pins

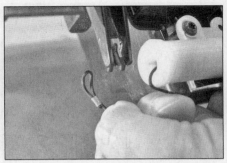

34.90 Unhook the damper cord

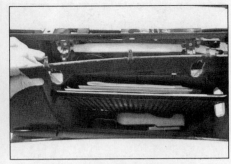

34.92 Unclip the lock cover

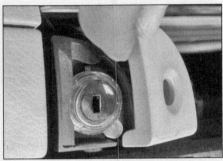

34.95 Prise the lock cover rearwards

34.98 Sunvisor outer mounting screws

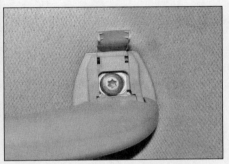

34.100 Open the cover and undo the screw each end of the grab handle

89 Using a suitable pair of pliers, press the pins from the hinges (see illustration).
90 Unhook the damper (see illustration), and remove the lid.
91 Refitting is a reversal of removal.

Glovebox lock

92 Open the glovebox, the prise the lock cover from place (see illustration).
93 Undo the retaining bolts, manoeuvre the lock from place, and disconnect any wiring plugs as they become accessible.
94 Refitting is a reversal of removal.

Glovebox lock cylinder

95 Open the glovebox, then carefully prise the lock cylinder cover rearwards and remove it (see illustration).
96 Insert the 'emergency key' into the lock cylinder, then rotate it 45° clockwise and pull the lock cylinder from place.
97 Refitting is a reversal of removal. The lock cylinder should emit an audible 'click' when refitted correctly.

Sunvisors

98 The sunvisors are secured by 1 screw at the inner end, and 2 screws at the outer (see illustration). Undo the screws and remove the sunvisor.
99 Refitting is a reversal of removal.

Grab handles

100 Fold open the covers, undo the bolts

and remove the grab handle (see illustration).
101 Refitting is a reversal of removal.

Carpet

102 The passenger compartment floor carpet is in one piece (with a separate piece used in the luggage area), and is secured at its edges by screws or clips, usually the same fasteners used to secure the various adjoining trim panels.
103 Carpet removal and refitting is reasonably straightforward, but very time-consuming, due to the fact that all adjoining trim panels must be removed first, as must components such as the seats, the centre console and seat belt lower anchorages.

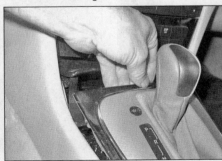

35.2 Pull up the front edge of the panel

35 Centre console – removal and refitting

Removal

1 Fully apply the parking brake, then move the selector lever to position 'D' (where applicable).
2 Open the ashtray at the front of the console, and starting at the front edge, pull up the gearchange/selector lever surround panel (see illustration). Disconnect any wiring plugs as the panel is lifted.
3 Rotate the gearchange/selector lever gaiter locking collar anti-clockwise (see illustration), then remove the surround panel, gaiter and pull the lever knob upwards.

35.3 Rotate the locking collar anti-clockwise

35.4 Release the clips and pull the astray upwards

35.5 Centre console front retaining bolts

35.6 Release the clips and lift out the base plate

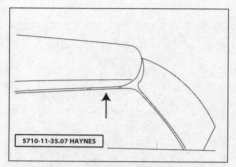

5710-11-35.07 HAYNES

35.7 Release the clip each side of the upper section

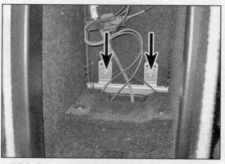

35.9 Centre console rear retaining bolts

2 bolts at the rear (see illustration). Undo the bolts, and with the help of an assistant, manoeuvre the console from place.

Refitting

10 Refitting is a reversal of removal. Ensure all wiring is securely reconnected, and the harness correctly routed.

36 Facia panel assembly – removal and refitting

4 Release the clip each side and pull the ashtray at the front of the console upwards from position (see illustration). Disconnect any wiring plugs as the ashtray is withdrawn.
5 Undo the 2 bolts at the front, upper side of the console (see illustration).

Models with a rear storage box

6 On models with a rear storage box, open the box, lift out the mat, then release the clip each side and remove the base plate (see illustration).

Models without a rear storage box

7 On models without the rear storage box, release the clip each side at the rear, then using a blunt, flat-bladed tool, carefully prise the centre console upper section upwards to release the retaining clips (see illustration).

All models

8 Disconnect the console wiring plugs, and release the plug brackets as necessary.
9 The centre console is now secured by

Upper section

1 Remove the instrument cluster as described in Chapter 12 Section 10.
2 Remove the A-pillar trim panels as described in Section 34.
3 Carefully prise the facia end panels from place (see illustration).
4 Using a blunt, flat-bladed tool, carefully prise the decorative strip from the drivers side of the facia (see illustration).
5 Prise the right-hand end of the passengers side decorative strip from the facia, then slide

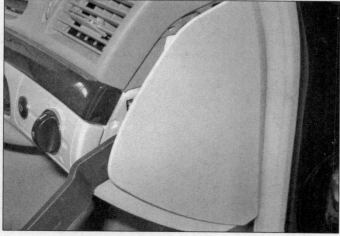

36.3 Prise the end panels from the facia

36.4 Prise the decorative strip rearwards

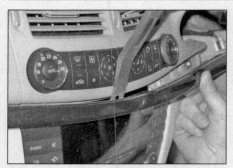

36.5a Prise the right-hand end of the decorative strip rearwards...

36.5b...then slide it to the left from the retaining clips

36.8a The upper facia panel is secured by 2 bolts at the drivers end...

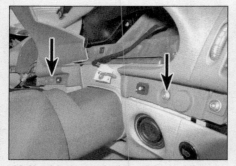

36.8b...2 bolts each side of the instrument cluster aperture...

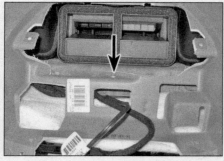

36.8c...a bolt in the centre aperture..

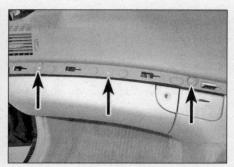

36.8d...3 bolts above the passengers glovebox...

it to the left and manoeuvre it from place (see illustrations).

6 Remove the facia central speaker as described in Chapter 12 Section 17.

7 Remove the heating/air conditioning control panel as described in Chapter 3 Section 8.

8 The upper facia panel is secured by 10 bolts (see illustrations). Undo the bolts, and with the help of an assistant, manoeuvre the upper facia panel from place. Release the clips and detach the LED lighting units from the facia end vents as it's withdrawn.

Caution: Take care not to damage the headlining airbag wiring plugs as the upper section of the facia is manoeuvred from place.

Lower section

Drivers side

9 Remove the facia panel upper section as previously described in this Section.

10 Remove the centre console as described in Section 35.

11 Remove the facia mounted audio unit and infotainment unit as described in Chapter 12 Section 16.

12 Remove the accelerator pedal assembly as described in Chapter 4A Section 5.

13 Pull open the bonnet release lever, and undo the bolt exposed (see illustration 8.2a).

14 Detach the bonnet release handle from the panel, and disconnect the cable (see illustration 8.2b).

15 Prise out the clip, undo the 3 bolts and

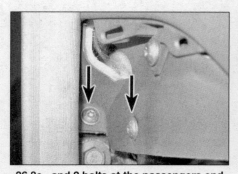

36.8e...and 2 bolts at the passengers end

fold down the panel beneath the facia (see illustration).

16 Unclip the central gateway control unit,

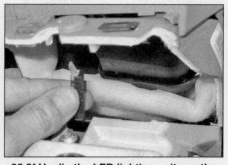

36.8f Unclip the LED lighting units as the facia is withdrawn

and the diagnostic plug, disconnecting any other wiring plugs as the panel is withdrawn (see illustration).

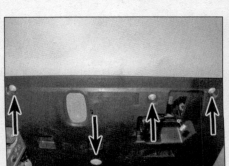

36.15 Drivers lower facia panel bolts/clip

36.16 Unclip the control unit and wiring plugs

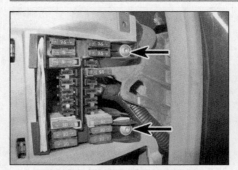

36.19a Undo the fusebox screws

36.19b Remove the screw at the lower, outer edge of the facia panel

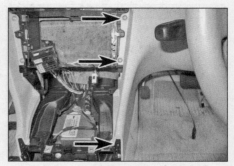

36.19c Undo the screws at the inner edge of the panel

17 Where applicable, unclip and remove the air duct below the drivers side of the facia.

18 On models with 5-speed automatic transmission, remove the EIS (Electronic Ignition Switch) unit as described in Chapter 12 Section 5.

19 Undo the 3 bolts at the outer edge of the facia lower panel, and the 3 bolts at the inner edge **(see illustrations)**.

20 Detach the lower part of the facia panel from the rear footwell air duct.

21 Pull out the handle, undo the screws, pull out the lever, then unhook the parking brake release cable from the operating lever **(see illustrations)**.

22 Unclip the fusebox from the outer end of the facia panel. There's no need to disconnect the wiring plugs.

23 Undo the 2 bolts in the instrument cluster aperture, lower the facia panel, and disconnect any wiring plugs **(see illustration)**.

Passengers side

24 Refer to 'Glovebox removal' as described in Section 34.

Refitting

25 Refitting is a reversal of removal, noting the following points:

a) Ensure that all wiring is correctly routed, and is not trapped as the facia panels are refitted.

b) Reconnect the battery negative lead as described in Chapter 5A Section 4. Ensure no-one is in the car.

c) Upon completion, check that all the electrical components and switches function correctly.

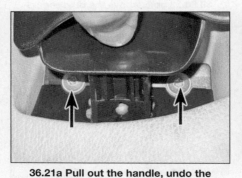

36.21a Pull out the handle, undo the screws...

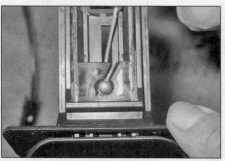

36.21b ...and disconnect the parking brake cable

36.23 Remove the bolt each side of the steering column

Chapter 12
Body electrical systems

Contents

Degrees of difficulty

Easy, suitable for novice with little experience	**Fairly easy,** suitable for beginner with some experience	**Fairly difficult,** suitable for competent DIY mechanic	**Difficult,** suitable for experienced DIY mechanic	**Very difficult,** suitable for expert DIY or professional

Specifications

System type .... 12 volt negative earth

Fuses .... See inside fusebox lid

Bulbs   **Wattage**

Exterior lights:

Direction indicator – Front	21 PY
Directional indicator – Rear	HiP
Direction indicator side repeater	LED
Front foglight	55 H11
Front sidelight	5 capless or LED
Headlight:	
Main beam	55 H7
Dipped beam:	
Halogen	55 H7
Bi-Xenon	35 DS2
High level stop light	LED
Number plate light	5 festoon
Rear fog light	HiP
Reverse	HiP
Stop/tail light	HiP

Interior lights:

Door puddle lights	5 festoon
Glovebox light	5 festoon
Interior lights	5 capless
Luggage compartment lights	5 festoon
Overhead console lights	5 capless
Tailgate lights	5 capless
Vanity lights	5 festoon
Footwell lights	5 festoon

Torque wrench settings

	Nm	lbf ft
Airbag control unit bolts	8	6
Impact sensor bolts:		
Front	8	6
Rear	4	3
Passengers airbag bolts	4	3
Steering wheel airbag screws	8	6
Wiper arm nuts:		
Front wiper arms	19	14
Rear wiper arm	12	9

1 General information and precautions

⚠ *Warning: Before carrying out any work on the electrical system, read through the precautions given in Safety first! at the beginning of this manual and in Chapter 5A Section 1.*

1 The electrical system is of the 12 volt negative-earth type. Power for the lights and all electrical accessories is supplied by a lead-acid or AGM (Absorbent Glass Matt) type battery, which is located in the luggage compartment, and is charged by the alternator.

2 This Chapter covers repair and service procedures for the various electrical components not associated with the engine. Information on the battery, alternator and starter motor can be found in Chapter 5A.

3 It should be noted that prior to working on any component in the electrical system, the battery negative terminal should first be disconnected to prevent the possibility of electrical short-circuits and/or fires.

2 Electrical fault finding – general information

Note: *Refer to the precautions given in Safety first! and in Chapter 5A Section 1 before starting work. The following tests relate to testing of the main electrical circuits, and should not be used to test delicate electronic circuits (such as anti-lock braking systems), particularly where an electronic control unit/module (ECU/ECM) is used.*

General

1 A typical electrical circuit consists of an electrical component; any switches, relays, motors, fuses, fusible links or circuit breakers related to that component, and the wiring and connectors which link the component to both the battery and the chassis. To help to pin-point a problem in an electrical circuit, wiring diagrams are included at the end of this Chapter.

2 Before attempting to diagnose an electrical fault, first study the appropriate wiring diagram to obtain a complete understanding of the components included in the particular circuit concerned. The possible sources of a fault can be narrowed down by noting if other components related to the circuit are operating properly. If several components or circuits fail at one time, the problem is likely to be related to a shared fuse or earth connection.

3 Electrical problems usually stem from simple causes, such as loose or corroded connections, a faulty earth connection, a blown fuse, a melted fusible link, or a faulty relay (refer to Section 3 for details of testing relays). Visually inspect the condition of all fuses, wires and connections in a problem circuit before testing the components. Use the wiring diagrams to determine which terminal connections will need to be checked in order to pin-point the trouble spot.

4 The basic tools required for electrical fault finding include a circuit tester or voltmeter (a 12 volt bulb with a set of test leads can also be used for certain tests); a self-powered test light (sometimes known as a continuity tester); an ohmmeter (to measure resistance); a battery and set of test leads; and a jumper wire, preferably with a circuit breaker or fuse incorporated, which can be used to bypass suspect wires or electrical components. Before attempting to locate a problem with test instruments, use the wiring diagram to determine where to make the connections.

⚠ *Warning: Under no circumstances may live measuring instruments such as ohmmeters, voltmeters or a bulb and test leads be used to test any of the airbag circuitry. Any testing of these components must be left to a Mercedes dealer or specialist, as there is a danger of activating the system if the correct procedures are not followed.*

5 To find the source of an intermittent wiring fault (usually due to a poor or dirty connection, or damaged wiring insulation), a 'wiggle' test can be performed on the wiring. This involves wiggling the wiring by hand to see if the fault occurs as the wiring is moved. It should be possible to narrow down the source of the fault to a particular section of wiring. This method of testing can be used in conjunction with any of the tests described in the following sub-Sections.

6 Apart from problems due to poor connections, two basic types of fault can occur in an electrical circuit – open-circuit, or short-circuit.

7 Open-circuit faults are caused by a break somewhere in the circuit, which prevents current from flowing. An open-circuit fault will prevent a component from working, but will not cause the relevant circuit fuse to blow.

8 Short-circuit faults are caused by a 'short' somewhere in the circuit, which allows the current flowing in the circuit to 'escape' along an alternative route, usually to earth. Short-circuit faults are normally caused by a breakdown in wiring insulation, which allows a feed wire to touch either another wire, or an earthed component such as the bodyshell. A short-circuit fault will normally cause the relevant circuit fuse to blow.

Caution: The E-Class electrical system is extremely complex. Many of the ECMs are connected via a 'Databus' system, where they are able to share information from the various sensors, and communicate with each other. For instance, as the automatic gearbox approaches a gear ratio shift point, it signals the engine management ECM via the Databus. As the gearchange is made by the transmission ECM, the engine management ECM retards the injection timing, momentarily reducing engine output, to ensure a smoother transition from one gear ratio to the next. Due to the design of the Databus system, it is not advisable to backprobe the ECMs with a multimeter, in the traditional manner. Instead, the electrical systems are equipped with a sophisticated self-diagnosis system, which can interrogate the various ECMs to reveal stored fault codes, and help pin-point faults. In order to access the self-diagnosis system, specialist test equipment (Mercedes STAR – or equivalent) is required.

Finding an open-circuit

9 To check for an open-circuit, connect one lead of a circuit tester or voltmeter to either the negative battery terminal or a known good earth.

10 Connect the other lead to a connector in the circuit being tested, preferably nearest to the battery or fuse.

11 Switch on the circuit, bearing in mind that some circuits are live only when the ignition switch is moved to a particular position.

12 If voltage is present (indicated either by the tester bulb lighting or a voltmeter reading, as applicable), this means that the section of the circuit between the relevant connector and the battery is problem-free.

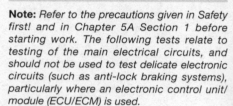

13 Continue to check the remainder of the circuit in the same fashion.

14 When a point is reached at which no voltage is present, the problem must lie between that point and the previous test point with voltage. Most problems can be traced to a broken, corroded or loose connection.

Finding a short-circuit

15 To check for a short-circuit, first disconnect the load(s) from the circuit (loads are the components which draw current from a circuit, such as bulbs, motors, heating elements, etc).

16 Remove the relevant fuse from the circuit, and connect a circuit tester or voltmeter to the fuse connections.

17 Switch on the circuit, bearing in mind that

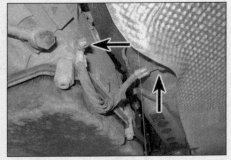

2.20a Earth connections are located in various places, including the transmission/body...

some circuits are live only when the ignition switch is moved to a particular position.

18 If voltage is present (indicated either by the tester bulb lighting or a voltmeter reading, as applicable), this means that there is a short-circuit.

19 If no voltage is present, but the fuse still blows with the load(s) connected, this indicates an internal fault in the load(s).

Finding an earth fault

20 The battery negative terminal is connected to 'earth' – the metal of the engine/transmission and the car body – and most systems are wired so that they only receive a positive feed, the current returning through the metal of the car body **(see illustrations)**. This means that the component mounting and the body form part of that circuit. Loose or corroded mountings can therefore cause a range of electrical faults, ranging from total failure of a circuit, to a puzzling partial fault. In particular, lights may shine dimly (especially when another circuit sharing the same earth point is in operation), motors (eg, wiper motors or the heater fan motor) may run slowly, and the operation of one circuit may have an apparently unrelated effect on another.

21 Note that on many vehicles, earth straps are used between certain components, such as the engine/transmission and the body, usually where there is no metal-to-metal contact between components due to flexible rubber mountings, etc.

22 To check whether a component is

properly earthed, disconnect the battery and connect one lead of an ohmmeter to a known good earth point. Connect the other lead to the wire or earth connection being tested. The resistance reading should be zero; if not, check the connection as follows.

23 If an earth connection is thought to be faulty, dismantle the connection and clean back to bare metal both the bodyshell and the wire terminal or the component earth connection mating surface. Be careful to remove all traces of dirt and corrosion, and then use a knife to trim away any paint, so that a clean metal-to-metal joint is made.

24 On reassembly, tighten the joint fasteners securely; if a wire terminal is being refitted, use serrated washers between the terminal and the bodyshell to ensure a clean and secure connection. When the connection is remade, prevent the onset of corrosion in the future by applying a coat of petroleum jelly or silicone-based grease or by spraying on (at regular intervals) a proprietary ignition sealer or a water-dispersant lubricant.

3 Fuses, relays and SAM control units – general information

Main fuses

1 Most of the fuses are situated in the main fusebox, located under the drivers side of the facia; there is also another fusebox in

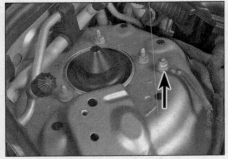

2.20b...left-hand front suspension turret...

2.20c...left-hand side of the luggage compartment...

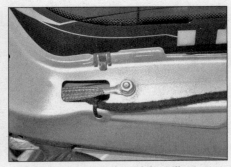

2.20d...upper section of the tailgate...

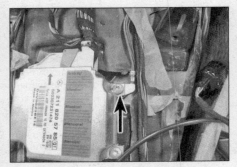

2.20e...SRS control unit mounting bolt...

2.20f...inner right-hand front wing...

2.20g...and left-hand front chassis member

3.1b Luggage compartment fuse box

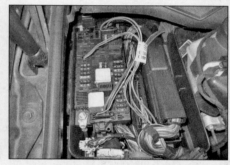

3.1c Engine compartment fusebox

the luggage compartment, and a fuse/relay box in the left-hand corner of the engine compartment **(see illustrations)**. Fusible links (Pre-fuse) are located under the passengers floor panel, and in the luggage compartment.

2 To gain access to the main fuses, carefully prise the end panel from the drivers side of the facia. To access the luggage compartment fuses, unclip the left-hand access panel from luggage compartment **(see illustrations)**.

3 A list of the circuits each fuse protects is given on a diagram sheet inside of the fusebox cover on the drivers end of the facia panel **(see illustration 3.1a)**.

4 To remove a fuse, first switch off the circuit concerned (or the ignition), and then pull the fuse out of its terminals. The wire within the fuse should be visible; if the fuse is blown it will be broken or melted.

5 Always renew a fuse with one of an identical rating; never use a fuse with a different rating from the original or substitute anything else. Never renew a fuse more than once without tracing the source of the trouble. The fuse rating is stamped on top of the fuse; note that the fuses are also colour-coded for easy recognition.

6 If a new fuse blows immediately, find the cause before renewing it again; a short to earth as a result of faulty insulation is most likely. Where a fuse protects more than one circuit, try to isolate the defect by switching on each circuit in turn (if possible) until the fuse blows again. Always carry a supply of spare fuses of each relevant rating on the vehicle; a spare of each rating should be clipped into the base of the fusebox.

Relays

7 The majority of the relays are located in the engine compartment fuse/relay box.

8 In order to access the relays, press the release levers rearwards, and remove the cover from the box located in the left-hand rear corner of the engine compartment **(see illustration)**.

9 If a circuit or system controlled by a relay develops a fault and the relay is suspect, operate the system; if the relay is functioning it should be possible to hear it click as it is energised. If this is the case the fault lies with the components or wiring of the system. If the relay is not being energised then either the relay is not receiving a main supply or a switching voltage or the relay itself is faulty. Testing is by the substitution of a known good unit but be careful; while some relays are identical in appearance and in operation, others look similar but perform different functions.

10 To renew a relay, first ensure that the ignition switch is off. The relay can then simply be pulled out from the socket and the new relay pressed in.

SAM control units

11 A SAM (Signal Acquisition and Actuation Module) functions much as a network router does on a computer or communications network. It monitors input from various switches, controls, monitoring devices, and warning systems. When a switch is activated, the signal goes through a SAM before the device you are controlling responds. If there is a fault with the device you are attempting to operate, there will probable be an error message delivered through the SAM to the CAN (Controller Area Network) databus. The CAN bus will send the error message to the "error screen" on the instrument cluster.

12 SAM units are integrated into the fuse/relay boxes, and are therefore located in the luggage compartment, engine compartment, and beneath the floor panel on the passengers side.

13 No repair or overhaul of the SAM units is possible. If a fault is suspected, have the self-diagnosis system interrogated using Mercedes STAR (or equivalent) diagnostic equipment, using the 16-pin socket located under the drivers side of the facia **(see illustration)**.

3.2a Prise the panel away to access the drivers side fusebox

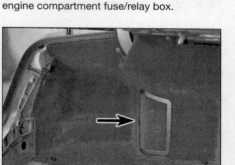

3.2b Unclip the panel to access the luggage compartment fusebox

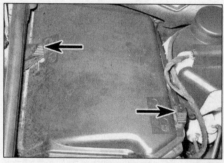

3.8 Move the levers to the 'unlocked' positions

3.13 Unclip the cover to access the diagnostic socket

4 Electrical connectors – general information

1 Most electrical connections on these vehicles are made with multiwire plastic connectors. The mating halves of many connectors are secured with locking clips molded into the plastic connector shells. The mating halves of some large connectors, such as some of those under the instrument panel, are held together by a bolt through the center of the connector.

2 To separate a connector with locking clips, use a small screwdriver to pry the clips apart carefully, then separate the connector halves. Pull only on the shell, never pull on the wiring harness, as you may damage the individual wires and terminals inside the connectors. Look at the connector closely before trying to separate the halves. Often the locking clips are engaged in a way that is not immediately clear. Additionally, many connectors have more than one set of clips.

3 Each pair of connector terminals has a male half and a female half. When you look at the end view of a connector in a diagram, be sure to understand whether the view shows the harness side or the component side of the connector. Connector halves are mirror images of each other, and a terminal shown on the right side end-view of one half will be on the left side end-view of the other half.

4 It is often necessary to take circuit voltage measurements with a connector connected. Whenever possible, carefully insert a small straight pin (not your meter probe) into the rear of the connector shell to contact the terminal inside, then clip your meter lead to the pin. This kind of connection is called "backprobing." When inserting a test probe into a terminal, be careful not to distort the terminal opening. Doing so can lead to a poor connection and corrosion at that terminal later. Using the small straight pin instead of a meter probe results in less chance of deforming the terminal connector. "T" pins are a good choice as temporary meter connections. They allow for a larger surface area to attach the meter leads too.

Electrical connectors

5 Typical electrical connectors:

4.5a Most electrical connectors have a single release tab that you depress to release the connector

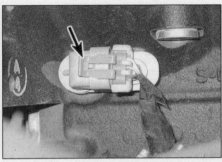

4.5b Some electrical connectors have a retaining tab which must be pried up to free the connector

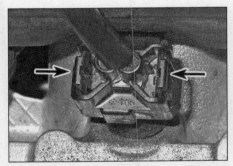

4.5c Some connectors have two release tabs that you must squeeze to release the connector

4.5d Some connectors use wire retainers that you squeeze to release the connector

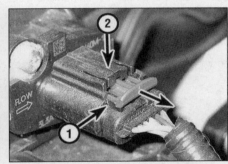

4.5e Critical connectors often employ a sliding lock (1) that you must pull out before you can depress the release tab (2)

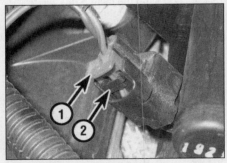

4.5f Here's another sliding-lock style connector, with the lock (1) and the release tab (2) on the side of the connector

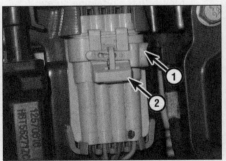

4.5g On some connectors the lock (1) must be pulled out to the side and removed before you can lift the release tab (2)

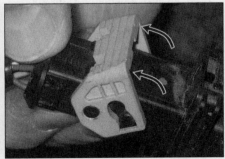

4.5h Some critical connectors, like the multi-pin connectors at the Electronic Control Module employ pivoting locks that must be flipped open

5.2 Unscrew the ESI unit collar

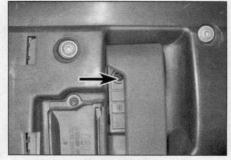

5.4 Undo the bonnet release lever bolt

5.6 Undo the retaining bolts and remove the panel clip

5 Switches –
removal and refitting

Electronic ignition switch control unit

Note: *If a new EIS unit is to be fitted, connect Mercedes STAR diagnostic equipment and transfer the basic data from the EIS to the STAR. Upon completion reverse the process.*

1 Disconnect the battery negative lead as described in Chapter 5A Section 4.

2 Using a pair pliers (or similar) unscrew the collar from around the ESI unit on the facia **(see illustration)**.

3 Remove the accelerator pedal assembly as described in Chapter 4A Section 5.

4 Operate the bonnet release lever, and undo the bolt exposed **(see illustration)**.

5 Unclip the release lever from the facia panel, and detach the release cable from the lever.

6 Undo the 3 retaining bolts, prise out the clip and fold down the facia lower panel, unclip the central gateway control unit and disconnect any wiring plugs **(see illustration)**. Remove the panel.

7 Where applicable, unclip the footwell air duct from under the steering column.

8 Lower the EIS unit from the facia until the wiring plugs etc. are accessible.

9 On models with 5-speed automatic transmission, unclip the selector lever release cable from the EIS unit **(see illustration)**.

10 Disconnect the wiring plugs and manoeuvre the EIS unit from place.

11 Refitting is a reversal of removal.

Steering column combination switch

12 Remove the steering wheel as described in Chapter 10 Section 21.

13 Undo the retaining screw and slide the steering column switch module from place **(see illustrations)**. Disconnect the wiring plugs as the module is withdrawn.

Vehicles upto 2004 model year

14 With reference to Section 20, remove the airbag rotary contact unit.

15 Undo the screw and pull the steering angle sensor from the switch assembly **(see illustrations)**.

16 Slide the cruise control switch from the column **(see illustration)**.

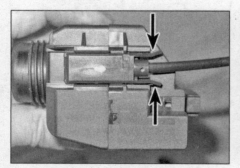

5.9 Squeeze together the tabs and disconnect the release cable

5.13a Undo the retaining screw...

5.13b...and slide the switch module from the column

5.15a Undo the screw...

5.15b...and remove the steering angle sensor

5.16 Remove the cruise control switch

5.17 Combination switch retaining screws

5.19 Module trim retaining screws

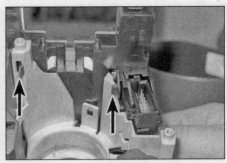

5.21 Release the steering angle sensor clips

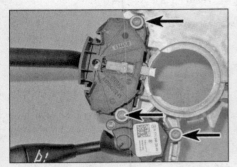

5.22 Column adjustment/combination switch retaining screws

5.25 Prise the decorative trim strip rearwards from the facia

26 Undo the retaining bolt, then working at the lower edge, carefully prise the lighting control switch upwards and out from the facia **(see illustrations)**. Disconnect the wiring plugs as the switch unit is withdrawn.
27 Refitting is a reversal of removal.

Door contact switch

28 Insert a thin, flat-bladed screwdriver through the aperture at the top of the switch, depress the clip and ease the switch from the pillar **(see illustration)**.
29 Disconnect the wiring plug from the switch.
30 Refitting is a reversal of removal.

Facia switches

Upper control panel (Hazard warning/ ESP/heated seats/central locking switch assembly)

Note: *If a new upper control panel is to be fitted, stored data from the panel must be transferred to Mercedes STAR diagnostic equipment (or equivalent), then reloaded to the panel upon completion.*

31 Move the gear change/selector lever fully rearwards.
32 Open the ashtray, and pull up the front edge of the gear change/selector lever surround panel upwards.
33 Release the clip each side, reach

17 Undo the 3 retaining screws and withdraw the combination switch **(see illustration)**.
18 Refitting is a reversal of removal.

Vehicles from 2004 model year

19 Undo the screws and slide the module trim from place **(see illustration)**.
20 With reference to Section 20, undo the screws and detach the airbag rotary contact unit from the module.
21 Undo the retaining screw (where fitted), release the clips and detach the steering angle sensor from the module **(see illustration)**. If the centre position of the sensor is lost during removal, gently rotate the inner race of the sensor anti-clockwise to the stop, then rotate it clockwise approximately 2 turns

until the arrows on the sensor and inner race align.
22 If required, detach the steering column adjustment/wheel heater switch assembly from the combination switch (where applicable) **(see illustration)**.
23 Undo the 2 screws and detach the combination switch from the carrier plate.
24 Refitting is a reversal of removal.

Lighting control switch

25 Using a blunt, flat-bladed tool, carefully prise the decorative trim strip from the drivers side of the facia **(see illustration)**. Use a piece of cardboard to protect the facia.

5.26a Undo the bolt...

5.26b ...and prise the lighting control switch from place

5.28 Depress the contact switch clip with a small screwdriver

5.33 Release the clips and pull the ashtray upwards

5.34 Upper control panel retaining bolts

5.44 Pull up the front edge of the lever surround panel

underneath and pull the front ashtray from the facia **(see illustration)**. Unclip the 'Keyless Go' unit (where applicable) and disconnect any wiring plugs as the ashtray is withdrawn.

Vehicles up to 06/08

34 Undo the 2 retaining bolts at the lower edge of the control panel **(see illustration)**.
35 Pull the control panel and bracket assembly rearwards, until the wiring plugs become accessible. Note their fitted positions, and disconnect the various wiring plugs.
36 If required, undo the 2 retaining bolts and detach the control panel from the bracket, then undo the 3 retaining screws and detach the cover from the panel.
37 Refitting is a reversal of removal.

Vehicles from 06/08

38 Unclip the wiring/optic plugs from the bracket under the control panel.

5.45 Rotate the gaiter locking collar anti-clockwise

39 Undo the bolts on the underside, then pull the Kinematics stowage compartment/ CD changer rearwards until the wiring plugs/ fibre optic connectors become accessible. Disconnect the wiring plugs/connectors, and remove the stowage compartment/CD changer.
40 Open the stowage compartment/CD changer flap completely, then undo the 4 retaining bolts (2 at the upper edge, 2 at the lower edge) and remove the bezel from the panel.
41 Disconnect the wiring plugs and remove the control panel.
42 Refitting is a reversal of removal.

Heating/air conditioning switches

43 The heating/air conditioning switches are integral with the control panel. Removal of the control panel is described in Chapter 3 Section 8.

Centre console switches

44 Open the ashtray at the front of the console, and starting at the front edge, pull up the gearchange/selector lever surround panel **(see illustration)**. Disconnect any wiring plugs as the panel is lifted.
45 Rotate the gearchange/selector lever gaiter locking collar anti-clockwise **(see illustration)**, then pull up the gear knob and remove the surround panel and gaiter.
46 Invert the surround panel, undo the screws and remove the relevant switch assembly **(see illustration)**.

47 Refitting is a reversal of removal.

Stop light switch

48 Removal of the stop light switch is described in Chapter 9 Section 18.

Steering wheel switches

49 Remove the drivers airbag as described in Section 20.
50 The gearchange buttons simply prise from place **(see illustration)**. Disconnect the wiring plug as the button(s) are withdrawn.
51 The switches on the airbag unit are secured by 2 screws each **(see illustration)**. Disconnect the wiring plug as the switch is withdrawn.
52 Refitting is a reversal of removal.

Parking brake-on warning switch

53 Removal of the switch is described in Chapter 9 Section 18.

Oil pressure warning switch

54 Removal of the switch is described in Chapter 2A Section 17, or Chapter 2B Section 16 as applicable.

Door panel switches

55 Remove the door inner trim panel as described in Chapter 11 Section 17.
56 Carefully pull away the door insulation material from the panel.
57 Disconnect the wiring plug, undo the

5.46 Console rear switch panel retaining screws

5.50 Prise the gearchange buttons from the steering wheel

5.51 Airbag switch retaining screws

5.57a Undo the nuts and remove the door panel switch assembly

5.57b The window switch assembly is secured by 1 screw

5.59 Prise the speaker cover from the panel

retaining screw/nuts and detach the relevant switch assembly from the trim panel **(see illustrations)**.

58 Refitting is a reversal of removal.

Boot lid/tailgate switch

59 Carefully prise the lower speaker cover from the door trim panel **(see illustration)**.

60 Disconnect the wiring plug, undo the screw and detach the switch from the speaker cover **(see illustration)**.

61 Refitting is a reversal of removal.

Overhead console switches

62 Remove the interior mirror as described in Chapter 11 Section 28.

63 Disconnect the wiring plugs from the overhead console.

64 Release the retaining clips and detach the switch assembly from the console.

65 Refitting is a reversal of removal.

6 Bulbs (exterior lights) – renewal

General

1 Whenever a bulb is renewed, note the following points:

a) *Disconnect the battery negative lead as described in Chapter 5A Section 4 before starting work.*

b) *Remember that if the light has just been in use, the bulb may be extremely hot.*

5.60 Boot lid/tailgate release switch retaining screw

c) *Always check the bulb contacts and holder, ensuring that there is clean metal-to-metal contact between the bulb and the socket contacts. Clean off any corrosion or dirt before fitting a new bulb.*

d) *Wherever bayonet-type bulbs are fitted, ensure that the live contact(s) bear firmly against the bulb contact.*

e) *Always ensure that the new bulb is of the correct rating and that it is completely clean before fitting it; this applies particularly to headlight/foglight bulbs (see below).*

f) *With quartz halogen bulbs (headlights and similar applications), use a tissue or clean cloth when handling the bulb; do not touch the bulb glass with the fingers. Even small quantities of grease from the fingers will cause blackening and premature failure. If a bulb is accidentally touched, clean it with methylated spirit and a clean rag.*

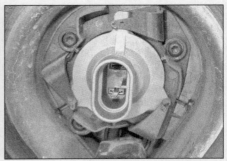

6.2 Rotate the bulbholder anti-clockwise

Headlight

Main beam

2 Rotate the bulbholder anti-clockwise and pull it from the reflector **(see illustration)**.

3 Pull the bulb from the holder **(see illustration)**. Take care not to touch the glass with your fingers.

4 Refitting is a reversal of removal. Note that the bulb will only fit correctly in one position.

Dipped beam

Halogen bulb

5 Rotate the cover on the rear of the headlight anti-clockwise and remove it **(see illustration)**.

6 Rotate the bulbholder anti-clockwise and pull it from the headlight **(see illustration)**.

7 Pull the bulb from the holder. Take care not to touch the glass with your fingers.

8 Refitting is a reversal of removal.

6.3 Pull the bulb from the holder

6.5 Rotate the cover anti-clockwise

6.6 Rotate the bulbholder anti-clockwise and pull it from the reflector

6.10 Rotate the cover anti-clockwise

Bi-Xenon High-intensity discharge bulb

Caution: Bi-Xenon bulbs are pressurised to approximately 22 bar. Take extreme care when handling these bulbs – wear safety glasses and gloves.

9 Due to the high-voltages required to produce the electric arc between the bulbs electrodes, disconnect the battery as described in Chapter 5A Section 4, then wait at least 10 minutes for any residual electrical energy to dissipate.

10 Rotate the cover behind the dipped beam location anti-clockwise and remove it **(see illustration)**.

Vehicles upto 06/06

11 Rotate the ignition unit anti-clockwise and remove it from the rear of the bulb **(see illustration)**. Note that the electrical connector will automatically disconnect as the unit is withdrawn.

6.17 Rotate the side light bulbholder anti-clockwise, pull it from the reflector...

6.20 Reach behind the headlight and twist the directional indicator bulbholder anti-clockwise

6.11 The wiring plug will disconnect as the ignition unit is rotated

12 Release the retaining springs and manoeuvre the Xenon bulb from place **(see illustration)**. Take care not to touch the bulb with bare fingers.

13 Refitting is a reversal of removal.

Vehicles from 06/06

14 On these vehicles, the Xenon ignition unit is integral with the bulb. Disconnect the wiring plug from the unit.

15 Rotate the ignition unit anti-clockwise and carefully manoeuvre it from the headlight. Take care not to touch the bulb with bare fingers.

16 Refitting is a reversal of removal. If a new unit/bulb has been fitted, the systems operating counter must be reset to zero using Mercedes STAR diagnostic equipment (or equivalent). Entrust this task to a Mercedes dealer or suitably equipped specialist.

Front side lights

Note: On models with Bi-Xenon HID dipped

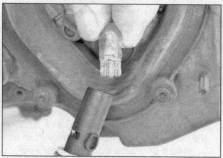

6.18...then pull the bulb from the holder

6.21 Press-in the bulb and rotate it anti-clockwise

6.12 Release the springs and remove the Xenon bulb

beam headlights, the traditional side light bulbs have been replaced by LED units, which are designed to last the lifetime of the vehicle. If the light should fail, the complete headlight may need to be replaced. Consult a Mercedes dealer or parts specialist.

17 Rotate the bulbholder anti-clockwise and pull it from the rear of the headlight **(see illustration)**.

18 Pull the capless bulb from the holder **(see illustration)**.

19 Refitting is a reversal of removal.

Front directional indicator

20 Rotate the bulbholder anti-clockwise and pull it from the rear of the headlight **(see illustration)**. Access is limited.

21 Press the bulb into the holder slightly, rotate it anti-clockwise and pull it from the holder **(see illustration)**.

22 Refitting is a reversal of removal. Note that the bulb bayonet pins are offset – the bulb will only fit correctly in one position.

Side repeater

23 On all models, the side repeaters are LEDs, designed to last the lifetime of the vehicle. Should the unit fail, replace the side repeater as described in Section 8.

Front foglight

24 Raise the front of the vehicle and support it securely on axle stands (see *'Vehicle jacking and support'*). Undo the fasteners and open the access flaps in the engine undershield **(see illustration)**.

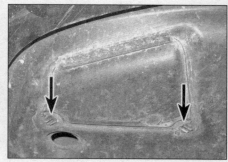

6.24 Rotate the fasteners and open the flap

6.25 Rotate the front foglight bulbholder anti-clockwise

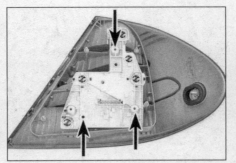

6.31 Rear bulbholder/carrier retaining screws

6.34 Undo the screws and remove the number plate light

25 Disconnect the wiring plug, rotate the bulbholder anti-clockwise and remove it from the rear of the fog light **(see illustration)**.
26 Note that the bulb is integral with the holder.
27 Refitting is a reversal of removal.

Rear light assembly

28 The rear fog lamp, tail light, brake light, directional indicator and reversing lights are either LEDs or HiP bulbs (High internal Pressure). Should a fault develop the complete bulb holder assembly must be renewed.
29 Remove the rear light assembly as described in Section 8.

30 Remove the rubber seal around the light assembly.
31 Undo the screws and detach the bulb holder/lamp carrier from the light **(see illustration)**. Disconnect any wiring plugs as the unit is withdrawn.
Caution: The HiP bulbs are highly pressurised. Take care not to damage them by rough handling. It would be prudent to wear safety glasses and gloves.
32 Refitting is a reversal of removal.

High level stop light

33 The high-level stop light is illuminated by

LEDs. If faulty, the complete assembly must be renewed as described in Section 8.

Number plate light

34 Undo the retaining screws, and prise the light from the tailgate/boot lid **(see illustration)**.
35 Carefully prise the festoon bulb from the lens **(see illustration)**.
36 Refitting is a reversal of removal.

7 Interior lights – general information, removal and refitting

General information

1 Illumination of some of the interior lights is provided by LED's. Consequently, should a fault develop the complete assembly may need to be renewed. Consult a Mercedes dealer or parts specialist.

Front overhead console lights

2 Remove the front overhead console as described in Section 5, then rotate the bulbholder anti-clockwise, pull it from place, then pull the capless bulb from the holder **(see illustrations)**.
3 Prise the interior mirror light lens from place, then pull out the capless bulb **(see illustration)**.

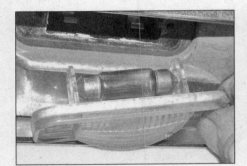

6.35 Remove the festoon bulb

7.2a Rotate the bulbholder(s) anti-clockwise...

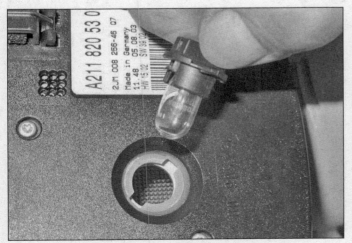

7.2b...and pull the capless bulb from the holder

7.3 Prise the mirror light lens from place

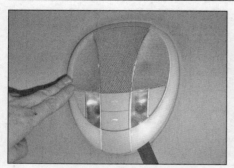

7.4a Prise the rear overhead light console from place

7.4b Rear overhead console bulbholders

7.5 Prise the vanity light unit from the headlining

7.6 Prise the luggage compartment light from the trim panel

7.9 Rotate the D-pillar light bulbholder anti-clockwise

Rear overhead light console

4 Using a blunt, flat-bladed tool, carefully prise the rear overhead light console from the headlining, the rotate the bulbholder(s) anti-clockwise, remove the bulbholder, and pull the capless bulb from the holder (see illustrations).

Vanity lights

5 Carefully prise the vanity light unit from the headlining, then pull the festoon bulb from the contacts (see illustration).

Luggage compartment light

6 Carefully prise the light unit from the trim panel (see illustration). Disconnect the wiring plug as the light unit is withdrawn, then remove the festoon bulb.
7 Refitting is a reversal of removal.

Glovebox light

8 Open the glovebox, slide out the shelf (where fitted), then prise out the light unit and remove the festoon bulb.

D-pillar lights (Estate models)

9 Carefully prise the light unit from the pillar trim panel (see illustration). Rotate the bulbholder anti-clockwise, and pull the capless bulb from place.
10 Refitting is a reversal of removal.

Door puddle lights

11 Use a flat-bladed screwdriver to prise the light unit from the base of the door trim panel (see illustration).
12 Pull the festoon light bulb from the contacts.
13 Refitting is a reversal of removal.

Tailgate light

14 Carefully prise the light unit from the tailgate trim panel (see illustration). Pull the capless bulb from the contacts.
15 Refitting is a removal of refitting.

| 8 | Exterior light units – removal and refitting | |

Headlight

1 Remove the front bumper as described in Chapter 11 Section 16.

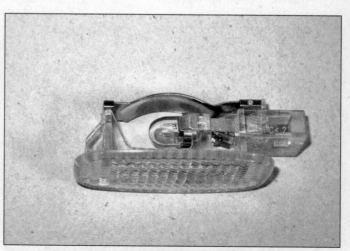

7.11 Prise the puddle light from the door panel

7.14 Pull out the capless bulb

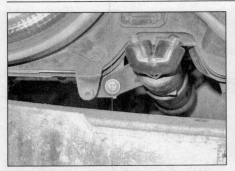

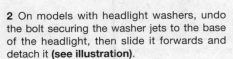

8.2 Undo the screw securing the headlight washer jet

8.3a Headlight retaining bolts

8.3b The outer headlight retaining bolt is accessed from the rear

2 On models with headlight washers, undo the bolt securing the washer jets to the base of the headlight, then slide it forwards and detach it **(see illustration)**.

3 Undo the bolts and manoeuvre the headlight forwards from position **(see illustrations)**. Disconnect the wiring plugs as the headlight is withdrawn, then rotate the directional indicator bulbholder anti-clockwise and detach it from the rear of the headlight.

4 Refitting is a reversal of removal. If necessary, have the headlight alignment checked at the earliest opportunity.

Side repeater light

5 Remove the exterior mirror cover as described in Chapter 11 Section 27.

6 Undo the retaining screws and detach the side repeater from the cover **(see illustration)**.

7 Refitting is a reversal of removal.

Tail light

Saloon

8 Remove the luggage compartment lights as described in Section 7.

9 Prise up the centre pins, lever out the plastic expansion rivets, and remove the boot sill trim panel **(see illustration)**.

10 Remove the plastic expansion rivets, unclip the hinge aperture frame and pull the rear of the luggage compartment side trim panel away to access the tail lights.

11 Where applicable, move the dynamic seat control pneumatic pump and bracket to one side.

12 Disconnect the wiring plug, undo the 5 retaining nuts and manoeuvre the tail light from place **(see illustration)**.

13 Refitting is a reversal of removal.

8.6 Side repeater retaining screws

Estate

Tailgate lights

14 Remove the tailgate lower trim panel as described in Chapter 11 Section 34.

15 Disconnect the tail light wiring plug.

16 Undo the nut, remove the retaining bracket and detach the tail light from the tailgate **(see illustration)**.

17 Refitting is a reversal of removal. Ensure the outer lugs engage correctly with the tailgate.

8.9 Remove the expansion rivets securing the boot sill trim panel

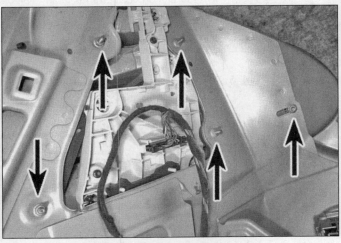

8.12 Saloon rear light retaining nuts

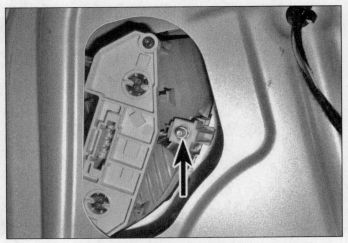

8.16 Tailgate light retaining nut

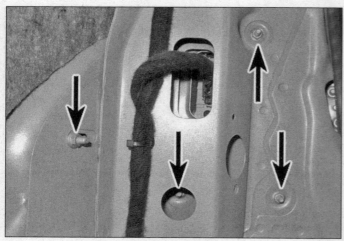

8.21a Undo the retaining nuts...

8.21b...and remove the body-mounted light assembly

Body mounted lights

18 Remove the rear section of the luggage compartment side trim panel as described in Chapter 11 Section 34.

19 Where applicable, move the bass speaker module on the right-hand side to access the tail lights.

20 Where applicable, move the dynamic seat pneumatic pump and bracket to one side to access the left-hand tail lights.

21 Undo the 4 retaining nuts, manoeuvre the tail light assembly rearwards, and disconnect the wiring plugs as they become accessible **(see illustrations)**.

22 Refitting is a reversal of removal.

8.24 Slide the catches apart and remove the cover

8.28c Prise the spoiler away to release the retaining clips

High-level brake light
Saloon

23 Remove the boot lid trim panel as described in Chapter 11 Section 34.

24 Slide the catches apart, and remove the cover from the high-level brake light **(see illustration)**. Disconnect the wiring plug as the cover is withdrawn.

25 If required, unclip the light lens from the boot lid.

26 Refitting is a reversal of removal.

Estate

27 Remove the tailgate upper trim panel as described in Chapter 11 Section 34.

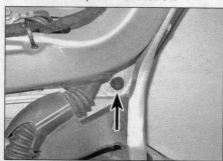

8.28a The spoiler is secured by 3 nuts – 1 at each end, and 1 in the centre

Models up to 06/06

28 Disconnect the washer hose, then undo the nuts and prise the rear spoiler from the tailgate **(see illustrations)**. Disconnect the wiring plug as the spoiler is removed.

29 Undo the retaining bolts and detach the high-level brake light from the spoiler **(see illustration)**.

30 Refitting is a reversal of removal.

Models from 06/06

31 Disconnect the wiring plug, and the washer hose, undo the 3 retaining nuts, then pull the spoiler from the tailgate to release the retaining clips.

32 Undo the 2 retaining bolts, and starting at the outer edges, detach the seal from the spoiler.

33 Release the clips and detach the high-level brake light from the spoiler.

34 Refitting is a reversal of removal.

Front fog light

35 Raise the front of the vehicle and support it securely on axle stands (see *'Vehicle jacking and support'*). Undo the fasteners and remove the front section of the engine undershield.

36 Disconnect the wiring plug from the rear of the fog light.

8.29 High-level brake light retaining screws

8.28b Open the clip and disconnect the washer hose

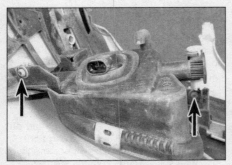

8.37 Front fog light retaining screws – models upto 06/06

8.38a Access to the fog light adjustment screw is through a hole in the trim panel on some models...

8.38b...or from the rear on other models

37 Undo the screws and manoeuvre the fog light from place **(see illustration)**.
38 Refitting is a reversal of removal. Note that if required, the fog light aim can be adjusted by rotating the screw at the front, inner, top corner of the light unit, or on some models, the adjusting screw is access from behind, via the access flap beneath **(see illustrations)**.

the top of the headlight unit **(see illustration)**. There would appear to be only one adjustment screw – check on the UK models
3 All models have an electrically-operated headlight beam adjustment system which is controlled through the switch in the facia. On these models ensure that the switch is set to the off position before adjusting the headlight aim.

1 Move the drivers seat fully rearwards, and to its lowest position.
2 Disconnect the battery negative lead as described in Chapter 5A Section 4.
3 Insert fingers into the gap between the instrument panel and the surround trim, then gently pull the trim rearwards to release the retaining clips **(see illustration)**. Take care as the clips are easily damaged.
4 Undo the 4 retaining bolts, and manoeuvre the instrument panel/cluster rearwards until the wiring plugs are accessible **(see illustration)**. Disconnect the wiring plugs, and remove the panel/cluster.
5 Refitting is a reversal of removal.

9 Headlight beam adjustment – general information

1 Accurate adjustment of the headlight beam is only possible using optical beam setting equipment and this work should therefore be carried out by a Mercedes dealer or suitably-equipped workshop.
2 For reference, the headlights can be adjusted by rotating the adjuster screw on

10 Instrument panel – removal and refitting

Removal

Note: *If a new instrument panel/cluster is to be fitted, the stored data must be transferred to Mercedes STAR diagnostic equipment (or equivalent), then reloaded to the new panel/cluster upon completion.*

Refitting

6 Refitting is a reversal of removal. If the panel has been renewed, it will need to be configured using Mercedes diagnostic equipment (or equivalent).

11 Rain sensor – removal and refitting

Removal

1 Carefully unclip the cover from in front of the interior mirror base **(see illustration)**.
2 Disconnect the sensor wiring plug.
3 Carefully unclip the rain/light sensor **(see illustration)**. Take care as the clips are easily damaged. Note that the sensor lens is fixed to the windscreen – no attempt must be made to remove it.

9.2 Headlight beam adjustment screw

10.3 Pull the surround trim rearwards

10.4 Instrument panel/cluster retaining bolts

11.1 Unclip the mirror base cover

11.3 Rain sensor

12.1 Undo the bolt and remove the horn

Refitting

4 Refitting is a reversal of removal. If a new sensor has been fitted, it must be configured using Mercedes STAR diagnostic equipment or equivalent.

12 Horns – removal and refitting

Removal

1 Open the bonnet, undo the retaining bolt and remove the right-hand horn **(see illustration)**. Disconnect the wiring plugs as the horn is withdrawn.

2 Undo the fasteners and pull back the front section of the left-hand front wheelarch liner. To improve access, remove the front wheel.

13.4 Undo the wiper spindle nut

14.3 Multi-function sensor unit

13.2 Depress the catch and fully open the bonnet

3 Undo the retaining bolt and remove the left-hand horn. Disconnect the wiring plugs as the horn is withdrawn.

Refitting

4 Refitting is a reversal of removal. If the front road wheel has been removed, tighten the bolt to the specified torque.

13 Wiper arm – removal and refitting

Removal

Front wiper arms

1 With the wipers in the 'at rest' position, switch off the ignition switch, and remove the key. On models with 'Keyless Go' system

13.6 Lift up the cover and undo the spindle nut

14.4a Pull up the rubber seal...

move the transmitter out of range of the vehicle.

2 Open the bonnet and raise it to the vertical position. This is achieved by opening the bonnet to the normal position, then depressing the catch on each hinge and lift the bonnet to the vertical position **(see illustration)**.

3 Mark the position of the wipers arm on the windscreen using a strip of insulating tape.

4 Undo the drivers side spindle nut and pull the arm from the spindle **(see illustration)**.

5 Undo the passengers side wiper arm linkage nuts, then pull the arms from the spindles.

Tailgate wiper arm

6 With the tailgate wiper in the 'at rest' position, prise open the spindle cover and undo the arm retaining nut **(see illustration)**.

7 Pull the wiper arm from the spindle. If necessary use a suitable puller to release the wiper arm.

Refitting

8 Refit the wiper arms to the spindles, aligning the blades to the marks/tape on the windscreen. Tighten the retaining nuts to the specified torque.

14 Windscreen wiper motor and linkage – removal and refitting

Removal

Front wiper motor

1 Remove the front wiper arms as described in Section 13.

2 Open the bonnet and raise it to the vertical position. This is achieved by opening the bonnet to the normal position, then depressing the catch on each hinge and lift the bonnet to the vertical position **(see illustration 13.2)**.

3 Where applicable (models with Convenience auto air conditioning), disconnect the wiring plug, undo the 3 retaining bolts and remove the multi-function sensor from the scuttle trim panel **(see illustration)**.

4 Pull up the rubber seal at the front edge of the scuttle trim panel, and remove the rubber grommets around the wiper spindles **(see illustrations)**.

14.4b...and prise out the wiper spindle grommets

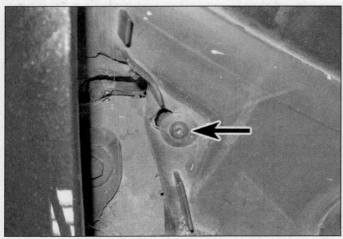

14.6 Remove the plastic expansion rivets at each end, and in the centre of the scuttle trim panel

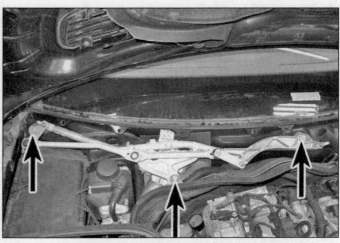

14.7 Wiper motor linkage retaining nuts/bolt

5 Unclip the washer hose from the scuttle trim panel.
6 Unscrew the centre pins, lever out the plastic expansion rivets, and pull the scuttle trim panel upwards from place **(see illustration)**. Disconnect the drain hose from the panel as it's withdrawn.
7 Undo the retaining nuts/bolt, and manoeuvre the wiper linkage/motor from place **(see illustration)**. Disconnect the wiring plug as the assembly is withdrawn
8 If required, prise the linkage arms from the motor arm, then note its fitted position, undo the nut and detach the arm from the motor **(see illustration)**.
9 Undo the bolts and detach the motor from the linkage.

Rear wiper motor
10 Remove the rear wiper arm as described in Section 13.
11 Remove the tailgate lower trim panel as described in Chapter 11 Section 34.
12 Disconnect the wiper motor wiring plug.
13 Undo the 3 bolts and remove the rear wiper motor **(see illustration)**.

Refitting
14 Refitting is a reversal of removal.

15 Windscreen/tailgate washer system components – removal and refitting

Washer reservoir
Removal
Main reservoir

1 As this procedure involves detaching coolant pipes, wait until the engine is cold before starting.
2 Remove the pollen filter as described in Chapter 1 Section 19.
3 Remove the plastic expansion rivet securing the screenwash reservoir filler neck to the inner wing **(see illustration)**.
4 Using a flat-bladed screwdriver, prise the plastic plate around the hoses from the inner wing **(see illustration)**.
5 Pull the filler neck from the fluid reservoir. Renew the seal.
6 Apply clamps to the fluid reservoir heater coolant hoses, then disconnect the hoses **(see illustration)**. Be prepared for fluid spillage.

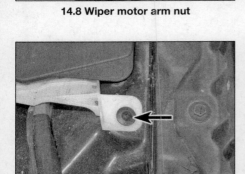

14.8 Wiper motor arm nut

14.13 Rear wiper motor retaining bolts

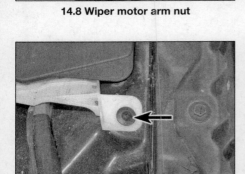

15.3 Remove the filler neck rivet

15.4 Prise away the plastic plate around the hoses

15.6 Apply clamps to the reservoir heater hoses

15.9 Disconnect the wiring and hoses

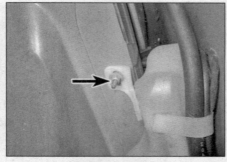

15.10 Reservoir retaining nut

15.12 Additional reservoir retaining nut

7 Slacken the front right-hand roadwheel bolts, raise the front of the vehicle and support it securely on axle stands (see *'Vehicle jacking and support'*). Remove the roadwheel.

8 Release the fasteners and release the rear section of the right-hand wheelach liner.

9 Note their fitted positions, then disconnect the wiring plugs and hoses from the fluid reservoir **(see illustration)**. Be prepared for fluid spillage.

10 Undo the retaining nut and manoeuvre the reservoir from place **(see illustration)**.

Additional reservoir

11 Remove the main reservoir filler neck as previously described in this Section.

12 Unclip/disconnect the hoses from the additional reservoir, then undo the retaining

nut and manoeuvre the reservoir from place **(see illustration)**.

Refitting

13 Refitting is a reversal of removal.

Windscreen and headlight washer pumps – removal and refitting

Removal

14 One pump provides fluid to the front and rear windscreens, and another pump supplies fluid to the headlight washers (where fitted). Begin by removing the right-hand front roadwheel and wheelarch liner as described earlier in this Section.

15 Note their fitted positions, then

disconnect the wiring plug and hoses from the relevant pump. The innermost pump is for the headlight washers, and the outermost for the windscreens.

16 Pull the relevant pump from the fluid reservoir. Be prepared for fluid spillage. Examine the rubber sealing grommet, and renew if necessary.

Refitting

17 Refitting is a reversal of removal.

Jets

Windscreen jets

18 Open the bonnet, fold back the insulation material, and remove the cover beneath the jet locations **(see illustrations)**.

19 Disconnect the wiring plug and hose from the relevant jet **(see illustration)**.

20 Release the clip each side and remove the jet **(see illustration)**.

21 Refitting is a reversal of removal. If necessary, the aim of the washer jets can be adjusted using a pin.

Tailgate screen jet

22 Remove the rear spoiler as described in Section 8.

23 Unclip the jet from the spoiler **(see illustration)**.

24 Refitting is a reversal of removal.

15.18a Fold back the insulation material

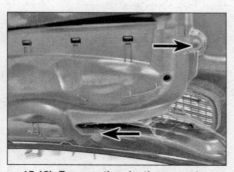

15.18b Remove the plastic expansion rivets each side of the cover

15.19 Disconnect the wiring plug and hose

15.20 Release the clip each side

15.23 Release the jet retaining clip(s)

16.3 Undo the screws to the 'stop'

16.19 The radio antenna amplifier is located on the upper section of the tailgate

17.15 Rotate the speaker anti-clockwise to remove it

16 Infotainment units – removal and refitting

Caution: Do not bend the fibre optic cables at a radius of sharper than 25 mm.

Facia Radio/Audio/display unit

Note: If a new radio/audio/display unit is to be fitted, the basic data must be transferred to Mercedes STAR diagnostic equipment, then loaded into the new radio/audio unit upon completion.

1 Remove the heater control panel as described in Chapter 3 Section 8.
2 Remove the upper control panel as described in Section 5.
3 Working on the underside of the radio/audio/display unit, undo the screw each side to the 'stop' (see illustration).
4 Manoeuvre the radio/audio/display unit rearwards from the facia, and disconnect the various wiring plugs/fibre optic cables as they become accessible.
5 Refitting is a reversal of removal.

CD changer

6 Move the gear change/selector lever to the rearmost position, then open the front ashtray and pull up the front edge of the gear change/selector lever surround panel upwards (see illustration 5.44).
7 Pull the ashtray rearwards, and disconnect the wiring plugs. Where applicable, unclip the 'Keyless Go' control unit from the ashtray.
8 Unclip the wiring and fibre optic cables from the bracket on the underside of the CD changer.
9 Undo the bolt each side at the underside of the CD changer.
10 Manoeuvre the CD changer rearwards from the facia. Disconnect the various wiring plugs/fibre optic cables from the unit as they become accessible.
11 Refitting is a reversal of removal.

Antenna amplifier module

Saloon models

12 Remove the left hand C-pillar trim panel as described in Chapter 11 Section 34.

13 Disconnect the wiring plugs, undo the retaining nuts and remove the amplifier. Release any wiring harness retaining clips as necessary.
14 Refitting is a reversal of removal.

Estate models

Antenna amplifier

15 The antenna amplifier may be fitted behind the left-, or right-hand D-pillar trim panel, depending on vehicle specification. Remove the relevant D-pillar trim panel as described in Chapter 11 Section 34.
16 Undo the retaining nut, disconnect the wiring plug and remove the amplifier.
17 Refitting is a reversal of removal.

Radio antenna amplifier

Note: This procedure applies only to vehicles with Mercedes 50 APS radio, or COMAND system.

18 Remove the tailgate upper trim panel as described in Chapter 11 Section 34.
19 Undo the retaining nut, disconnect the wiring plug and remove the amplifier from the upper section of the tailgate (see illustration).
20 Refitting is a reversal of removal.

Antennas/aerials

21 All antennas/aerials are integrated into the rear screen, and cannot be renewed separately.

17 Speakers and amplifiers – removal and refitting

Note: The following procedure descriptions apply to various vehicle specification levels. Therefore, the actual fitment of components will vary greatly.
Caution: Do not bend the fibre optic cables at a radius of sharper than 25 mm.

Bass speaker amplifier – Saloon models

1 Remove the left-hand side luggage compartment trim panel as described in Chapter 11 Section 34.
2 Disconnect the wiring plug, undo the 3 retaining nuts and remove the amplifier.
3 Refitting is a reversal of removal.

Bass speaker module – Estate models

4 Remove the right-hand side rear section of the luggage compartment side trim panel as described in Chapter 11 Section 34.
5 Disconnect the wiring plug, undo the 4 retaining nuts and remove the bass speaker module.
6 Refitting is a reversal of removal.

Speaker amplifier control unit

7 Remove the left-hand side luggage compartment trim panel as described in Chapter 11 Section 34.
8 Fold back the insulation material to access the control unit.
9 Release the locking clamp, disconnect the wiring plug, followed by the fibre optic cable.
10 Undo the 4 retaining nuts and remove control unit.
11 Refitting is a reversal of removal.

Footwell speaker

12 The speakers are located in the front footwells, in front of the centre console. Using a blunt-, flat-bladed tool, carefully prise the speaker from the trim panel. Disconnect the wiring plug as it becomes accessible.
13 Refitting is a reversal of removal.

Door speakers

Main speakers

14 Remove the front door trim panel and weathershield as described in Chapter 11 Section 17. Note that it's only necessary to release the weathershield in the area of the speaker.
15 Disconnect the wiring plug, prise out the clips, rotate the speaker anti-clockwise and remove it (see illustration).

Tweeters

Front door

16 Carefully prise the mirror mounting triangular trim from the door. Disconnect the wiring plug as the trim panel is withdrawn.
17 Detach the tweeter from the trim.

Rear door

18 Carefully prise the speaker trim cover from the lower section of the door trim panel. Disconnect any wiring plugs as the cover is withdrawn.

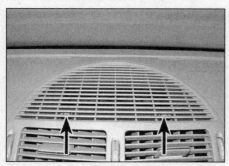

17.20 Release the clip each side and prise up the speaker grille

19 Release the clips and detach the tweeter from the speaker trim cover.

Facia speaker

Vehicles up to 06/04

20 Using a thin screwdriver, release the clip each side at the lower edge of the facia speaker grille (see illustration).

Vehicles from 06/04

21 Starting at the front, outer-edges, carefully prise the speaker grille from the facia using a blunt, flat-bladed tool (see illustration).

All vehicles

22 Undo the 2 retaining screws, and lift the speaker from the facia (see illustration). Disconnect the wiring plug as it becomes accessible.

23 Refitting is a reversal of removal.

Parcel shelf speaker

24 Remove the parcel shelf as described in Chapter 11 Section 34.

25 Disconnect the wiring plugs, rotate the speaker housing anti-clockwise and remove it (see illustration).

26 Refitting is a reversal of removal.

Headlining speaker

27 Using a blunt, flat-bladed tool, carefully prise the speaker cover from the headlining.

28 Undo the retaining screws, lower the speaker from the headlining, and disconnect the wiring plug.

29 Refitting is a reversal of removal.

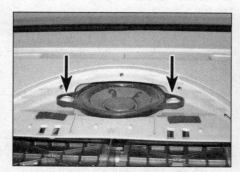

17.22 Facia speaker retaining screws

17.21 Prise up the front, outer edges of the speaker grille

18 Anti-theft alarm –
general information

Note: This information is applicable only to the anti-theft alarm system fitted by Mercedes-Benz as standard equipment.

1 All models are fitted with an anti-theft alarm system as standard equipment. The alarm has switches on all the doors (including the boot lid), the bonnet, the audio unit and the ignition switch, and also a tilt switch, which is sensitive to shocks. If the boot lid, bonnet or either of the doors are opened, the ignition switch or audio unit are switched on whilst the alarm is set, or if the tilt switch senses the vehicle is being tampered with, the alarm horn will sound and the hazard warning lights will flash. The alarm also has an immobiliser function, which makes the ignition/starter (as applicable) system inoperable whilst the alarm is triggered.

2 On later models, the scope of alarm functions is increased, with switchable interior motion sensors and anti-jacking/tilt sensor.

3 The alarm is set using the key in the front door lock or boot/tailgate lock; on later models, the alarm is also set when the doors are locked using the remote central locking device. The LED on the centre console will flash to indicate that the alarm system is operational.

4 Models are equipped with the Mercedes-Benz Driver Authorisation System

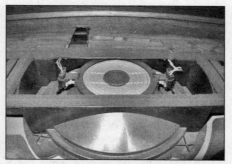

17.25 Rotate the speaker housing anti-clockwise

(DAS). This advanced security system does away with a conventional key for locking and unlocking the doors and, instead, a sophisticated electronic remote-control handset/electronic key is provided. Without this handset, the engine cannot be started.

5 Should the alarm system become faulty, the vehicle should be taken to a Mercedes-Benz dealer for examination. They will have access to a special diagnostic tester, which will quickly trace any fault present in the system.

19 Airbag system – general information and precautions

1 A driver's airbag, passenger airbag, front side airbags (incorporated into the seats), rear side airbags (behind the door trims) and window air bags are fitted as standard to all models.

2 Airbag units have the word AIRBAG or SRS-AIRBAG stamped on them. The airbag system comprises of the airbag unit(s) (each with a gas generator), the control unit (with an integral roll-over sensor), front and side impact sensors, and a warning light in the instrument panel. The airbag control unit features 'intelligent' software, and also operates the front seat belt tensioner mechanisms at the same time as the airbag (see Chapter 11).

3 The driver's and passenger's front airbags will only be triggered in the event of a heavy frontal impact above a predetermined force; depending on the point of impact (rear impacts will not usually trigger the airbag system). The side airbags will only be triggered if the car is hit from the side, and only on the side from which the car has been hit. The passenger airbags and seat belt tensioner will only be triggered if the passenger seat is occupied – a sensor built into the seat cushion informs the control unit of this. Light impacts, such as those which might be sustained when parking, will not trigger the system.

4 The airbag is inflated within milliseconds, and forms a safety cushion between the driver, steering wheel and door, or between the passenger, facia and door, depending on the severity of the accident. This prevents contact between the upper body and wheel/facia/door, and therefore greatly reduces the risk of injury. The airbag then deflates almost immediately.

5 Every time the ignition is switched on, the airbag control unit performs a self-test. The self-test takes approximately 4 seconds and during this time the airbag warning light in the instrument panel is illuminated. After the self-test has been completed the warning light should go out. If the warning light fails to come on, remains illuminated after the initial period or comes on at any time when the vehicle is being driven, there is a fault in the airbag system. The vehicle should be taken to a Mercedes-Benz dealer for examination at the earliest possible opportunity.

⚠️ **Warning: Before carrying out any operations on the airbag system, disconnect the battery negative terminal, and wait for at least 2 minutes. This will allow any residual electrical energy to dissipate. When operations are complete, make sure no one is inside the vehicle when the battery is reconnected.**
Note *that the airbag(s) must not be subjected to temperatures in excess of 90°C (194°F). When the airbag is removed, ensure that it is stored the correct way up to prevent possible inflation (padded surface uppermost).*

● *The airbags, impact sensors and control unit are both sensitive to impact. If either is dropped or damaged they should be renewed.*
● *Disconnect the airbag control unit wiring plug prior to using arc-welding equipment on the vehicle.*
● *Do not allow any solvents or cleaning agents to contact the airbag assemblies. They must be cleaned using only a damp cloth.*

20 Airbag system components – removal and refitting 🔧

Caution: Refer to the warnings in the previous Section before carrying out the following operations.
1 Disconnect the battery negative lead as described in Chapter 5A Section 4.

Steering wheel airbag

2 Fully extend the steering column.
3 Insert a T27 Torx bit into the the front face of the steering wheel boss, and unscrew the airbag retaining screw each side **(see illustration).**
4 Lift the airbag unit from the steering wheel, release the locking tabs and disconnect the wiring plugs **(see illustration).** Note that the airbag must not be knocked or dropped, and should be stored the correct way up (padded surface uppermost).
5 Refitting is a reversal of removal. Tighten the airbag unit retaining screws to the specified torque.

Passengers airbag

6 Remove the upper section of the facia as described in Chapter 11 Section 36.
7 Prise out the locking tabs and disconnect the wiring plug from each end of the airbag unit **(see illustration).**
8 Undo the 4 retaining bolts and manoeuvre the airbag unit from the facia crossmember **(see illustration).**
9 Refitting is a reversal of removal. Tighten the airbag unit retaining bolts to the specified torque.

Front seat airbags

10 Removal of the seat airbags requires the seat upholstery to be removed. This is a complex task, requiring patience and experience. Consequently, we recommend

this is entrusted to a Mercedes dealer or specialist.

Rear side airbags

11 Remove the rear door trim panel and weathershield as described in Chapter 11 Section 34.
12 Disconnect the wiring plug from the airbag unit **(see illustration).**
13 Unclip the interior handle cable from the support bracket.
14 Drill out the 3 rivets, and remove the airbag unit **(see illustration).**
15 Refitting is a reversal of removal, using new rivets to secure the airbag unit.

Headlining airbags

16 On each side of the passenger cabin, a window airbag is fitted. The airbag runs from the lower part of the windscreen pillar to the C/D-pillar. To remove the airbag, the entire headlining must be removed. This task is outside the scope of the DIY'er, and therefore we recommend that the task be entrusted to a Mercedes dealer or specialist.

Airbag/tensioner control unit

17 Move the gear change/selector lever fully rearwards, then open the front ashtray, and pull up the front edge of the gear change/selector lever surround panel.
18 Release the clips and pull the front ashtray from the facia, disconnecting the wiring plugs as they become accessible **(see illustration 5.33).**

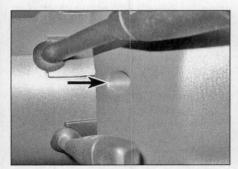
20.3 Use a T27 Torx bit to undo the airbag retaining screw each side

20.4 Prise up the locking tabs and disconnect the wiring plugs

20.7 Slide down the grey catch, then prise out the locking tab

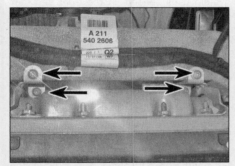
20.8 Passengers airbag retaining bolts

20.12 Disconnect the airbag wiring plug

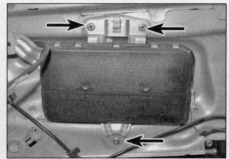
20.14 Drill out the airbag rivets

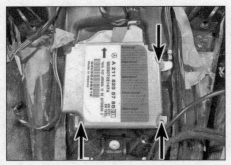

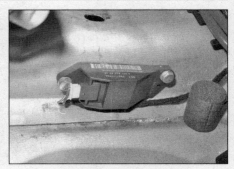

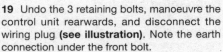

20.19 Airbag control unit retaining bolts

20.25 Left-hand impact sensor retaining bolts

20.31 Side impact sensor

19 Undo the 3 retaining bolts, manoeuvre the control unit rearwards, and disconnect the wiring plug **(see illustration)**. Note the earth connection under the front bolt.
20 Refitting is a reversal of removal. If a new control unit has been fitted, it must be configured using Mercedes STAR diagnostic equipment or equivalent. Tighten the control unit retaining bolts to the specified torque.

Impact sensors

Front sensors

21 An impact sensor is fitted each side of the engine compartment, adjacent to the radiator.
22 Open the bonnet.

Right-hand sensor

23 Unclip the air intake duct adjacent to the cooling fan shroud.
24 Where fitted, disconnect the wiring plug,

detach the coolant circulation pump/rubber bracket and position it to one side.

Left-, and right-hand sensor

25 Undo the retaining bolts and remove the sensor **(see illustration)**. Disconnect the wiring plug as the sensor(s) is withdrawn.
26 Refitting is a reversal of removal. Tighten the sensor retaining bolts to the specified torque.

Side sensors

27 Remove the relevant front seat as described in Chapter 11 Section 29.
28 Pull up the front, and rear door sill trim panels.
29 Unclip the rear footwell air grille.
30 Pull back the carpet from the B-pillar area.
31 Undo the screws and remove the side impact sensor **(see illustration)**. Disconnect the wiring plug as the sensor is withdrawn.

32 Refitting is a reversal of removal, tightening the sensor retaining bolts to the specified torque.

Rotary contact unit (clockspring)

33 Remove the steering column switch module as described in Section 5.
34 Undo the screws and detach the rotary contact unit from the switch assembly **(see illustrations)**.

Vehicles from 2004 model year

35 If the central position of the rotary contact unit has been lost, gently turn the clockspring clockwise to the stop, then turn it anti-clockwise until the arrows are opposite each other, and the cable loop black points are visible in the window **(see illustration)**.

Vehicles upto 2004 models year

36 With the 3 locking screws fully screwed-in, rotate the contact unit anti-clockwise unit light resistance is felt, then rotate it 3 – 3.5 revolutions clockwise unit the locking screws can be unscrewed again through the openings and the contact unit fixed in the centre position.

20.34a Undo the screws...

20.34b...and remove the rotary contact unit – upto 2004 model year

20.34c Rotary contact unit screws – 2004 model year-on

20.35 The arrows must align, and the cable loop black points must be visible

---

21 Parktronic (PTS) system
– general information and component renewal

General information

1 Available as an option, the Parktronic system is an ultrasonic parking aid. The system uses sensors in the front and rear bumpers to transmit a signal which then bounces off any objects in range in front of or behind the car. The sensors receive the reflected signal, and the control unit can then calculate the distance of the object from the car. The system works at speeds up to 9 mph. The resulting distance information is conveyed to the driver by visual display and audio signal.
2 There are six sensors in the front bumper, and four at the rear. The control unit is located under the luggage area floor or behind the left-hand side trim panel. The audio/visual warning units are located in the instrument panel incorporated in the rear interior light.

21.5 Unclip the PTS control unit

21.16 Unclip the rubber cover...

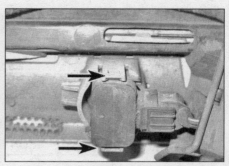

21.17...then release the sensor retaining clips

3 When the ignition is switched on, the system performs a self-test. If the system develops a fault, this will be indicated by just the red sections of the visual warning units staying on. In the event of a fault, first check the connections at the bumper-mounted sensors, as these may be subject to dirt and water entry. After checking this, and the wiring as far as possible, it is advisable to take the car to a Mercedes-Benz dealer for testing using diagnostic equipment.

Electronic control module

Note: *If a new PTS control unit is to be fitted, the existing basic data must be transferred to Mercedes STAR diagnostic equipment (or equivalent), then transferred to the new control unit upon completion.*

4 Remove the left-hand side luggage compartment side trim panel as described in Chapter 11 Section 34.

Vehicles upto 2009 model year

5 Disconnect the wiring plugs, and unclip the PTS control unit **(see illustration)**.

Vehicles from 2009 model year

6 Undo the 2 retaining bolts, and unhook the bracket from the rear SAM control unit, with the fuse and relay module. Position the assemble to one side to access the PTS control unit.

Models with 'Keyless Go' system

7 Disconnect the wiring plugs, undo the nuts and detach the PTS control unit from the bracket.

Models without 'Keyless Go' system

8 Detach the PS control unit from the SAM control unit/fuse/relay module.

All models

9 Refitting is a reversal of removal. See the note at the beginning of this Section.

Ultrasonic sensors

Front sensors

Vehicles up to 06/06

10 Protect the bumper paintwork with masking tape, then starting at the outer edges, carefully release the clips securing the protective strip to the bumper using a blunt, flat-bladed tool.

11 Disconnect the wiring plugs, then unclip the relevant sensor from the protective strip.

Vehicles from 06/06

12 Remove the front bumper as described in Chapter 11 Section 16.

13 Detach the impact absorber from the bumper until the relevant sensor is accessible.

14 Disconnect the wiring plug from the relevant sensor.

15 Release the clips and detach the sensor from the bumper.

Rear sensors

Vehicles up to 06/06

16 Unclip the rubber cover from the sensor location **(see illustration)**.

17 Disconnect the wiring plugs, then unclip the relevant sensor from the bumper **(see illustration)**.

Vehicles from 06/06

18 Remove the rear bumper as described in Chapter 11 Section 16.

19 Disconnect the wiring plug, then unclip the relevant sensor from the bumper.

All sensors

20 Refitting is a reversal of removal.

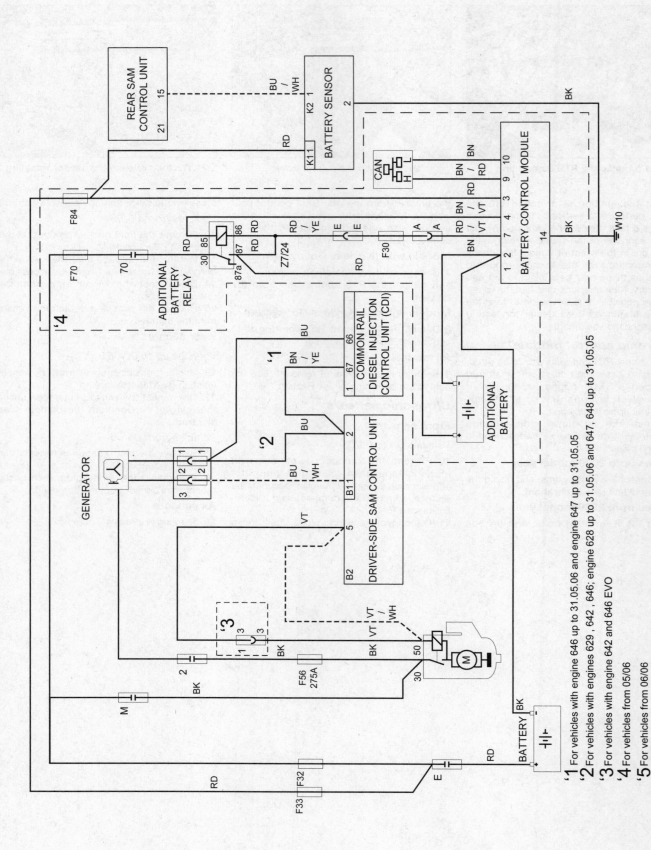

Starting and charging – Model 211 assembly G2 without interface

'1 For vehicles with engine 646 up to 31.05.06 and engine 647 up to 31.05.05
'2 For vehicles with engines 629, 642, 646; engine 628 up to 31.05.05
'3 For vehicles with engine 646 up to 31.05.06 and engine 647, 648 up to 31.05.05
'4 For vehicles from 05/06
'5 For vehicles from 06/06

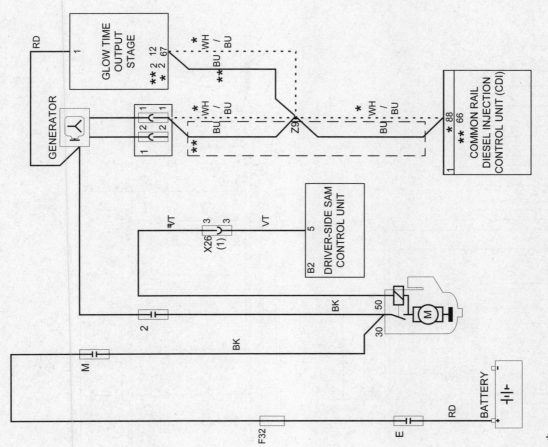

Starting and charging – Model 211 Assembly G2 with LIN

* For vehicles with engine 642 as of 1.6.05 in MODEL 211, not valid for M642 BLUETEC

** For vehicles with engine 646.820 /821 as of 1.6.06 in MODEL 211

* For vehicles with engine 642 as of 1.6.05 in MODEL 211, not valid for M642 BLUETEC

** For vehicles with engine 646.820 /821 as of 1.6.06 in MODEL 211

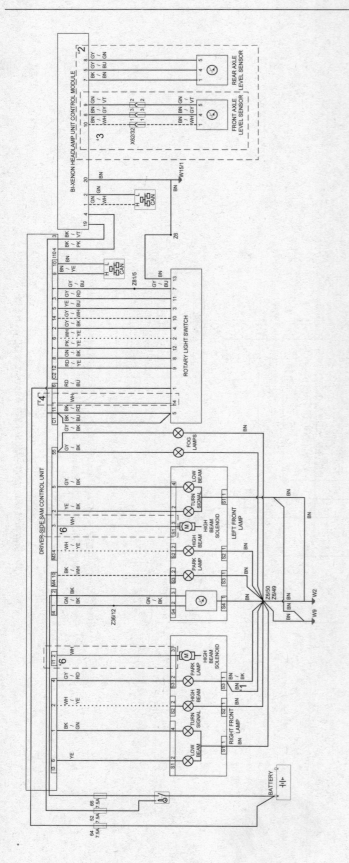

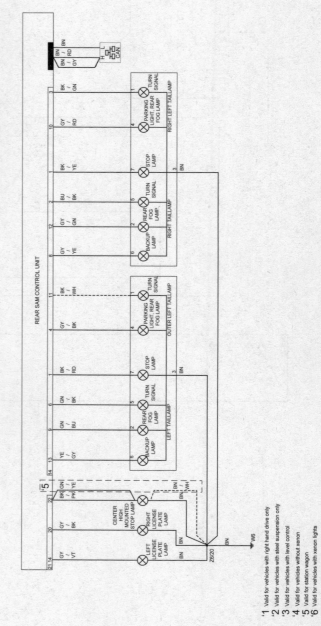

Exterior lights until 05.06

*1 Valid for vehicles with right hand drive only.
*2 Valid for vehicles with steel suspension only
*3 Valid for vehicles with level control
*4 Valid for vehicles without xenon
*5 Valid for station wagon
*6 Valid for vehicles with xenon lights

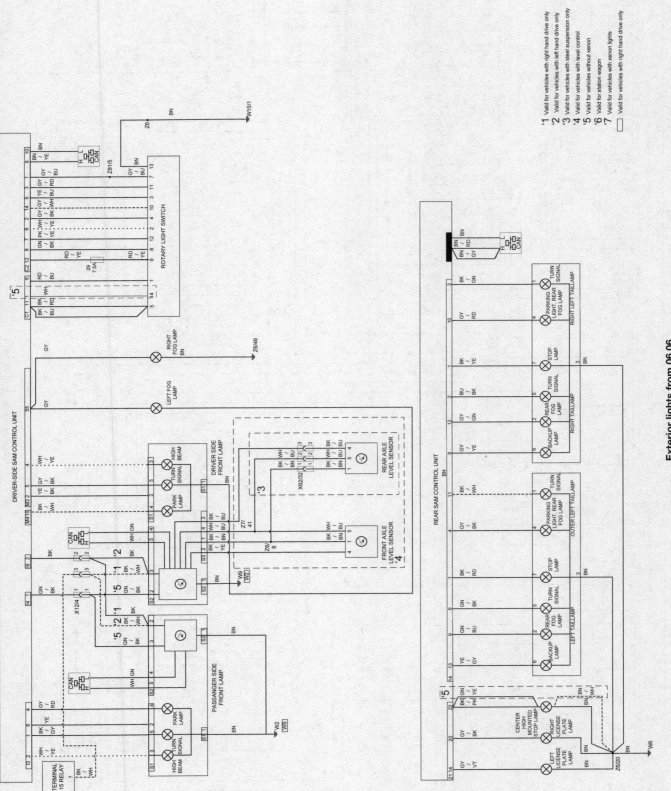

Exterior lights from 06.06

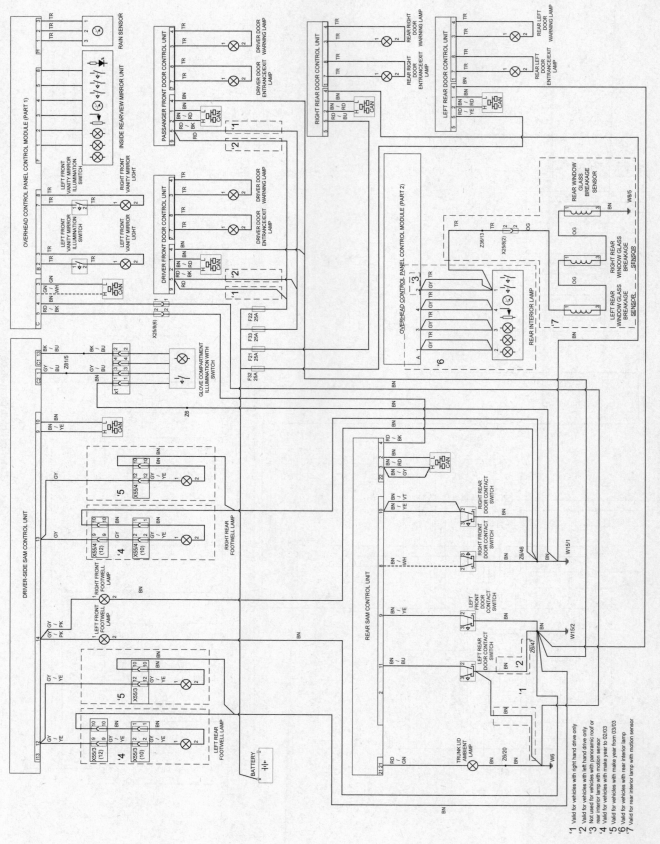

Interior lights until 05.06

*1 Valid for vehicles with right hand drive only
*2 Valid for vehicles with left hand drive only
*3 Not used for vehicles with panoramic roof or
   rear interior lamp with motion sensor
*4 Valid for vehicles with make year to 02/03
*5 Valid for vehicles with make year from 03/03
*6 Valid for vehicles with rear interior lamp
*7 Valid for rear interior lamp with motion sensor

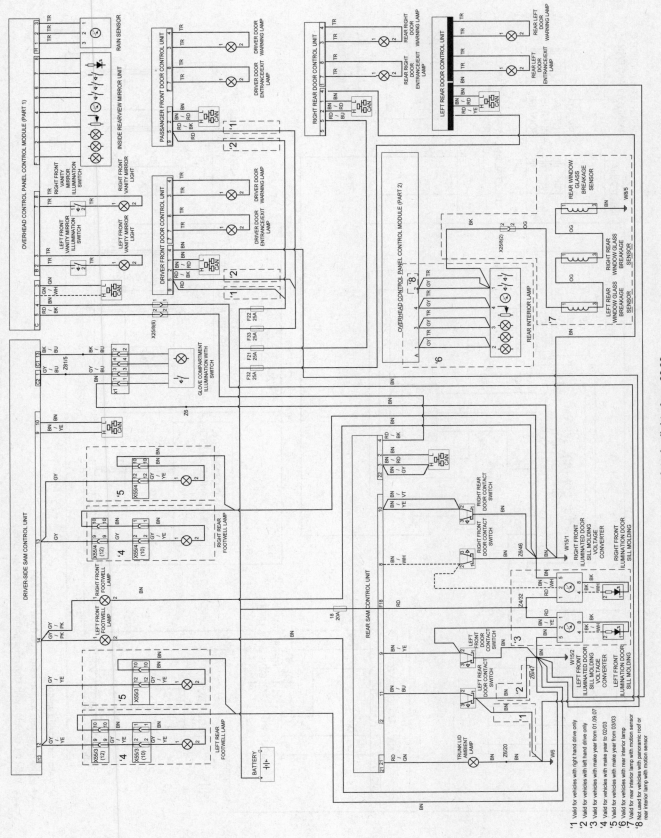

Interior lights from 06.06

*1 Valid for vehicles with right hand drive only
*2 Valid for vehicles with left hand drive only
*3 Valid for vehicles with make year from 01.09.07
*4 Valid for vehicles with make year to 02/03
*5 Valid for vehicles with make year from 03/03
*6 Valid for rear interior lamp
*7 Valid for vehicles with panoramic roof or rear interior lamp with motion sensor
*8 Not used for vehicles with motion sensor

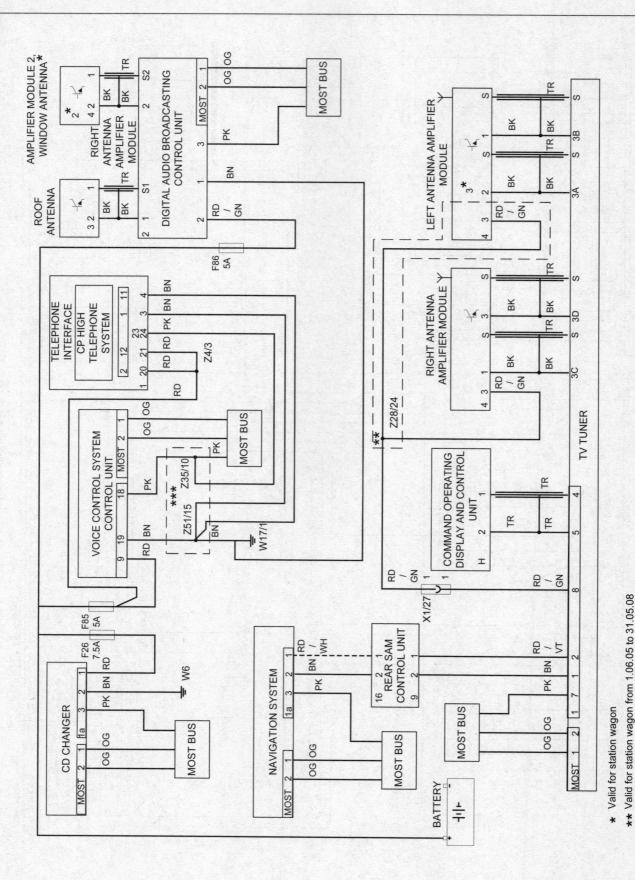

Audio add-on up to 31.05.08

* Valid for station wagon
** Valid for station wagon from 1.06.05 to 31.05.08
*** Valid for vehicles with Universal portable CTEL interface

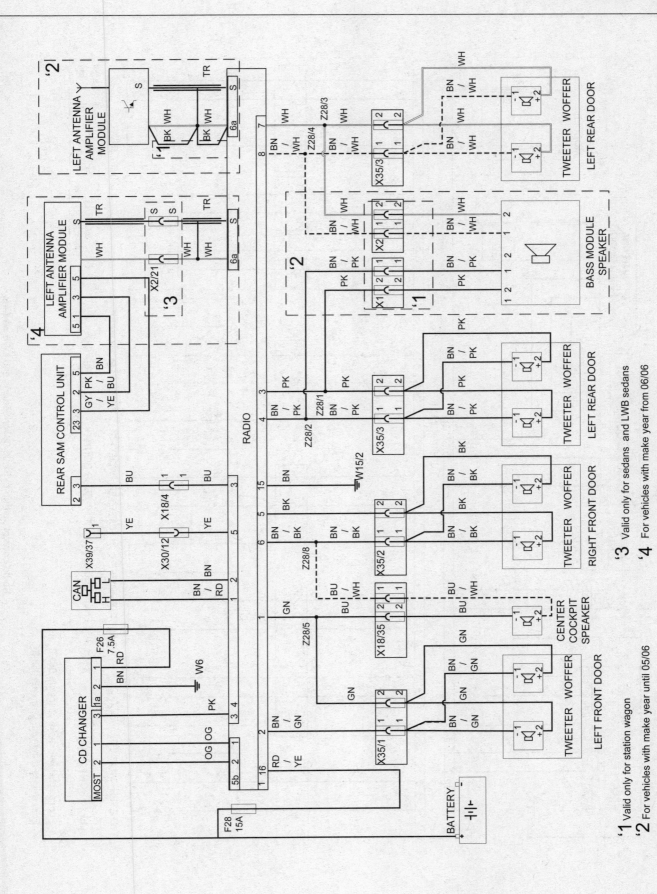

Basic Radio up to 31.05.08

'3 Valid only for sedans and LWB sedans

'4 For vehicles with make year from 06/06

'1 Valid only for station wagon

'2 For vehicles with make year until 05/06

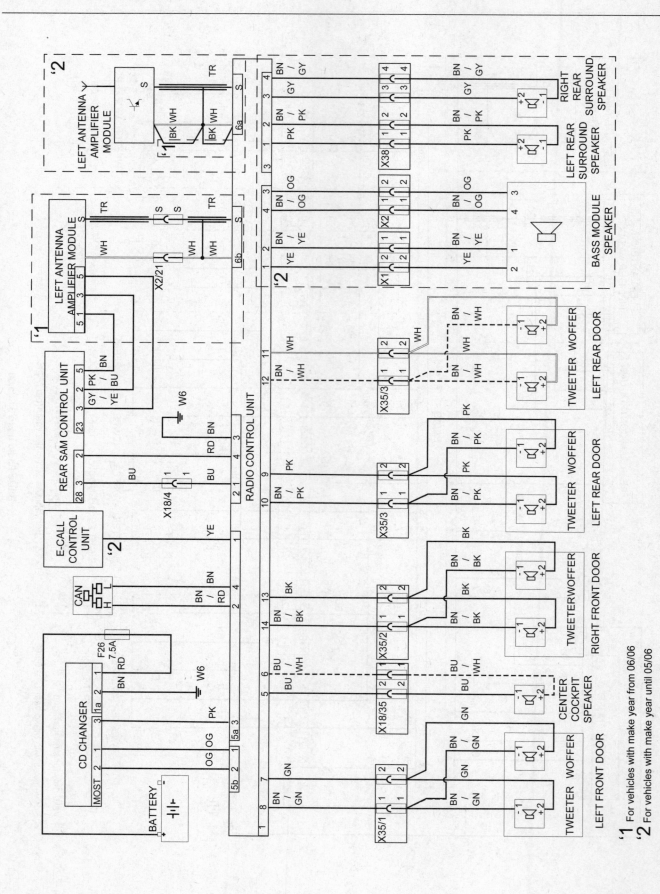

Radio control unit up to 31.05.08 for Sedans and LWB sedans

'1 For vehicles with make year from 06/06
'2 For vehicles with make year until 05/06

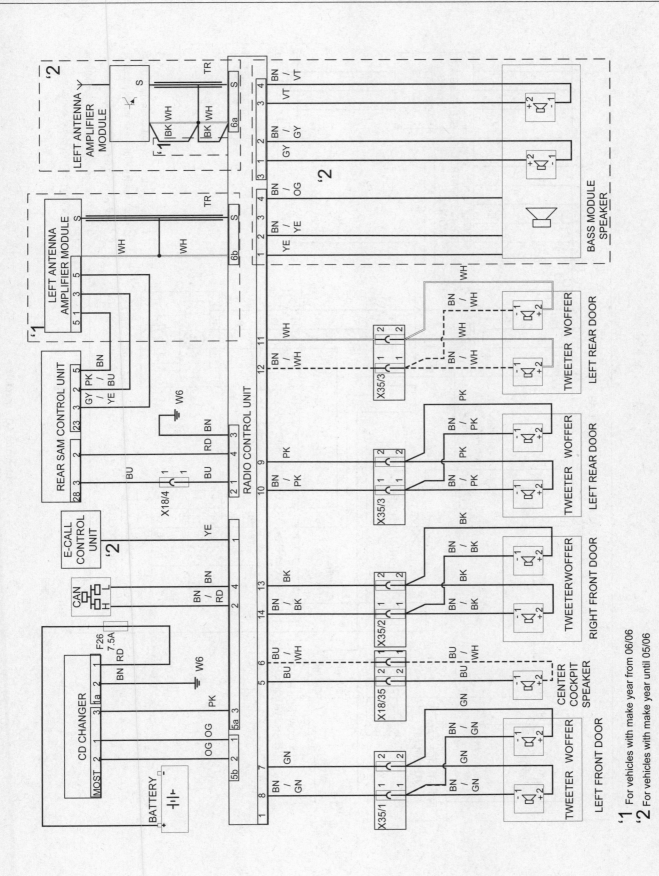

Radio control unit up to 31.05.08 for station wagons

'1 For vehicles with make year from 06/06
'2 For vehicles with make year until 05/06

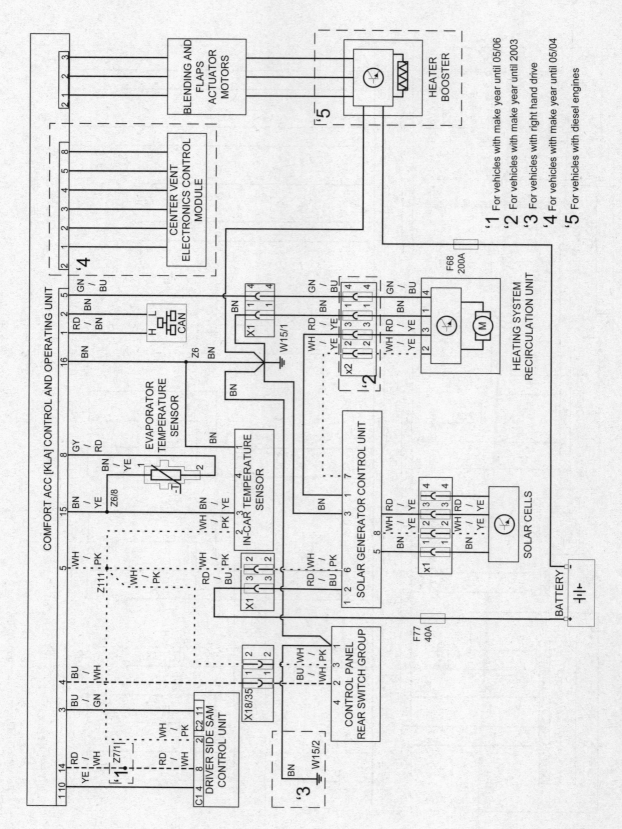

Automatic AC – comfort

'1 For vehicles with make year until 05/06
'2 For vehicles with make year until 2003
'3 For vehicles with right hand drive
'4 For vehicles with make year until 05/04
'5 For vehicles with diesel engines

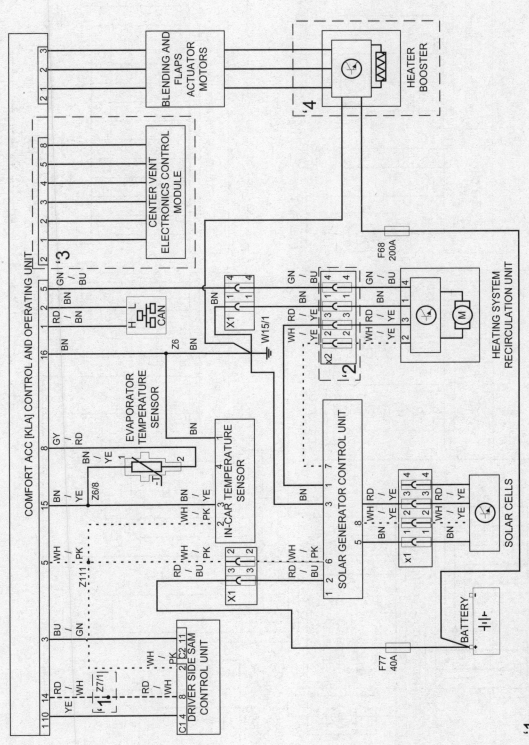

Automatic AC

'1 For vehicles with make year until 05/06
'2 For vehicles with make year until 2003
'3 For vehicles with make year until 05/04
'4 For vehicles with diesel engines

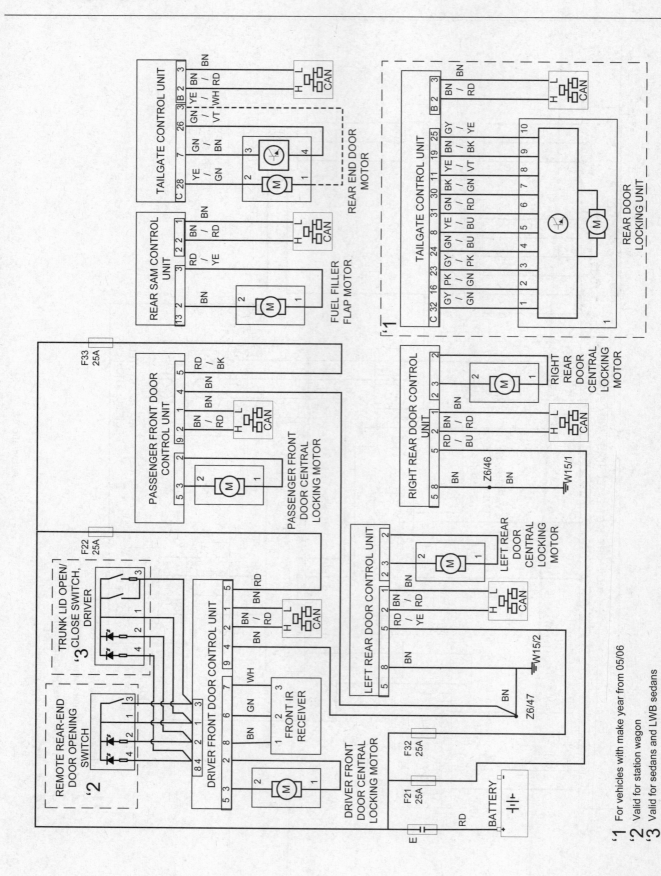

Central locking RHD

'1 For vehicles with make year from 05/06
'2 Valid for station wagon
'3 Valid for sedans and LWB sedans

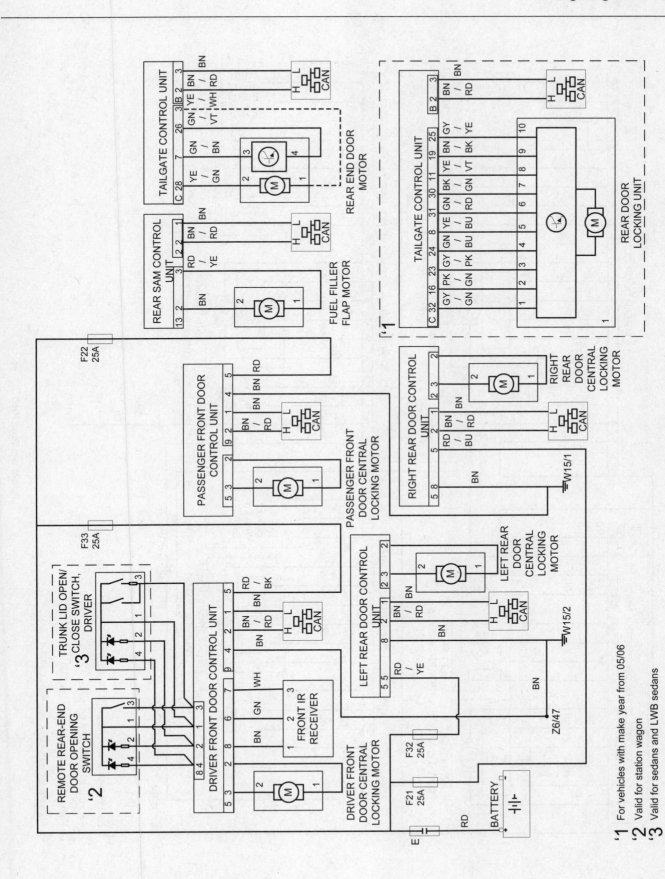

Central locking LHD

'1 For vehicles with make year from 05/06

'2 Valid for station wagon

'3 Valid for sedans and LWB sedans

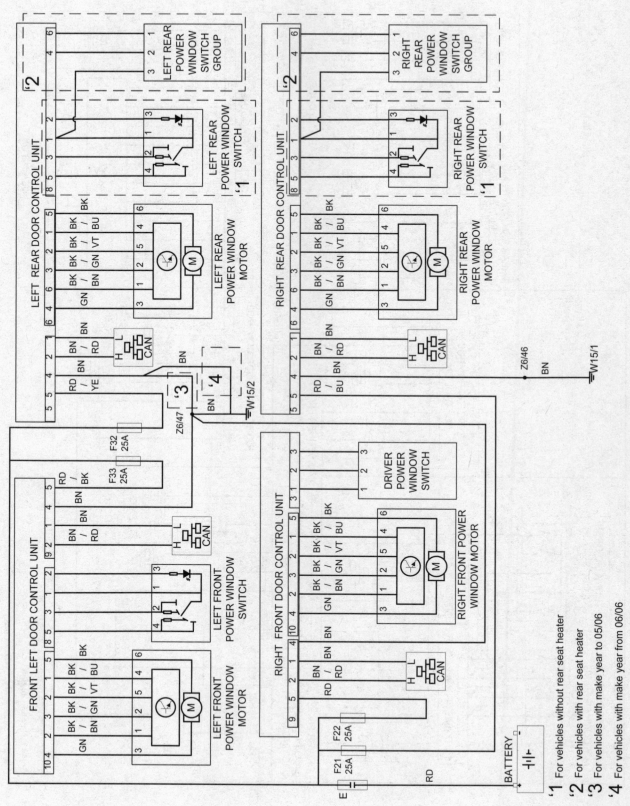

Power windows RHD

'1 For vehicles without rear seat heater
'2 For vehicles with rear seat heater
'3 For vehicles with make year to 05/06
'4 For vehicles with make year from 06/06

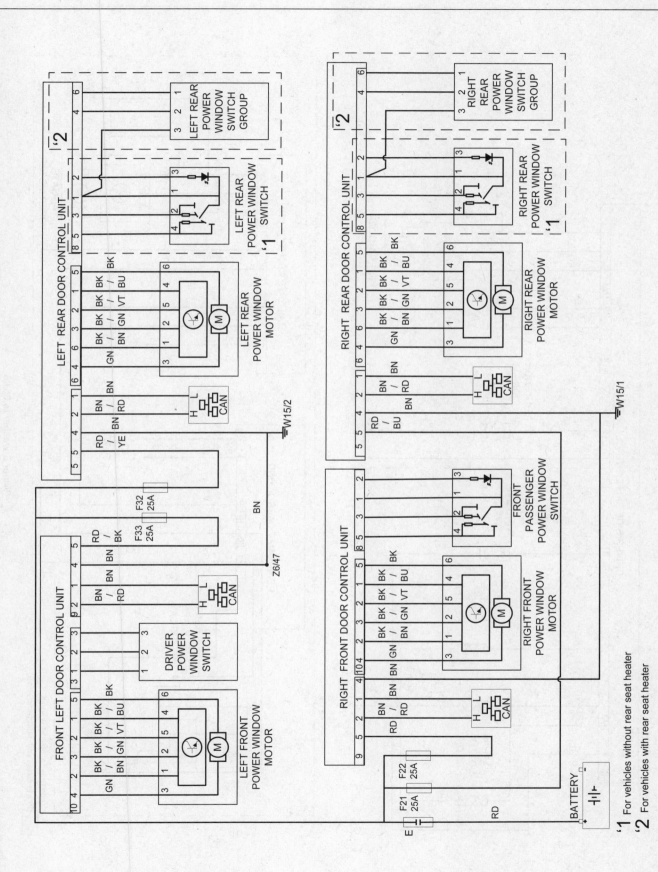

Power windows LHD

'1 For vehicles without rear seat heater
'2 For vehicles with rear seat heater

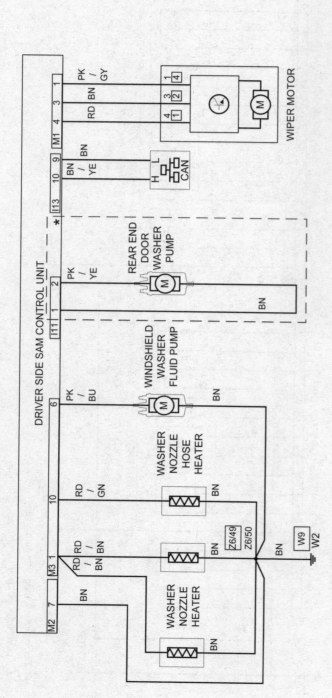

Wiper & washer to 05.06

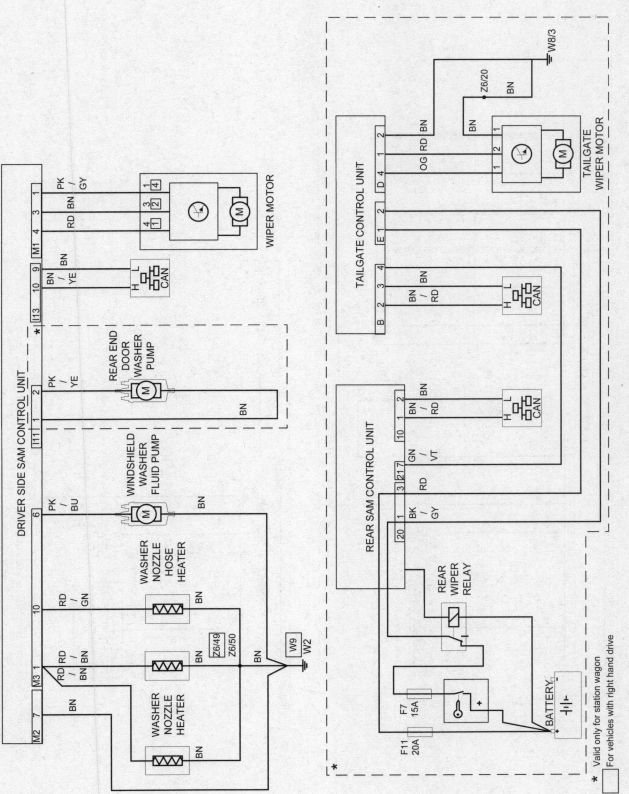

Wiper & washer from 05.06

DRIVER SIDE SAM CONTROL UNIT

WIPER MOTOR

REAR END DOOR WASHER PUMP

WINDSHIELD WASHER FLUID PUMP

WASHER NOZZLE HOSE HEATER

WASHER NOZZLE HEATER

TAILGATE CONTROL UNIT

TAILGATE WIPER MOTOR

REAR SAM CONTROL UNIT

REAR WIPER RELAY

BATTERY

* Valid only for station wagon

* For vehicles with right hand drive

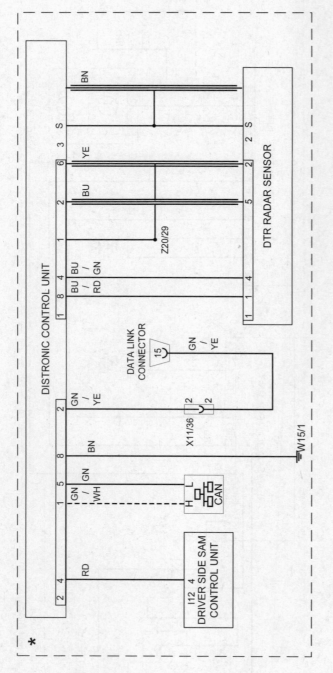

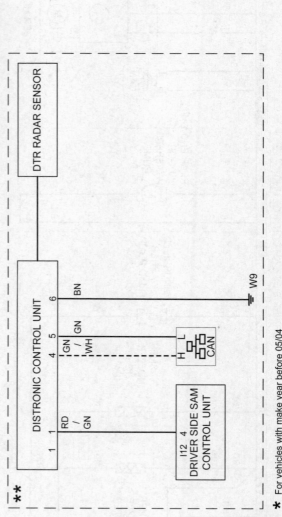

Cruise Control

* For vehicles with make year before 05/04

** For vehicles with make year from 06/04

Dimensions and weights

Note: *All figures are approximate, and may vary according to model. Refer to manufacturer's data for exact figures.*

Dimensions

Overall length:
    Saloon . . . . 4852 mm
    Estate . . . . 4884 mm
Overall width. . . . . 1822 mm
Overall height:
    Saloon . . . . 1484 mm
    Estate . . . . 1506 mm
Wheelbase . . . . 2854 mm

Weights

Unladen . . . . 1615 to 1980 kg
Gross vehicle weight . . . . 2140 to 2460 kg
Maximum roof rack load . . . . 100 kg

Fuel economy

Although depreciation is still the biggest part of the cost of motoring for most car owners, the cost of fuel is more immediately noticeable. These pages give some tips on how to get the best fuel economy.

Working it out

Manufacturer's figures

Car manufacturers are required by law to provide fuel consumption information on all new vehicles sold. These 'official' figures are obtained by simulating various driving conditions on a rolling road or a test track. Real life conditions are different, so the fuel consumption actually achieved may not bear much resemblance to the quoted figures.

How to calculate it

Many cars now have trip computers which will

display fuel consumption, both instantaneous and average. Refer to the owner's handbook for details of how to use these.

To calculate consumption yourself (and maybe to check that the trip computer is accurate), proceed as follows.

1. Fill up with fuel and note the mileage, or zero the trip recorder.
2. Drive as usual until you need to fill up again.
3. Note the amount of fuel required to refill the tank, and the mileage covered since the previous fill-up.
4. Divide the mileage by the amount of fuel used to obtain the consumption figure.

For example:

Mileage at first fill-up (a) = 27,903
Mileage at second fill-up (b) = 28,346
Mileage covered (b - a) = 443
Fuel required at second fill-up = 48.6 litres

The half-completed changeover to metric units in the UK means that we buy our fuel in litres, measure distances in miles and talk about fuel consumption in miles per gallon. There are two ways round this: the first is to convert the litres to gallons before doing the calculation (by dividing by 4.546, or see Table 1). So in the example:

48.6 litres ÷ 4.546 = 10.69 gallons
443 miles ÷ 10.69 gallons = 41.4 mpg

The second way is to calculate the consumption in miles per litre, then multiply that figure by 4.546 (or see Table 2).

So in the example, fuel consumption is:

443 miles ÷ 48.6 litres = 9.1 mpl
9.1 mpl x 4.546 = 41.4 mpg

The rest of Europe expresses fuel consumption in litres of fuel required to travel 100 km (l/100 km). For interest, the conversions are given in Table 3. In practice it doesn't matter what units you use, provided you know what your normal consumption is and can spot if it's getting better or worse.

Table 1: conversion of litres to Imperial gallons

litres	1	2	3	4	5	10	20	30	40	50	60	70
gallons	0.22	0.44	0.66	0.88	1.10	2.24	4.49	6.73	8.98	11.22	13.47	15.71

Table 2: conversion of miles per litre to miles per gallon

miles per litre	5	6	7	8	9	10	11	12	13	14
miles per gallon	23	27	32	36	41	46	50	55	59	64

Table 3: conversion of litres per 100 km to miles per gallon

litres per 100 km	4	4.5	5	5.5	6	6.5	7	8	9	10
miles per gallon	71	63	56	51	47	43	40	35	31	28

Maintenance

A well-maintained car uses less fuel and creates less pollution. In particular:

Filters

Change air and fuel filters at the specified intervals.

Oil

Use a good quality oil of the lowest viscosity specified by the vehicle manufacturer (see *Lubricants and fluids*). Check the level often and be careful not to overfill.

Spark plugs

When applicable, renew at the specified intervals.

Tyres

Check tyre pressures regularly. Under-inflated tyres have an increased rolling resistance. It is generally safe to use the higher pressures specified for full load conditions even when not fully laden, but keep an eye on the centre band of tread for signs of wear due to over-inflation.

When buying new tyres, consider the 'fuel saving' models which most manufacturers include in their ranges.

Driving style

Acceleration

Acceleration uses more fuel than driving at a steady speed. The best technique with modern cars is to accelerate reasonably briskly to the desired speed, changing up through the gears as soon as possible without making the engine labour.

Air conditioning

Air conditioning absorbs quite a bit of energy from the engine – typically 3 kW (4 hp) or so. The effect on fuel consumption is at its worst in slow traffic. Switch it off when not required.

Anticipation

Drive smoothly and try to read the traffic flow so as to avoid unnecessary acceleration and braking.

Automatic transmission

When accelerating in an automatic, avoid depressing the throttle so far as to make the transmission hold onto lower gears at higher speeds. Don't use the 'Sport' setting, if applicable.

When stationary with the engine running, select 'N' or 'P'. When moving, keep your left foot away from the brake.

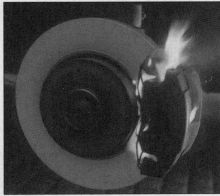

Braking

Braking converts the car's energy of motion into heat – essentially, it is wasted. Obviously some braking is always going to be necessary, but with good anticipation it is surprising how much can be avoided, especially on routes that you know well.

Carshare

Consider sharing lifts to work or to the shops. Even once a week will make a difference.

Electrical loads

Electricity is 'fuel' too; the alternator which charges the battery does so by converting some of the engine's energy of motion into electrical energy. The more electrical accessories are in use, the greater the load on the alternator. Switch off big consumers like the heated rear window when not required.

Freewheeling

Freewheeling (coasting) in neutral with the engine switched off is dangerous. The effort required to operate power-assisted brakes and steering increases when the engine is not running, with a potential lack of control in emergency situations.

In any case, modern fuel injection systems automatically cut off the engine's fuel supply on the overrun (moving and in gear, but with the accelerator pedal released).

Gadgets

Bolt-on devices claiming to save fuel have been around for nearly as long as the motor car itself. Those which worked were rapidly adopted as standard equipment by the vehicle manufacturers. Others worked only in certain situations, or saved fuel only at the expense of unacceptable effects on performance, driveability or the life of engine components.

The most effective fuel saving gadget is the driver's right foot.

Journey planning

Combine (eg) a trip to the supermarket with a visit to the recycling centre and the DIY store, rather than making separate journeys.

When possible choose a travelling time outside rush hours.

Load

The more heavily a car is laden, the greater the energy required to accelerate it to a given speed. Remove heavy items which you don't need to carry.

One load which is often overlooked is the contents of the fuel tank. A tankful of fuel (55 litres / 12 gallons) weighs 45 kg (100 lb) or so. Just half filling it may be worthwhile.

Lost?

At the risk of stating the obvious, if you're going somewhere new, have details of the route to hand. There's not much point in achieving record mpg if you also go miles out of your way.

Parking

If possible, carry out any reversing or turning manoeuvres when you arrive at a parking space so that you can drive straight out when you leave. Manoeuvering when the engine is cold uses a lot more fuel.

Driving around looking for free on-street parking may cost more in fuel than buying a car park ticket.

Premium fuel

Most major oil companies (and some supermarkets) have premium grades of fuel which are several pence a litre dearer than the standard grades. Reports vary, but the consensus seems to be that if these fuels improve economy at all, they do not do so by enough to justify their extra cost.

Roof rack

When loading a roof rack, try to produce a wedge shape with the narrow end at the front. Any cover should be securely fastened – if it flaps it's creating turbulence and absorbing energy.

Remove roof racks and boxes when not in use – they increase air resistance and can create a surprising amount of noise.

Short journeys

The engine is at its least efficient, and wear is highest, during the first few miles after a cold start. Consider walking, cycling or using public transport.

Speed

The engine is at its most efficient when running at a steady speed and load at the rpm where it develops maximum torque. (You can find this figure in the car's handbook.) For most cars this corresponds to between 55 and 65 mph in top gear.

Above the optimum cruising speed, fuel consumption starts to rise quite sharply. A car travelling at 80 mph will typically be using 30% more fuel than at 60 mph.

Supermarket fuel

It may be cheap but is it any good? In the UK all supermarket fuel must meet the relevant British Standard. The major oil companies will say that their branded fuels have better additive packages which may stop carbon and other deposits building up. A reasonable compromise might be to use one tank of branded fuel to three or four from the supermarket.

Switch off when stationary

Switch off the engine if you look like being stationary for more than 30 seconds or so. This is good for the environment as well as for your pocket. Be aware though that frequent restarts are hard on the battery and the starter motor.

Windows

Driving with the windows open increases air turbulence around the vehicle. Closing the windows promotes smooth airflow and

reduced resistance. The faster you go, the more significant this is.

And finally...

Driving techniques associated with good fuel economy tend to involve moderate acceleration and low top speeds. Be considerate to the needs of other road users who may need to make brisker progress; even if you do not agree with them this is not an excuse to be obstructive.

Safety must always take precedence over economy, whether it is a question of accelerating hard to complete an overtaking manoeuvre, killing your speed when confronted with a potential hazard or switching the lights on when it starts to get dark.

Conversion factors

Length (distance)

Inches (in)	x 25.4	=	Millimetres (mm)	x 0.0394 =	Inches (in)
Feet (ft)	x 0.305	=	Metres (m)	x 3.281 =	Feet (ft)
Miles	x 1.609	=	Kilometres (km)	x 0.621 =	Miles

Volume (capacity)

Cubic inches (cu in; in³)	x 16.387	=	Cubic centimetres (cc; cm³)	x 0.061 =	Cubic inches (cu in; in³)
Imperial pints (Imp pt)	x 0.568	=	Litres (l)	x 1.76 =	Imperial pints (Imp pt)
Imperial quarts (Imp qt)	x 1.137	=	Litres (l)	x 0.88 =	Imperial quarts (Imp qt)
Imperial quarts (Imp qt)	x 1.201	=	US quarts (US qt)	x 0.833 =	Imperial quarts (Imp qt)
US quarts (US qt)	x 0.946	=	Litres (l)	x 1.057 =	US quarts (US qt)
Imperial gallons (Imp gal)	x 4.546	=	Litres (l)	x 0.22 =	Imperial gallons (Imp gal)
Imperial gallons (Imp gal)	x 1.201	=	US gallons (US gal)	x 0.833 =	Imperial gallons (Imp gal)
US gallons (US gal)	x 3.785	=	Litres (l)	x 0.264 =	US gallons (US gal)

Mass (weight)

Ounces (oz)	x 28.35	=	Grams (g)	x 0.035 =	Ounces (oz)
Pounds (lb)	x 0.454	=	Kilograms (kg)	x 2.205 =	Pounds (lb)

Force

Ounces-force (ozf; oz)	x 0.278	=	Newtons (N)	x 3.6 =	Ounces-force (ozf; oz)
Pounds-force (lbf; lb)	x 4.448	=	Newtons (N)	x 0.225 =	Pounds-force (lbf; lb)
Newtons (N)	x 0.1	=	Kilograms-force (kgf; kg)	x 9.81 =	Newtons (N)

Pressure

Pounds-force per square inch (psi; lbf/in²; lb/in²)	x 0.070	=	Kilograms-force per square centimetre (kgf/cm²; kg/cm²)	x 14.223 =	Pounds-force per square inch (psi; lbf/in²; lb/in²)
Pounds-force per square inch (psi; lbf/in²; lb/in²)	x 0.068	=	Atmospheres (atm)	x 14.696 =	Pounds-force per square inch (psi; lbf/in²; lb/in²)
Pounds-force per square inch (psi; lbf/in²; lb/in²)	x 0.069	=	Bars	x 14.5 =	Pounds-force per square inch (psi; lbf/in²; lb/in²)
Pounds-force per square inch (psi; lbf/in²; lb/in²)	x 6.895	=	Kilopascals (kPa)	x 0.145 =	Pounds-force per square inch (psi; lbf/in²; lb/in²)
Kilopascals (kPa)	x 0.01	=	Kilograms-force per square centimetre (kgf/cm²; kg/cm²)	x 98.1 =	Kilopascals (kPa)
Millibar (mbar)	x 100	=	Pascals (Pa)	x 0.01 =	Millibar (mbar)
Millibar (mbar)	x 0.0145	=	Pounds-force per square inch (psi; lbf/in²; lb/in²)	x 68.947 =	Millibar (mbar)
Millibar (mbar)	x 0.75	=	Millimetres of mercury (mmHg)	x 1.333 =	Millibar (mbar)
Millibar (mbar)	x 0.401	=	Inches of water (inH₂O)	x 2.491 =	Millibar (mbar)
Millimetres of mercury (mmHg)	x 0.535	=	Inches of water (inH₂O)	x 1.868 =	Millimetres of mercury (mmHg)
Inches of water (inH₂O)	x 0.036	=	Pounds-force per square inch (psi; lbf/in²; lb/in²)	x 27.68 =	Inches of water (inH₂O)

Torque (moment of force)

Pounds-force inches (lbf in; lb in)	x 1.152	=	Kilograms-force centimetre (kgf cm; kg cm)	x 0.868 =	Pounds-force inches (lbf in; lb in)
Pounds-force inches (lbf in; lb in)	x 0.113	=	Newton metres (Nm)	x 8.85 =	Pounds-force inches (lbf in; lb in)
Pounds-force inches (lbf in; lb in)	x 0.083	=	Pounds-force feet (lbf ft; lb ft)	x 12 =	Pounds-force inches (lbf in; lb in)
Pounds-force feet (lbf ft; lb ft)	x 0.138	=	Kilograms-force metres (kgf m; kg m)	x 7.233 =	Pounds-force feet (lbf ft; lb ft)
Pounds-force feet (lbf ft; lb ft)	x 1.356	=	Newton metres (Nm)	x 0.738 =	Pounds-force feet (lbf ft; lb ft)
Newton metres (Nm)	x 0.102	=	Kilograms-force metres (kgf m; kg m)	x 9.804 =	Newton metres (Nm)

Power

Horsepower (hp)	x 745.7	=	Watts (W)	x 0.0013 =	Horsepower (hp)

Velocity (speed)

Miles per hour (miles/hr; mph)	x 1.609	=	Kilometres per hour (km/hr; kph)	x 0.621 =	Miles per hour (miles/hr; mph)

Fuel consumption*

Miles per gallon, Imperial (mpg)	x 0.354	=	Kilometres per litre (km/l)	x 2.825 =	Miles per gallon, Imperial (mpg)
Miles per gallon, US (mpg)	x 0.425	=	Kilometres per litre (km/l)	x 2.352 =	Miles per gallon, US (mpg)

Temperature

Degrees Fahrenheit = (°C x 1.8) + 32   Degrees Celsius (Degrees Centigrade; °C) = (°F - 32) x 0.56

It is common practice to convert from miles per gallon (mpg) to litres/100 kilometres (l/100km), where mpg x l/100 km = 282

The jack supplied with the vehicle tool kit should only be used for changing the roadwheels – see "Wheel changing" at the front of this manual. When carrying out any other kind of work, raise the vehicle using a hydraulic trolley jack, and always supplement the jack with axle stands positioned under the vehicle jacking points.

When using a trolley jack or axle stands, always position the jack head or axle stand head under, or adjacent to one of the relevant wheel changing jacking points under the sills. Use a block of wood between the jack or axle stand and the sill. It is permissible to raise the front or rear of the vehicle with a trolley jack head under the front body crossmember or rear subframe

crossmember, providing axle stands are placed under the sill jacking points (see illustration).

Do not attempt to jack the vehicle under the sump, final drive unit, or any of the suspension components.

Never work under, around, or near a raised vehicle, unless it is adequately supported in at least two places.

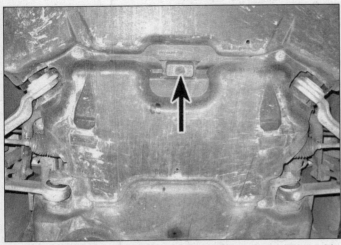

A rubber pad is provided under the front subframe for lifting with a workshop jack

Position axle stands under the rubber pads in the sill

Buying spare parts

Spare parts are available from many sources, including maker's appointed garages, accessory shops, and motor factors. To be sure of obtaining the correct parts, it will sometimes be necessary to quote the vehicle identification number. If possible, it can also be useful to take the old parts along for positive identification. Items such as starter motors and alternators may be available under a service exchange scheme – any parts returned should be clean.

Our advice regarding spare parts is as follows.

Officially appointed garages

This is the best source of parts which are peculiar to your car, and which are not otherwise generally available (eg, badges, interior trim, certain body panels, etc). It is also the only place at which you should buy parts if the vehicle is still under warranty.

Accessory shops

These are very good places to buy materials and components needed for the maintenance of your car (oil, air and fuel filters, light bulbs,

drivebelts, greases, brake pads, tough-up paint, etc). Components of this nature sold by a reputable shop are of the same standard as those used by the car manufacturer.

Besides components, these shops also sell tools and general accessories, usually have convenient opening hours, charge lower prices, and can often be found close to home. Some accessory shops have parts counters where components needed for almost any repair job can be purchased or ordered.

Motor factors

Good factors will stock all the more important components which wear out comparatively quickly, and can sometimes supply individual components needed for the overhaul of a larger assembly (eg, brake seals and hydraulic parts, bearing shells, pistons, valves). They may also handle work such as cylinder block reboring, crankshaft regrinding, etc.

Tyre and exhaust specialists

These outlets may be independent, or members of a local or national chain. They

frequently offer competitive prices when compared with a main dealer or local garage, but it will pay to obtain several quotes before making a decision. When researching prices, also ask what 'extras' may be added – for instance fitting a new valve and balancing the wheel are both commonly charged on top of the price of a new tyre.

Other sources

Beware of parts or materials obtained from market stalls, car boot sales, internet auction sites or similar outlets. Such items are not invariably sub-standard, but there is little chance of compensation if they do prove unsatisfactory. In the case of safety-critical components such as brake pads, there is the risk not only of financial loss, but also of an accident causing injury or death

Second-hand components or assemblies obtained from a car breaker can be a good buy in some circumstances, but this sort of purchase is best made by the experienced DIY mechanic.

Whenever servicing, repair or overhaul work is carried out on the car or its components, observe the following procedures and instructions. This will assist in carrying out the operation efficiently and to a professional standard of workmanship.

Joint mating faces and gaskets

When separating components at their mating faces, never insert screwdrivers or similar implements into the joint between the faces in order to prise them apart. This can cause severe damage which results in oil leaks, coolant leaks, etc upon reassembly. Separation is usually achieved by tapping along the joint with a soft-faced hammer in order to break the seal. However, note that this method may not be suitable where dowels are used for component location.

Where a gasket is used between the mating faces of two components, a new one must be fitted on reassembly; fit it dry unless otherwise stated in the repair procedure. Make sure that the mating faces are clean and dry, with all traces of old gasket removed. When cleaning a joint face, use a tool which is unlikely to score or damage the face, and remove any burrs or nicks with an oilstone or fine file.

Make sure that tapped holes are cleaned with a pipe cleaner, and keep them free of jointing compound, if this is being used, unless specifically instructed otherwise.

Ensure that all orifices, channels or pipes are clear, and blow through them, preferably using compressed air.

Oil seals

Oil seals can be removed by levering them out with a wide flat-bladed screwdriver or similar implement. Alternatively, a number of self-tapping screws may be screwed into the seal, and these used as a purchase for pliers or some similar device in order to pull the seal free.

Whenever an oil seal is removed from its working location, either individually or as part of an assembly, it should be renewed.

The very fine sealing lip of the seal is easily damaged, and will not seal if the surface it contacts is not completely clean and free from scratches, nicks or grooves. If the original sealing surface of the component cannot be restored, and the manufacturer has not made provision for slight relocation of the seal relative to the sealing surface, the component should be renewed.

Protect the lips of the seal from any surface which may damage them in the course of fitting. Use tape or a conical sleeve where possible. Where indicated, lubricate the seal lips with oil before fitting and, on dual-lipped seals, fill the space between the lips with grease.

Unless otherwise stated, oil seals must be fitted with their sealing lips toward the lubricant to be sealed.

Use a tubular drift or block of wood of the appropriate size to install the seal and, if the seal housing is shouldered, drive the seal down to the shoulder. If the seal housing is unshouldered, the seal should be fitted with its face flush with the housing top face (unless otherwise instructed).

Screw threads and fastenings

Seized nuts, bolts and screws are quite a common occurrence where corrosion has set in, and the use of penetrating oil or releasing fluid will often overcome this problem if the offending item is soaked for a while before attempting to release it. The use of an impact driver may also provide a means of releasing such stubborn fastening devices, when used in conjunction with the appropriate screwdriver bit or socket. If none of these methods works, it may be necessary to resort to the careful application of heat, or the use of a hacksaw or nut splitter device. Before resorting to extreme methods, check that you are not dealing with a left-hand thread!

Studs are usually removed by locking two nuts together on the threaded part, and then using a spanner on the lower nut to unscrew the stud. Studs or bolts which have broken off below the surface of the component in which they are mounted can sometimes be removed using a stud extractor.

Always ensure that a blind tapped hole is completely free from oil, grease, water or other fluid before installing the bolt or stud. Failure to do this could cause the housing to crack due to the hydraulic action of the bolt or stud as it is screwed in.

For some screw fastenings, notably cylinder head bolts or nuts, torque wrench settings are no longer specified for the latter stages of tightening, "angle-tightening" being called up instead. Typically, a fairly low torque wrench setting will be applied to the bolts/nuts in the correct sequence, followed by one or more stages of tightening through specified angles.

When checking or retightening a nut or bolt to a specified torque setting, slacken the nut or bolt by a quarter of a turn, and then retighten to the specified setting. However, this should not be attempted where angular tightening has been used.

Locknuts, locktabs and washers

Any fastening which will rotate against a component or housing during tightening should always have a washer between it and the relevant component or housing.

Spring or split washers should always be renewed when they are used to lock a critical component such as a big-end bearing retaining bolt or nut. Locktabs which are folded over to retain a nut or bolt should always be renewed.

Self-locking nuts can be re-used in non-critical areas, providing resistance can be felt when the locking portion passes over the bolt or stud thread. However, it should be noted that self-locking stiffnuts tend to lose their effectiveness after long periods of use, and should then be renewed as a matter of course.

Split pins must always be replaced with new ones of the correct size for the hole.

When thread-locking compound is found on the threads of a fastener which is to be re-used, it should be cleaned off with a wire brush and solvent, and fresh compound applied on reassembly.

Special tools

Some repair procedures in this manual entail the use of special tools such as a press, two or three-legged pullers, spring compressors, etc. Wherever possible, suitable readily-available alternatives to the manufacturer's special tools are described, and are shown in use. In some instances, where no alternative is possible, it has been necessary to resort to the use of a manufacturer's tool, and this has been done for reasons of safety as well as the efficient completion of the repair operation. Unless you are highly-skilled and have a thorough understanding of the procedures described, never attempt to bypass the use of any special tool when the procedure described specifies its use. Not only is there a very great risk of personal injury, but expensive damage could be caused to the components involved.

Environmental considerations

When disposing of used engine oil, brake fluid, antifreeze, etc, give due consideration to any detrimental environmental effects. Do not, for instance, pour any of the above liquids down drains into the general sewage system, or onto the ground to soak away. Many local council refuse tips provide a facility for waste oil disposal, as do some garages. You can find your nearest disposal point by calling the Environment Agency on 08708 506 506 or by visiting www.oilbankline.org.uk.

Note: It is illegal and anti-social to dump oil down the drain. To find the location of your local oil recycling bank, call 08708 506 506 or visit www.oilbankline.org.uk.

Modifications are a continuing and unpublicised process in vehicle manufacture, quite apart from major model changes. Spare parts manuals and lists are compiled upon a numerical basis, the individual vehicle identification numbers being essential to correct identification of the component concerned.

When ordering spare parts, always give as much information as possible. Quote the car model, year of manufacture, body and engine numbers as appropriate.

The vehicle identification plate is situated at the bottom of the drivers side door B-pillar. It gives the VIN (vehicle identification number), vehicle weight information and paint and trim colour codes. The vehicle identification number also stamped into the vehicle body beneath the drivers seat **(see illustrations)**.

The engine number is stamped on the left-hand side of the cylinder block.

The VIN is located on a plate at the base of the drivers door B-pillar...

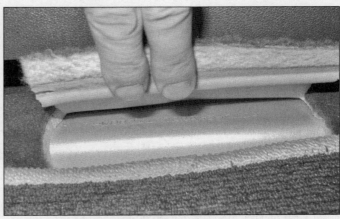

...and stamped in to the vehicle floor under the drivers seat

Introduction

A selection of good tools is a fundamental requirement for anyone contemplating the maintenance and repair of a motor vehicle. For the owner who does not possess any, their purchase will prove a considerable expense, offsetting some of the savings made by doing-it-yourself. However, provided that the tools purchased meet the relevant national safety standards and are of good quality, they will last for many years and prove an extremely worthwhile investment.

To help the average owner to decide which tools are needed to carry out the various tasks detailed in this manual, we have compiled three lists of tools under the following headings: *Maintenance and minor repair*, *Repair and overhaul*, and *Special*. Newcomers to practical mechanics should start off with the *Maintenance and minor repair* tool kit, and confine themselves to the simpler jobs around the vehicle. Then, as confidence and experience grow, more difficult tasks can be undertaken, with extra tools being purchased as, and when, they are needed. In this way, a *Maintenance and minor repair* tool kit can be built up into a *Repair and overhaul* tool kit over a considerable period of time, without any major cash outlays. The experienced do-it-yourselfer will have a tool kit good enough for most repair and overhaul procedures, and will add tools from the *Special* category when it is felt that the expense is justified by the amount of use to which these tools will be put.

Maintenance and minor repair tool kit

The tools given in this list should be considered as a minimum requirement if routine maintenance, servicing and minor repair operations are to be undertaken. We recommend the purchase of combination spanners (ring one end, open-ended the other); although more expensive than open-ended ones, they do give the advantages of both types of spanner.

- [ ] *Combination spanners:*
  Metric - 8 to 19 mm inclusive
- [ ] *Adjustable spanner - 35 mm jaw (approx.)*
- [ ] *Spark plug spanner (with rubber insert) - petrol models*
- [ ] *Spark plug gap adjustment tool - petrol models*
- [ ] *Set of feeler gauges*
- [ ] *Brake bleed nipple spanner*
- [ ] *Screwdrivers:*
  Flat blade - 100 mm long x 6 mm dia
  Cross blade - 100 mm long x 6 mm dia
  Torx - various sizes (not all vehicles)
- [ ] *Combination pliers*
- [ ] *Hacksaw (junior)*
- [ ] *Tyre pump*
- [ ] *Tyre pressure gauge*
- [ ] *Oil can*
- [ ] *Oil filter removal tool (if applicable)*
- [ ] *Fine emery cloth*
- [ ] *Wire brush (small)*
- [ ] *Funnel (medium size)*
- [ ] *Sump drain plug key (not all vehicles)*

Repair and overhaul tool kit

These tools are virtually essential for anyone undertaking any major repairs to a motor vehicle, and are additional to those given in the *Maintenance and minor repair* list. Included in this list is a comprehensive set of sockets. Although these are expensive, they will be found invaluable as they are so versatile - particularly if various drives are included in the set. We recommend the half-inch square-drive type, as this can be used with most proprietary torque wrenches.

The tools in this list will sometimes need to be supplemented by tools from the *Special* list:

- [ ] *Sockets to cover range in previous list (including Torx sockets)*
- [ ] *Reversible ratchet drive (for use with sockets)*
- [ ] *Extension piece, 250 mm (for use with sockets)*
- [ ] *Universal joint (for use with sockets)*
- [ ] *Flexible handle or sliding T "breaker bar" (for use with sockets)*
- [ ] *Torque wrench (for use with sockets)*
- [ ] *Self-locking grips*
- [ ] *Ball pein hammer*
- [ ] *Soft-faced mallet (plastic or rubber)*
- [ ] *Screwdrivers:*
  Flat blade - long & sturdy, short (chubby), and narrow (electrician's) types
  Cross blade – long & sturdy, and short (chubby) types
- [ ] *Pliers:*
  Long-nosed
  Side cutters (electrician's)
  Circlip (internal and external)
- [ ] *Cold chisel - 25 mm*
- [ ] *Scriber*
- [ ] *Scraper*
- [ ] *Centre-punch*
- [ ] *Pin punch*
- [ ] *Hacksaw*
- [ ] *Brake hose clamp*
- [ ] *Brake/clutch bleeding kit*
- [ ] *Selection of twist drills*
- [ ] *Steel rule/straight-edge*
- [ ] *Allen keys (inc. splined/Torx type)*
- [ ] *Selection of files*
- [ ] *Wire brush*
- [ ] *Axle stands*
- [ ] *Jack (strong trolley or hydraulic type)*
- [ ] *Light with extension lead*
- [ ] *Universal electrical multi-meter*

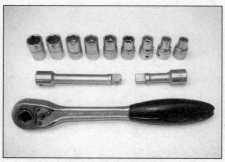

Sockets and reversible ratchet drive

Brake bleeding kit

Torx key, socket and bit

Hose clamp

Angular-tightening gauge

Special tools

The tools in this list are those which are not used regularly, are expensive to buy, or which need to be used in accordance with their manufacturers' instructions. Unless relatively difficult mechanical jobs are undertaken frequently, it will not be economic to buy many of these tools. Where this is the case, you could consider clubbing together with friends (or joining a motorists' club) to make a joint purchase, or borrowing the tools against a deposit from a local garage or tool hire specialist.

The following list contains only those tools and instruments freely available to the public, and not those special tools produced by the vehicle manufacturer specifically for its dealer network. You will find occasional references to these manufacturers' special tools in the text of this manual. Generally, an alternative method of doing the job without the vehicle manufacturers' special tool is given. However, sometimes there is no alternative to using them. Where this is the case and the relevant tool cannot be bought or borrowed, you will have to entrust the work to a dealer.

- [ ] *Angular-tightening gauge*
- [ ] *Valve spring compressor*
- [ ] *Valve grinding tool*
- [ ] *Piston ring compressor*
- [ ] *Piston ring removal/installation tool*
- [ ] *Cylinder bore hone*
- [ ] *Balljoint separator*
- [ ] *Coil spring compressors (where applicable)*
- [ ] *Two/three-legged hub and bearing puller*
- [ ] *Impact screwdriver*
- [ ] *Micrometer and/or vernier calipers*
- [ ] *Dial gauge*
- [ ] *Tachometer*
- [ ] *Fault code reader*
- [ ] *Cylinder compression gauge*
- [ ] *Hand-operated vacuum pump and gauge*
- [ ] *Clutch plate alignment set*
- [ ] *Brake shoe steady spring cup removal tool*
- [ ] *Bush and bearing removal/installation set*
- [ ] *Stud extractors*
- [ ] *Tap and die set*
- [ ] *Lifting tackle*

Buying tools

Reputable motor accessory shops and superstores often offer excellent quality tools at discount prices, so it pays to shop around.

Remember, you don't have to buy the most expensive items on the shelf, but it is always advisable to steer clear of the very cheap tools. Beware of 'bargains' offered on market stalls, on-line or at car boot sales. There are plenty of good tools around at reasonable prices, but always aim to purchase items which meet the relevant national safety standards. If in doubt, ask the proprietor or manager of the shop for advice before making a purchase.

Care and maintenance of tools

Having purchased a reasonable tool kit, it is necessary to keep the tools in a clean and serviceable condition. After use, always wipe off any dirt, grease and metal particles using a clean, dry cloth, before putting the tools away. Never leave them lying around after they have been used. A simple tool rack on the garage or workshop wall for items such as screwdrivers and pliers is a good idea. Store all normal spanners and sockets in a metal box. Any measuring instruments, gauges, meters, etc, must be carefully stored where they cannot be damaged or become rusty.

Take a little care when tools are used. Hammer heads inevitably become marked, and screwdrivers lose the keen edge on their blades from time to time. A little timely attention with emery cloth or a file will soon restore items like this to a good finish.

Working facilities

Not to be forgotten when discussing tools is the workshop itself. If anything more than routine maintenance is to be carried out, a suitable working area becomes essential.

It is appreciated that many an owner-mechanic is forced by circumstances to remove an engine or similar item without the benefit of a garage or workshop. Having done this, any repairs should always be done under the cover of a roof.

Wherever possible, any dismantling should be done on a clean, flat workbench or table at a suitable working height.

Any workbench needs a vice; one with a jaw opening of 100 mm is suitable for most jobs. As mentioned previously, some clean dry storage space is also required for tools, as well as for any lubricants, cleaning fluids, touch-up paints etc, which become necessary.

Another item which may be required, and which has a much more general usage, is an electric drill with a chuck capacity of at least 8 mm. This, together with a good range of twist drills, is virtually essential for fitting accessories.

Last, but not least, always keep a supply of old newspapers and clean, lint-free rags available, and try to keep any working area as clean as possible.

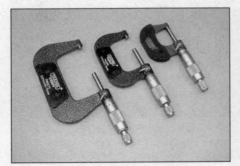

Micrometers

Dial test indicator ("dial gauge")

Oil filter removal tool (strap wrench type)

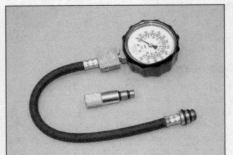

Compression tester

Bearing puller

This is a guide to getting your vehicle through the MOT test. Obviously it will not be possible to examine the vehicle to the same standard as the professional MOT tester. However, working through the following checks will enable you to identify any problem areas before submitting the vehicle for the test.

It has only been possible to summarise the test requirements here, based on the regulations in force at the time of printing. Test standards are becoming increasingly stringent, although there are some exemptions for older vehicles.

An assistant will be needed to help carry out some of these checks.

The checks have been sub-divided into four categories, as follows:

1 Checks carried out **FROM THE DRIVER'S SEAT**

2 Checks carried out **WITH THE VEHICLE ON THE GROUND**

3 Checks carried out **WITH THE VEHICLE RAISED AND THE WHEELS FREE TO TURN**

4 Checks carried out on **YOUR VEHICLE'S EXHAUST EMISSION SYSTEM**

---

1 Checks carried out **FROM THE DRIVER'S SEAT**

Handbrake (parking brake)

☐ Test the operation of the handbrake. Excessive travel (too many clicks) indicates incorrect brake or cable adjustment.
☐ Check that the handbrake cannot be released by tapping the lever sideways. Check the security of the lever mountings.

☐ If the parking brake is foot-operated, check that the pedal is secure and without excessive travel, and that the release mechanism operates correctly.
☐ Where applicable, test the operation of the electronic handbrake. The brake should engage and disengage without excessive delay. If the warning light does not extinguish when the brake is disengaged, this could indicate a fault which will need further investigation.

Footbrake

☐ Depress the brake pedal and check that it does not creep down to the floor, indicating a master cylinder fault. Release the pedal, wait a few seconds, then depress it again. If the pedal travels nearly to the floor before firm resistance is felt, brake adjustment or repair is necessary. If the pedal feels spongy, there is air in the hydraulic system which must be removed by bleeding.

☐ Check that the brake pedal is secure and in good condition. Check also for signs of fluid leaks on the pedal, floor or carpets, which would indicate failed seals in the brake master cylinder.
☐ Check the servo unit (when applicable) by operating the brake pedal several times, then keeping the pedal depressed and starting the engine. As the engine starts, the pedal will move down slightly. If not, the vacuum hose or the servo itself may be faulty.

Steering wheel and column

☐ Examine the steering wheel for fractures or looseness of the hub, spokes or rim.
☐ Move the steering wheel from side to side and then up and down. Check that the steering wheel is not loose on the column, indicating wear or a loose retaining nut. Continue moving the steering wheel as before, but also turn it slightly from left to right.

☐ Check that the steering wheel is not loose on the column, and that there is no abnormal movement of the steering wheel, indicating wear in the column support bearings or couplings.
☐ Check that the ignition lock (where fitted) engages and disengages correctly.
☐ Steering column adjustment mechanisms (where fitted) must be able to lock the column securely in place with no play evident.

Windscreen, mirrors and sunvisor

☐ The windscreen must be free of cracks or other significant damage within the driver's field of view. (Small stone chips are acceptable.) Rear view mirrors must be secure, intact, and capable of being adjusted.

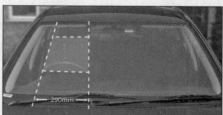

☐ The driver's sunvisor must be capable of being stored in the "up" position.

Seat belts and seats

Note: *The following checks are applicable to all seat belts, front and rear.*

☐ Examine the webbing of all the belts (including rear belts if fitted) for cuts, serious fraying or deterioration. Fasten and unfasten each belt to check the buckles. If applicable, check the retracting mechanism. Check the security of all seat belt mountings accessible from inside the vehicle, ensuring any height adjustable mountings lock securely in place.

☐ Seat belts with pre-tensioners, once activated, have a "flag" or similar showing on the seat belt stalk. This, in itself, is not a reason for test failure.

☐ The front seats themselves must be securely attached and the backrests must lock in the upright position.

Doors

☐ Both front doors must be able to be opened and closed from outside and inside, and must latch securely when closed.

Bonnet and boot/tailgate

☐ The bonnet and boot/tailgate must latch securely when closed.

---

2 Checks carried out **WITH THE VEHICLE ON THE GROUND**

Vehicle identification

☐ Number plates must be in good condition, secure and legible, with letters and numbers correctly spaced – spacing at (A) should be 33 mm and at (B) 11 mm. At the front, digits must be black on a white background and at the rear black on a yellow background. Other background designs (such as honeycomb) are not permitted.

☐ The VIN plate and/or homologation plate must be permanently displayed and legible.

Electrical equipment

☐ Switch on the ignition and check the operation of the horn.

☐ Check the windscreen washers and wipers, examining the wiper blades; renew damaged or perished blades. Also check the operation of the stop-lights.

☐ Check the operation of the sidelights and number plate lights. The lenses and reflectors must be secure, clean and undamaged.

☐ Check the operation and alignment of the headlights. The headlight reflectors must not be tarnished and the lenses must be undamaged.

☐ Switch on the ignition and check the operation of the direction indicators (including the instrument panel tell-tale) and the hazard warning lights. Operation of the sidelights and stop-lights must not affect the indicators - if it does, the cause is usually a bad earth at the rear light cluster. Indicators should flash at a rate of between 60 and 120 times per minute – faster or slower than this could indicate a fault with the flasher unit or a bad earth at one of the light units.

☐ Check the operation of the rear foglight(s), including the warning light on the instrument panel or in the switch.

☐ The warning lights must illuminate in accordance with the manufacturer's design. For most vehicles, the ABS and other warning lights should illuminate when the ignition is switched on, and (if the system is operating properly) extinguish after a few seconds. Refer to the owner's handbook.

Footbrake

☐ Examine the master cylinder, brake pipes and servo unit for leaks, loose mountings, corrosion or other damage. If ABS is fitted, this unit should also be examined for signs of leaks or corrosion.

☐ The fluid reservoir must be secure and the fluid level must be between the upper (**A**) and lower (**B**) markings.

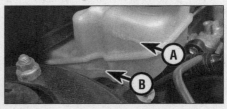

☐ Inspect both front brake flexible hoses for cracks or deterioration of the rubber. Turn the steering from lock to lock, and ensure that the hoses do not contact the wheel, tyre, or any part of the steering or suspension mechanism. With the brake pedal firmly depressed, check the hoses for bulges or leaks under pressure.

Steering and suspension

☐ Have your assistant turn the steering wheel from side to side slightly, up to the point where the steering gear just begins to transmit this movement to the roadwheels. Check for excessive free play between the steering wheel and the steering gear, indicating wear or insecurity of the steering column joints, the column-to-steering gear coupling, or the steering gear itself.

☐ Have your assistant turn the steering wheel more vigorously in each direction, so that the roadwheels just begin to turn. As this is done, examine all the steering joints, linkages, fittings and attachments. Renew any component that shows signs of wear or damage. On vehicles with power steering, check the security and condition of the steering pump, drivebelt and hoses.

☐ Check that the vehicle is standing level, and at approximately the correct ride height.

Shock absorbers

☐ Depress each corner of the vehicle in turn, then release it. The vehicle should rise and then settle in its normal position. If the vehicle continues to rise and fall, the shock absorber is defective. A shock absorber which has seized will also cause the vehicle to fail.

Exhaust system

☐ Start the engine. With your assistant holding a rag over the tailpipe, check the entire system for leaks. Repair or renew leaking sections.

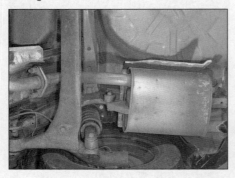

3 Checks carried out
WITH THE VEHICLE RAISED AND THE WHEELS FREE TO TURN

Jack up the front and rear of the vehicle, and securely support it on axle stands. Position the stands clear of the suspension assemblies. Ensure that the wheels are clear of the ground and that the steering can be turned from lock to lock.

Steering mechanism

☐ Have your assistant turn the steering from lock to lock. Check that the steering turns smoothly, and that no part of the steering mechanism, including a wheel or tyre, fouls any brake hose or pipe or any part of the body structure.
☐ Examine the steering rack rubber gaiters for damage or insecurity of the retaining clips. If power steering is fitted, check for signs of damage or leakage of the fluid hoses, pipes or connections. Also check for excessive stiffness or binding of the steering, a missing split pin or locking device, or severe corrosion of the body structure within 30 cm of any steering component attachment point.

Front and rear suspension and wheel bearings

☐ Starting at the front right-hand side, grasp the roadwheel at the 3 o'clock and 9 o'clock positions and rock gently but firmly. Check for free play or insecurity at the wheel bearings, suspension balljoints, or suspension mount-ings, pivots and attachments.
☐ Now grasp the wheel at the 12 o'clock and 6 o'clock positions and repeat the previous inspection. Spin the wheel, and check for roughness or tightness of the front wheel bearing.

☐ If excess free play is suspected at a component pivot point, this can be confirmed by using a large screwdriver or similar tool and levering between the mounting and the component attachment. This will confirm whether the wear is in the pivot bush, its retaining bolt, or in the mounting itself (the bolt holes can often become elongated).

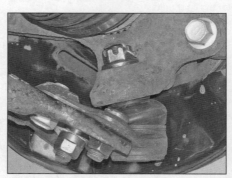

☐ Carry out all the above checks at the other front wheel, and then at both rear wheels.

Springs and shock absorbers

☐ Examine the suspension struts (when applicable) for serious fluid leakage, corrosion, or damage to the casing. Also check the security of the mounting points.
☐ If coil springs are fitted, check that the spring ends locate in their seats, and that the spring is not corroded, cracked or broken.
☐ If leaf springs are fitted, check that all leaves are intact, that the axle is securely attached to each spring, and that there is no deterioration of the spring eye mountings, bushes, and shackles.

☐ The same general checks apply to vehicles fitted with other suspension types, such as torsion bars, hydraulic displacer units, etc. Ensure that all mountings and attachments are secure, that there are no signs of excessive wear, corrosion or damage, and (on hydraulic types) that there are no fluid leaks or damaged pipes.
☐ Inspect the shock absorbers for signs of serious fluid leakage. Check for wear of the mounting bushes or attachments, or damage to the body of the unit.

Driveshafts (fwd vehicles only)

☐ Rotate each front wheel in turn and inspect the constant velocity joint gaiters for splits or damage. Also check that each driveshaft is straight and undamaged.

Braking system

☐ If possible without dismantling, check brake pad wear and disc condition. Ensure that the friction lining material has not worn excessively, (A) and that the discs are not fractured, pitted, scored or badly worn (B).

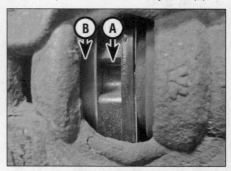

☐ Examine all the rigid brake pipes underneath the vehicle, and the flexible hose(s) at the rear. Look for corrosion, chafing or insecurity of the pipes, and for signs of bulging under pressure, chafing, splits or deterioration of the flexible hoses.
☐ Look for signs of fluid leaks at the brake calipers or on the brake backplates. Repair or renew leaking components.
☐ Slowly spin each wheel, while your assistant depresses and releases the footbrake. Ensure that each brake is operating and does not bind when the pedal is released.

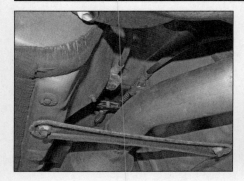

☐ Examine the handbrake mechanism, checking for frayed or broken cables, excessive corrosion, or wear or insecurity of the linkage. Check that the mechanism works on each relevant wheel, and releases fully, without binding.

☐ It is not possible to test brake efficiency without special equipment, but a road test can be carried out later to check that the vehicle pulls up in a straight line.

Fuel and exhaust systems

☐ Inspect the fuel tank (including the filler cap), fuel pipes, hoses and unions. All components must be secure and free from leaks. Locking fuel caps must lock securely and the key must be provided for the MOT test.

☐ Examine the exhaust system over its entire length, checking for any damaged, broken or missing mountings, security of the retaining clamps and rust or corrosion.

Wheels and tyres

☐ Examine the sidewalls and tread area of each tyre in turn. Check for cuts, tears, lumps, bulges, separation of the tread, and exposure of the ply or cord due to wear or damage. Check that the tyre bead is correctly seated on the wheel rim, that the valve is sound and properly seated, and that the wheel is not distorted or damaged.

☐ Check that the tyres are of the correct size for the vehicle, that they are of the same size and type on each axle, and that the pressures are correct.

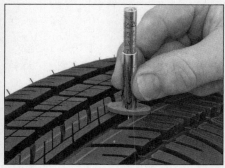

☐ Check the tyre tread depth. The legal minimum at the time of writing is 1.6 mm over the central three-quarters of the tread width. Abnormal tread wear may indicate incorrect front wheel alignment or wear in steering or suspension components.

☐ If the spare wheel is fitted externally or in a separate carrier beneath the vehicle, check that mountings are secure and free of excessive corrosion.

Body corrosion

☐ Check the condition of the entire vehicle structure for signs of corrosion in load-bearing areas. (These include chassis box sections, side sills, cross-members, pillars, and all suspension, steering, braking system and seat belt mountings and anchorages.) Any corrosion which has seriously reduced the thickness of a load-bearing area (or is within 30 cm of safety-related components such as steering or suspension) is likely to cause the vehicle to fail. In this case professional repairs are likely to be needed.

☐ Damage or corrosion which causes sharp or otherwise dangerous edges to be exposed will also cause the vehicle to fail.

Towbars

☐ Check the condition of mounting points (both beneath the vehicle and within boot/hatchback areas) for signs of corrosion, ensuring that all fixings are secure and not worn or damaged. There must be no excessive play in detachable tow ball arms or quick-release mechanisms.

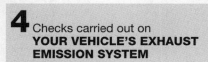

4 Checks carried out on **YOUR VEHICLE'S EXHAUST EMISSION SYSTEM**

Petrol models

☐ The engine should be warmed up, and running well (ignition system in good order, air filter element clean, etc).

☐ Before testing, run the engine at around 2500 rpm for 20 seconds. Let the engine drop to idle, and watch for smoke from the exhaust. If the idle speed is too high, or if dense blue or black smoke emerges for more than 5 seconds, the vehicle will fail. Typically, blue smoke signifies oil burning (engine wear);

black smoke means unburnt fuel (dirty air cleaner element, or other fuel system fault).

☐ An exhaust gas analyser for measuring carbon monoxide (CO) and hydrocarbons (HC) is now needed. If one cannot be hired or borrowed, have a local garage perform the check.

CO emissions (mixture)

☐ The MOT tester has access to the CO limits for all vehicles. The CO level is measured at idle speed, and at 'fast idle' (2500 to 3000 rpm). The following limits are given as a general guide:

At idle speed – Less than 0.5% CO
At 'fast idle' – Less than 0.3% CO
Lambda reading – 0.97 to 1.03

☐ If the CO level is too high, this may point to poor maintenance, a fuel injection system problem, faulty lambda (oxygen) sensor or catalytic converter. Try an injector cleaning treatment, and check the vehicle's ECU for fault codes.

HC emissions

☐ The MOT tester has access to HC limits for all vehicles. The HC level is measured at 'fast idle' (2500 to 3000 rpm). The following limits are given as a general guide:

At 'fast idle' – Less then 200 ppm

☐ Excessive HC emissions are typically caused by oil being burnt (worn engine), or by a blocked crankcase ventilation system ('breather'). If the engine oil is old and thin, an oil change may help. If the engine is running badly, check the vehicle's ECU for fault codes.

Diesel models

☐ The only emission test for diesel engines is measuring exhaust smoke density, using a calibrated smoke meter. The test involves accelerating the engine at least 3 times to its maximum unloaded speed.

Note: *On engines with a timing belt, it is VITAL that the belt is in good condition before the test is carried out.*

☐ With the engine warmed up, it is first purged by running at around 2500 rpm for 20 seconds. A governor check is then carried out, by slowly accelerating the engine to its maximum speed. After this, the smoke meter is connected, and the engine is accelerated quickly to maximum speed three times. If the smoke density is less than the limits given below, the vehicle will pass:

Non-turbo vehicles: 2.5m-1
Turbocharged vehicles: 3.0m-1

☐ If excess smoke is produced, try fitting a new air cleaner element, or using an injector cleaning treatment. If the engine is running badly, where applicable, check the vehicle's ECU for fault codes. Also check the vehicle's EGR system, where applicable. At high mileages, the injectors may require professional attention.

Engine

- ☐ Engine fails to rotate when attempting to start
- ☐ Engine rotates, but will not start
- ☐ Engine difficult to start when cold
- ☐ Engine difficult to start when hot
- ☐ Starter motor noisy or excessively rough in engagement
- ☐ Engine starts, but stops immediately
- ☐ Engine idles erratically
- ☐ Engine misfires at idle speed
- ☐ Engine misfires throughout the driving speed range
- ☐ Engine lacks power
- ☐ Engine backfires
- ☐ Oil pressure warning light illuminated with engine running
- ☐ Engine runs-on after switching off
- ☐ Whistling or wheezing noises
- ☐ Tapping or rattling noises
- ☐ Knocking or thumping noises

Cooling system

- ☐ Overheating
- ☐ Overcooling
- ☐ External coolant leakage
- ☐ Internal coolant leakage
- ☐ Corrosion

Fuel and exhaust systems

- ☐ Excessive fuel consumption
- ☐ Fuel leakage and/or fuel odour
- ☐ Excessive noise or fumes from the exhaust system

Clutch

- ☐ Pedal travels to the floor – no pressure or very little resistance
- ☐ Clutch fails to disengage (unable to select gears)
- ☐ Clutch slips (engine speed increases, with no increase in vehicle speed)
- ☐ Judder as clutch is engaged
- ☐ Noise when depressing or releasing clutch pedal

Manual transmission

- ☐ Noisy in neutral with the engine running
- ☐ Noisy in one particular gear
- ☐ Difficulty in engaging gears
- ☐ Jumps out of gear
- ☐ Vibration
- ☐ Lubricant leaks

Automatic transmission

- ☐ Fluid leakage
- ☐ General gear selection problems
- ☐ Engine will not start in any gear, or starts in gears other than Park or Neutral
- ☐ Transmission slips, shifts roughly, is noisy, or has no drive in forward or reverse gears

Transfer case

- ☐ Fluid leakage
- ☐ Noisy operation

Final drive

- ☐ Fluid leakage
- ☐ Noisy operation

Driveshafts/Propeller shaft

- ☐ Vibration when accelerating or decelerating
- ☐ Clicking or knocking noise on turns (at low speed on full lock)
- ☐ Knock or clunk when taking up drive
- ☐ Metallic grating sound, consistent with vehicle speed
- ☐ Vibration consistent with vehicle speed

Braking system

- ☐ Vehicle pull to one side under braking
- ☐ Noise (grinding or high-pitched squeal) when brakes applied
- ☐ Excessive brake pedal travel
- ☐ Brake pedal feels spongy when depressed
- ☐ Excessive brake pedal effort required to stop vehicle
- ☐ Judder felt through brake pedal or steering wheel when braking
- ☐ Pedal pulsates when braking hard
- ☐ Brakes binding

Steering and suspension

- ☐ Vehicle pulls to one side
- ☐ Wheel wobble and vibration
- ☐ Excessive pitching and/or rolling around corners, or during braking
- ☐ Wandering or general instablity
- ☐ Excessively stiff steering
- ☐ Excessive play in steering
- ☐ Lack of power assistance
- ☐ Tyre wear excessive

Electrical system

- ☐ Battery will not hold charge for more than a few days
- ☐ Ignition/no-charge warning light remains illuminated with the engine running
- ☐ Lights inoperative
- ☐ Fuel or temperature gauge inaccurate
- ☐ Horn operates continuously
- ☐ Horn inoperative
- ☐ Wipers fail to operate, or operate very slowly
- ☐ Wiper blades sweep over too large, or too small an area of glass
- ☐ Wiper blades fail to clean the glass effectively
- ☐ Screen or headlight washers inoperative, or unsatisfactory in operation
- ☐ Window glass moves only in one direction
- ☐ Window glass slow to move
- ☐ Window glass fails to move
- ☐ Central locking system inoperative, or unsatisfactory in operation.

Introduction

The vehicle owner who does his or her own maintenance according to the recommended service schedules should not have to use this section of the manual very often. Modern component reliability is such that, provided those items subject to wear or deterioration are inspected or renewed at the specified intervals, sudden failure is comparatively rare. Faults do not usually just happen as a result of sudden failure, but develop over a period of time. Major mechanical failures in particular are usually preceded by characteristic symptoms over hundreds or even thousands of miles. Those components which do occasionally fail without warning are often small and easily carried in the vehicle.

With any fault-finding, the first step is to decide where to begin investigations. Sometimes this is obvious, but on other occasions, a little detective work will be necessary. The owner who makes half a dozen haphazard adjustments or replacements may be successful in curing a fault (or its symptoms), but will be none the wiser if the fault recurs, and ultimately may have spent more time and money than was necessary.

A calm and logical approach will be found to be more satisfactory in the long run. Always take into account any warning signs or abnormalities that may have been noticed in the period preceding the fault – power loss, high or low gauge readings, unusual smells, etc – and remember that failure of components such as fuses or spark plugs may only be pointers to some underlying fault.

The pages which follow provide an easy-reference guide to the more common problems which may occur during the operation of the vehicle. These problems and their possible causes are grouped under headings denoting various components or systems, such as Engine, Cooling system, etc. The Chapter and/or Section which deals with the problem is also shown in brackets. Whatever the fault, certain basic principles apply. These are as follows:

Verify the fault. This is simply a matter of being sure that you know what the symptoms are before starting work. This is particularly important if you are investigating a fault for someone else, who may not have described it very accurately.

Don't overlook the obvious. For example, if the vehicle won't start, is there fuel in the tank? (Don't take anyone else's word on this particular point, and don't trust the fuel gauge either!) If an electrical fault is indicated, look for loose or broken wires before digging out the test gear.

Cure the disease, not the symptom. Substituting a flat battery with a fully-charged one will get you off the hard shoulder, but if the underlying cause is not attended to, the new battery will go the same way. Similarly, changing oil-fouled spark plugs for a new set will get you moving again, but remember that the reason for the fouling (if it wasn't simply an incorrect grade of plug) will have to be established and corrected.

Don't take anything for granted. Particularly, don't forget that a 'new' component may itself be defective (especially if it's been rattling around in the boot for months), and don't leave components out of a fault diagnosis sequence just because they are new or recently-fitted. When you do finally diagnose a difficult fault, you'll probably realise that all the evidence was there from the start.

Engine

Engine fails to rotate when attempting to start

☐ Battery terminal connections loose or corroded (Chapter 5A Section 4).
☐ Battery discharged or faulty (Chapter 5A Section 3).
☐ Broken, loose or disconnected wiring in the starting circuit (Chapter 12 Section 2).
☐ Defective starter solenoid or switch (Chapter 5A Section 2).
☐ Defective starter motor (Chapter 5A Section 9).
☐ Starter pinion or flywheel ring gear teeth loose or broken (Chapter 5A Section 10 and Chapter 2A Section 13).
☐ Engine earth strap broken or disconnected (Chapter 12 Section 2).

Engine rotates, but will not start

☐ Fuel tank empty.
☐ Battery discharged (engine rotates slowly) (Chapter 5A Section 3).
☐ Battery terminals loose or corroded (see "Weekly checks").
☐ Pre-heating system faulty (Chapter 5B Section 2).

☐ Fuel injection system faulty (Chapter 4A Section 9).
☐ Air in the fuel system (Chapter 4A Section 7).
☐ Major mechanical failure (Chapter 2A or Chapter 2B).

Engine difficult to start when cold

☐ Battery discharged (Chapter 5A Section 3).
☐ Battery terminal connections loose or corroded (see "Weekly checks").
☐ Pre-heating system faulty (Chapter 5B Section 2).
☐ Fuel injection system faulty (Chapter 4A Section 9).
☐ Low cylinder compressions (Chapter 2A Section 2 or Chapter 2B Section 2).

Engine difficult to start when hot

☐ Air filter element dirty or clogged (Chapter 1 Section 24).
☐ Fuel injection system faulty (Chapter 4A Section 9).
☐ Low cylinder compressions (Chapter 2A Section 2 or Chapter 2B Section 2).

Engine (continued)

Starter motor noisy or excessively rough in engagement

☐ Starter pinion or flywheel ring gear teeth loose or broken (Chapter 5A Section 8 or Chapter 2A Section 13 and Chapter 2B Section 13).
☐ Starter motor mounting bolts loose or missing (Chapter 5A Section 9).
☐ Starter motor internal components worn or damaged (Chapter 5A Section 10).

Engine starts, but stops immediately

☐ Blocked injector/fuel injection system fault (Chapter 4A).
☐ Air in the fuel system (Chapter 4A Section 7).
☐ Immobiliser fault – refer to a Mercedes dealer or specialist.

Engine idles erratically

☐ Air filter element clogged (Chapter 1 Section 24).
☐ Uneven or low compressions (Chapter 2A Section 2 or Chapter 2B Section 2).
☐ Camshaft lobes worn (Chapter 2A or Chapter 2B).
☐ Blocked injector/fuel injection system fault (Chapter 4A).

Engine misfires at idle speed

☐ Faulty injectors/fuel injection system fault (Chapter 4A).
☐ Uneven or low compressions (Chapter 2A Section 2 or Chapter 2B Section 2).

Engine misfires throughout the driving speed range

☐ Fuel filter choked (Chapter 1 Section 25).
☐ Fuel tank vent blocked, or fuel pipes restricted (Chapter 4A Section 2).
☐ Fault injector/fuel injection system fault (Chapter 4A).
☐ Uneven or low compressions (Chapter 2A Section 2 or Chapter 2B Section 2).

Engine lacks power

☐ Timing chain incorrectly fitted (Chapter 2A Section 7 or Chapter 2B Section 7).
☐ Fuel filter choked (Chapter 1 Section 25).
☐ Air filter blocked (Chapter 1 Section 24).
☐ Uneven or low compressions (Chapter 2A Section 2 or Chapter 2B Section 2).
☐ Faulty injectors/injection system fault (Chapter 4A).
☐ Brakes binding (Chapter 9).Clutch slipping (Chapter 6).
☐ Turbocharger fault (Chapter 4A Section 16)
☐ Turbocharger air ducts leaking.

Engine backfires

☐ Timing chain incorrectly fitted or tensioned (Chapter 2A Section 7 or Chapter 2B Section 8).
☐ Blocked injector/fuel injection system fault (Chapter 4A).

Oil pressure warning light illuminated with engine running

☐ Low oil level, or incorrect oil grade (see "Weekly checks").
☐ Faulty oil pressure sensor (Chapter 2A Section 17 or Chapter 2B Section 17).
☐ Worn engine bearings and/or oil pump (Chapter 2C).
☐ High engine operating temperature (Chapter 3).
☐ Oil pressure relief valve defective (Chapter 2A Section 12 or Chapter 2B Section 13).
☐ Oil pick up strainer clogged (Chapter 2A Section 12 or Chapter 2B Section 13).

Engine runs-on after switching off

☐ Excessive carbon build-up in engine (Chapter 2C).
☐ High engine operating temperature (Chapter 3).
☐ Fuel injection system fault (Chapter 4A).
☐ Incorrect oil level (see "Weekly checks").

Whistling or wheezing noises

☐ Leaking exhaust manifold or turbocharger gaskets (Chapter 4A).
☐ Leaking vacuum hose (Chapter 4A).
☐ Leaking air intake hose//intercooler ducts (Chapter 4A).

Tapping or rattling noises

☐ Worn valve gear or camshaft (Chapter 2C).
☐ Ancillary component fault (coolant pump, alternator etc.) (Chapter 3 and Chapter 5A).

Knocking or thumping noises

☐ Worn big-end bearings (regular heavy knocking, perhaps more under load) (Chapter 2C).
☐ Worn main bearings (rumbling and knocking, perhaps less under load) (Chapter 2C).
☐ Piston slap (most noticeable when cold) (Chapter 2C).
☐ Ancillary component fault (coolant pump, alternator, etc.) (Chapter 3 and Chapter 5A).

Cooling system

Overheating

☐ Insufficient coolant in the system (see "Weekly checks").
☐ Thermostat faulty (Chapter 3 Section 4).
☐ Radiator core blocked, or grille restricted (Chapter 3 Section 3).
☐ Electric cooling fan faulty (Chapter 3 Section 6).
☐ Air lock in cooling system (Chapter 1 Section 30).
☐ Expansion tank pressure cap faulty (Chapter 1 Section 30).
☐ Engine coolant temperature sensor faulty (Chapter 3 Section 7).

Overcooling

☐ Thermostat faulty (Chapter 3 Section 4).
☐ Engine coolant temperature sensor faulty (Chapter 3 Section 7).

External coolant leakage

☐ Deteriorated or damaged hoses or hose clips (Chapter 3 Section 2).
☐ Radiator core or heater matrix leaking (Chapter 3 Section 8).
☐ Pressure cap faulty (Chapter 1 Section 30).
☐ Coolant pump leaking (Chapter 3 Section 5).
☐ Boiling due to overheating.
☐ Core plug leaking (Chapter 2C Section 12).

Internal coolant leakage

☐ Leaking cylinder head gasket (Chapter 2A Section 10 or Chapter 2B Section 10).
☐ Cracked cylinder head or cylinder block (Chapter 2C).

Corrosion

☐ Infrequent draining and flushing (Chapter 1 Section 30).
☐ Incorrect coolant mixture or inappropriate coolant type (Chapter 1 Section 30).

Fuel and exhaust systems

Excessive fuel consumption

- [ ] Air filter dirty or clogged (Chapter 1 Section 24).
- [ ] Faulty injector/fuel injection system fault (Chapter 4A).
- [ ] Brakes binding (Chapter 9).
- [ ] Tyres under-inflated (see "Weekly checks").

Fuel leakage and/or fuel odour

- [ ] Damaged or corroded fuel tank, pipes or connections (Chapter 4A).

Excessive noise or fumes from the exhaust system

- [ ] Leaking exhaust system or manifold leaks (Chapter 4A).
- [ ] Leaking or corroded silencers or pipe (Chapter 4A Section 19).
- [ ] Broken mountings causing body or suspension contact (Chapter 4A Section 19).

Clutch

Pedal travels to the floor – no pressure or very little resistance

- [ ] Faulty master or slave cylinder (Chapter 6 Section 2 or Chapter 6 Section 3).
- [ ] Faulty hydraulic release system (Chapter 6).
- [ ] Broken clutch release bearing (Chapter 6).
- [ ] Broken diaphragm spring in clutch pressure plate (Chapter 6 Section 5).

Clutch fails to disengage (unable to select gears)

- [ ] Faulty master or slave cylinder (Chapter 6 Section 2 or Chapter 6 Section 3).
- [ ] Faulty hydraulic hose.
- [ ] Clutch disc sticking on the gearbox input shaft splines (Chapter 6 Section 5).
- [ ] Clutch disc sticking on the flywheel or pressure plate (Chapter 6 Section 5).
- [ ] Faulty pressure plate assembly (Chapter 6 Section 5).
- [ ] Air in hydraulic system (Chapter 6 Section 4).

Clutch slips (engine speed increases, with no increase in vehicle speed)

- [ ] Faulty hydraulic release system (Chapter 6).
- [ ] Clutch disc linings excessively worn (Chapter 6 Section 5).
- [ ] Clutch disc lining contaminated with oil or grease (Chapter 6 Section 5).
- [ ] Faulty pressure plate or weak diaphragm spring (Chapter 6 Section 5).

Judder as clutch is engaged

- [ ] Clutch disc linings contaminated with oil or grease (Chapter 6 Section 5).
- [ ] Clutch disc linings excessively worn (Chapter 6 Section 5).
- [ ] Faulty or distorted pressure plate or diaphragm spring (Chapter 6 Section 5).
- [ ] Worn or loose engine or gearbox mountings (Chapter 2A Section 16 or Chapter 2B Section 15).
- [ ] Clutch disc or gearbox input shaft splines worn (Chapter 6 Section 5).

Noise when depressing or releasing clutch pedal

- [ ] Worn clutch release bearing (Chapter 6).
- [ ] Worn or dry clutch pedal pivot.
- [ ] Faulty pressure plate assembly (Chapter 6 Section 5).
- [ ] Pressure plate diaphragm spring broken (Chapter 6 Section 5).

Manual transmission

Noisy in neutral with the engine running

- [ ] Input shaft bearings worn (noise apparent with clutch pedal released, but not when depressed) (Chapter 7A Section 8).*
- [ ] Clutch release bearings worn (noise apparent with clutch pedal depressed, possibly less when released (Chapter 6 Section 3).

Noisy in one particular gear

- [ ] Worn, damaged or chipped gear teeth (Chapter 7A Section 8).*

Difficulty in engaging gears

- [ ] Clutch faulty (Chapter 6).
- [ ] Clutch hydraulic hose faulty.
- [ ] Worn synchroniser units (Chapter 7A Section 8).*

Jumps out of gear

- [ ] Worn synchroniser units (Chapter 7A Section 8).*
- [ ] Worn selector forks (Chapter 7A Section 8).*

Vibration

- [ ] Lack of oil (Chapter 7A Section 2).
- [ ] Worn bearings (Chapter 7A Section 8).*

Lubricant leaks

- [ ] Leaking oil seal (Chapter 7A Section 5).
- [ ] Leaking housing joint (Chapter 7A Section 8).*
- [ ] Leaking input shaft oil seal (Chapter 7A).

Note: *Although the corrective action necessary to remedy the symptoms described in beyond the scope of the home mechanic, then above information should be helpful in isolating the cause of the condition, so that the owner can communicate clearly with a professional mechanic.*

Automatic transmission

Fluid leakage

☐ Automatic transmission fluid is usually dark in colour. Fluid leaks should not be confused with engine oil, which can easily be blown onto the transmission by airflow. To determine the source of a leak, first remove all built-up dirt and grime from the transmission housing and surrounding areas using a degreasing agent, or by steam-cleaning. Drive the vehicle at low speed, so airflow will not blow the leak far from its source. Raise and support the vehicle, and determine where the leak is coming from.

Engine will not start in any gear, or starts in gears other than Park or Neutral

☐ Selector lever/housing problem (Chapter 7B Section 2).Transmission control module problem (Chapter 7B Section 9).

Transmission slips, shifts roughly, is noisy, or has no drive in forward or reverse gears

☐ There are many probable causes for the above problems, but unless there is a very obvious reason (such as a loose or corroded wiring plug connection on or near the transmission), the car should be taken to a franchise dealer or specialist for the fault to be diagnosed. The transmission control module incorporates a self-diagnosis facility, and any fault codes can quickly be read and interpreted by a dealer or specialist with the proper diagnostic equipment.

Note: *Due to the complexity of the automatic transmission, it is difficult for the home mechanic to properly diagnose and service this unit. For problems other then the following, the vehicle should be taken to a dealer service department or automatic transmission specialist. Do not be too hasty in removing the transmission if a fault is suspected, as most of the testing is carried out with the unit still fitted.*

Final drive

Fluid leakage

☐ Oil seal leaking (Chapter 8 Section 4).

Noisy operation

☐ Low oil level (Chapter 8 Section 2).
☐ Worn bearings/differential gears (Chapter 8 Section 3).

Driveshafts/Propeller shaft

Vibration when accelerating or decelerating

☐ Worn constant velocity joint (Chapter 8 Section 5).
☐ Bent or distorted driveshaft (Chapter 8 Section 5).

Knock or clunk when taking up drive

☐ Worn propeller shaft universal joint bearings (Chapter 8 Section 10).
☐ Loose propeller shaft flange bolts (Chapter 8 Section 7).

Metallic grating sound, consistent with vehicle speed

☐ Severe wear in the propeller shaft universal joint bearings (Chapter 8 Section 10).
☐ Worn propeller shaft centre support bearing (Chapter 8 Section 9).

Vibration consistent with vehicle speed

☐ Propeller shaft out of balance (Chapter 8 Section 7).
☐ Wheels out of balance.
☐ Propeller shaft or driveshaft joints worn (Chapter 8).

Braking system

Vehicle pull to one side under braking

☐ Worn, defective, damaged or contaminated brake pads on one side (Chapter 9 Section 5 or Chapter 9 Section 6).
☐ Seized or partially seized front or rear brake caliper (Chapter 9 Section 9 or Chapter 9 Section 10).
☐ A mixture of brake pad lining materials fitted between sides (Chapter 9 Section 5 or Chapter 9 Section 6).
☐ Brake caliper mounting bolts loose (Chapter 9 Section 9 or Chapter 9 Section 10).
☐ Worn or damaged steering or suspension components (Chapter 10).

Noise (grinding or high-pitched squeal) when brakes applied

☐ Brake pad friction material worn down to metal backing (Chapter 9 Section 5 or Chapter 9 Section 6).
☐ Excessive corrosion of brake disc – may be apparent after the vehicle has been standing for some time (Chapter 9 Section 7).
☐ Foreign object (stone chipping, etc.) trapped between the brake disc and shield.

Braking system (continued)

Excessive brake pedal travel

- [ ] Faulty master cylinder (Chapter 9 Section 11).
- [ ] Air in hydraulic system (Chapter 9 Section 2).
- [ ] Faulty vacuum servo unit (Chapter 9 Section 12).
- [ ] Faulty vacuum pump (Chapter 9 Section 21).

Brake pedal feels spongy when depressed

- [ ] Air in hydraulic system (Chapter 9 Section 2).
- [ ] Deteriorated flexible rubber brake hoses (Chapter 9 Section 3).
- [ ] Master cylinder mountings loose (Chapter 9 Section 11).
- [ ] Faulty master cylinder (Chapter 9 Section 11).

Excessive brake pedal effort required to stop vehicle

- [ ] Faulty vacuum servo unit (Chapter 9 Section 12).
- [ ] Faulty servo unit check valve (Chapter 9 Section 12).
- [ ] Disconnected, damaged or insecure brake servo vacuum hose (Chapter 9 Section 13).
- [ ] Faulty vacuum pump (Chapter 9 Section 21).
- [ ] Faulty brake pipe or hose (Chapter 9 Section 3).
- [ ] Seized brake caliper (Chapter 9 Section 9 or Chapter 9 Section 10).
- [ ] Brake pads incorrectly fitted (Chapter 9 Section 5, 6).
- [ ] Incorrect grade of brake pads fitted (Chapter 9 Section 5, 6).
- [ ] Brake pads contaminated (Chapter 9 Section 5, 6).

Judder felt through brake pedal or steering wheel when braking

- [ ] Excessive run-out or distortion of brake disc (Chapter 9 Section 7, 8).
- [ ] Brake pad linings worn (Chapter 9 Section 5, 6).
- [ ] Brake caliper mountings loose (Chapter 9 Section 9, 10).
- [ ] Wear in suspension or steering components or mountings (Chapter 10).

Pedal pulsates when braking hard

- [ ] Normal feature of ABS – no fault.

Brakes binding

- [ ] Seized brake caliper (Chapter 9 Section 9, 10).
- [ ] Incorrectly adjusted parking brake (Chapter 9 Section 14).
- [ ] Faulty master cylinder (Chapter 9 Section 11).

Note: *Before assuming that a brake problem exists, make sure that the tyres are in good condition and correctly inflated, that the front wheel alignment is correct, and that the vehicle is not loaded with weight in an unequal manner. Apart from checking the condition of all pipe and hose connections, any faults occurring on the anti-lock braking system should be referred to a Mercedes dealer or specialist for diagnosis.*

Steering and suspension

Vehicle pulls to one side

- [ ] Defective tyre (see "*Weekly checks*").
- [ ] Excessive wear in suspension or steering components (Chapter 1 Section 13).
- [ ] Incorrect front wheel alignment (Chapter 10 Section 29).
- [ ] Accident damage to steering or suspension components.

Wheel wobble and vibration

- [ ] Front roadwheels out of balance (vibration felt mainly through the steering wheel).
- [ ] Rear roadwheels out of balance (vibration felt mainly throughout the vehicle).
- [ ] Roadwheels damaged or distorted (Chapter 1 Section 13).
- [ ] Faulty or damaged tyre (see "*Weekly checks*").
- [ ] Worn steering or suspension joints, bushes or components (Chapter 1 Section 13).
- [ ] Wheel bolts loose (Chapter 1 Section 13).

Excessive pitching and/or rolling around corners, or during braking

- [ ] Defective shock absorbers (Chapter 10 Section 5, 14).
- [ ] Broken or weak coil spring and/or suspension components (Chapter 10).
- [ ] Worn or damaged anti-roll bar or mountings (Chapter 10 Section 9, 10, 18, 19).

Wandering or general instablity

- [ ] Incorrect wheel alignment (Chapter 10 Section 29).
- [ ] Worn steering or suspension components (Chapter 1 Section 13).
- [ ] Roadwheels out of balance.
- [ ] Faulty or damaged tyre (see "*Weekly checks*").
- [ ] Wheel bolts loose.
- [ ] Defective shock absorbers (Chapter 10 Section 5, 14).

Excessively stiff steering

- [ ] Seized track rod end balljoint or suspension balljoint (Chapter 10).
- [ ] Broken or incorrectly adjusted auxiliary drivebelt (Chapter 1 Section 6).
- [ ] Incorrect front wheel alignment (Chapter 10 Section 29).
- [ ] Steering gear damaged (Chapter 10 Section 24).

Excessive play in steering

- [ ] Worn steering column universal joints (Chapter 10 Section 22).
- [ ] Worn steering track rod end balljoints (Chapter 10 Section 28).
- [ ] Worn steering gear (Chapter 10 Section 24).
- [ ] Worn steering or suspension joints, bushes or components (Chapter 10).

Lack of power assistance

- [ ] Broken or incorrectly adjusted auxiliary drivebelt (Chapter 1 Section 6).
- [ ] Incorrect power steering fluid level (see "*Weekly checks*").
- [ ] Restriction in power steering hoses.
- [ ] Faulty power steering pump (Chapter 10 Section 26).
- [ ] Faulty steering gear (Chapter 10 Section 24).
- [ ] Air in hydraulic system (Chapter 10 Section 27).

Tyre wear excessive

- [ ] Tyres under inflated (wear on both edges) (see "*Weekly checks*").
- [ ] Incorrect camber or castor angles (wear on one edge) (Chapter 10 Section 29).
- [ ] Worn steering or suspension joints, bushes or components (Chapter 1 Section 13).
- [ ] Accident damage.
- [ ] Incorrect wheel alignment (feathered edges) (Chapter 10 Section 29).
- [ ] Tyres over-inflated (worn in centre of tread) (see "*Weekly checks*").
- [ ] Worn shock absorbers (Chapter 10 Section 5, 14).
- [ ] Tyres/wheel out of balance (tyres worn unevenly).
- [ ] Tyre/wheel damage (see "*Weekly checks*").

Electrical system

Battery will not hold charge for more than a few days

- [ ] Battery defective internally (Chapter 5A Section 3).
- [ ] Battery terminal connections loose or corroded (see "Weekly checks").
- [ ] Auxiliary drivebelt worn or incorrectly tensioned (Chapter 1 Section 6).
- [ ] Alternator not charging at correct output (Chapter 5A Section 5, 7).
- [ ] Short circuit causing continual current drain (Chapter 12 Section 2).

Ignition/no-charge warning light remains illuminated with the engine running

- [ ] Auxiliary drivebelt broken, worn, or incorrectly adjusted (Chapter 1 Section 6).
- [ ] Internal fault in alternator or voltage regulator (Chapter 5A Section 7).
- [ ] Broken, disconnected, or loose wiring in charging circuit (Chapter 12 Section 2).

Lights inoperative

- [ ] Blown bulb (Chapter 12 Section 6).
- [ ] Corrosion of bulbholder contacts (Chapter 12 Section 6).
- [ ] Blown fuse (Chapter 12 Section 3).
- [ ] Faulty relay (Chapter 12 Section 3).
- [ ] Broken, loose or disconnected wiring (Chapter 12 Section 2).
- [ ] Faulty switch (Chapter 12 Section 5).

Fuel or temperature gauge inaccurate

- [ ] Faulty fuel level sensor(s) (Chapter 4A Section 4).
- [ ] Faulty engine coolant temperature sensor (Chapter 3 Section 7).
- [ ] Faulty instrument cluster (Chapter 12 Section 10).

Horn operates continuously

- [ ] Horn contacts faulty (Chapter 12 Section 5).

Horn inoperative

- [ ] Horn switch contact faulty (Chapter 12 Section 5).
- [ ] Horn faulty (Chapter 12 Section 12).
- [ ] Fuse blown (Chapter 12 Section 3).

Wipers fail to operate, or operate very slowly

- [ ] Wiper blades stuck to screen, or seized linkage (Chapter 12 Section 14).
- [ ] Blown fuse (Chapter 12 Section 3).
- [ ] Faulty relay (Chapter 12 Section 3).
- [ ] Faulty wiper motor (Chapter 12 Section 14).

Wiper blades sweep over too large, or too small an area of glass

- [ ] Wiper arms incorrectly positioned on spindles (Chapter 12 Section 13).
- [ ] Excessive wear of wiper linkage (Chapter 12 Section 14).
- [ ] Wiper motor or linkage mountings loose (Chapter 12 Section 14).

Wiper blades fail to clean the glass effectively

- [ ] Wiper blade rubbers worn or perished (see "Weekly checks").
- [ ] Wiper arms defective (Chapter 12 Section 13).
- [ ] Insufficient windscreen washer additive to adequately remove road film (see "Weekly checks").

Screen or headlight washers inoperative, or unsatisfactory in operation

- [ ] Blocked washer jet (Chapter 12 Section 15).
- [ ] Disconnected, kinked or restricted fluid hose.
- [ ] Insufficient fluid in washer reservoir (see "Weekly checks").
- [ ] Blown fuse (Chapter 12 Section 3).
- [ ] Faulty washer pump (Chapter 12 Section 15).
- [ ] Faulty switch (Chapter 12 Section 5).

Window glass moves only in one direction

- [ ] Faulty switch (Chapter 12 Section 5).

Window glass slow to move

- [ ] Regulator seized or damaged, or in need of lubrication (Chapter 11 Section 18, 19).
- [ ] Door internal components or trim fouling regulator (Chapter 11 Section 17).
- [ ] Window guide rubber dirty or in need of lubrication (Silicone spray).
- [ ] Faulty motor (Chapter 11 Section 18, 19).

Window glass fails to move

- [ ] Blown fuse (Chapter 12 Section 3).
- [ ] Faulty CJB (Chapter 12 Section 3).
- [ ] Broken or disconnected wiring or connections (Chapter 12 Section 2).
- [ ] Faulty motor (Chapter 11 Section 18, 19).

Central locking system inoperative, or unsatisfactory in operation.

- [ ] Blown fuse (Chapter 12 Section 2).
- [ ] Faulty SAM (Chapter 12 Section 3).
- [ ] Broken or disconnected wiring or connectors (Chapter 12 Section 2).
- [ ] Faulty door/boot/tailgate lock (Chapter 11 Section 12, 14, 21, 23).
- [ ] Faulty relay (Chapter 12 Section 3).

Note: *References throughout this index are in the form "Chapter number" • "Page number". So, for example, 2C•15 refers to page 15 of Chapter 2C.*

Note: *References throughout this index are in the form "Chapter number" • "Page number". So, for example, 2C•15 refers to page 15 of Chapter 2C.*

Note: *References throughout this index are in the form "Chapter number" • "Page number". So, for example, 2C•15 refers to page 15 of Chapter 2C.*

REF•26 Notes

Preserving Our Motoring Heritage

> <
> The Model J Duesenberg
> Derham Tourster.
> Only eight of these
> magnificent cars were
> ever built – this is the
> only example to be found
> outside the United States
> of America

Almost every car you've ever loved, loathed or desired is gathered under one roof at the Haynes Motor Museum. Over 300 immaculately presented cars and motorbikes represent every aspect of our motoring heritage, from elegant reminders of bygone days, such as the superb Model J Duesenberg to curiosities like the bug-eyed BMW Isetta. There are also many old friends and flames. Perhaps you remember the 1959 Ford Popular that you did your courting in? The magnificent 'Red Collection' is a spectacle of classic sports cars including AC, Alfa Romeo, Austin Healey, Ferrari, Lamborghini, Maserati, MG, Riley, Porsche and Triumph.

A Perfect Day Out

Each and every vehicle at the Haynes Motor Museum has played its part in the history and culture of Motoring. Today, they make a wonderful spectacle and a great day out for all the family. Bring the kids, bring Mum and Dad, but above all bring your camera to capture those golden memories for ever. You will also find an impressive array of motoring memorabilia, a comfortable 70 seat video cinema and one of the most extensive transport book shops in Britain. The Pit Stop Cafe serves everything from a cup of tea to wholesome, home-made meals or, if you prefer, you can enjoy the large picnic area nestled in the beautiful rural surroundings of Somerset.

> John Haynes O.B.E.,
> Founder and
> Chairman of the
> museum at the wheel
> of a Haynes Light 12.
> >

> <
> Graham Hill's Lola
> Cosworth Formula 1
> car next to a 1934
> Riley Sports.

The Museum is situated on the A359 Yeovil to Frome road at Sparkford, just off the A303 in Somerset. It is about 40 miles south of Bristol, and 25 minutes drive from the M5 intersection at Taunton.

Open 9.30am - 5.30pm (10.00am - 4.00pm Winter) 7 days a week, *except Christmas Day, Boxing Day and New Years Day*

Special rates available for schools, coach parties and outings Charitable Trust No. 292048